The Emergence of Historical Forensic Expertise

This book scrutinizes the emergence of historical forensic contribution in some of the most important national and international legal ventures of the last century. It aims to advance the debate from discussions on whether historians should testify or not toward nuanced understanding of the history of the practice and making the best out of its performance in the future.

Vladimir Petrović is a Senior Researcher at the Institute for Contemporary History in Belgrade, Serbia.

Routledge Approaches to History

For a full list of titles in this series, please visit www.routledge.com

11 **The Struggle for the Long-Term in Transnational Science and Politics**
Forging the Future
Edited by Jenny Andersson and Eglė Rindzevičiūtė

12 **'A New Type of History'**
Fictional Proposals for dealing with the Past
Beverley Southgate

13 **Beyond Memory: Silence and the Aesthetics of Remembrance**
Edited by Alexandre Dessingué and Jay Winter

14 **The Soviet Past in the Post-Socialist Present**
Methodology and Ethics in Russian, Baltic and Central European Oral History and Memory Studies
Edited by Melanie Ilic and Dalia Leinarte

15 **Theoretical Perspectives on Historians' Autobiographies**
From Documentation to Intervention
Jaume Aurell

16 **How History Works**
The Reconstitution of a Human Science
Martin L. Davies

17 **History, Ethics, and the Recognition of the Other**
A Levinasian View on the Writing of History
Anton Froeyman

18 **The Historiography of Transition**
Critical Phases in the Development of Modernity (1494–1973)
Edited by Paolo Pombeni

19 **The Emergence of Historical Forensic Expertise**
Clio Takes the Stand
Vladimir Petrović

The Emergence of Historical Forensic Expertise

Clio Takes the Stand

Vladimir Petrović

Routledge
Taylor & Francis Group
LONDON AND NEW YORK

First published 2017 by Rougledge

2 Park Square, Milton Park, Abingdon, Oxfordshire OX14 4RN
52 Vanderbilt Avenue, New York, NY 10017

Routledge is an imprint of the Taylor & Francis Group, an informa business

First issued in paperback 2019

Library of Congress Cataloging-in-Publication Data
Names: Petrović, Vladimir, 1979– author.
Title: The emergence of historical forensic expertise : Clio takes the stand / By Vladimir Petrovic.
Description: New York : Routledge, 2016. | Includes bibliographical references and index.
Identifiers: LCCN 2016034241 (print) | LCCN 2016034394 (ebook) | ISBN 9781138690646 (alk. paper) | ISBN 9781315536828
Subjects: LCSH: Forensic historians. | Evidence, Expert. | Evidence (Law) | Historiography.
Classification: LCC K2290.H57 P48 2016 (print) | LCC K2290.H57 (ebook) | DDC 347/.067—dc23
LC record available at https://lccn.loc.gov/2016034241

ISBN: 978-1-138-69064-6 (hbk)
ISBN: 978-0-367-26405-5 (pbk)

Typeset in Sabon
by Apex CoVantage, LLC

Contents

Figures

Acknowledgments

My passion for studying the past transformed into reflective historiographical thinking gradually and under multiple influences. The initial impetus to think about the social role of historians came from my first mentor Andrej Mitrović, and my brother Ljubomir Petrović, who are sadly no longer among us. Further stimulus appeared during the course of my studies at Central European University, where I developed an interest in the role of historians in dealing with the atrocious past, prompted by Sorin Antohi and Balázs Trencsényi. This interest was chanelled into a doctoral project through the the inspiring mentorship of István Rév, as well as the collegial support of Maria Falina, Simina Radu-Bucurenci, Bogdan Iacob, Ferenc Laczó, Zsofia Lorand, Katalin Straner and Marko Zubak. Taking the reverberating advice of my supervisor, I proceeded to investigate the topic from the inside, interning and working in the War Crimes Prosecutor's Office in Serbia, as well as at the International Criminal Tribunal for the former Yugoslavia. Among people working either in it or on it, Predrag Dojčinović, Barbora Hola, Christian Nielsen, Novak Vučo, and Richard Wilson were of huge help. I also happily acknowledge the intellectual debt to Nanci Adler, Berber Bevernage, Enrico Corniani, Ramses Delafontaine, Nenad Dimitrijević, Norbert Frei, Morgan Kousser, Diana Mishkova, Werner Renz, Dubravka Stojanović, and Renata Uitz, who challenged me to explore different aspects of the historical profession. The Institute for Contemporary History in Belgrade enabled me to profess it, as my colleagues, particularly Mladen Acković, Dragan Bogetić, Dragomir Bondžić, Srđan Cvetković, Vladimir Ivanović, Predrag Marković, Kosta Nikolić, Ivana Pantelić and Momčilo Pavlović, showed exceptional understanding for my prolonged research abroad. Turning this research into a book was finalized within the project *Understanding the Age of Transitional Justice* of the NIOD Institute for War, Holocaust and Genocide Studies of the Royal Netherlands Academy for Arts and Sciences. Nanci Adler, NIOD's head of research, along with Ugur Ümit Üngör and Thijs Bouwknegt, transformed that process into pure pleasure. Jura Avizienis skillfully proofread the manuscript, which was carefully edited by Max Novick and Jennifer Morrow, but could not have been completed without the steady support of Ashley Mears and a motivating presence of our newborn Nola.

Introduction

Is there a place for the historian in a courtroom? The subject generates heated, albeit disconnected debates characterized by all-too-quick and decisive responses, affirmative as well as dismissive. Opinions are equally divided among practitioners. "A historian? In my courtroom?" The judge in Belgrade was staring at me, genuinely bewildered. "Who ever heard of such a thing?" His colleague, a prosecutor at The Hague, was musing at length about the merits of historical expert testimony, even claiming that he personally introduced this innovation into international criminal law. Although my interlocutors differed sharply over the role of historical forensics, they were equally in the dark about its evolution. This struck me as strange, given that historians actively participated in some of the most important legal ventures of the last century, from the Dreyfus case to the Milošević trial. However, as their contribution remains obscured and controversial, I grew convinced that a monographic overview of the evolution of historical expert witnessing is in order. Therefore, shedding some light on the neglected history of historical expert witnessing is a principal theme of this book. Its aim is to advance the discussion, in hope that nuanced understanding of this practice's past could improve its future courtroom manifestations.

The Topic and the Debate

Debates about historians as expert witnesses are characterized with unusually dramatic wording, reflecting persistent uneasiness. Despite a respectable number of precedents, the practice has never fully achieved legitimization. Instead it has triggered a set of tellingly disconnected exchanges. Surprisingly enough, their opposed protagonists largely agree on treating the practice as a zero-sum issue: historians are usually either perceived as useful expert witnesses, or not. The tone was set by scholars who participated in such ventures or declined to do so, like prominent French contemporary historian Henry Rousso, who famously refusal to appear in the Papon trial: "In my soul and conscience, I believe that historians cannot be 'witnesses' and that the role of 'expert witness' rather poorly suits the rules and objective of a court trial. It is one thing to try to understand history in the context of a research project or course lesson, with the intellectual freedom that such activities presuppose: it is quite another to try to do so under oath when an individual's fate hangs in the balance."[1] However, equally confident are historians who have taken the stand: "Being an expert witness in a judicial case allows historians to use their historical training and historical judgment to benefit society," wrote Charles Bolton, who took the stand in creationist cases. Morgan Kousser, historical expert on the voting rights trials, expressed his view in an article entitled "Are Expert Witnesses Whores?" By no means, he concluded; testifying is an opportunity to "do justice and scholarship at the same time."[2]

Not all first-hand accounts are so unequivocal. Appointed as historical consultant for war crimes prosecution in Australia, Jonathan Steinberg "accepted at once and without hesitation. It seemed to me to be a call I could not refuse; it was a chance to offer what professional skill I had in an important public transaction." However, he soon grasped the complexities of the experience of historical expert witnessing: "The experience as an expert witness in court tested my professional skills to the limit and raised questions about the very practice of history itself. The methods, approaches, techniques and indeed, the stamina required of a historian who goes to court—I was in a witness box for six and a half hours—went well beyond any claims previously made on me in my professional career. Nothing I had done before nor anything since demanded so much of me. After all, most of the time what an academic historian says or does matters little. In the case I had to meet the demands of a court of law in which a man's life and freedom were at stake."[3]

More nuanced reflections were yet to come from various sources, as the topic was cutting through several disciplines and concerned diverse subject matter, occurring in even more diverse contexts. The most consistent intellectual dialogue on the issue is to be found in the Anglo-American legal literature, within the wider discussion of the constantly shifting criteria of the admissibility of expert testimonies.[4] Meanwhile, European contributions echo the same concerns mostly through spasmodic exchanges over concrete cases, although they do contribute significantly to reframing the issue of historical expert witnessing in a transnational setting.[5] Still the desired closure has remained elusive, as the scholarly dialogue on the appropriateness of a historian playing the role of expert witness remains not only largely polarized between the supporters and adversaries of the practice, but also constrained by the boundaries of particular legal and historical disciplinary requirements, as it is scattered through different jurisdictions. Morgan Kousser thoughtfully noted that "the literature on the use of social scientists and historians as expert witnesses is wider than it is deep."[6] The chronological broadness, thematic fragmentation, and interdisciplinary character of the topic indeed present a mighty deterrent. Among attempts to bridge that gap, a special place belongs to edited volumes which contain contributions that cut through different manifestations of historical expert witnessing, thus opening the way for a more nuanced approach.[7] However, much more needs to be done to grasp the elusive genealogy of historical expert witnessing.[8]

Firstly, there is a need to move past some commonplaces. "The first, but perhaps least appreciated fact about historians as expert witnesses is how often they assume the role. Although colleagues and even litigators presume that historians rarely enter the courtroom, in fact it has been a common occurrence for some fifty years," observes David J. Rothman, himself a historian of medicine and an expert witness in a number of trials.[9] The second, equally underappreciated fact concerns the growing variety of manifestations of historical expert witnessing. According to Hal Rothman, "Historians are no longer an unusual sight in the courtroom. Since the 1950s, historians have been active in legal proceedings as experts and adversaries. Historians now function in a range of roles and cases, offering their expertise to prosecution and defense in civil, criminal, and administrative proceedings."[10] Furthermore, it is crucial to grasp these varieties, as recently suggested by Richard Evans, who testified as an expert witness in *Irving v. Lipstadt*. Summarizing his experiences in a forum of the journal *History and Theory*, he questioned the applicability of Henry Rousso's criticism of the practice to the trial in which he himself took part: "Does it apply to other cases in other jurisdictions?" he asked, stressing that the trial he participated in "was not a criminal, but a civil action."[11] Indeed, the role of experts is defined differently in various legal contexts, in criminal and civil cases alike. Common law and continental law have different takes on the institution of expert, reflected in their adversarial or inquisitorial procedures: in the former, experts are usually employed by the parties, whereas in the latter they are summoned by the judge. Within these great legal traditions there are further differentiations within national jurisdictions, and their blending in international law also creates a particular position for expert witnesses. The purpose of this expertise varies greatly from civil to criminal proceedings, from military tribunals to civilian courts, from jury trials to bench trials, even from trial to trial.[12] This nuancing is an important precondition for any scrutiny of expert forensic contributions.

The form and the content of the historian's contribution also offer important elements of differentiation: It can be given in written form or delivered orally or both. It can be concerned with the recent or quite distant past. It can be a summary of already published material or it can be composed solely for the trial. It can be an individual endeavor or a collective work. It can perform a fact-finding purpose or provide context. It can be central or peripheral to the proceedings. In short, historians' forensic contributions come in all shapes and sizes. Hence every generalization holds the obvious risk of pushing the debate into an unhelpful holistic confinement, resulting in the fallacy of proscriptive blanket solutions. This book attempts to avoid that path by scrutinizing historical expert witnessing through the lens of its rather neglected yet all too rich history in order to secure the ground for a scrutiny of the origins, scope, transformation, variety, and impact of historians' courtroom performances. Its starting point is a revival of a somewhat forgotten question: How did the once unthinkable idea of historical expert testimony become an established, albeit debatable, practice in so many different legal and political contexts?

Roadmap: (In)compatibility Tension and Beyond

"To follow the story of the Western legal tradition," writes Harold Berman, "is to confront implicit theories both of law and of history."[13] Being a historian, yet working with prosecutors, judges, and lawyers, I was more than aware of a curious combination of persistent interest and almost instinctive disciplinary unease, pervasive among my historian colleagues as well. "In many ways, the disciplines of law and history have a natural affinity," agrees Jonathan Martin. "This close relationship is nonetheless suffused with tension. Lawyers and historians are in many respects odd bedfellows." Robert Gordon similarly concluded that "lawyers and historians have always cohabited in a relationship of intimate antagonism."[14] Where did the antagonism come from? Recent works of Richard Wilson and Gerry Simpson have helped unearth this implicit resistance grounded in the complex framing of relations between history and law.[15] Among these, in particular the *presumption of incompatibility between history and law*, is a sort of an interpretative fiber which runs through my entire book. Deriving from the long, intimate, but also ambiguous relations between the two disciplines, the presumption that they simply do not mix well was keeping historians out of courtrooms at a time when other human sciences stabilized their legal applications. This accounts not just for the belated forensication of historiography, but also for the ongoing struggle to legitimize the practice of historical expert witnessing. Its main generator is the antagonistic multilayered proximity between the disciplines summarized well by Austin Sarat and Thomas Kearns: "While law lives in history, it has a history of its own. While law responds to history, it also makes history."[16] Therefore, one can speak of *History on Trial*, meaning a judicial process that adjudicates matters which are traditionally of interest to historians, but there is also *History of Trial*, which is the historiographical analysis of judicial proceedings. Lastly, one can speak of *History in Trial*, which consists of the deployment of historiographical elements in judicial proceedings. These come in many forms and could be introduced by all the participants in a given trial—prosecutors or defendants and their attorneys, judges, eyewitnesses, and experts. In this variety, the performance of professional historians as experts on the stand accounts for the most structured manifestation of history in the courtroom.

Da mihi facta, dabo tibi ius—give me the facts, and I will give you the law. Such is the classical division of labor between the court and the parties, inscribed as early as 1234 in the papal codification *Decretalia Gregorii*. In striving to do so, "intuitively, at least for lawyers, the record book of history appears as a treasury of very sound points of reference," observes Renata

Uitz.[17] Such intuition has occasionally led to a true fetishization of history. Justice Oliver Wendell Holmes, one of the most prominent legal figures of the late nineteenth century, expressed this philosophy in a nutshell: "Upon this point a page of history is worth a volume in logic," he said, asserting that "rational study of law is still to a large extent the study of history." However, a century later this confidence got destabilized, as it became clear that as "the non-historian assumes that historical facts are objectively knowable, 'out there,' so to speak, and that they will disclose themselves to anyone who seeks diligently (. . .) a first-year graduate student in History learns the fallacy of these assumptions in the first week of the methods seminar."[18] István Rév captured the crux of the matter: "Facts, in the field of history, come wrapped in words."[19]

Thus no wonder that many authors drew incompatibility implications, perhaps most famously Carlo Ginzburg: "Law and history, it seems, have different rules and different epistemological foundations (. . .) this is the reason why legal principles cannot be safely transferred into historical research." Ginzburg famously concluded: "The paths of judge and historian, which run side by side for a certain distance, eventually and inevitably diverge. If one attempts to reduce the role of the historian to that of a judge, one simplifies and impoverishes historiographical knowledge, but if one attempts to reduce the role of the judge to that of a historian, one contaminates—and irreparably so—the administration of justice."[20] Paul Ricoeur also considered the "confrontation between the judge's task and the historian's task. (. . .) The judge has to pass judgment (. . .) this historians do not do, cannot do, do not want to do."[21] This clash seems even more dramatic in practice. M. C. Mirrow, who served as a historical expert witness, drew the depressing conclusion that "forensic truth is not the same as truth sought by academic historians. (. . .) Thus, there is an inherent incompatibility between the forensic goal of the best possible result given the time limits of a judicial proceedings and the 'true' result sought by the historian regardless of the time constraints."[22] For many observers, nothing but a complete divorce is merited.

Still, many a practitioner has come out of the witness box with a less rigid take, like Douglas Littlefield, who concluded that "undertaking historical research and writing for an academic purpose and pursuing those same endeavors in a legal setting are, of course, not mutually exclusive activities. Nonetheless, the practice of history in the legal arena operates on a set of basic assumptions and is guided by rules different from those characteristic of history in an academic environment."[23] Similarly James Gow and Ivan Zverzhanovski maintain that "the same evidence serves two purposes: the quest for 'truth' by those involved in the judicial process, on one side, and those engaged in academic historical interpretations on the other. (. . .) The two frameworks for truth are neither necessarily competitive nor complementary, and the test of their validity may differ. But the raw material they use may be identical and the outcome of each may be parallel and consistent. And the two varieties of truth may reinforce one another in the quest to restore peace and security, to establish justice and to compile a broadly accepted account of contentious, awful events."[24] A shared fascination with the evidence seems to provide a lasting bridge between the disciplines. Ksenija Turković maintained that "traditionally the relationship between law and history has been very close—judges as well as historians attempt to establish the truth about past events with the help of evidence."[25] Communalities in dealing with evidence also impressed Paul Connerton: "Historians (. . .) proceed inferentially. They investigate evidence much as lawyers cross-question witnesses in a court of law, extracting from that evidence information which it does not explicitly contain."[26] Similar analogies led Judge Richard Posner to the conclusion that "the law is the most historically oriented, or if you like the most backward looking, the most 'past dependent' of the professions."[27]

The attempt to transcend the irreconcilable positions of the proponents of the compatibility and incompatibility of history and law is slowly picking up pace. Certainly, it is impossible to overlook the troubled features of relations between history and law. However, uncoupling them is equally not possible, observes Alain Wijfells: "Discussions on History and Law often tend to consider that both areas would seem to cultivate their own brand of truth: there would thus be a historical truth and a legal truth." Still, he observed that "in spite of the acknowledged differences, the destinies of historical research and legal proceedings are not to such extent foreign to each other. (. . .) On the contrary, a great many human activities show that the two can meet, or at least come close to each other in a variety of circumstances."[28] Historical expert witnessing is exactly one such human activity. Not necessarily aware of its complexities, its practitioners are working under the long shadow of theories about the (in)compatibility between history and law. As long as that is the case, historical forensic contribution will be perceived in a binary code—either as a synergic reunion, or as the irreparable clash of incompatible disciplines. In order to move past such constraints, this book proposes three maneuvers.

Firstly, it opens by taking a step back. Its first part—*Inceptions*—contextualizes historical testimony into the early development in forensics, noting the inherent general tensions in expert witnessing, and their particular manifestations in historiography. Why did historians take the stand belatedly and what made their courtroom appearance more controversial? First courtroom performances of historians, such as Gabriel Monod in a famous Dreyfus case and the much less known tribulations of Heinrich Friedjung at his own trial, are examined in light of the presumed disciplinary intimacy between history and law that gave birth to the implicit theory of their incompatibility. This presumption was reached in the interwar period, under the influence of fiercely politicized debate about the guilt for the outbreak of the war *(Kriegsschuldfrage)*, delaying the forensication of historiography and eventually making it more controversial. The second chapter of the same part of the book deals with the great shift that opened the first cracks in the theory of incompatibility. Expressed in the activity of International Military Tribunals in Nuremberg and Tokyo through initiatives of Robert Jackson, Jacob Robinson, Robert Kempner, and other historically minded jurists, the past was introduced in a courtroom as a decisive trigger which preconditioned the emergence of historical forensic expertise.

The second part of the book—*Improvisations*—explores the impact of the postwar shift toward universal human rights, and particularly a momentum for critical reexamination of the past. It manifested in a number of trials held in Germany, whose courtrooms witnessed an unsteady stream of historians exercising an expert function, from the Fritz Bauer–inspired Remer case to the Ulm trial. Around the same time, the gradual admittance of historians into American courtrooms in cases regarding past injustices, from Brown v. Board of Education to Native American claims, heralded the formation of a distinctive brand of historical expert witnessing, characterized by the adversarial character of these proceedings, yet equally inspired with human rights concerns and the ambition to address the past wrongs fostered by Thurgood Marshall and conducted by historians as prominent as Alfred Kelly, John Hope Franklin, and C. Vann Woodward. This part of the book attempts to establish the channels through which historiography was introduced into the legal process, with particular stress on the emergence of organized institutional research into contemporary history, which provided a legitimization for the first postwar appearances of historians as experts in both common and continental law, resulting in two distinct paradigms of the usage of historical forensic contributions.

The third and final part of the book dwells on the intersection of these two paradigms, searching for a turning point that normalized historical expert witnessing in both adversarial and inquisitorial legal procedure. To that end, a rebirth of Holocaust-related prosecutions in early 1960s is examined, emphasizing the importance of the Eichmann trial and the Frankfurt Auschwitz trial and the interplay between them. This merger of paradigms secured the necessary visibility of historical experts, who performed in both adversarial and inquisitorial courtrooms to secure the necessary context for the prosecution's case. They testified either as individuals (like Salo Baron, invited by Israeli authorities to appear in the Eichmann trial) or as a group (like historians the Munich Institute for Contemporary History prompted by prosecutor Fritz Bauer to partake in Frankfurt Auschwitz trial). Such interventions not only led to the renewal of the debate on the role of history in legal proceedings, but also fostered gradual maturing of contemporary historiography and even its remoralization. A similar tendency was observable on the other side of the Atlantic, with growing number of U.S. historians picking up the civil rights cause. The impact of these changes on relations between history and law was reflected in debates of that time, featuring Hannah Arendt, Otto Kircheimer, Carl Friedrich, or Judith Shklar, which focused on the role of trials in fostering social change. Expressed in the global abolishment of statutes of limitations for war crimes and crimes against humanity, such change indeed marked a new stage in relations between history and law and a point of no return in normalization of historical forensics.

It is apparent that the book maneuvers between generalized and particularized approaches, in order to preserve the cohesion of the phenomenon, but also to honor the complexities of its different manifestations. Some risks are inherent to such zigzag: "Whoever wishes to perceive the phenomenon of war crimes and their adjudication based on historiographical finding must be aware that he or she stands on a shifting ground," noted two researchers who recently delved into this topic.[29] To stabilize that ground, I paid attention not only to famous trials in which famous historians appeared, but also to prominent trials in which the participation of historians was obscured, as well as much less known proceedings in which well-known historians took part. Such is the intention behind the selection of the cases scattered over various jurisdictions around the globe, which are broadly set in chronological order but at the same time chaptered in accordance with their thematic proximity.

The overarching theme that cuts through all the cases is the continuing struggle to overcome the extreme injustices of the first half of the previous century. Legal confrontation with this bad past eventually dragged the historians into the arena, for better or worse: "The implications of the rise of the historical 'expert' are only beginning to be understood and it seems clear that, as new controversies and explosive questions appear on the agenda of public debate, this new role of historians is not going to go away. (. . .) It is essential that we continue to reflect upon our role in this context because there is going to be a lot more work for the expert historians, concluded the editors of a recent volume entitled *Contemporary History on Trial.*"[30] As this work mounts, we move toward acknowledging the complexities of this sensitive junction between history and the law. Whether historians can testify is answered by the legal community. Whether they should take the stand remains for individual practitioners to decide according to their interpretation of professional responsibility. With this in mind, the aim of the book is simply to foster making informed choices in this field by offering a comparative and nuanced understanding of the origin, scope, and variety of historical forensics.

Notes

1 Henry Rousso, *The Haunting Past: History, Memory, and Justice in Contemporary France* (Philadelphia: University of Pennsylvania Press, 2002), 85.

2 Charles Bolton, "The Historians as Expert Witnesses: Creationism in Arkansas," *The Public Historian* 4 (1982): 59; Morgan J. Kousser, "Are Expert Witnesses Whores? Reflections on Objectivity in Scholarship and Expert Witnessing," *The Public Historian* 6 (1984): 18.

3 Jonathan Steinberg, "The Historian at Court: Expert Witness in an Australian War Crimes Trial," in *History in Court: Historical Expertise and Methods in a Forensic Context*, ed. Alain Wijffels (Leiden: Ius Deco, 2001), 203–204.

4 Daniel A. Farber, "Adjudication of Things Past: Reflections on History as Evidence" and Reuel E. Schiler, "The Strawhorsemen of the Apocalypse: Relativism and the Historian as Expert Witness" in *Hastings Law Journal* 49 (1998): 1009–1026, 1169–1181; Brian W. Martin, "Working with Lawyers: A Historian's Perspective," *Organization of American Historians Newsletter* 30 (May, 2002): 4–5; and John A. Neuenschwander, "Historians as Expert Witnesses: The View from the Bench," *Organization of American Historians Newsletter* (August 2002): 1–6. Also see forums in journals *Law and History Review* 18 (2000): 559–626, *History and Theory* 41 (2002): 326–345 and most recently *The Public Historian* 37.1 (2015): 8–104. Another recapitulation of the debates in Jonathan D. Martin, "Historians at the Gate: Accommodating Expert Testimony in Federal Courts," *New York University Law Review* 78 (2003): 1518–1543. The most recent impressive addition to the growing literature on historical expert witnessing: Ramses Delafontaine, *Historians as Expert Judicial Witnesses in Tobacco Litigation: A Controversial Legal Practice* (New York: Springer, 2015).

5 Such a tendency was reflected through a number of conferences and workshops, or through thematic volumes and specialized editions of journals: Claudia Kurtsidis-Haider, "Überlegungen zu Justiz und Zeitgeschichte im europäischen Vergleich," in *Keine "Abrechnung" NS-Verbrechen, Justiz und Gesellschaft in Europa nach 1945*, ed. Winfried R. Garscha (Wien: Akademishe Verlag Anst, 1998), 430–434; Carlo Ginzburg, *The Judge and the Historian: Marginal Notes on a Late-Twentieth-Century Miscarriage of Justice* (London: Verso, 1999). Also see the contributions in thematic volumes of *Droit et société* 38 (1998), *Rechtsgeschichte* 3 (2004), *Časopis za suvremenu povijest* 1 (2004), and *Ab Imperio* 3 (2007), all dedicated to the relation between history and law.

6 Morgan Kousser, "Expert Witnesses, Rational Choice, and the Search for Intent," *Constitutional Commentary* 5 (1988): 349.

7 Norbert Frei, Dirk van Laak and Michael Stolleis (eds.), *Geschichte vor Gericht: Historiker, Richter und suche nach Gerechtigkeit* (München: Verlag C.H. Beck, 2000); Alain Wijffels (ed.), *History in Court: Historical Expertise and Methods in a Forensic Context* (Leiden: Ius Deco Publications, 2001); Harriet Jones, Kjell Östberg, and Nico Randeraad (eds.), *Contemporary History on Trial: Europe since 1989 and the Role of the Expert Historian* (Manchester: Manchester University Press, 2007).

8 Olivier Dumoulin provides an analysis of the changes of the public role of French historians throughout the twentieth century, stressing the importance of the influence from the U.S. on postwar historical expertise in France. Olivier Dumoulin, *Le rôle social de l'historien: De la chaire au prétoire* (Paris: Albin Michel, 2003). I also tackled the issue of transnational genealogy of historical expert witnessing in the Eichmann case and Frankfurt Auschwitz trial. Vladimir Petrović, "Juridical Memory Making and the Transformation of Historical Expert Witnessing: Contextualizing the Eichmann Case and the Frankfurt Auschwitz Trial," in *Erinnern und Vergessen: Jahrbuch Junge Rechtsgeschichte*, eds. Oliver Brupbacher et al. (München: Martin Meidenbauer, 2007), 326–347.

9 David J. Rothman, "Serving Clio and the Client: The Historian as Expert Witness," *Bulletin of the History of Medicine* 77 (2003): 25.

10 Hal K. Rothman, "Historian v. Historian: Interpreting the Past in the Courtroom," *Public Historian* 15 (1993): 39.

11 Richard J. Evans, "History, Memory, and the Law: The Historian as Expert Witness," *History and Theory* 41 (2002): 340.

12 Many of these considerations have been the subject of valid research in comparative legal studies, a realm of immense help in differentiating between the varieties of historical expert witnessing. See Morris Ploscowe, "The Expert Evidence in Criminal Cases in France, Germany and Italy," *Law and Contemporary*

Problems 2 (1935): 504–509. This comparative aspect in legal studies developed significantly: Robert F. Taylor, "A Comparative Study of Expert Testimony in France and the United States," *Texas International Law Journal* 31 (1996): 181–212.

13 Harold J. Berman, *Law and Revolution: The Formation of the Western Legal Tradition* (Cambridge, MA: Harvard University Press 1983), 10.

14 Martin, Historians at the Gate . . ., 1523–1524. Robert W. Gordon, "The Past as Authority and as Social Critic: Stabilizing and Destabilizing Functions of History in Legal Argument," in *The Historic Turn in the Human Sciences*, ed. Terrence J. McDonald (Ann Arbor: University of Michigan Press, 1996), 339.

15 Richard Ashby Wilson, "Judging History: The Historical Record of the International Criminal Tribunal for the Former Yugoslavia," *Human Rights Quarterly* 27 (2005): 908–942; Gerry Simpson, *Law, War and Crime: War Crimes, Trials and the Reinvention of International Law* (Cambridge: Polity Press, 2007), 85–88; Richard Ashby Wilson, *Writing History in International Criminal Trials* (Cambridge: Cambridge University Press, 2011), 1–8.

16 Austin Sarat and Thomas Kearns (eds.), *History, Memory and the Law* (Ann Arbor: University of Michigan Press, 2002), 3.

17 Renata Uitz, *Constitutions, Courts and History, Historical Narratives in Constitutional Adjudication* (CEU Press: Budapest 2005), ix.

18 William M. Wiecek, "Clio as Hostage: The United States Supreme Court and the Uses of History," *California Western Law Review* 24 (1987): 236–237, 266–267.

19 István Rév, *Retroactive Justice: Prehistory of Post-Communism* (Stanford: Stanford University Press, 2005), 2.

20 Ginzburg, *The Judge and the Historian*, 19, 117–118.

21 Paul Ricoeur, *Memory, History, Forgetting* (Chicago: University of Chicago Press, 2004), 320. Michael Wildt argues that the truth of the historian differs from the truth of the prosecutor in terms of their object of research, knowledge interests, goals, and modes of argumentation. Michael Wildt, "Differierende Wahrheiten: Historiker und Staatsanwälte als Ermittler von NS Verbrechen," in *Geschichte vor Gericht*, ed. Norbert Frei, 51–55. More on shifting notions of time in law and history in Berber Bevernage, "Time, Presence and Historical Injustice," *History and Theory* 47 (2008): 149–167 and Berber Bevernage, *History, Memory, and State-Sponsored Violence* (New York: Routledge, 2012).

22 M. C. Mirrow, "Kennewick Man, Identity and the Failure of Forensic History," in *History in Court*, ed. Alain Wijffels, 243.

23 Douglas R. Littlefield, "The Forensic Historian: Clio in Court," *Western Historical Quarterly* 25 (1994): 507.

24 James Gow and Ivan Zverzhanovski, "The Milošević Trial: Purpose and Performance," *Nationalities Papers* 32 (2004): 897.

25 Ksenija Turković, "Historians in Search for Truth about Conflicts in the Territory of Former Yugoslavia as Expert Witnesses in front of the ICTY," *Časopis za suvremenu povijest* 36 (2004): 42.

26 Paul Connerton, *How Societies Remember* (Cambridge: Cambridge University Press, 1989), 13.

27 Richard A. Posner, "Past-Dependency, Pragmatism, and Critique of History in Adjudication and Legal Scholarship," *The University of Chicago Law Review* 67 (2000), 573.

28 *History in Court*, ed. Alain Wijffels, 13–15.

29 Patricia Heberer and Jürgen Matthäus, "Introduction: War Crimes Trials and Historian," in *Atrocities on Trial: Historical Perspectives on the Politics of Prosecuting War Crimes*, eds. Heberer Patricia and Jürgen Matthäus (Lincoln: University of Nebraska Press, 2008), xvi.

30 "Conclusion" in *Contemporary History on Trial: Europe since 1989 and the Role of the Expert Historian*, eds. Harriet Jones, Kjell Östberg and Nico Randeraad, 198–199.

Bibliography

Berman, Harold J. *Law and Revolution: The Formation of the Western Legal Tradition*. Cambridge, MA: Harvard University Press, 1983.

Bevernage, Berber. "Time, Presence and Historical Injustice." *History and Theory* 47 (2008): 149–167.

Bevernage, Berber. *History, Memory, and State-Sponsored Violence*. New York/London: Routledge, 2012.

Bolton, Charles. "The Historians as Expert Witnesses: Creationism in Arkansas." *The Public Historian* 4 (1982): 59–67.

Brupbacher, Oliver, et al., eds. *Erinnern und Vergessen: Jahrbuch Junge Rechtsgeschichte*. München: Martin Meidenbauer, 2007.

Connerton, Paul. *How Societies Remember*. Cambridge: Cambridge University Press, 1989.

Delafontaine, Ramses. *Historians as Expert Judicial Witnesses in Tobacco Litigation: A Controversial Legal Practice*. New York: Springer, 2015.

Dumoulin, Olivier. *Le rôle social de l'historien: De la chaire au prétoire*. Paris: Albin Michel, 2003.

Evans, Richard J. "History, Memory, and the Law: The Historian as Expert Witness." *History and Theory* 41 (2002): 326–345.

Farber, Daniel A. "Adjudication of Things Past: Reflections on History as Evidence." *Hastings Law Journal* 49 (1998): 1009–1026.

Frei, Norbert, Dirk van Laak and Michael Stolleis, eds. *Geschichte vor Gericht: Historiker, Richter und suche nach Gerechtigkeit*. München: Verlag C.H. Beck, 2000.

Garscha, Winfried R., ed. *Keine "Abrechnung" NS-Verbrechen, Justiz und Gesellschaft in Europa nach 1945*. Wien: Akademishe Verlag Anst, 1998.

Ginzburg, Carlo. *The Judge and the Historian: Marginal Notes on a Late-Twentieth-Century Miscarriage of Justice*. London: Verso, 1999.

Gow, James and Ivan Zverzhanovski. "The Milošević Trial: Purpose and Performance." *Nationalities Papers* 32 (2004): 897–919.

Heberer, Patricia and Jürgen Matthäus, eds. *Atrocities on Trial: Historical Perspectives on the Politics of Prosecuting War Crimes*. Lincoln: University of Nebraska Press, 2008.

Jones, Harriet, Kjell Östberg and Nico Randeraad, eds. *Contemporary History on Trial: Europe since 1989 and the Role of the Expert Historian*. Manchester: Manchester University Press, 2007.

Kousser, Morgan J. "Are Expert Witnesses Whores? Reflections on Objectivity in Scholarship and Expert Witnessing." *The Public Historian* 6 (1984): 5–19.

Kousser, Morgan J. "Expert Witnesses, Rational Choice, and the Search for Intent." *Constitutional Commentary* 5 (1988): 349–373.

Littlefield, Douglas R. "The Forensic Historian: Clio in Court." *Western Historical Quarterly* 25 (1994): 507–512.

Martin, Brian W. "Working with Lawyers: A Historian's Perspective." *Organization of American Historians Newsletter* 30 (May, 2002): 4–5.

Martin, Jonathan D. "Historians at the Gate: Accommodating Expert Testimony in Federal Courts." *New York University Law Review* 78 (2003): 1518–1543.

McDonald, Terrence J., ed. *The Historic Turn in the Human Sciences*. Ann Arbor: University of Michigan Press, 1996.

Neuenschwander, John A. "Historians as Expert Witnesses: The View from the Bench." *Organization of American Historians Newsletter* (August, 2002): 1–6.

Ploscowe, Morris. "The Expert Evidence in Criminal Cases in France, Germany and Italy." *Law and Contemporary Problems* 2 (1935): 504–509.

Posner, Richard A. "Past-Dependency, Pragmatism, and Critique of History in Adjudication and Legal Scholarship." *The University of Chicago Law Review* 67 (2000): 573–606.

Rév, István. *Retroactive Justice: Prehistory of Post-Communism*. Stanford: Stanford University Press, 2005.

Ricoeur, Paul. *Memory, History, Forgetting*. Chicago: University of Chicago Press, 2004.

Rothman, David J. "Serving Clio and the Client: The Historian as Expert Witness." *Bulletin of the History of Medicine* 77 (2003): 25–44.

Rothman, Hal K. "Historian v. Historian: Interpreting the Past in the Courtroom." *Public Historian* 15 (1993): 39–53.

Rousso, Henry. *The Haunting Past: History, Memory, and Justice in Contemporary France*. Philadelphia: University of Pennsylvania Press, 2002.

Sarat, Austin and Thomas Kearns, eds. *History, Memory and the Law*. Ann Arbor: University of Michigan Press, 2002.

Schiler, Reuel E. "The Strawhorsemen of the Apocalypse: Relativism and the Historian as Expert Witness." *Hastings Law Journal* 49 (1998): 1169–1181.

Simpson, Gerry. *Law, War and Crime: War Crimes and the Reinvention of International Law*. Cambridge: Polity Press, 2007.

Taylor, Robert F. "A Comparative Study of Expert Testimony in France and the United States." *Texas International Law Journal* 31 (1996): 181–212.

Turković, Ksenija. "Historians in Search for Truth about Conflicts in the Territory of Former Yugoslavia as Expert Witnesses in Front of the ICTY." *Časopis za suvremenu povijest* 36 (2004): 41–67.

Uitz, Renata. *Constitutions, Courts and History, Historical Narratives in Constitutional Adjudication*. Budapest: CEU Press, 2005.

Wiecek, William M. "Clio as Hostage: The United States Supreme Court and the Uses of History." *California Western Law Review* 24 (1987): 227–267.

Wijffels, Alain, ed. *History in Court: Historical Expertise and Methods in a Forensic Context*. Leiden: Ius Deco, 2001.

Wilson, Richard Ashby. "Judging History: The Historical Record of the International Criminal Tribunal for the former Yugoslavia." *Human Rights Quarterly* 27 (2005): 908–942.

Wilson, Richard Ashby. *Writing History in International Criminal Trials*. Cambridge: Cambridge University Press, 2011.

Part I

Inceptions

Preconditions for the Emergence of Historical Forensics

1 The Long Path to Forensic Historiography

Fierce debates characterize the development of the peculiar institution of the expert in various legal traditions ranging from the hard sciences to the humanities. Developments in the forensic sciences deemed relevant for understanding the emergence of the courtroom role of historians create the background against which the "forensication" of historiography appears by no means a unique phenomenon. It does resurface, however, as a complex case burdened with the specificities of the entangled relationship between history and law.

Who Guards the Guardians? Transformations and Varieties of Expert Evidence

It is surprisingly difficult to generically define the courtroom role of experts beyond the all-purpose truism that an expert is a person who assists in the rendering of justice by providing specific knowledge for legal use. The type of knowledge, its content, the ways it has been provided, the types of assistance, and the legal contexts have varied significantly throughout history, and many of these differences persist in contemporary jurisdictions. Even terminologically, the label "expert witness," customary in common law, becomes misleading in the realm of continental law, where such a person is typically defined not as a witness, but solely as expert.[1] This peculiar position is readily noted in the literature, but not necessarily detailed for the reasons summarized by Tal Golan: "Situated at the intersection between the two dominant institutions of science and law, scientific expert testimony has long been overlooked by both. Historians of science ignored it because they did not consider courts of law to be important sites of scientific activity before the twentieth century. Historians of law ignored it because they never considered science to be a significant factor of judicial practices and jurisprudence related to the evidence. As a result, there is relatively little scholarship about the history of the relations between the two most authoritative institutions in modern Western culture—science and the law."[2]

It is therefore not an easy task to provide a comprehensive account of the development of this peculiar institution, which is probably best understood by contrasting it with the institution of the eyewitness. An expert is a person whose contribution to the establishment of legally relevant facts is not based on physical proximity to the case at stake. Experts usually do not testify about what they saw, heard, or felt. On the contrary, they step forward as bearers of specific general knowledge that can be applied to a given case, hence constructing an insight that might assist the rendering of justice. The historical variety of the contributions of experts derives exactly from such a highly contextual concept—the nature of courtroom expertise was largely dependent on the brand of knowledge acknowledged by different cultures or needed under different circumstances. Such examples are legion. Meticulous legal historians suggest there was no legal system that did not rely on some kind of expert assistance. Among the "founding fathers" of courtroom expertise one could therefore enlist Imhotep, Grand Vizier of the Pharaoh Zoser, but also biblical figures like Joseph and Daniel. Traces of expertise are present in Mesopotamia as well as in ancient Greece. Under Roman law the practice obtained its name—*forensics*—meaning "what is for the forum." In the times of the Republic and Empire, "what was for the forum" were the estimates of sanity and various medical issues, as well as parentage, handwriting, and other technical matters that the judges relegated to specialists, recognized under different names—*aestimator, numnarius, peritus, disceptor*, and ultimately *expertus*.[3] The blending of whatever remained of Roman law with various German and Celtic institutions in the Middle Ages produced new types of expertise. For instance, at the end of this long road, the fifteenth-century *Malleus Maleficarium* offers a variety of means for an expert inquisitor to recognize witches and to perform exorcisms. Admitting the complexity of the cases at stake, the authors of this booklet leave the possibility of "lawful exorcism" conducted by laymen, in which "not only physicians and astronomers be the judges, but especially Theologians."[4] On the other hand, under the auspices of humanism, a substantially different kind of expertise developed through the critical scrutiny of medieval texts, especially with the purpose of debunking their forgeries.[5]

As early modern states all over Europe were gradually assuming a monopoly over criminal prosecution, vesting the judicial process in the hands of professional judges and systematizing its procedure, the institution of expert witnessing began to resemble its contemporary shape, and in Article 147 of *Constitutio Criminalis Carolina*, from 1532, it is explicitly mentioned as such *(sachverständige Person)*.[6] At their discretion, judges could rely on medical expertise where deemed necessary, but by no means were they constrained by its findings. In continental law, the experts were summoned by the judges, however cautiously. For instance, the Civil Ordinance of Louis XIV (1667) encouraged judges to seek expert opinion, but trust in this institution diminished, among other reasons, because the function of expert became a hereditary title. This decay was reversed during the subsequent codifications of legal procedure, such as the *Constitutio Criminalis Theresiana* in German lands from 1765 and ultimately in Napoleon's *Code Civile*.[7]

Undoubtedly influenced by a growing confidence in science in the Enlightenment, these legal settings provided for experts to submit reports or to appear before judges to answer their questions. Still, their impact on the inquisitorial system was significantly curbed by the judges.

At about the same time, the first clear differences could be observed between what would become common law and the legal practice in continental Europe. As trial by jury emerged in England, jurors at this early stage were not simply considered to be laymen, but helpers to the court, and therefore were often chosen for their understanding of the dispute. They were thus considered expert jurors—"those were to be summoned who could best tell the fact."[8] In addition, the court started to call upon skilled persons to provide insights onto problems. Gradually, the jurors were de-expertized during the course of the seventeenth century as judges began to consult experts, much as in continental Europe. However, the system in Britain was leading toward a different understanding of expertise. Experts could be summoned by the judge, but also engaged by the parties. This principle was at work in the 1678 case of *Rex v. Pembroke*, a murder trial, in which both the prosecution and the defense called upon physicians to testify to the causes of symptoms observed in an autopsy. This adversarial aspect eventually prevailed by the end of the eighteenth century. Its virtues were forcefully defended in the famous *Folkes v. Chadd* case (1782), where the judge, Lord Mansfield, provided a rationale for such practice: "For in matters of science the reasoning of men of science can only be answered by men of science."[9] As a lasting trait in common law, as opposed to continental practice, the men of science became "expert witnesses" called upon by the party to testify before the jury of laymen, whereas the other side would call upon its own expert in the adversarial system which prevailed in the British Empire, and therefore in the U.S. as well. Despite these differences, the institution of expert in both criminal and civil proceedings became the norm in common and continental law by the beginning of the nineteenth century. The scientific revolution resulted in an increasing confidence in the impact of experts on rendering justice, so beautifully embodied in Arthur Conan Doyle's character Sherlock Holmes, the omnipotent detective who solves the most mysterious cases through shrewd logic and up-to-date scientific discoveries.

Growing hope in contribution of the experts was accompanied by doubts and criticism, resembling a problem neatly expressed in Juvenal's mocking of the ideal character of Plato's ideal state, defended by its guardians. "But who guards the guardians?" exclaimed Juvenal, underpinning the basic problem of expert witnessing. Experts, as well as expert witnesses, were called upon because the court, unable to grasp a certain specialized problem, was in need of information, hence raising the question of whether the trials might ultimately be decided by the experts. The old dictum *da mihi facta, dabo tibi ius* (give me the facts, I'll give you the law), meant to reassert and confirm the role of the court in the process of rendering justice, was also revealing the dependency of the court on the providers of those facts, causing an apparent tension between judge and expert.

This problem deepened with the abrupt professionalization of scholarship in the nineteenth century, and with the increasing number of criminal proceedings and civil cases appearing before the courts. It grew to particular prominence in the common law countries. "Discontent with scientific expertise in the courts has existed as long as there have been scientific expert witnesses, and by the mid-nineteenth century, the debate over the meaning of these conflicts and the ways to resolve them had all the features that today are assumed to be new," remarks Tal Golan.[10] Expert witnessing became one of the most enigmatic parts of common law procedure, treated by legal scholars as "anomalous in Anglo-Saxon law."[11] Unlike in the inquisitorial procedure of continental countries, in which such tensions were regulated through civil and criminal codes, wherein the proceedings themselves were largely in the hands of judges, adversarial procedure considered the parties as principally gatherers of evidence. The parties were finding, coaching, and examining the witnesses, as well as the experts. There was a fear that the experts would be willing to be hired and to testify on behalf of their side, setting aside scholarly criteria. Even if this partisan malpractice would be set aside, the possibility remained that the experts might start dominating the proceedings by pulling the judges and jurors into the quagmire of their esoteric debates. Such concern appeared more or less simultaneously with the full institutionalization of expert witnessing by the end of the nineteenth century in the U.S. Its early proliferation had many discontents and led to a famous remark by Judge William Foster from 1897: "There are three kinds of liars: the common liar, the damned liar, and the scientific expert."[12] Even sharper was Lee M. Friedman, who observed that "to the jury an expert is an expert—a kind of intellectual prostitute ready to sell his opinion and enlist in the services of the side that pays him."[13] Jurists as reputed as Learned Hand warned in 1900 that "no one will deny that the law should in some way effectively use expert knowledge wherever it will aid in settling disputes. The only question is as to how it can do so best." He also noted with concern the danger that "the expert becomes a hired champion of one side." Finally, he asked: "How can the jury judge between two statements each founded upon an experience confessedly foreign in kind to their own? It is just because they are incompetent for such a task that the expert is necessary at all."[14] He called for the formation of an advisory board of neutral experts, which would be of assistance to the jury in scientific matters.

Actually, a similar solution prevailed in continental law countries. The inquisitorial procedure of civil law countries (such as France or Germany) favored enlisting the experts by the courts whenever an issue exceeding the knowledge of a judge should arise. Experts were summoned by the judges, chosen from an established list, with parties given the opportunity to object to the choice of expert. The final decision nonetheless rested with the court, which not only decided on the expert, but also outlined the scope of his expertise. In general, the continental expert was to be chosen by the judge, who also instructed him about the requirements of the trial; additionally, his report was to be submitted to the judge. The parties could recommend an expert, but they did not play a role in his appointment. They could challenge the admissibility of the report or its content and attempt to invalidate it, but the final decision was in the hands of the judge.[15] However, the judge was also not bound by the findings of the report and could make the ruling contrary to the expert's findings. The experts were usually chosen from the list drawn up by the courts or justice ministries. Such a legal context put experts, judges, and the parties in a very different situation than in the common law countries, but it was not free of controversy either. In France, for instance, a relatively wide judicial reliance on expert fact-finders granted by the *Code Napoléon* was transformed through the Law of July 15, 1944, in order to ensure that "recourse to expertise was limited to those issues clearly beyond the technical competence of the court. The legislature (. . .) sought to ensure that the judge's duties could not be delegated to an expert."[16]

In both common and continental legal systems "the scientific community and the increasingly irritated judges both remained relatively oblivious to the uncertainties of scientific evidence as long as these were limited to civil litigation. But by mid-19th century, the problems of expert testimony also began to surface in the criminal system, where not only property but also life and liberty were at stake."[17] Requiring a verdict that was beyond a reasonable doubt in such cases, common law devised the custom that in criminal cases expert testimony could not provide the primary evidence (the so-called smoking gun). On the other hand, criminal trials would be quite unimaginable without the contribution of forensic pathology, clinical forensic medicine, forensic psychiatry, criminal issues in traffic accidents, dactyloscopy, document examination, firearms evidence, breath alcohol measurement, and others.[18] The list of sciences with a forensic dimension seems as endless as the ability of human beings to engage in different legal disputes. In fact, the forensic aspect became a relevant test for the very purpose of a given realm of scholarship.

It is no wonder then that in such a context the courtroom introduction of each and every branch of such knowledge was accompanied by lively debate. The uproar was particularly loud when the realm of forensics was about to embrace the social sciences, the contribution of which seemed less obvious then ballistics or medicine. Even the introduction of forensic psychology at the beginning of the twentieth century was accompanied by a significant controversy.[19] Admittedly, in the famous case *Muller v. Oregon*, argued in 1907 before the U.S. Supreme Court, Louis D. Brandeis successfully deployed his famous brief supporting the constitutionality of the limitation of working hours based on statistics from medical and sociological journals.[20] After some years of ambivalent courtroom practice, in the 1923 case of *Frye v. United States* the judges of the Appeals Court of the District of Columbia provided a ruling that has served as the lasting standard for the use of expert knowledge, which "must be sufficiently established to have gained general acceptance in the particular field in which it belongs."[21] The principle of the general acceptance of expert knowledge within its own fields was to guide the American courts for decades to come. However, many questions remained unanswered: What is generally accepted knowledge in a particular field? How are the judges and juries to recognize it? Frye's opinion rested on a static and cumulative view of the development of knowledge, and was therefore quite hostile toward spearheading up-to-date research. It was not easily applicable to the social sciences either, as demonstrated in the famous 1925 *Scopes Monkey Trial* about teaching evolution in Tennessee public schools. A number of expert witnesses from various disciplines ranging from zoology and geology to anthropology and religious studies appeared in this case, but their testimonies were not admitted into evidence, as the judge was convinced that there could be no viable expertise on the Bible.[22] As the expert role of social scientists was disputed, with both jurists and practitioners questioning whether such a contribution was legally useful, professionally justified, or methodologically sound, this debate was bound to rage in any new field that achieved a forensic component. In that respect, history was no exception.

Engaged Historians in the Courtroom and Outside

History was an exception, however, in another respect. Its practitioners could claim that unlike sociology, anthropology, or even psychology, which around the turn of the century all fought for institutionalization, history enjoyed a rich and recognizable tradition, as well as a long-standing relationship with the law. In a book with a telling title, *The Judge and the Historian*, Carlo Ginzburg noted that "the ties between history and law have always been close—they date back two thousand five hundred years, to their emergence in Greece."[23] And indeed, even etymologically, a complex interdependence between historical and legal inquiry can be traced back to their emergence in antiquity; the meaning of the ancient Greek word for historian—ἵστωρ *(hístōr)*— denotes "the one who knows," hence the expert, and in some contexts, even investigator and judge.[24] This bond was also rediscovered in the Renaissance: "Historical studies must be placed upon a solid foundation of law, and jurisprudence must be joined to history," wrote François Baudouin in 1561.[25] Ever since, there is hardly a shortage of references to the proximity between these modes of human experience. As early as 1814 Joseph von Hormayr was praising "history, that pure two-sided mirror of judgments past and judgments still to come, that inexhaustible source of universally beneficial experience, and incorruptible judge of those who have no other judge."[26] A similarly powerful understanding was immortalized in Schiller and Hegel's vision of *Weltgeschichte als Weltgericht* (global history as global court). This vision persisted in frequent, if implicit, metaphors of the tribunal of history or the judgment of history. Scaled down from the high ground of philosophy of history to pedestrian concerns of historiographers, frequently compared with judges, advocates, prosecutors, detectives, and witnesses, this analogy was growing in complexity, as observed in 1808 by Lord Henry Brougham:

> There is this general distinction between contemporary history and all other history,—that the former is a witness, the latter a judge. The opinions of a contemporary author on the events which he records, are only then authority, when the impression made on a bystander happens to be a material part of the case; nor is this any exception to the maxim, that his business is to testify, not to lecture. On facts, however, he is paramount evidence; and that, not only in the age immediately succeeding him, but also, which is generally forgotten, to the latest times. The modern historian, who consults original authorities through the medium of some later predecessor, descends from the character of a judge to that of a faithful reporter of decisions.[27]

"Yet it must be owed," cautioned Brougham, himself a jurist who was to become Lord Chancellor, "that the distinction which has been mentioned between the writer of the past and those of contemporary history, is not always perfect. In many cases, therefore, our witness is compelled to act the part of a judge. There are others, in which the judge must become a witness."[28] Such instability of roles did not fit well into the project of transformation of historiography into a fully institutionalized academic discipline, spearheaded later in the century by the creators of the most influential historical seminars in Europe. In the view of their founding figures, if it was to become a science, historiography was to be based on the meticulous but chronologically distanced investigation of as many available sources as possible with the purpose of creating an objective account of past events. "To history has been assigned the office of judging the past, of instructing the present for the benefit of future ages. To such high offices this work does not aspire: It wants only to show what actually happened *(wie es eigentlich gewesen)*," wrote Leopold von Ranke in his much-quoted dictum, which has guided generations of practitioners, well beyond his Friedrich Wilhelms University of Berlin.[29] One such admirer, Lord Acton, agreed in his famous 1895 inaugural speech at Cambridge that "history, to be above evasion or dispute, must stand on documents, not on opinions." However, for him this was a path for historians to move from the biased role of hanging judge to become "an accepted tribunal, and the same for all."[30] He therefore diverted from otherwise revered Ranke: "He will not judge, he only relates"[31]. Either way, a new professional ideal, described by Peter Novick, envisaged "the objective historian's role (. . .) of a neutral, or disinterested, judge; it must never degenerate into that of advocate or, even worse, propagandist. The historian's conclusions are expected to display the standard judicial qualities of balance and evenhandedness. As with judiciary, these qualities are guarded by the insulation of the historical profession from social pressure or political influence, and by the individual historian avoiding partisanship or bias."[32]

The availability of sources and their impartial analysis was to be secured by a detachment created through the temporal remoteness between the researcher and the topic—the famed historical distance. This detachment created a gap between historians and the legal and political concerns of contemporary society. The influential methodological textbook of Charles Langlois and Charles Seignobos echoes this idea: "It is an obsolete illusion to suppose that history supplies information of practical utility in the conduct of life."[33] Lastly, Peter Novick observes that "with the development of new, autonomous, policy-oriented social science disciplines, there was a migration out of history on the part of those of more activist inclination. The tension between advocacy and objectivity existed among political scientists, sociologists, and economists—not historians."[34] Due to this increasing gap, historians were not perceiving themselves as helpful experts for the courtroom.

Lawyers seemed to concur. Words Petrarch wrote in the fourteenth century seemed to apply well half a millennia later: "The majority of our jurists, caring little or nothing for the origins of law and the first fathers of jurisprudence, or anything except professional gain (. . .) did not believe that knowledge of the arts and of literature would be of use."[35] Even in England, where judges like Francis Buller maintained that "a general history may be admitted to prove a matter relating to the kingdom at large," this principle was challenged in the famous case of the impeachment of Warren Hastings, in which Edmond Burke attempted to introduce extracts from the historical work of Prince Demetris Cantemir as evidence. Against the substantial opposition by Hastings' attorney, who dismissed these writings as "reveries," he succeeded to read and introduce excerpts, retorting that "Prince Cantemir was a man of great learning (. . .) the history of such a man could not without much decency called reveries."[36] This was however an exception, as similar practice was challenged in later cases.[37] The legal value of historical arguments was challenged by as persuasive an authority as Frederic William Maitland, whose inaugural lecture at Cambridge in 1888 offered a warning against the temptation to "mix up two different logics, the logic of authority, and the logic of evidence. What the lawyer wants is authority and the newer the better; what the historian wants is evidence and the older the better. A mixture of legal dogma and legal history is in general an unsatisfactory compound. I do not say that there are not judgments and text-books which have achieved the difficult task of combining the results of deep historical research with a luminous and accurate exposition of existing law—neither confounding the dogma nor perverting the history; but the task is difficult."[38] Perhaps therefore it does not come as a surprise that this gap was breached across the Channel, in France, where Montesquieu famously expressed the need to "illuminate history by laws and laws by history," recognized in a vivid scholarly production of the postrevolutionary period.[39] By the end of the nineteenth century, this recipe was to be tested in the most dramatic legal event that was shaking the French public and shaping its political and intellectual landscape—the Dreyfus affair.

The Dreyfus Affair: Historians Debunking Forgeries

Launched in 1894 with the suspicion that confidential information was leaked to the German embassy from the French General Staff, the affair took off as the finger of accusation was pointed toward Captain Alfred Dreyfus, a French artillery officer of Jewish origin. By the end of the year, he was arrested, tried for treason by a military tribunal, and sentenced to life imprisonment.[40] However, such a prompt rendering of justice, surrounded with chauvinistic and anti-Semitic campaigning, raised suspicions about foul play. It was becoming apparent that Dreyfus was not convicted on solid evidence, that the trial was not transparent, and that he was scapegoated and even framed by the top echelons of the French military. Hence the reopening of his case became a rallying cry for a group of intellectuals assembled around the newly formed *Ligue des droits de l'homme* (Human Rights League), pursuing the revision of the case with growing zeal. In the legal quagmire that followed the arrest of Dreyfus, the crux of the case revolved around written evidence of dubious authenticity. Examination of those documents was conducted hastily by inadequate specialists.[41] Many grew convinced that the crucial documents, among others the infamous *bordereau* found at the German embassy, were either forged or falsely attributed to Dreyfus. When Émile Zola started writing his articles in late 1897, culminating with the famous *J'accuse!*, he warned the French president that "France has this stain on its cheek. History will write that it is under your presidency that such social crime could be committed."[42]

Zola hoped that not only history, but also historians would support him. As he was promptly accused of defaming the military and was to appear at court, he wrote to a number of historians that he "would cite as witnesses before the jury of the Seine, scholars, paleographers, historians accustomed to these scientific methods."[43] His chances to find allies in these quarters were good. It is much less known that he was not the first intellectual to speak publicly for Dreyfus. Three weeks before him, Gabriel Monod (1844–1912) had done so. One of the most distinguished French historians, famed medievalist, and founder of the chair of history at École des hautes etudes, Monod was also creator of *Revue Historique*. In his 1876 opening article of this venerable periodical he wrote: "It is in this manner that history, without assumptions to any profit apart of the one that we draw from the truth works in a discrete and certain manner toward the greatness of the nation, and at the same time towards the progress of the human race."[44] Two decades later, he was challenged to translate this ideal into practice. In late 1897 Mathieu Dreyfus, the brother of the accused, showed the letters with his brother's handwriting to Monod, who compared it to the facsimile of the bordereau published in *Le Matain* a year before. After initial graphological analysis Monod was convinced that Dreyfus could not be its author; he made this public in an open letter to *Le Temps*, becoming thus the first among intellectuals to advocate the revision of the process, weeks before Zola: "I have read carefully the facsimile of the bordereau attributed to Captain Dreyfus. (. . .) I believe I can determine that it was not written by his hand (. . .) and that he was a victim of most tragic judicial error. (. . .) I'd also add that the content of the document even increased my suspicion. I was silent until now (. . .) convinced that my personal conviction was not enough to secure the revision of the trial."[45] Together with Albert Sorel, his colleague from the French Institute, he joined the ranks of Dreyfusards, alongside classicist Louis Havet, archaeologist Salamon Reinach, and chemist Émile Duclaux from the Institute, as well as poet Anatole France, educationalist Ferdinand Buisson, journalist Octave Mirbeau, librarian Lucien Herr, archivist Paul Viollet, essayist Edmond Fleg, and politician Léon Blum.[46] Among them, historians were perhaps less publicly visible, but legally they had the most relevant role. As the case was about to be appealed, Monod started preparing his expert opinion for the Court of Cassation.[47]

With graphology still in its cradle, it made sense to turn to historians, who by virtue of their training specialized in debunking the famous forgeries of the Middle Ages.[48] Historians boasted great experience in working on the fringes of the law, as emphasized in one of the first French textbooks on historical methodology, written in 1897: "The notion of *witness* has been borrowed from the procedure of the law-courts. (. . .) We apply to authors that juridical procedure which divides witnesses into admissible and inadmissible. Instinctively we take sides with the author on whom we have bestowed our approval, and we go so far as to say, as in the law courts, that the burden of proof rests with those who reject valid testimony."[49]

However, even the authors of this textbook, Charles Langlois and Charles Seignobos, were initially reluctant to put these pronouncements into practice on a case as contemporary and as hot as the Dreyfus affair. Others, galvanized by Monod, volunteered to serve as experts in several trials related to the affair. Enthusiastically responding to Zola's invitation, many historians, particularly medievalists from École des chartes, had an opportunity to offer their expertise at his defamation trial in early 1898. The trial against Zola, who was accused in 1898 of defaming the Army, was therefore an opportunity for this group to act and to widen. Alongside experts from other disciplines, a number of respected French historians took on the challenge of witnessing. Famed historians Arthur Giry, Paul Meyer, and the brothers Molinier—paleographer Auguste and historian and Louvre curator Émile—applied the historical method to critique the sources of the disputed documents, primarily arguing that the author of the incriminating bordereau was not Dreyfus, but another officer, Major Esterhazy. They were called by Zola and all accepted his invitation, except Abel Lefranc, who worried he would

Figure 1.1 Professor Gabriel Monod and Captain Alfred Dreyfus, 1910

not be seen as competent enough.[50] As the date of the trial approached, they went public as well, sometimes even forgetting necessary caution. "Meyer, for example, told *L'Aurore* before Zola's trial that even an ignoramus would be able to see that the writing on the bordereau belonged to Esterhazy, a statement that invited the question of why, in that case, expert skills were needed in court."[51] This provoked Robert de Lasteyrie, also an alumnus of École des chartes and a member of the Institute de France to attack historians for testifying about a document "that they only know from a crude facsimile. (. . .) I can scarcely understand how they could have forgotten to such an extent all the critical traditions honored at the École des chartes." To protect this tradition, he organized a Manifesto of the Chartists published in *L'éclair* on March 22, 1898, calling for methodological restraint in contemporary matters. Still, historians who would be testifying in Zola trials would not be easily deterred. Molinier claimed the "applicability of universal critical method: knowledge of thousands of documents from different eras did indeed qualify someone to judge the bordereau."[52]

Historians exhibited the same determination on the stand. Arthur Giry, a professor at École des hautes études who testified in the Zola case about the authorship, passionately asserted their professional authority over the documents: "The study and the composition of the text are naturally one important part in our branch of erudition; we teach our pupils to determine the age, the origin, and provenience, to discern between authentic, false, interpolated and sincere documents. The method is always the same. It does not vary, because we have such a particular education that gives habit to observe in a text the most detailed particularities. We can as well apply this method to the contemporary text as much as to the Ancient text."[53] However, as persuasive as he was, he could not sway the judges, who were not necessarily as impressed as his students. Paul Meyer, the director of the École des chartes, got a similar treatment when reprimanded by the presiding judge for using notes: "I am not reading. Mr. President, I am just a professor, and as I have a poor memory, I am always obliged to write down, in a sentence or two, the ideas I am about to convey."[54] At the very beginning of their expert role, historians were to learn an important lesson: the courtroom was no classroom. Zola was convicted, and had fled to England before the verdict was rendered on his appeal. However, this development aroused more public sympathy for the revisionists, and had opened up the avenue for their original goal—the review of the Dreyfus case.

Historians were even blunter during this review, held from August to September 1899 in Rennes. In particular, its sixteenth session, held on August 30, allowed Paul Meyer, August Molinier, and Arthur Giry to substantiate their argument that Esterhazy was the author of the bordereau.[55] Émile Molinier also restated the arguments on the issue of the authenticity of the disputed documents, claiming that they could not possibly have been written by Dreyfus on the basis of his professional authority: "I will allow myself to remind you on this topic that the rules of historical critique which I apply to the expertise of commander Esterhazy's paper are the same rules that historians have been applying to all forms of historical writings during the previous centuries." He was challenging the authority of previous experts: "You may perhaps tell me that I am not an expert. This is the third time that I had come to testify and the first in which I have offered my expertise in a case of writing. But if I allow myself to put this opinion in front of you with such a force, that is because it is a result of very long personal study."[56] No less than ten graphological experts were again depositing lengthy but conflicting evidence, hence historians made a much better impression among the spectators.[57] Jean Jaurès wrote: "They were not divided as experts in the Dreyfus case, and they do not operate behind closed doors as did the experts in the Esterhazy case."[58] Young Julien Benda was even more impressed, comparing "patient historical research with disgust to those 'men of letters' who distorted reason to serve their political agenda" with "history and its rigor as a discipline."[59]

In the short run, public reactions were of little help, as the judges were not so impressed. "The court listened to them with scrupulous but mistrustful attention, for it regards them primarily as 'intellectuals,' presumptuous pedants and members of a cast who believe that they constitute an aristocracy of the intellect and are all more or less lost to patriotism," observed Maurice Paleologue, perceptive observer of the affair.[60] Dreyfus was reconvicted, his sentence lowered to ten years. However, the tide was turning, as more evidence on Dreyfus' innocence was coming to light. After fierce public pressure, Dreyfus was eventually pardoned by the French president in 1899, and was finally fully rehabilitated by the court in 1906, knighted with the *Légion d'Honneur* and reintegrated into the French army in the same year.

In the Dreyfus affair, historians contributed significantly to the undoing of the miscarriage of justice. "Detectives at work, they thoroughly enjoyed showing the usefulness of their technique. (. . .) It was a glorious time for those men whose participation in political life so far had been so limited."[61] The rationale of their engagement was spelled out by Zola's friend, one of the founders of the Human Rights League and one of the Sorbonne's foremost professors of history, Gabriel Séailles: "Our teaching would lose all authority if we were not ready to confirm it by our deeds."[62] Through this confrontation with the most traditionalist parts of the French society, these intellectuals were also asserting their cosmopolitan attitudes and credentials—it is by no means a coincidence that Gabriel Monod was in the forefront of the initiative to organize the International Historical Congress, first structural cross-border cooperation of historians. The inaugural meeting was held in The Hague in 1898, as Monod reported, with "no friction resulting from the presence of scholars of different nationalities, languages and conceptions."[63] The first congress was held in Paris in 1900, with a strong emphasis on comparative transnational historical research.

There were powerful countertendencies. The nationalist fervor of the period was threatening to compromise the high standards of historical scholarship, as historians were tempted to put their skills and credentials to the service of the national cause, leaving the ones who declined exposed to lasting hatred from the right wing.[64] This trend was by no means restricted to France. As Harold Berman reminds, "the emergence in the nineteenth century of the so-called scientific history, that is of systematic and painstaking research (. . .) coincided with the emergence of the most intense nationalism that Europe had yet experienced. It was simply assumed that history meant national history."[65] In a sense, emancipation and the commitment of historians in the Dreyfus case, who overcame disciplinary conservatism, nationalistic bias, and racial prejudice, was more an exception than the rule.

The Friedjung Trial: Forgeries That Debunked a Historian

In late 1909, shortly after Dreyfus was rehabilitated, a libel suit was brought against well-known Austrian historian Heinrich Friedjung (1851–1920).[66] Friedjung was one of the first historians of the contemporary period, the author of widely respected monographs on the recent history of Central Europe *(Der Kampf um die Vorherschaft in Deutschland 1859–1866, Der Kriemkrieg und die österreichischen Politik*, and *Österreich von 1848 bis 1860)*. He entered political life as a pan-German, but was excluded from the Greater German Party due to his Jewish origins. Eventually, he found a new cause in defending the Habsburg monarchy from the perceived Slavic danger.[67] To that end, he joined the campaign fought by a number of Vienna journals, closely aligned with the proponents of bellicose action within the administration of Austria-Hungary. The aim was to implicate Croatian and Serbian politicians, who were acting in a coalition from 1905 in Austro-Hungary in maintaining treasonous connections with Serbia.[68]

Such articles appeared by the beginning of 1909 in the daily *Reichpost*, and were backed by Friedjung's article "Österreich-Ungarn und Serbien," published in the *Neue Freie Presse* in March 1909. His essays presented an overview of contemporary foreign policy, sprinkled with sensational claims and exclusive documents. Friedjung was analyzing the impact of the change of Serbian dynasties and their implication for the region, stressing that this change marked the beginning of instabilities caused by constant conspiracies launched against the Habsburg monarchy; these conspiracies were allegedly assisted by insiders in the monarchy, chiefly the presumably bought representatives of the Croato-Serbian coalition, presumed to have been receiving money from the Serbian government through the organization "Slovene South," whose ultimate purpose was the dismembering of the Dual Monarchy. His article was not only descriptive, but also prescriptive. As he states, "It would be a cultural deed of the highest value if Austrian weapons would be ordered to annihilate the conspiratorial center in Belgrade and help the healthy elements of Serbian society to prevail."[69]

The warmongering article appeared at the peak of the crisis that erupted in 1908 when Bosnia was annexed by Austria-Hungary, bringing it to the brink of war with Serbia, but also with Russia. As the crisis was resolved, instead of announcing sequels, Miroslav Spalajković, official of the Serbian Ministry for Foreign Affairs and depicted by Friedjung as the key conspirator, reacted immediately. Denying the entire content of the article, Spalajković demanded "arbitrage by experts on the documents." Friedjung accepted the challenge and even raised the stakes, showing his readiness not only for arbitrage over the documents, but for no less than a trial: "While Mr. Spalajković has the right to deny everything even under the arbitrage, I am in a contrary position. (. . .) That is the difference between him, who was the soul of the war party against Austria-Hungary in his Ministry, and me, as a historian who aspires to the truth." Asked to provide evidence for his accusations of the Parliamentarians of the Croato-Serbian coalition, Friedjung stated: "If I were to be called in front of the court, I would bring out my documentary material in its entirety in order to establish legal and historical facts." He maintained that his article was based on scholarly scrutiny, "just as any of the documents in my historical books. Having in mind the course of my studies, I believe that I am recognized for my ability to distinguish true historical sources and documents from false ones. I gather one will also acknowledge that I am not led by political passion and personal hatred in establishing the facts. Therefore I dare demand that my article is given full historical credibility."[70] Friedjung got what he called for, as fifty-two parliamentarians sued him and the editors of *Reichpost* and *Neue Freie Presse* for libel. He had put his professional reputation at stake, guaranteeing the professional quality of his interpretations and the reliability and authenticity of his sources, which he assembled in a volume that he presented to a Landsgericht in Vienna, where a jury trial was held between December 9 and 22, 1909.[71]

At the outset of the trial, which opened with his defense, Friedjung confidently explained that "it is no business of the historian to reduce men's words and deeds to the provisions of a penal code; his task is to examine documents, to establish facts and illustrate characters." He finished his plaidoyer with outmost confidence: "Experts and historians are there to give judgments if I did my job well. I think I was building on a sound ground, and let it be the base for jurors to reach their verdict."[72] However, it was exactly on this front line that Friedjung started losing ground. In the course of the trial it emerged that his essay was based on material that seemed to be confidential correspondence and documentation of high Serbian officials.[73] Photographed and supplied to the Austrian legation in Belgrade through shady intelligence channels, they were taken at face value in Vienna due to their explosive character and ultimately their translations were leaked to Friedjung directly from the Austrian Foreign Office, on the instructions of its head, Count Ährenthal. Unable to read Serbian, Friedjung took the translations at face value. As he said in the trial, "I was chosen to publish these protocols and reveal Serbian conspiracies as the intention was to use my name to uplift the importance of the publication (. . .) I published the article

Wiener Bilder

Illustrirtes Familienblatt

Nr. 50. Wien, Mittwoch, 15. Dezember 1909. XIV. Jahrgang.

Redaktion und Administration: III. Beatrixgasse 14b. — Telephon Nr. 1048 röm. VI. — K. k. Postsparkassen-Konto Nr. 54.151.

Ein Monstre-Ehrenbeleidigungsprozess.

Der Angeklagte Dr. Heinrich Friedjung hält seine Verteidigungsrede.

Im Innern des Blattes:

Giftmordversuche an Generalstäblern. Die Brandkatastrophe in Hamburg.

Weihnachts-Preisrätsel.

Figure 1.2 Professor Heinrich Friedjung questioned on the stand, front page of *Wiener Bilder*, 15 December 1909

as at the time the danger of war with Serbia was culminating. If it were not for that danger, I would not publish."[74] Asked to provide the originals of the facsimiles of the documents, he desperately attempted to obtain them, writing personally to Count Ährenthal, pleading that his professional career was at stake: "As in the article I explicitly said that I have the documents at my disposal, I need them to cover myself as a historian. This is an important point which decides if the article is written by a historian or by a publicist. It has been only a few months since the Austrian Academy of Sciences elected me as associate member, and there will be great surprise among their circles if I appear before jurors without convincing material."[75] Despite the plea, he could present only three facsimiles and one transcription, whereas other documents were withheld by the Ministry, whose officials started doubting their authenticity and attempted to control political damage at the expense of cutting Friedjung loose. In reality, Ährenthal, who knew Friedjung from 1898, used his professional credentials, assessing him as a vain and naïve academic suitable for manipulation.[76]

During the rest of the trial, witness after witness appeared, challenging the authenticity of the documents which were used, analyzing anachronisms in the text and inconsistencies of the content. Friedjung could only fume as he questioned them: "I hold it unheard of that witnesses from Serbia simply dismiss as mystifications and crude forgery all the documents used by the leading persons of this Monarchy in shaping policy toward Serbia." Spalajković retorted: "There are forgers all over the world, who deceive even politicians and people in the highest positions. This is what happened now as well, and I pity the victims of this deceit."[77] This view was supported by Tomáš Masaryk, for whom this case was yet another cause célèbre to demonstrate pressure on the Slavic population of the Habsburg monarchy. He testified about his own inquiries in Belgrade on the nature of the documents, which he considered to be crude forgeries. In the final stage of the trial, this opinion was also supported through the expertise provided to the court by Milan Rešetar (1860–1942), professor of Slavistics at Vienna University, and the court's translator, Dr. Kraus. Their joint opinion related to a supposed copy of Spalajković's report was read on December 20. Analyzing its grammar, linguistics, expressions, orthography, and style, they reached the conclusion that the author of the text had no profound knowledge of the Serbian language; the expressions used in the documents were highly atypical for the vocabulary of Serbian diplomacy. They also claimed that the other documents submitted by Friedjung were likely to be forgeries. Another expert called by the court, a reputed young historian, Dr. Hans Übersberger (1877–1962), a docent specializing in the history of Eastern Europe at the University of Vienna, attempted to offer a counter-version, insisting: "[There are] methodological differences between Professor Reshetar and me. He is a philologist, I am a historian."[78] He was much readier to consider the documents authentic transcriptions; apparently without much success, as the day after the President of the Court assisted in brokering the settlement between the parties, according to which the plaintiffs withdrew their charges in return for Professor Friedjung's statement of apology, publicly recognizing the questionable nature of his sources.

The pro-Yugoslav press was jubilant: "Was Herr Friedjung a dupe or accomplice of the exalted purveyors of the documents? The papers were drawn up in Serbian, of which Herr Friedjung confessedly did not understand a word. Did that excuse him? Could he exonerate himself by pleading blind confidence in his patrons? A justification of this kind was his death-warrant as a historian."[79] Even Friedjung's admirers, like A. J. P. Taylor, who translated his seminal book into English, were forced to conclude that "the contrast between Friedjung the historian and Friedjung the politician is at first sight overwhelming."[80] Indeed, Friedjung's professional reputation was badly bruised, to the extent that even a pro-Slav observer such as Seton-Watson felt compelled to console him after the trial: "As a fellow soldier in an army of historians, I wanted to convey to my General that in my view the process did not damage your stature as a man and historian at the least. This cannot be said for those who had put a historian of such a position in so disgraceful a manner."[81] However, in other writings Seton-Watson contributed this blunder to a particular patriotic fever which overtook Friedjung: "Not being in the position to defend his fatherland, sword in hand, he conceived it to be his plain duty as a historian and publicist, to place his pen at the service of Austria, and in so doing he was only continuing his life's work of strengthening the consciousness of his fellow citizens with an interpretation of their past history."[82] Such an attitude was not atypical for historians of the time, and was increasing as the crisis leading to the First World War was mounting. According to Ernst Breisach, until then most historians "agreed that history was an endeavor with the purely theoretical interest of reconstructing the past and without any practical interests, be it lessons, devotion, entertainment, or propaganda. Yet since 1914 adherents of both answers have confronted problems."[83] Older historians, like Heinrich Friedjung or Hans Übersberger, joined the ranks in writing proposals for the postwar order, after the presumed victory of their country.[84] Their younger colleagues went to the trenches.

Reaching the Incompatibility Presumption

For historians across the front lines, the Great War hardly ended in 1918. The wartime explosion of nationalist hysteria was followed by postwar resentment and bitterness. "The war posed a fundamental and sweeping challenge to the profession's posture of disinterested objectivity."[85] Although some attempts to patch prewar academic cooperation were made, most visibly through recommencing of international congresses and even creation of the International Commission on Historical Sciences in 1926, the ideal of impartiality was too easily giving way to the promotion of the national cause.[86] Historians entered this minefield through the publication of edited volumes of documentation, typically called White, Red, and Yellow Books of documents, mostly tailored to demonstrate the wrongdoings of the other side.[87] Instead of providing a critical reading of the crisis and the outbreak of war, many historians frequently followed this logic and remained confined by immediate political concerns, producing arguments favorable to "their" side and avoiding responsibility for the outbreak of war.[88] This "world war of documents" was also prompted with another novelty, as the Soviet government advanced the principle of open diplomacy, revealing in the process a bulk of secret treaties, correspondence, and documentation created by previous governments.[89] In order to deal with this disruption into the secrecy of diplomatic transactions and into the notion of historical distance, other governments followed with undertakings of selective releases of governmental material, by definition of an exonerating nature. Such tendencies outlasted the war, and indeed they were the driving force behind the spread of contemporary historiography in the interwar period by promoting large state-sponsored projects of publishing sources on foreign policies, conceived within the idea of legitimizing their national standpoints.[90] This tendency reached its heights in so-called *Kriegsshuldfrage*—the debate over the guilt for the outbreak of war.

This debate started immediately with the end of hostilities, through the demands by the victorious Entente powers that Germany should acknowledge responsibility for the outbreak of the war, punish the perpetrators, and suffer legal and economic consequences. In early 1919, the German government probed into the idea of forming a special court to investigate the matter. However, the majority of German jurists expressed the view that "the question was political and historical, and in no case a legal problem."[91] Initially it seemed that Inter-Allied Commission on the Authorship of War seemed to share their view, reporting that aggression was not an act but "the consequence of social, political and economic forces beyond the ken of any court or commission" which "public consciousness reproves and history will condemn," and therefore "a matter for historians and statesmen, and not courts."[92] However, as negotiations in Paris were progressing, it was clear that a tougher approach would prevail in the final text of a peace treaty. And indeed, Article 231 of the Versailles Treaty stated: "The Allied and Associated Governments affirm and Germany accepts the responsibility of Germany and her allies for causing all the loss and damage to which the Allied and Associated Governments and their nationals have been subjected as a consequence of the war imposed upon them by the aggression of Germany and her allies."[93] Reparation demands were based on that claim.

At first, all that the German side could do was sign the treaty on June 28, 1919, and accept the related obligations. However, in August 1919, the German parliament had already created a commission to investigate the causes of the war, and gave commissionaires privileged access to the newly founded *Reichsarchiv*. Soon after, the German Ministry of Foreign Affairs created a specialized service for the question of war guilt, supporting simultaneously the seemingly private institution named *Zentralstelle für Erforschung der Kriegsursachen* (1921–1937).[94] The goal was the same—securing the ground for the revision of clauses in the Versailles peace treaty by shifting the responsibility for the outbreak of the war.

A number of historians were engaged in this work. The oldest and most reputed among them was Hans Delbrück (1848–1929), who was overseeing the activity of Zentralstelle, engaged in editing the growing collection of primary diplomatic sources.[95] Whereas seasoned Delbrück contributed with his reputation, the much younger Justus Hashagen (1877–1961) brought in zeal and a new approach. Already in 1915 he had pioneered the term *Zeitgeschichte* (contemporary history) in a combatant booklet, arguing for the acceleration of scholarly production in this field against the British and the French, "because such literature is political power."[96] Not discouraged by the defeat in war, during which he was managing patriotic education within the military, he continued to advocate historical engagement on a national front in a programmatic essay written at the end of the war: "New obligations are arising from the war for the German historian as well. The external would be that he would have to investigate the international history of the recent past with greater zeal than before. (. . .) Contemporary history, once the favorite subject of study of German historians (. . .), has to be elevated from the neglected prewar position of step-child."[97] In the early interwar period, he even attempted to give a theoretical edge to such activism, arguing that after all, every history is engaged and biased, the more so as it deals with contemporary issues.[98] Hashagen was soon given an opportunity to apply his teaching, as he was consulting the Ministry of Foreign Affairs on the war guilt question, editing their documents, but also contributing to Zentralstelle's journal *Kriegsschuldfrage* (the Question of War Guilt). Although the journal, renamed in 1929 to *Berliner Monatshefte für international Aufklärung die Kriegsschuldfrage*, was declaratively open to impartial debate, it was tasked to help exonerate Germany. Such concentrated action even mobilized limited support from non-German authors, such as Sidney Fay, Harry Elmer Barnes, Charles Beard, Pierre Renouvin, and in particular James Mackinnon, who in 1923 conceeded that "the question of war guilt cannot yet be definitely settled from the objective point of view simply for the lack of the full documentary evidence which lies hidden in the various European chanceries. But there are already indications which tend to throw doubt on the dogma on exclusive responsibility of the Central Powers."[99]

Working as the extended arms of their foreign ministry, Hashagen and others were experimenting with methodological innovations, reaching out to the recent past and consciously breaking the previously sacrosanct demand of historical detachment and emotional distance. However, mixing historical with legal arguments, in order to provide a sustainable explanation for the outbreak of the war, led to a failure to resolve these differences on the heuristic and interpretative levels, and considerably added to frustration and revanchism. It became part of an earthquake well described by Ernst Troeltsch in the article *Crisis of Historicism* (1922), where he emphasized that "the crisis is, of course, sharpest in Germany, the motherland of modern history. (. . .) The World War here has in particular completely cluttered all historical thinking, devalued old structures and standards, and completely abandoned new problems, but at the same time it created a twofold or even threefold skepticism toward any history."[100] Much of this disarray was visible in the activity of the German Parliament's Commission for Research on the Question of Responsibility for the World War, which worked from 1919 to 1932 in four working groups, engaging in obtaining documents, questioning eyewitnesses, and ordering expert reports *(Gutachten)* and hearing their authors in the capacity of experts *(Sachversständige)*. Among the approximately thirty-five experts who appeared in front of the commission, reputed professionals like Delbrück were greatly outnumbered by self-styled historians, including Dietrich Schäfer, Max von Montgelas, and Ernst Fischer. Needless to say, their arguments were supporting the growing officialized narrative of government, shifting the blame for war responsibility away from Germany. There were exceptions, however, including legal historian Hermann Kantorowicz (1877–1940), who warned of the dangers in crossing the boundaries between history, politics, and law: "It is a great, but deeply rooted mistake to think that the essence of this question is historical, that it can be decided by 'history,' that in practice professors of history should be included in its solution. A historian can only establish the facts, the judgment on these facts is not his task. (. . .) At this court, historical science must appear as the witness, which assists in the making of the judgment with relevant expert help, but does not sit in the court as a judge."[101] His 1923 report challenged the nationalist orthodoxy, claiming that a large part of the responsibility for the outbreak of war was indeed with Germany, documenting this claim with embarrassing data, such as that over 75% of documents from the official 1914 German White Book were forged. His moderate analysis of the causes of war, which did not meet nationalist expectations, earned him many enemies. There was certainly no love lost between him and the revisionists of the Zentralstelle. He had no illusions about "the articles published by the German Review Die Kriegsschuldfrage," stating: "It is most depressing to observe how many Englishmen and Americans, for whose 'enlightenment' this review is mainly intended, have allowed themselves to be misled by it. (. . .) This group disposes not merely of a great deal of capital, but of much learning, industry, ingenuity and skill, and above all, ardent patriotism. But the aims which they pursue have very little to do with learning and truth (. . .) The present reaction in Germany rests to a great extent upon this propaganda. (. . .) It is my conviction that the future of our country rests not upon propaganda, however skilful and patriotic, but solely upon the truth."[102]

In the short run, Kantorowicz's position was self-defeating. His report was excluded from the Reichstag's publication of reports and Commission documents. His professional advancement hindered, he obtained a professorship in Kiel but was blacklisted by the Nazis both due to his activity and his Jewish descent. Consequently, upon the *Machtergreiffung* (Nazi takeover of power in 1933), Kantorowicz's books were burned during the Nazi-staged rallies, and he himself was forced out of his professorship into emigration; his report remained unpublished for forty years.[103] Ironically, emigration was also the destiny of some of the most prolific contributors to the German side of the *Kriegsschuldfrage*. Many of the upcoming and most promising German historians like Gerhard Ritter and Hans Rothfels were sympathetic toward a favorable resolution of the *Kriegsschuldfrage* and occasionally contributed to the journal. In 1932, German historians collectively pleaded from Historikertag, held in Göttingen, for "a clean scholarly exploration of the reasons for war," arguing that "the expression Kriegsschuldfrage is non-scholarly and does not belong to the language of historians. The craft works with categories of causes and consequences, and not with moralistic concepts like guilt and atonement."[104] Historiographic resistance toward the Versailles treaty became mainstream even before Hitler came to power.

However, by that time historians like Hans Rothfels and Hans Herzfeld discovered they had to leave their academic posts, and eventually Germany as well, due to their Jewish origins. The journal *Kriegsschuldfrage* was also discontinued, in 1934. Zentralstelle lingered for some years but without much relevance, as Hitler's rise to power rendered any debate about wartime responsibility obsolete.[105] Even the champions of engaged nationalist historiography like Justus Hashagen hardly profited from the rise of Nazis. Not ready to follow completely the vehemently anti-Semitic party line, Hashagen was pushed out of his university in 1936, and criminal proceedings against him were suspended only because he was found mentally unstable and forced into retirement.[106]

Such an epilogue seemed to justify a cautiousness of the old guard of German conservative historians, who found the topic to be too recent and politicized to be academically handled. *Historische Zeitschrift*, the most venerable and influential journal of the country, dedicated only nine articles to the First World War during the period between 1914 and 1933. As the extremes of the twentieth century brought the activities of history writing and rendering justice back together, the retreat to the Ivory Tower seemed more appealing. In Germany, the neo-Rankean approach was advocated by Friedrich Meinecke, emblematic historian of the Weimar period, alarmed "that for years there has been sounding that historism must be transcended." On the contrary, said Meinecke, "the rise of historism was one of the greatest intellectual revolutions that has ever taken place in Western thought."[107] Following this trajectory from Leibniz and Vico through Goethe and Herder until Leopold von Ranke, Meinecke was praising the distance of non-engaged historiography, most tellingly in his 1936 address to the Prussian Academy of Sciences: "In the midst of the vast historical and intellectual transformations in which we are involved. Our hearts may be full of this question, and we may well feel that each of us in our inmost selves could find a definite answer. Yet it is right and proper on this occasion to avoid all controversy, and to let our thoughts rest in the peace of true contemplation."[108] In the short run, this strategy kept traditional historians floating above the swamp of the Third Reich. The time for contemplation, however, was running out. As one of the Swiss hosts of the last interwar International Historical Congress held in Zurich in 1938 observed: "We noticed how little the historians from the various national camps socialized with one another, how frostily they faced each other. (. . .) Most of the lectures by the Germans were only attended by their fellow countrymen and political friends. (. . .) Renouvain explained that he couldn't speak German, and Srbik said he didn't understand French. (. . .) I had intended to ask him why Meinecke had been dismissed so silently from the editorial board of *Historische Zeitschrift*. His hesitant answer astounded me: 'Well, isn't it true, after all, Meinecke had quite a number of Jewish students.' "[109] In such an atmosphere "it was said, Congress had lacked in an essential element; for if one could expect historiography to contribute to our understanding of the world we live in, then the Zurich Congress had failed precisely in this endeavor (. . .) by the lack of concern for contemporary history."[110]

The German experience was extreme but also indicative for the general trend of the self-isolation of interwar historiographies. In the neighboring Netherlands, Johan Huizinga in 1931 flatly refused a proposal to teach his students a course in contemporary history, sharing his reasoning: "Lecturing on the recent past, no, I have nothing to say about that that they cannot read in the papers. What they need is distance, perspective, well-defined historical forms."[111] As European historiographies were regressing back into their national Ivory Towers, their colleagues across the Atlantic were undermining the methodological optimism which was a trademark of the generation of founding fathers. A historicist undercurrent of relativity and pragmatism became the creed of a new generation of American historians, heralded by Charles Beard and Carl Becker. "Many historians lost optimism and faith in progress which (. . .) had grounded their faith in objectivity. And the war itself became the subject of interminable historical controversy, undermining faith that professional historical scholarship would converge on a consensual objective truth."[112] For these and similar reasons, many reputed and cautious practitioners were actively discouraged from stepping into the field of the recent past, and slowing down the development of the field of contemporary history. Detachment evolved into a true, implicit but powerful theory of distance.[113]

This gulf was broadened and theorized in Michael Oakeshott's influential concept of the differing historical, scientific, and practical experience (1933). Oakeshott was challenging the compatibility of these modes of experience, and was particularly suspicious of the ability of historians to create objective knowledge about the past: "Since history is an experience, it is presence (. . .). What the historian does when he imagines it (. . .) in reality is only the self-explication of his present consciousness." Oakeshott cautioned that "each world of those abstract ideas (. . .) so long as it is content to mind its own business, is unassailable. None but historical thinking can achieve historical truth. And in this respect every mode of experience is free from the relevant interference both of every other mode and of the concrete totality itself (. . .) Actual error, then appears, and appears only when what is asserted in a mode is asserted also beyond the mode, is asserted absolutely and without qualification."[114] This incompatibility was further articulated by Benedetto Croce: "Those who on the plea of narrating history bustle about as judges, condemning here and giving absolution there, because they think that this is the office of history (. . .) are generally recognized as devoid of historical sense." He was fuming over the false objectivity employed by "judge-like historians [which is] incompatible with the logic of historiography." He warned: "The togaed historian (. . .) this old type of historian, so suited for servile times, must be prevented from reappearing in our times, which we may wish to consider unservile; but the desire shown for restoration of the court-of-justice type of history certainly favors his re-appearance."[115] He attributed this tendency to "an appeal to history. History is supposed to be the great High Court which reviews all the troubled judgments arising out of the passions and errors of men, corrects them, and pronounces a final verdict as in a universal judgment, separating the elect from reprobates. Die Weltgeschichte, das Weltgericht: world history, world judgment. Neither the future, nor history can carry this utterly intolerable burden of a task intrinsically absurd and impracticable."[116]

Even authors like Robin Collingwood, who stood as the lone defender of historical judgments, doubted their immediate applicability. He claimed that historian's task is "not only of discovering what actually happened, but of judging it in the light of our own moral ideals. (. . .) If we feel that we cannot shoulder it, we ought to drop historical studies and do something else."[117] However, although he recognized that "the analogy between legal methods and historical methods is of some value for understanding of history," he was quick to point out that "the methods of criminal detection are not at every point identical with those of scientific history, because their ultimate purpose is not the same. (. . .) The student of historical method would hardly find it worth his while, therefore, to go closely into the rules of evidence, as these are recognized in courts of law. For the historian is under no obligation to make up his mind within any stated time."[118]

Such reflections were particularly hindering to the development of contemporary history. Enthusiasts who advocated for an engagement with the pressing issues of the present, like R.W. Seton-Watson in his passionate 1928 plea for the engagement of historians with contemporary issues, had to conclude that prevailing opinion found it an "unworthy subject for the true historian's pen (. . .), incompatible with the detachment and calm of academic life."[119] Even the periodical *Journal for Modern History*, created in

1929 to explore the recent past, was careful to define its scope to cover "the history of Europe and its expansion from the Renaissance to the close of the World War."[120] Not even the journal *Annales*, created in the same year as an outlet to most innovative trends of French historiography, was dedicating much space to the recent past, with the notable exception of a 1937 special volume on Nazism.[121] This contradiction was well reflected in the views of one of the key persons of the Annales school, Marc Bloch. Although convinced that the study of the past derives out of present concerns, the famed medievalist was cautious about the recent past: "Bloch, who rejected any conception of historiography as art for art's sake and demanded that history make a contribution to informed action in the present, warned against too much contemporary history."[122]

Actually, what Bloch was warning against was the habit of passing historical judgments, as he explicated in his famous *Craft of the Historian:* "There are two ways of being impartial: that of the scholar and that of the judge. They have a common root in their honest submission to the truth. (. . .) However, there comes a moment when their paths divide. When the scholar has observed and explained, his task is finished. It yet remains for the judge to pass sentence. (. . .) Now, for a long time, the historian has passed for a sort of judge in Hades, charged with meting out praise or blame to dead heroes. (. . .) How absurd it is, by elevating the entirely relative criteria of one individual, one party or one generation to the absolute, to inflict standards upon the way in which Sulla governed Rome, or Richelieu the States of the Most Christian King (. . .) Robespierrists! Anti-Robespierrists! For pity's sake, simply tell us what Robespierre was."[123] It is interesting to observe that around the same time Herbert Butterfield, an author who, unlike Bloch, abhorred presentism, arrived at a similar conclusion: "The study of the past with one eye, so to speak, upon the present is the source of all sins and sophistries in history. It is the fallacy into which we slip when we are giving the judgments that seem the most assuredly self-evident. The historian like every other specialist is quick to over-step the bounds of his subject and elicit from history more than history can really give." Concerned about this tendency, Butterfield concluded that the historian "is neither judge nor jury; he is in the position of a man called upon to give evidence; and even so he may abuse his office and he requires the closest cross-examination, for he is one of these 'expert witnesses' who persist in offering opinions concealed within their evidence." In his view, such history "will lie to us until the very end of the last cross-examination."[124]

Both the proponents of positivism and relativism, as well as the adherents of historicism and presentism, seemed to agree that passing judgment on the past is neither possible nor desirable. Hence by implication, history and law ended up on a collision course characterized by deep structural misunderstanding. Instead of prompting further refining of the relation between the two disciplines, their insulation was provoked. The barriers of institutional webs and constitutive rules of those two types of inquiries into the past led to a recognizable division without much interaction outside of the subfield of legal history. Interestingly, the professionalization of historical scholarship somehow excluded the development of its forensic expertise. Namely, it went as a matter of course that a historian might help the proceedings by using some of his auxiliary faculties, for instance verifying the authenticity of the records.[125] But whether more could be done was strongly suspected, from both sides. The expert role of the historian seemed to contradict the very core of self-understanding of the historian's craft, as being too engaged, too partisan, and too subsumed into the political and legal issues of the day. Theory of incompatibility was convincing enough to delay the forensication of history for quite some time. Therefore, paradoxically, in the period in which the majority of sciences were assuming their forensic dimension, historians were held remote from actual expert witnessing. The idea that a historian and a judge may both look into the past, but see different things, was embedded so strongly that it took a global shift to make the confluence between the disciplines possible and the courtroom appearance of the historian imaginable.

Acknowledgments

Parts of this chapter were originally published in Vladimir Petrović, "Witnessing a Troubled Century: Historians as Expert Witnesses in France 1898–1998," *Istorija 20.veka*, 1 (2009), 173–188.

Notes

1 The history of the continental institute of the expert is thoroughly researched in German legal literature. Cf. Konstantinos Kerameus, *Die Entwicklung des Sachverständigenbeweises im deutschen und griechischen Zivilprozessrecht* (Cologne: Carl Heymanns Verlag, 1963); Karlhans Dippel, *Die Stellung des Sachverständingen im Strafprozess* (Heidelberg: Dekker, 1986). Expert witnessing in common law is probably best researched in the American context: Sheila Jasanoff, *Science at the Bar: Law, Science and Technology in America* (Cambridge, MA: Harvard University Press, 1997). For a bold attempt to account for the development of expert witnessing in common law see Robert Kargon, "Expert Testimony in Historical Perspective," *Law and Human Behaviour* 10 (1986): 15–27. For a comparative aspect see Robert F. Taylor, "A Comparative Study of Expert Testimony in France and the United States," *Texas International Law Journal* 31 (1996): 181–213; Lirieka Meintjes-Van der Walt, *Expert Evidence in the Criminal Justice Process: A Comparative Approach* (Amsterdam: Rozenberg Publishers, 2001), 13.

2 Tal Golan, *Laws of Men and Laws of Nature: The History of Scientific Expert Testimony in England and America* (Cambridge: Harvard University Press, 2004), 1. However, these obstacles are somewhat alleviated by a trend in recent inquiries to scrutinize this nexus through edited volumes: Cf. Roger Smith and Brian Wyanne (eds.), *Expert Evidence: Interpreting Science in the Law* (London and New York: Routledge, 1989); Helen Reece (ed.), *Law and Science* (Oxford: Oxford University Press, 1998).

3 Dippel, *Die Stellung des Sachverständingen im Strafprozess*, 6–8.

4 Jacobus Sprenger and Heinrich Kramer, *Malleus Maleficarum* (London: The Folio Society, 1968), 191–192.
5 Perhaps the most famous such example was Lorenzo Valla's *De falso credita et ementita Constantini donation declamation*, which appeared in 1440. Cf. Lorenzo Valla, *Discourse on the Forgery of the Alleged Donation of Constantine* (New Haven: Yale University Press, 1922).
6 Friedrich Toepel, *Grundsrukturen des Sachverständigenbeweises im Strasfprozessrecht* (Tübingen: Mohr Siebeck, 2002), 259–261.
7 Enno Poppen, *Die Geschichte de Sachverständigenbeweises im Strafprozess des deutsch-sprachigen Raumes* (Göttingen: Musterschmidt 1984), 58–63.
8 Golan, *Laws of Men and Laws of Nature*, 19.
9 The case is studied at length in Golan, *Laws of Men and Laws of Nature*, 7–52.
10 Ibid., 4.
11 Lee M. Friedman, "Expert Testimony: Its Abuse and Reformation," *The Yale Law Journal* 19 (1910): 247.
12 Golan, *Laws of Men and Laws of Nature*, 255.
13 Friedman, "Expert Testimony: Its Abuse and Reformation," 247.
14 Learned Hand, "Historical and Practical Considerations Regarding Expert Testimony," *Harvard Law Review* 15 (1901): 40, 53–54.
15 Morris Ploscowe, "The Expert Evidence in Criminal Cases in France, Germany and Italy," *Law and Contemporary Problems* 2 (1935): 504–509.
16 Taylor, "A Comparative Study of Expert Testimony in France and the United States," 181.
17 Golan, *Laws of Men and Laws of Nature*, 96.
18 Extensive list in Ian Freckelton (ed.), *Expert Evidence in Criminal Law* (Melbourn: LBC, 1994).
19 On resistance to its introduction see Golan, Laws of Men and Laws of Nature,. 211–253. A recent attempt to compare forensic psychiatry to historiography is Albert M. Drukteinis, "Forensic Historiography: Narratives and Science," *Journal of American Academy of Psychiatry and the Law* 42 (2014): 427–436.
20 The text of Brandeis' brief and related documents from this case can be found in Nancy Woloch, *Muller v. Oregon: A Brief History with Documents* (Boston: Bedford Books, 1996).
21 *Frye v. United States*, http://www.daubertontheweb.com/frye_opinion.htm, accessed on 21.2.2016.
22 Cf. Douglas O. Linder, *State v. John Scopes*, http://law2.umkc.edu/faculty/projects/ftrials/scopes/evolut.htm, accessed on 21.2.2016. A list of experts is available at http://law2.umkc.edu/faculty/projects/ftrials/scopes/metcalfm.html. The recollections of Professor Fay-Cooper Cole, the founder of the Department of Anthropology at the University of Chicago, are in *Scientific American*, January 1959, http://www.scientificamerican.com/article/50-years-ago-scope-trial-witness.
23 Carlo Ginzburg, *The Judge and the Historian: Marginal Notes on a Late-Twentieth-Century Miscarriage of Justice* (London: Verso, 1999), 12.
24 Henry George Liddell and Robert Scott (eds.), *A Greek-English Lexicon* (Oxford: Clarendon Press, 1996), s.v. ἵστωρ. See also Gerald Press, "History and the Development of the Idea of History in Antiquity," *History and Theory* 16.3 (October, 1977): 280–296; Cf. François Hartog, "Le temoin et l'historien," *Gradhiva* 27 (2000): 1–14.
25 Donald R. Kelley, *Foundations of Modern Historical Scholarship: Language, Law, and History* (New York: Columbia University Press, 1970), 116.
26 Joseph von Hormayr, "Austria and Germany," in *National Romanticism: The Formation of National Movements*, eds. Balázs Trencsényi and Michal Kopeček (Budapest: Central European University Press, 2006), 30.
27 "Mitford's History of Greece," *Edinburgh Review* 12 (July, 1808): 480.

28 Ibid.
29 Leopold von Ranke, *Sämtliche Werke* (Leipzig: Duncker und Humblot, 1885), vol. 33, 7. On the role of seminars of founding persons, see Michael Bentley, *Modern Historiography: An Introduction* (New York: Routledge, 1999), 71–79. The professionalization of historiography was scrutinized in comparative perspective by Georg G. Iggers and Q. Edward Wanq, *A Global History of Modern Historiography* (London: Pearson, 2008), 128–133, and its propagation by Rolf Torstendahl, *The Rise and Propagation of Historical Professionalism* (New York: Routledge, 2014), 3–67.
30 John Edward Emerich Acton, *Inaugural Lecture on the Study of History* (London: Macmillan, 1906), 16.
31 "Acton on Ranke", in Herbert Butterfiled, *Man on his Past. The Study of the History of Historical Scholarship* (Cambridge: Cambridge University Press, 1955), 219
32 Peter Novick, *That Noble Dream: The "Objectivity Question" and the American Historical Profession* (Cambridge: Cambridge University Press, 1993), 2.
33 Charles V. Langlois and Charles Seignobos, *Introduction to the Study of History* (New York: Holt, 1898), 319.
34 Novick, *That Noble Dream*, 69.
35 Kelley, *Foundations of Modern Historical Scholarship*, 88.
36 The book in question was Demetris Cantemir's *History of the Growth and Decay of the Ottoman Empire*. Cf. *The Trial of Warren Hastings, Esq: Late Governor General of Bengal, before the Curt of Peers Sitting in Westminster Hall* (London: J. Ridgway, 1788), vol. II, 343–346. More on Burke's role in the Hastings trial in Lida Maxwell, *Public Trials: Burke, Zola, Arendt and the Politics of Lost Causes* (Oxford: Oxford University Press, 2014), 37–80. Cf. Johannes Houwink Ten Cate, "Genocide in the Courtroom: On the Interaction between Legal Experts and Historians," *International Journal of Legal Information* 39 (2011): 187–188. Burke's role in emphasizing the historical method within common law tradition is scrutinized in detail by Renata Uitz, *Constitutions, Courts and History, Historical Narratives in Constitutional Adjudication* (CEU Press: Budapest 2005), 49–53.
37 In the 1835 Evans v. Getting case of disputed manor boundaries in Wales, see failed attempt to read into evidence parts of History of Brecknockshire in Samuel March Phillipps, Andrew Amos, *A Treatise on the Law of Evidence* (London: Saunders and Benning, 1838), 605–606. However, in other cases, such as the 1890 Read v. Bishop of Lincoln, considerable weight was given to the "authorities to be found in the writings of authoritative and eminent writers." Edward Stanley Roscoe, *The Bishop of Lincoln's Case* (London: William Clowes and Sons, 1891), 6.
38 Frederic W. Maitland, "Why the History of English Law Is Not Written," in *The Collected Papers of Frederic William Maitland*, ed. H. A. L. Fisher (Cambridge: Cambridge University Press, 1991), vol. I, 491–492.
39 Donald R. Kelley, *Historians and the Law in Postrevolutionary France* (Princeton: Princeton University Press, 1984), 3.
40 The most complete set of transcripts of trials and other proceedings and material related to the Dreyfus affair was reproduced in about 150 volumes published by Pierre-Victor Stock. Cf. *Le process Dreyfus: Devant le conseile de guerre de Rennes* (Paris: P.V. Stock, 1900), vol. 1–3; *La revision du procès Dreyfus: Enquête de la Cour de cassation* (Paris: P.V. Stock, 1899). A comprehensive selection of the documents is available at *Dreyfus Rehabilitated: France 1906*. http://www.dreyfus.culture.fr/en/. A comprehensive overview of the events is provided by George R. Whyte, *The Dreyfus Affair: A Chronological History* (London: Palgrave, 2008).

41 Louis Begley, *Why the Dreyfus Affair Matters* (New Haven: Yale University Press, 2009), 98–99.
42 Émile Zola, "J'accuse," *L'Aurore*, January 13, 1898, 1. More on Zola's intervention in Lida Maxwell, *Public Trials: Burke, Zola, Arendt and the Politics of Lost Causes* (Oxford: Oxford University Press, 2014), 81–95.
43 Laurent Ferri, "Émile Zola et 'ces messieurs de l'École des chartes' dans l'affaire Dreyfus: documents inédits," *Bibliothèque de l'École des chartes* 164 (2006): 598.
44 G. Monod, "Du progrès des études historiques en France depuis le XVIe siècle," *Revue historique* I (1876): 5–38.
45 "Le 2 novembre 1897 l'historien Gabriel Monod analyse l'écriture de Dreyfus et défend l'honorabilité du capitaine Dreyfus," *1906: Dreyfus Rehabilite*, http://www.dreyfus.culture.fr/fr/mediatheque/media-type1-html-Engagement_dreyfusard_de_G._Monod.htm, accessed on 21.2.2016. Published in *Le Temps*, 6 November, 1897.
46 On the role of intellectuals in the affair see Vincent Duclert, "De l'engagement des savants à l'intellectuel critique: Une histoire intellectuelle de l'affaire Dreyfus," *Historical Reflections/Réflexions Historiques* 24.1 (Spring 1998): 25–62.
47 His account under the pseudonym Pierre Mole, *Exposé impartial de l'affaire Dreyfus* (Paris: P. V. Stock, 1899).
48 For more on the state of French historiography around the time of the affair in Pim den Boer, see *History as a Profession: The Study of History in France 1818–1914* (Princeton: Princeton University Press, 1998), 224–359. On the role of historians in the Dreyfus case see Isabel Noronha-DiVanna, *Writing History in the Third Republic* (Cambridge: Cambridge Scholars Publishing, 2010), 42–47.
49 Charles V. Langlois and Charles Seignobos, *Introduction to the Study of History* (New York: Holt, 1898), 158–159.
50 Letters of acceptance and refusal can be found in Ferri, "*Émile Zola* . . .", 601–603.
51 Ruth Harris, *Dreyfus: Politics, Emotion, and the Scandal of the Century* (New York: Holt 2010), 143.
52 Bertrand Joly, "L'Ecole des chartes et l'Affaire Dreyfus," *Bibliothèque de l'école des chartes* 147 (1989): 629–637; Harris, *Dreyfus*, 141–146.
53 Extensive excerpts from the courtroom performance of historians in the Zola trial are available in Olivier Dumoulin, *Le rôle social de l'historien*, 165–166. Also see Jean-Noël Jeanneney, *La passé dans le prétoire* (Paris: Seuil 1998), 13–33. A full transcript of the Zola trial can be found in *Le procès Zola, devant la Cour d'assises de la Seine et la Cour de Cassation* (P. V. Stock: Paris, 1898), vol. I–II.
54 Quoted from Jeanneney, *La passé dans le prétoire*, 16.
55 Full record in *Le process Dreyfus: Devant le Conseile de guerre de Rennes* (Paris: P. V. Stock, 1900), vol. 3, 3–55.
56 Dumoulin, *Le rôle social de l'historien*, 167.
57 *Le process Dreyfus: Devant le Conseile de guerre de Rennes*, vol. 2, 297–496.
58 Dumoulin, *Le rôle social de l'historien*, 168.
59 Julien Benda, *La jeunesse d'un clerc* (Paris: Gallimard, 1968), 115.
60 Maurice Paleologue, *An Intimate Journal of the Dreyfus Case* (New York: Criterion Books, 1957), 271.
61 Noronha-DiVanna, *Writing History in the Third Republic*, 46.
62 George R. Whyte, *The Dreyfus Affair: A Chronological History* (London: Palgrave, 2008), 24.
63 Karl Dietrich Erdmann, *Toward a Global Community of Historians: The International Historical Congresses and the International Committee of Historical Sciences 1898–2000* (New York: Berghahn Books 2005), 10.

64 In 1899, a year after *La Ligue des droits de l'homme*, a movement of far right-wing intellectuals, *Action française*, was created. Monod, and even his Protestant descent, was viciously attacked by its founder Charles Maurras. "Genealogie des Monod," *Gazzete de France*, 16 November, 1897.

65 Harold J. Berman, *Law and Revolution: The Formation of the Western Legal Tradition* (Cambridge, MA: Harvard University Press 1983), 17.

66 Biographical details in Harry Ritter, "Progressive Historians and the Historical Imagination in Austria: Heinrich Friedjung and Richard Charmatz," *Austrian History Yearbook* 19.1 (1983): 45–90.

67 Friedjung's speeches, articles, and correspondence are assembled in Franz Adlgasser and Margret Friedrich (eds.), *Heinrich Friedjung, Geschichte in Gesprächen: Aufzeichnungen 1898–1919* (Wien: Böhlau, 1998), vols. 1–2. The evolution of Friedjung's attitudes toward southern Slavs was a subject of a doctoral dissertation by Franz Graf, *Heinrich Friedjung und die sudslawische Frage* (Wien: University of Vienna, 1950).

68 Ranka Gašić, *Novi kurs Srba u Hrvatskoj* (Zagreb: Prosvjeta, 2001), 52–54. More on the context in which this process was happening in Nicholas J. Miller, *Between Nation and State: Serbian Politics in Croatia before the First World War* (Pittsburgh: University of Pittsburgh Press, 1997), 125–134. For more on the political context, see Livia Kardum, "Aneksiona kriza i Friedjungov Process," *Politićka misao* 1 (1993): 133–147.

69 Heinrich Friedjung, "Österreich-Ungarn und Serbien," *Neue Freie Presse*, 25 March, 1909, 2–4.

70 *Neue Freie Presse*, 10 April, 1909, 4–5.

71 Extensive analysis of the trial was written by Hodimir Sirotković, "Pravni i politički aspekti procesa Rundpost-Fridjung," *Starine JAZU* 52 (1962): 49–184. The trial generated enormous interest by the press and was extensively covered. *Neue Freie Presse* published almost the entire stenographic record. Cf. "Der Prozeß Friedjung vor den Wiener Geschwornen," *Neue Freie Presse*, 19, 21, 22 December, 1909; *Obzor* and *Politika* also reported extensively.

72 Sirotković, *Pravni i politički aspekti . . .*, 121.

73 Heinrich Friedjung, *Aktenstücke zur grosserbischen Propaganda in Österreich-Ungarn, Vorgelegt dem Wiener Geschworenengericht von Heinrich Friedjung* (Wien: Selbstverlag, 1909).

74 Sirotković, *Pravni i politički aspekti . . .*, 90.

75 Ibid., 99–100.

76 Franz Adlgasser and Margret Friedrich (eds.), *Heinrich Friedjung, Geschichte in Gesprächen: Aufzeichnungen 1898–1919* (Wien: Böhlau, 1998), vol. 1, 12.

77 The testimonies and particularly Spalajković's role in the affair are analyzed by Zoran Bajin, "Miroslav Spalajković na Fridjungovom procesu," *Zbornik Matice srpske za istoriju* 85 (2012): 101–102.

78 "Der Prozeß Friedjung vor den Wiener Geschwornen," *Neue Freie Presse*, 21 December, 1909, 11–13; "Fridjungov pretres," *Politika* 8 [21] December, 1909, 2.

79 Ante Biankini, *Austro-Magyar Judicial Crimes. Persecution of the Yugoslavs: Political Trials 1908–1916* (Chicago: The Jugoslav Committee in North America, 1917), 33.

80 A. J. P. Taylor, "Introduction," in *The Struggle for Supremacy in Germany 1859–1866*, ed. Heinrich Fridejung (London: Macmillan and Co., 1935), xxviii.

81 "R. W. Seton Watson to Heinrich Friedjung," 25 December, 1909, in: *R. W. Seton-Watson and the Yugoslavs. Correspondence 1906–1941* (London-Zagreb: British Academy, 1976), vol. I, 65.

82 R. W. Seton-Watson, *The Southern Slav Question and the Habsburg Monarchy* (New York: Howard Fertis, 1969), 211.

83 Ernst Breisach, *Historiography: Ancient, Medieval and Modern* (Chicago and London: University of Chicago Press, 1994), 323.
84 Jingoistic outbursts were not at all limited to German historiography. Cf. "The Historians in World War One," Georg G. Iggers and Q. Edward Wanq, *A Global History of Modern Historiography* (London: Pearson, 2008), 172–175.
85 Novick, *That Noble Dream*, 111.
86 These tensions are described in Erdmann, *Toward a Global Community of Historians*, 68–75.
87 See the index to such material at The World War One Document Archive, http://wwi.lib.byu.edu/index.php/1914_Documents.
88 The complex web of interdependency between such scholarly attempts and predominant political moods is revealed in contributions in Keith Wilson (ed.), *Forging the Collective Memory: Government and International Historians through Two World Wars* (Providence, Oxford: Bergham Books, 1996).
89 Bernhard Schwertfeger, *Der Weltkrieg der Dokumente: Zehn Jahre Kriegsschuldforschung und ihr Ergenbis* (Berlin: Deutsche Verlagsgesellschaft für Politik und Geschichte,1929).
90 Index to such material is available at *The World War One Document Archive*, http://wwi.lib.byu.edu/index.php/Official_Papers.
91 Ulrich Heinemann, *Die verdrängte Niederlage: Politische Öffentlichkeit und Kriegsschuldfrage in der Weimarer Republik* (Göttingen: Vandenhoeck & Ruprech, 1983), 156.
92 Michael Marrus, *Nuremberg War Crimes Trial 1945–6: A Documentary History* (Boston: Bedford Books, 1997), 6.
93 *Der Vertrag von Versailles* (Berlin: Auftrage des Auswartigen Amtes, 1924), 206–221.
94 A detailed description of the establishment and the activity of Zentralstelle appears in Heinemann, Die verdrängte Niederlage,. 95–105. An account on the early activity in Germany by one of the protagonists is in August Bach, "Zentralstelle für Erforschung der Kriegsursachen," *Berliner Monatshefte* 1 (März, 1937): 272–283.
95 Crucial collections of sources are available in Max Montgelas, Walter Schuecking, Bernhard von Buelow and Karl Kautsky (eds.), *Die Deutschen Dokumente zum Kriegsausbruch 1914* (Berlin: Deutsche Verlagsgesellshaft für Politik und Geschichte, 1921); Johannes Lepsius, Albrecht Mendelssohn Bartoldy and Friedrich Thimme (eds.), *Die Große Politik der Europäischen Kabinette 1871–1914* (Berlin: Deutsche Verlagsgesellshaft für Politik und Geschichte, 1922–27).
96 Justus Hashagen, *Das Studium der Zeitgeschichte* (Bonn: Friedrich Cohen Verlag, 1915), 5. On the impact of the debate on the development of contemporary historiography see Klaus Grosse Kracht, *Kriegsschuldfrage und zeithistorische Forschung in Deutschland: Historiographische Nachwirkungen des Ersten Weltkriegs*, *Zeitgeschichte-Online*, 2004, http://www.zeitgeschichte-online.de/md=EKW-GKracht, accessed on 20.12.2014.
97 Justus Hashagen, "Neue Historikerpflichten," *Deutscher Wille: Des Kunstwarts* 19 (1918): 109.
98 Justus Hashagen, "Ausserwisenschaftliche Einflusse aud die neuere Geschichtswissenschaft," in Max Scheler *Versuche Zu Einer Soziologie Des Wissens* (München: Deutschland Duncker und Humblot, 1924), 233–255.
99 Quoted in Erdmann, *Toward a Global Community of Historians*, 94. Cf. Anthony D'Agostino, "The Revisionist Tradition in European Diplomatic History," *The Journal of the Historical Society* 2 (2004): 255–287. On the involvement of iconoclastic American historians see Novick, *That Noble Dream*, 208–219.

100 Ernst Troeltsch, "Die Krisis des Historismus," *Die neue Rundschau* 33 (1922): 572–590.
101 Hermann Kantorowicz, *Gutachten zur Kriegsschuldfrage* (Frankfurt: Europäische Verlagsanstalt, 1967), 99, 92.
102 Hermann Kantorowicz, "A German Expert on War Guilt," *The Slavonic Review* 5.13 (1926): 209–210.
103 More about Hermann Kantorowicz in Karlheinz H. Muscheler, *Hermann Ulrich Kantorowicz: Eine Biographie* (Berlin: Duncker & Humblot, 1984).
104 Heinemann, *Die verdrängte Niederlage*, 106.
105 Cf. Holger H. Herwig, "Clio Decieved: Patriotic Self-Censorship in Germany after the Great War," in *Forging the Collective Memory*, ed. Keith Wilson, 113–114.
106 Peter Borowsky, "Justus Hashagen, ein vergessener Hamburger Historiker," *Zeitschrift des Vereins für Hamburgische Geschichte* 84 (1998): 163–183.
107 Originally published as Friedrich Meinecke, *Die Entstehung des Historismus* (München: R. Oldenbourg, 1936); quote here from Friedrich Meinecke, *Historism* (New York, Herder and Herder, 1972), iv.
108 Ibid., 508. See also Georg Iggers, "The Dissolution of German Historicism," in *Ideas in History*, eds. Richard Harr and Harold Parker (Durham, NC: Duke University Press 1965), 288–329.
109 Quoted in Erdmann, *Toward a Global Community of Historians*, 175.
110 Ibid., 169.
111 Quoted from Jaap den Hollander, Herman Paul and Rik Peters, "Introduction: The Metaphor of Historical Distance," *History and Theory* 50 (December, 2011): 2.
112 Novick, *That Noble Dream*, 111.
113 Historical distancing is richly theorized and explored in the 2010 thematic volume of *History and Theory*. Cf. Mark Salber Phillips, "Rethinking Historical Distance: From Doctrine to Heuristics," *History and Theory* 50 (December, 2011), 11–23. See also Peter Burke, "A Short History of Distance," in *Rethinking Historical Distance*, eds. Mark Salber Phillips, Barbara Caine and Julia Adeney Thomas (London: Palgrave, 2013), 26–40. See also the most recent contribution of Mark Phillips, *On Historical Distance* (New Haven: Yale University Press, 2015).
114 Michael Oakeshott, *Experience and Its Modes* (Cambridge: Cambridge University Press, 2015), 254.
115 Benedetto Croce, *History as the Story of Liberty* (London: George Wallen and Ullen, 1941), 47–49.
116 Ibid., 209.
117 "Can Historians Be Impartial? (1936)," in R.G. Collingwood, *The Principles of History* (Oxford: Oxford University Press, 1999), 218.
118 Robin Collingwood, *The Idea of History* (Oxford: Oxford University Press, 1993), 268.
119 R.W. Seton-Watson, "A Plea for the Study of Contemporary History," *History* 14 (April, 1929): 2.
120 "Victuri Salutamus," *The Journal of Modern History* 1.1 (March, 1929): 2.
121 Bentley, *Modern Historiography*, 115.
122 Erdmann, *Toward a Global Community of Historians*, 197.
123 Marc Bloch, *The Historian's Craft* (New York: Alfred A. Knopf, 1959), 138–140.
124 Herbert Butterfield, *The Whig Interpretation of History* (London: G. Bell and Sons, 1931), 70, 131–132.
125 C. Ainsworth Mitchell, *The Expert Witness and the Application of Science and of Art to Human Identification, Criminal Investigation, Civil Actions and History* (Cambridge: W. Heffer and Sons, 1923).

Bibliography

Acton, John Edward Emerich. *Inaugural Lecture on the Study of History*. London: Macmillan, 1906.

Adlgasser, Franz and Margret Friedrich, eds. *Heinrich Friedjung, Geschichte in Gesprächen: Aufzeichnungen 1898–1919*. Wien: Böhlau, 1998.

Ainsworth, C. Mitchell. *The Expert Witness and the Application of Science and of Art to Human Identification, Criminal Investigation, Civil Actions and History*. Cambridge: W. Heffer and Sons, 1923.

Arrigo, Bruce A. *The Contours of Psychiatric Justice: A Postmodern Critique of Mental Illness, Criminal Insanity, and the Law*. New York and London: Garland Publishing, 1996.

Bach, August. "Zentralstelle für Erforschung der Kriegusrachen." *Berliner Monatshefte* 1 (März 1937): 272–283.

Bajin, Zoran. "Miroslav Spalajković na Fridjungovom procesu." *Zbornik Matice srpske za istoriju* 85 (2012): 101–102.

Begley, Louis. *Why the Dreyfus Affair Matters*. New Haven: Yale University Press, 2009.

Bentley, Michael. *Modern Historiography: An Introduction*. New York: Routledge, 1999.

Berman, Harold J. *Law and Revolution: The Formation of the Western Legal Tradition*. Cambridge, MA: Harvard University Press, 1983.

Biankini, Ante. *Austro-Magyar Judicial Crimes: Persecution of the Yugoslavs: Political Trials 1908–1916*. Chicago: The Jugoslav Ante Committee in North America, 1917.

Blay, Theodore H. *The Psychologist as Expert Witness*. New York: A Wiley-Interscience Publication, 1984.

Bloch, Marc. *The Historian's Craft*. New York: Alfred A. Knopf, 1959.

Boer, Pim den. *History as a Profession: The Study of History in France 1818–1914*. Princeton: Princeton University Press, 1998.

Borowsky, Peter. "Justus Hashagen, ein vergessener Hamburger Historiker." *Zeitschrift des Vereins für Hamburgische Geschichte* 84 (1998): 163–183.

Breisach, Ernst. *Historiography: Ancient, Medieval and Modern*. Chicago and London: University of Chicago Press, 1994.

Burke, Peter. "A Short History of Distance," in *Rethinking Historical Distance*, eds. Mark Salber Phillips, Barbara Caine and Julia Adeney Thomas. London: Palgrave, 2013, 26–40.

Butterfield, Herbert. *The Whig Interpretation of History*. London: G. Bell, 1931.

Butterfiled, Herbert. *Man on His Past. The Study of the History of Historical Scholarship*. Cambridge: Cambridge University Press, 1955).

Cate, Johannes Houwink Ten. "Genocide in the Courtroom: On the Interaction between Legal Experts and Historians," *International Journal of Legal Information* 39 (2011): 186–194.

Cole, Fay-Cooper. "*50 Years Ago: A Witness at the Scopes Trial.*" *Scientific American*, January 1959. http://www.scientificamerican.com/article/50-years-ago-scope-trial-witness.

Collingwood, R.G. *The Idea of History*. Oxford: Oxford University Press, 1993.

Collingwood, R.G. "Can Historians Be Impartial? (1936)," in *The Principles of History*, ed. R.G. Collingwood. Oxford: Oxford University Press, 1999.

Croce, Benedetto. *History as the Story of Liberty.* London: George Wallen and Ullen, 1941.
D'Agostino, Anthony. "The Revisionist Tradition in European Diplomatic History." *The Journal of the Historical Society* 2 (2004): 255–287.
"Depesche des Sektionschefs Spalajkovic," *Neue Freie Presse*, 22 December 1909.
"Der Prozeß Friedjung vor den Wiener Geschwornen," *Neue Freie Presse*, 19 December 1909.
Der Vertrag von Versailles: Amtlicher Text der Entante und amtliche deutsche Ubersetzung. Berlin: Auftrage des Auswartigen Amtes, 1924.
Dippel, Karlhans. *Die Stellung des Sachverständingen im Strafprozess.* Heidelberg: Dekker, 1986.
Dreyfus Rehabilitated: France 1906. http://www.dreyfus.culture.fr/en.
Drukteinis, Albert M. "Forensic Historiography: Narratives and Science," *Journal of American Academy of Psychiatry and the Law* 42 (2014): 427–436.
Duclert, Vincent. "De l'engagement des savants à l'intellectuel critique: Une histoire intellectuelle de l'affaire Dreyfus," *Historical Reflections/Réflexions Historiques, Intellectuals and the Dreyfus Affair* 24.1 (Spring 1998): 25–62.
Dumoulin, Olivier. *Le rôle social de l'historien: De la chaire au prétoire.* Paris: Albin Michel, 2003.
Erdmann, Karl Dietrich. *Toward a Global Community of Historians: The International Historical Congresses and the International Committee of Historical Sciences 1898–2000.* New York: Berghahn Books, 2005.
Ferri, Laurent. "Émile Zola et 'ces messieurs de l'École des chartes' dans l'affaire Dreyfus: documents inédits." *Bibliothèque de l'École des chartes* 164.2 (2006): 595–603.
Fisher, H. A. L., ed. *The Collected Papers of Frederic William Maitland.* Cambridge: Cambridge University Press, 1991.
Freckelton, Ian, ed. *Expert Evidence in Criminal Law.* Melbourne: LBC, 1994.
Friedjung, Heinrich. Aktenstücke zur grosserbischen Propaganda in Österreich-Ungarn, Vorgelegt dem Wiener Geschworenengericht von Heinrich Friedjung. Wien: Selbstverlag, 1909.
Friedjung, Heinrich. "Österreich-Ungarn und Serbien," *Neue Freie Presse*, 25 March 1909, 2–4.
Friedjung, Heinrich. *The Struggle for Supremacy in Germany* 1859–1866. London: Macmillan and Co., 1935.
"Fridjungov pretres," *Politika*, 8 [21] December 1909, 2.
Friedman, Lee M. "Expert Testimony: Its Abuse and Reformation." *The Yale Law Journal* 19 (1910): 247–257.
Gašić, Ranka. *Novi kurs Srba u Hrvatskoj.* Zagreb: Prosvjeta, 2001.
Ginzburg, Carlo. *The Judge and the Historian: Marginal Notes on a Late-Twentieth-Century Miscarriage of Justice.* London: Verso, 1999.
Golan, Tal. *Laws of Men and Laws of Nature: The History of Scientific Expert Testimony in England and America.* Cambridge: Harvard University Press, 2004.
Graf, Franz Heinrich. *Friedjung und die sudslawische Frage.* Wien: University of Vienna, 1950.
Hand, Learned. "Historical and Practical Considerations Regarding Expert Testimony." *Harvard Law Review* 15 (1901): 40–58.
Harris, Ruth. *Dreyfus: Politics, Emotion, and the Scandal of the Century.* New York: Holt, 2010.

Hartog, François. "Le temoin et l'historien." *Gradhiva* 27 (2000): 1–14.

Hashagen, Justus. *Das Studium der Zeitgeschihte*. Bonn: Friedrich Cohen Verlag, 1915.

Hashagen, Justus. "Neue Historikerpflichten," *Deutscher Wille: Des Kunstwarts* 19, Heft (1918).

Heinemann, Ulrich. *Die verdrängte Niederlage: politische Öffentlichkeit und Kriegsschuldfrage in der Weimarer Republik*. Göttingen: Vandenhoeck & Ruprech, 1983.

Heussi, Karl. *Die Krisis des Historismus*. Tübingen: Mohr, 1932.

Hollander, Jaap den, Herman Paul and Rik Peters. "Introduction: The Metaphor of Historical Distance." *History and Theory* 50 (December, 2011): 1–10.

Iggers, Georg G. and Q. Edward Wanq. *A Global History of Modern Historiography*. London: Pearson, 2008.

Jasanoff, Sheila. *Science at the Bar: Law, Science and Technology in America*. Cambridge, MA: Harvard University Press, 1997.

Jeanneney, Jean-Noël. *La passé dans le prétoire*. Paris: Seuil, 1998.

Joly, Bertrand. "L'Ecole des chartes et l'Affaire Dreyfus." *Bibliothèque de l'école des chartes* 147 (1989): 611–671.

Kantorowicz, Hermann. "A German Expert on War Guilt." *The Slavonic Review* 5.13 (1926): 209–210.

Kantorowicz, Hermann. *Gutachten zur Kriegsschuldfrage*. Frankfurt: Europäische Verlagsanstalt, 1967.

Kardum, Livia. "Aneksiona kriza i Friedjungov process." *Politicka misao* 1 (1993): 133–147.

Kargon, Robert. "Expert Testimony in Historical Perspective." *Law and Human Behaviour* 10 (1986): 15–27.

Kelley, Donald R. *Foundations of Modern Historical Scholarship: Language, Law, and History*. New York: Columbia University Press, 1970.

Kelley, Donald R. *Historians and the Law in Postrevolutionary France*. Princeton: Princeton University Press, 1984.

Kerameus, Konstantinos. *Die Entwicklung des Sachverständigenbeveises im deutschen und griechischen Zivilprozessrecht*. Cologne: Carl Heymanns Verlag, 1963.

Kracht, Klaus Grosse. "Kriegsschuldfrage und zeithistorische Forschung in Deutschland: Historiographische Nachwirkungen des Ersten Weltkriegs," *Zeitgeschichte-Online*, 2004. http://www.zeitgeschichte-online.de/md=EKW-GKracht (accessed on 20.12.2014)

La revision du procès Dreyfus: Enquête de la Cour de cassation. Paris: P. V. Stock, 1899.

Langlois, Charles V. and Seignobos, Charles. *Introduction to the Study of History*. New York: Holt, 1898.

Le procès Zola, devant la Cour d'assises de la Seine et la Cour de Cassation. Paris: P. V.Stock: Paris, 1898.

Le process Dreyfus: Devant le Conseile de gueree de Rennes. Paris: P. V. Stock, 1900.

Lepsius, Johannes, Albrecht Mendelssohn Bartoldy and Friedrich Thimme, eds. *Die Große Politik der Europäischen Kabinette 1871–1914*. Berlin: Deutsche Verlagsgesellshaft für Politik und Geschichte, 1922–1927.

Liddell, Henry George and Robert Scott, eds. *A Greek-English Lexicon*. Oxford: Clarendon Press, 1996.

Linder, Douglas O. "State vs John Scopes," *Famous Trials*. http://law2.umkc.edu/faculty/projects/ftrials/scopes/evolut.htm (accessed on 21.2.2016).

Marrus, Michael. *The Nuremberg War Crimes Trial 1945–6: A Documentary History*. Boston: Bedford Books, 1997.

Maurras, Charles. "Genealogie des Monod," *Gazzete de France*, 16 November, 1897.

Maxwell, Lida. *Public Trials: Burke, Zola, Arendt and the Politics of Lost Causes*. Oxford: Oxford University Press, 2014.

Meinecke, Friedrich. *Die Entstehung des Historismus*. München: R. Oldenbourg, 1936.

Meinecke, Friedrich. *Historism*. New York: Herder and Herder, 1972.

Meintjes-Van der Walt, Lirieka. *Expert Evidence in the Criminal Justice Process: A Comparative Approach*. Amsterdam: Rozenberg Publishers, 2001.

Miller, Nicholas J. *Between Nation and State: Serbian Politics in Croatia before the First World War*. Pittsburg: University of Pittsburg Press, 1997.

"Mitford's History of Greece." *Edinburgh Review* 12 (July, 1808): 478–517.

Mole, Pierre. *Exposé impartial de l'affaire Dreyfus*. Paris: P. V. Stock, 1899.

Monod, Gabriel. "Du progrès des études historiques en France depuis le XVIe siècle." *Revue historique* 1 (1876): 5–38.

Monod, Gabriel. *Le Temps*, 6 November 1897.

Montgelas, Max, Walter Schuecking, Bernhard von Buelow and Karl Kautsky, eds. *Die Deutschen Dokumente zum Kriegsausbruch 1914*. Berlin: Deutsche Verlagsgesellshaft für Politik und Geschichte, 1921.

Muscheler, Karlheinz H. *Hermann Ulrich Kantorowicz: Eine Biographie*. Berlin: Duncker & Humblot, 1984.

Noronha-DiVanna, Isabel. *Writing History in the Third Republic*. Cambridge: Cambridge Scholars Publishing, 2010.

Novick, Peter. *That Noble Dream: The "Objectivity Question" and the American Historical Profession*. Cambridge: Cambridge University Press, 1993.

Oakeshott, Michael. *Experience and Its Modes*. Cambridge: Cambridge University Press, 2015.

Paleologue, Maurice. *An Intimate Journal of the Dreyfus Case*. New York: Criterion Books, 1957.

Phillipps, Samuel March and Andrew Amos. *A Treatise on the Law of Evidence*. London: Saunders and Benning, 1838.

Phillips, Mark Salber. "Rethinking Historical Distance: From Doctrine to Heuristics." *History and Theory* 50 (December, 2011): 11–23.

Phillips, Mark Salber. *On Historical Distance*. New Haven: Yale University Press, 2015.

Ploscowe, Morris. "The Expert Evidence in Criminal Cases in France, Germany and Italy." *Law and Contemporary Problems* 2 (1935): 504–509.

Poppen, Enno. *Die Geschichte de Sachverständigenbeweises im Strafprozess des deutsch-sprachigen Raumes*. Göttingen: Musterschmidt, 1984.

Press, Gerald. "History and the Development of the Idea of History in Antiquity." *History and Theory* 16.3 (October, 1977): 280–296.

von Ranke, Leopold. *Sämtliche Werke*. vol. 31. Leipzig: Duncker und Humblot, 1885.

Reece, Helen, ed. *Law and Science*. Oxford: Oxford University Press, 1998.

Ritter, Harry. "Progressive Historians and the Historical Imagination in Austria: Heinrich Friedjung and Richard Charmatz." *Austrian History Yearbook* 19.1 (1983): 45–90.

Roscoe, Edward Stanley. *The Bishop of Lincoln's Case.* London: William Clowes, 1891.

Scheler, Max, ed. *Versuche Zu Einer Soziologie Des Wissens.* München: Deutschland Duncker und Humblot, 1924.

Schwertfeger, Bernhard. *Der Weltkrieg der Dokumente: Zehn JahreKiegsschuldforschung und ihr Ergenbis.* Berlin: Deutsche Verlagsgesellschaft für Politik und Geschichte, 1929.

Seaton-Watson, R. "A Plea for the Study of Contemporary History." *History* 14 (1929): 2.

Seaton-Watson, R.W. *The Southern Slav Question and the Habsburg Monarchy.* New York: Howard Fertis, 1969.

Seaton-Watson and the Yugoslavs: Correspondence 1906–1941. London-Zagreb: British Academy, 1976.

Siegel, Jay, ed. *Encyclopedia of Forensic Sciences.* London: Academic Press, 2000.

Sirotković, Hodimir. "Pravni i politički aspekti procesa Rundpost-Fridjung." *Starine JAZU* 52 (1962): 49–184.

Smith, Roger and Brian Wyanne, eds. *Expert Evidence: Interpreting Science in the Law.* London and New York: Routledge, 1989.

Sprenger, Jacobus and Kramer Heinrich. *Malleus Maleficarum.* London: The Folio Society, 1968.

Taylor, Robert F. "A Comparative Study of Expert Testimony in France and the United States." *Texas International Law Journal* 31 (1996): 181–213.

Toepel, Friedrich. Grundsrukturen des Sachverständigenbeweises im Strasfprozessrecht. Tübingen: Mohr Siebeck, 2002.

Torstendahl, Rolf. *The Rise and Propagation of Historical Professionalism.* New York: Routledge, 2014.

Trencsényi, Balázs and Michal Kopeček, eds. *National Romanticism: The Formation of National Movements.* Budapest: Central European University Press, 2006.

The Trial of Warren Hastings, Esq: Late Governor General of Bengal, before the Court of Peers Sitting in Westminster Hall. London: J. Ridgway, 1788.

Troeltsch, Ernst. "Die Krisis des Historismus." *Die neue Rundschau* 33 (1922): 572–590.

Uitz, Renata. *Constitutions, Courts and History, Historical Narratives in Constitutional Adjudication.* CEU Press: Budapest, 2005.

Valla, Lorenzo. *Discourse on the Forgery of the Alleged Donation of Constantine.* New Haven: Yale University Press, 1922.

Whyte, George R. *The Dreyfus Affair: A Chronological History.* London: Palgrave, 2008.

Wilson, Keith, ed. *Forging the Collective Memory: Government and International Historians through Two World Wars.* Providence. Oxford: Bergham Books, 1996.

Woloch, Nancy. *Muller v. Oregon: A Brief History with Documents.* Boston: Bedford Books, 1996.

The World War One Document Archive. http://wwi.lib.byu.edu/index.php/1914_Documents (accessed on 21.2.2016).

Zola, Émile. "J'accuse," *L'Aurore*, 13 January 1898, 1.

2 The Great Shift

The Concept of Universal Human Rights

In order for historians to reappear in court as experts, their field of expertise had to become an undisputed matter of legal interest. This development was cryptically anticipated by Friedrich Nietzsche in his 1873 book *On the Use and Abuse of History for Life:* "A person must have the power and from time to time use it to break a past and to dissolve it, in order to be able to live. He manages to do this by dragging the past before the court of justice, investigating it meticulously, and finally condemning it." Nietzsche's concept materialized in the aftermath of the Second World War in ways the author would probably have found much too literal. At least since Nuremberg, quite substantial elements of the past have been "dragged before the court of justice," as courtrooms are being increasingly perceived as the places to right the wrongs of the past by addressing historical injustices.

Dragging the Past before the Court of Justice

This was a lengthy dragging indeed. At the time of Nietzsche's writing, it was no more than a distant ideal expressed in famous documents of the American and French revolutions, as well as international agreements such as the Paris Declaration on Naval Warfare (1856), the First Geneva Convention on the treatment of the wounded (1864), or the Petersburg Declarations of 1868. By the turn of the century, *Regulations Respecting the Laws and Customs of War on Land* were signed in The Hague (1899), and in 1906 the Geneva conventions were reviewed and extended, creating the foundations of both international humanitarian law and human rights law.[1] However, instead of organizing the third conference in The Hague, which was planned for 1915, the European powers, breaching the majority of the signed conventions, dragged the world into its first war. The devastation of the war brought about new initiatives expressed through the establishment of the League of Nations and the signing of the Second Geneva Convention in 1929 regulating the treatment of prisoners of war. Even attempts to abolish warfare were expressed in the unanimous vote of the Assembly of the League of Nations for the *Protocol for the Peaceful Settlement of*

International Disputes in 1924 and through the multilateral treaty known as the Briand-Kellogg pact of 1928.[2]

A reexamination of the past through an attempt to punish crimes of the First World War complemented this forward-looking activity. *The Commission of Responsibilities of the Authors of the War and the Enforcement of Penalties* was unwilling to judge on the issue of responsibility for war. Instead of bringing history to trial, it was willing to leave these crimes to history: "The premeditation of a war of aggression (. . .) is conduct which the public conscience reproves and which history will condemn, but (. . .) a war of aggression may not be considered as an act directly contrary to positive law. (. . .) We therefore do not advise that the acts which provoked the war should be charged against their authors and made the subject of proceedings before a tribunal."[3] Still, the famous Articles 227–231 of the Versailles Treaty underscored the German responsibility for the outbreak of war, calling for punishing the Kaiser and the German High Command, as well as the direct perpetrators of war crimes.[4] The effects were mixed—the Kaiser found refuge in the Netherlands, and no actual readiness among the Entente powers to bring him to justice existed. As for less royal perpetrators, the first such list that the Entente drafted contained 3,000 names, to be further cut to 854 suspects, including the wartime German Chancellor Bethmann-Hollweg and top military commanders Erich Ludendorff and Paul von Hindenburg. After fierce protests in Germany this list dwindled to forty-five persons of lower rank, who were indeed tried in front of the German Supreme Court in Leipzig in 1921. However, the actual trials started only against twelve people, six of whom were convicted and sentenced to shorter prison terms. Two of these even escaped from prison with the help of guards and to the delight of the German public. On the other hand, the attempt to put Ottoman officials responsible for genocide of the Armenians on trial by the military court martial in Istanbul (1919–1923) was diverted into a power struggle through various means ranging from judicial murders to general amnesty. Equally disappointing was the attempt of the Allies to organize international trials at Malta.[5] The stark limitations of the Leipzig and Istanbul trials showed cleavages between universal standards and local applications. The realities of the interwar period, characterized by fervent nationalism, racism, anti-Semitism, discrimination, and persecution, strengthened with economic difficulties, closures behind national borders, and the building of authoritarian and totalitarian systems, contributed to the growing autarchy. It took another war and an even worse wave of atrocities committed during its course to create a global consensus on the necessity to face the evil past, and finally drag history before the courts of justice.

Never before had the world seen as much devastation and human misery as in the period of the Second World War, regarded by Shoshanna Felman and Dori Laub as "a trauma we consider as the watershed of our times (. . .) not as an event encapsulated in the past, but as a history which is essentially not over, a history whose repercussions are not simply omnipresent in all our cultural practices, but whose traumatic consequences are still actively evolving."[6] It was a total war in many respects—from the geographical aspect of the global theater of warfare, through the totality of the means of warfare regardless of their lethality and criminality, to the political level of the confrontation of mutually exclusive ideologies. As a result, the victory was also supposed to be total. The unconditional surrender of Nazi Germany was to symbolize the defeat over the ideology of exterminationist nationalism embedded in "scientific racism." One of the most important avenues through which this change was expressed in the aftermath of the Second World War was hectic legal activity all over Europe.[7]

In addition to national reckonings, the initiatives to coordinate the policy of punishment for perpetrators of war crime internationaly already started during the war, on the insistence of the exiled representatives of the occupied European countries, who formed the Inter-Allied Conference on war crimes. The Allies very early on expressed a commitment to prosecute jointly those responsible both for the outbreak of war and for perpetration of war crimes. This commitment was expressed in mid-1943 through the creation of the United Nations War Crimes Commission.[8]

Once the Allied troops reached Germany, it became apparent that the scope of the crimes committed in occupied Europe transgressed even the most pessimistic expectations, and it was equally clear that each and every means available would be employed in order to conduct a visible reckoning. The occupying powers started a hectic activity—in mid-1945, the British occupying powers in Germany prosecuted Josef Krammer and forty-five of his SS subordinates of the camp Bergen-Belsen. The American authorities did the same with the staff of the Hadamar sanatorium and with General Yamashita in Manila on the other side of the globe. The Soviets also started an unprecedented number of trials on the territory they occupied.[9] This was being done in accordance with the November 1943 Moscow declaration, declaring that all the war criminals would be punished on the territory on which they committed the gravest crimes. However, the declaration made particular observation regarding major war criminals, whose crimes were considered to transgress national borders. There was a wide consensus that the leadership of the Axis should be held responsible, although numerous debates arose in regards to how exactly to do so. The fate of the German leadership was debated from 1941, with different twists and ideas, the possibility of a trial being just one among many options.[10]

In deliberating the details of this approach, particularly tempting was the possibility of creating an international tribunal. On the one hand, there was no convincing historical precedent for such an endeavor, and the amount of potential legal and political complications was vast. Still, rather than leaving the punishment to extralegal retribution, the U.S. submitted an elaborate proposal to the British and Soviet representatives in San Francisco in April 1945, setting the stage for due process for those accused of war crimes. After tedious negotiations, involving many aspects of this legal novelty, officials in Moscow, London, and Paris agreed on the details, and with the signing of the *London Agreement on the Punishment of the Major War Criminals of the European Axis* on August 8, 1945, the basis for the International Military Tribunal was set.

At the same time, the Allied representatives wavered between different ideas on whom to prosecute and for which crimes. With Adolf Hitler, undisputed head of the Third Reich, as well as other important members of the Nazi elite already dead (Heinrich Himmler, Joseph Goebbels), a definitive list had to be negotiated.[11] This choice was to determine the very scope, nature, and impact of the trial. "Whom will we accuse and put to their defense? We will accuse a large number of individuals and officials who were in authority in the government, in the military establishment, including the General Staff, and in the financial, industrial and economic life of Germany who by all civilized standards are provable to be common criminals," wrote Robert Jackson, Judge of the U.S. Supreme Court, to President Truman, who designated him to head the U.S. prosecution team. Jackson made no secret of his overall goal—"the establishment of a well-documented history of what we are convinced was a grand, concerted pattern to incite and commit the aggressions and barbarities which have shocked the world."[12]

Key architects of the International Military Tribunal in Nuremberg were well aware of the historical significance of the proceedings, and prepared accordingly. Nuremberg was to become, in the frequently misquoted words of assistant prosecutor Robert Kempner, "the greatest historical seminar ever held in the history of the world." Actually, he called it "the world's greatest research institute," but the point remained the same.[13] During the preparations for the trial, Gordon Dean, chief prosecutor Jackson's spokesman, wrote that "one of the primary purposes of the trial of the major war criminals is to document and dramatize for contemporary consumption and for history the means and methods employed by the leading Nazis in their plan to dominate the world and to wage an aggressive war."[14] His colleague, associate prosecutor Telford Taylor, was even blunter: "We cannot here make history over again. But we can see that it is written true." He had no illusions about the pitfalls of dragging history to court: "I was no historian, but I remembered something of the successful attacks against the Versailles treaty's imposition of war guilt on Germany and her allies which had been brought by 'revisionist' historians such as Sidney B. Fay and Harry Elmer Barnes," Taylor wrote. To avoid this, on the eve of the trial he wrote to prosecutor Jackson, "It is important that the trial not become an inquiry into the causes of war (. . .). The question of causation is important and will be discussed for many years, but it has no place in this trial (. . .). Contributing causes may be pleaded by the defendants before the bar of history, but not before the tribunal."[15] Jackson agreed: "We certainly do not want to permit this to be turned into a trial of anyone except those accused (. . .). So far as we are concerned, we have never thought there was any basis in this case for trying the remote causes for this war. Our definition of crime does not involve causes; it involves only actual aggressive war." However, he insisted: "Unless we write the record of this movement with clarity and precision, we cannot blame the future if in days of peace it finds incredible the accusatory generalities uttered during the war. We must establish incredible events by credible evidence."[16] A similar process was happening on the other side of the globe, in the International Military Tribunal for the Far East, designed in Tokyo to bring Japanese wartime officials to justice. In the view of Judith Shklar, "In the two great Trials at Nuremberg and Tokyo the past was being judged."[17]

History on Trial: The Nuremberg Revolution

And indeed, in the courtroom of the Palace of Justice in Nuremberg, one of the rare undemolished buildings in the city, history was on many lips. Expectations were high, and not just among laymen. Sir Norman Birkett, British Judge who was to sit on the panel, wrote in his diary on the eve of the trial that he expected "a very great landmark in the history of International Law. There will be a precedent for all successive generations (. . .). The world must be patient (and so must I) for what is being done now assuredly belongs to history."[18]

A crucial conveyer of this historical message was the 25,000-word indictment. Lodged on October 18, 1945, it accused twenty-three high-ranking officials of various branches of the Nazi government. Headed by Herman Göring, Hitler's Reichsmarschall and top-ranking surviving Nazi leader, among them one could see party officials (Rudolf Hess, Martin Bormann, Baldur von Schirach), ideologues and propagators (Alfred Rosenberg, Julius Streicher, Hans Fritzsche), diplomats (Joachim von Ribbentrop, Konstantin von Neurath, Franz von Papen), masters of the wartime economy (Robert Ley, Hans Frank, Wilhelm Frick, Walter Funk, Albert Speer, Hjalmar Schacht), occupation enforcers (Arthur Seyss-Inquart, Fritz Saukel, Ernst Kaltenbrunner), and officers of the German military (Wilhelm Keitel, Karl Dönitz, Erich Raeder, Alfred Jodl). Despite much confusion in the process of choosing the defendants, they eventually presented a sort of a cross-section of the Nazi elite and stood as symbols of different pillars of a defeated regime. Additionally, several organizations (Reich Cabinet, Leadership Corps of the Nazi Party, Schutzstaffel [SS], Sicherheitsdienst [SD], Gestapo, SA, and the German General Staff) stood accused.[19]

The prosecutors were well aware that the accused were making history, and they were determined to prove this. In doing so, their goals and their means were criminal. Jackson was set to portray "the view of the Nazis as a band of brigands set on subverting in Germany every vestige of the rule of law (. . .) once these international brigands, the top leaders of the Nazi party, of the SS and Gestapo had firmly established themselves within Germany by terrorism and crime, they immediately set out on a course of international pillage."[20] Accordingly, the charges included crimes of conspiracy,

Figure 2.1 Prosecution, defense, and the accused in the International Military Tribunal

© Charles Alexander, Office of the United States Chief of Counsel, courtesy Harry S. Truman Library

crimes against peace, crimes against humanity, and war crimes. All but the last one were novelties, introduced as the prosecutors were aware of the unique character of their task. As Nazi leaders did not necessarily kill anyone with their own hands, and in many cases did not directly order anybody to be killed, their responsibility was to be proved as involvement in an overall conspiracy with the goal of waging an aggressive war, incriminated as a crime against peace. The means involved breaches of laws and customs of warfare toward combatants, as well as civilians, on a scale that merited a novel legal expression of crimes against humanity. Such a complex legal setting was bound to trigger a distinct historical narrative. According to the historical gist of the indictment, read on November 20, 1945:

> In 1921 Adolf Hitler became the supreme leader or Fuehrer of the Nationalsozialistische Deutsche Arbeiterpartei, also known as the Nazi Party, which had been founded in Germany in 1920. He continued as such throughout the period covered by this Indictment. The Nazi Party, together with certain of its subsidiary organizations, became the instrument of cohesion among the defendants and their co-conspirators and an instrument for the carrying out of the aims and purposes of their conspiracy. Each defendant became a member of the Nazi Party and of the conspiracy, with knowledge of their aims and purposes, or, with such knowledge, became an accessory to their aims and purposes at some stage of the development of the conspiracy. (. . .) All the defendants, with diverse other persons, during a period of years preceding 8 May 1945, participated as leaders, organizers, instigators,

> or accomplices in the formulation or execution of a common plan or conspiracy to commit, or which involved the commission of, Crimes against Peace, War Crimes, and Crimes against Humanity.[21]

The historical dimension of the indictment was not lost on Robert Jackson, and was reflected in his opening statement on the following day: "The privilege of opening the first trial in history for crimes against the peace of the world imposes a grave responsibility. (. . .) We must never forget that the record on which we judge these defendants is the record on which history will judge us tomorrow. (. . .) Never before in legal history has an effort been made to bring within the scope of a single litigation the developments of a decade, covering a whole continent, and involving a score of nations, countless individuals, and innumerable events."[22] The presentation of a case on such a vast scale was no small problem for Jackson, who worried that the message would be plausibly conveyed. Although a judge of the U.S. Supreme Court, Jackson had reservations about the relations between history and law: "Judges often are not thorough or objective historians."[23] His solution for the problem was substantiating the indictment with as much documentation as possible. In doing so, the captured archives of the Third Reich and elsewhere had been of enormous aid. As the war was reaching its end, the Allies were in possession of one of the greatest archival remnants in the world. "There is no parallel in history to this baring of contemporary official papers to the public eye and expert scrutiny," wrote one of the participant historians, young Peter Calvocoresi, who used his professional training as an officer of British intelligence service to sift through the piles of documents in search of useful material.[24] The bureaucracy of the Third Reich left more than enough of a paper trail to begin the investigation and launch a prosecution. Contrary to the orders received, the majority of German archivists did not destroy their holdings, due to "the professional psychology of archivists, who would rather eviscerate their own children than destroy the material entrusted to their charge."[25]

Consequently, the majority of the prosecution's case was, by Jackson's decision, conducted through the documents from the captured archives. Over one hundred thousand documents were screened, with ten thousand selected for their probative value, structured to reflect four distinctive groups of crimes (conspiracy, crimes against humanity, war crimes, and crimes against peace).[26] Although the roles of the prosecution teams of the four Great Powers were previously divided exactly along these lines in order to minimize overlaps, in the courtroom they did not resist the temptation to widen their approach. The Presiding Judge from Great Britain, Geoffrey Lawrence, noted that the selection of "these documents naturally took the prosecution many months and continued long after the case had begun."[27] For more than seventy days, until March 4, 1946, the bench was faced with piles of documents, earning the proceedings the nickname of "a citadel of boredom" from an observer as perceptive as Rebecca West: "Boredom on a huge, historic scale."[28] Still, the prosecution did not consider changing its strategy, convinced that "the documents and testimony of the Nuremberg record can be of the greatest value showing the Germans the truth about the recent past."[29] Other leading figures in the American prosecution, like Jackson's special assistant William Donovan, who bore the much more important title of the Head of the Office of Strategies Services, feared this approach to be too dull. He wrote to Jackson that "because it was a lawsuit plus something else it needed an affirmative human aspect with German as well as foreign witnesses."[30]

Eventually, submitted documents were supported with the testimonies of eyewitnesses, including highly ranked insiders such as Otto Ohlendorf, Walter Schellenberg, Dieter Wisliceny, Erich von dem Bach Zelewski, Rudolf Hoess, Friedrich Paulus, and Hans Gisevius, giving direct insight onto the horrors of the Third Reich. There were no experts, let alone historical experts, among the witnesses. Only one such expert, or alternatively amicus curiae "as an authority on the total picture of the Holocaust," was considered. In June 1945 the director of the Institute of Jewish Affairs, lawyer and historian Jacob Robinson (1889–1977), was appointed special consultant for Jewish affairs to the U.S. Chief of Counsel, Robert H. Jackson. Robinson supplied the prosecution with a number of documents, but also with numerous ideas about ways to structure the case.[31] Under this influence, "Jackson apparently agreed to call Chaim Weizmann, the aged president of the World Zionist Organization, to testify at Nuremberg. Weizmann, it was hoped, would prepare a 15,000-word statement and would address the tribunal for about three hours." However, Weizmann "was unwilling to subject himself to cross-examination without being adequately prepared. (. . .) In contrast to David Ben-Gurion who was enthusiastic about the idea, Weizmann hesitated. He wanted to bring to bear additional research and sought to put off an appearance before the tribunal."[32] Even Robinson was hesitant, noting "the unique opportunity of pronouncing an earth-shaking j'accuse," recognizing "a historic occasion" (. . .) which should appeal to both emotions and reason of the mankind," but fearing "severe cross-examination" on the stand: "Unless skillfully handled, the whole appearance might boomerang."[33] Torn, Robinson flew to Nuremberg, where he was initially approached "for the purpose of determining whether he would be available and valuable as a trial witness to the persecution of the Jews. (. . .) It is believed that Dr. Robinson qualifies as an expert witness on the Jewish problem and that his opinion and estimates carry considerable weight."[34] Robinson seemed enthusiastic, but eventually neither Robert Jackson nor the World Jewish Congress shared that enthusiasm, preferring him to work in a semi-official capacity on matters of considerable importance, including the questioning of Nazi officials regarding the Jewish demographic loss.[35] Robinson could only comment: "We, those who are competent, are on the outside, and those who are inside are incompetent."[36] The prosecution wanted history on trial, not historians on the stand.

However, so did the defense, which was using any means possible to promote their view of the past and to exonerate themselves. If the prosecution came to an understanding of the historical importance of the proceedings, so did many of the accused. It would not be an exaggeration to conclude that the defendants were obsessed with history, treating it as their last refuge. Although they challenged the legality and legitimacy of the proceedings, as well as the basis for the crime of conspiracy and crimes against peace, the accused did not even contest the existence of war crimes, but rather attempted to evade their individual responsibility by relegating the blame to Hitler and Himmler. Lacking a documentary basis, the defendants attempted to compensate through witnesses. In comparison with the 33 witnesses who testified for the prosecution, the defense called upon 61 persons, and the depositions of 143 other persons were heard in the court. Although several highly ranked Luftwaffe officers and Ministry of Foreign Affairs officials did step forward in defense of Göring and Ribbentrop, generally the accused testified on mutual behalf, which exposed them to a thorough cross-examination. However, they could not resist the temptation of stating their case and sending a message not just to the bench, but to history as well.

Such an approach was most consistently deployed by Hermann Göring, who considered himself the unofficial leader of the dock, and who made no secret of his opinion that he considered the trial to be no more than the vengeance of the victors over the vanquished. He maintained that the future would vindicate the Nazi leadership, exclaiming that in fifty years the squares would be covered with their monuments. He scorned Germans who testified for the prosecution, remarking during Gisevius' testimony: "Look at him sitting there like a traitor. Don't worry, in 10 or 12 years history will take an entirely different view of these traitors."[37] He explained the bellicose posture to a prison psychologist: "As I told you, it is not a question of dying but of my reputation in history."[38] He was equally blunt with the psychiatrist: "Yes, I know I shall hang. You know I shall hang. I am ready. But I am determined to go down in German history as a great man. If I cannot convince the court, I shall at least convince the German people that all I did was done for the Greater German Reich. In 50 or 60 years there will be statues of Hermann Göring all over Germany. Little statues, maybe, but one in every German home."[39] Eager to secure such a legacy, Göring took the stand in March 1946, testifying for more than three days, and also being subjected to cross-examination of approximately the same duration. This was the peak of the historical counter-narrative of a stubborn defendant, who defended Nazi Germany political and military goals on the stand.[40] His performance left a deep impression on other defendants, like Ribbentrop, who expressed similar views in the semi-private atmosphere of their detention unit: "Why all this fuss about breaking treaties?" he asked, conversing with prison psychiatrists. "Did you ever read about the history of the British Empire? Why, it's full of broken treaties, the oppression of minorities, mass murder, aggressive wars, and everything." Confronted with the most blatant breaches of treaties, such as the attack on the Soviet Union, he evaded personal responsibility, claiming that he had argued for furthering this alliance, but was overruled by Hitler: "Well, maybe history will show that Hitler was right and I was wrong. (. . .) History will have to decide. You must regard these things in proper perspective. It is not so easy to understand." Eventually, he made up his mind in light of mounting information on the beginning of Cold War: "The future looks so black for Europe. (. . .) Stalin is a tremendous power (. . .). I wanted policy of conciliation, but I think history will show the Führer was right."[41] After repeated interventions of the prosecution, irritated by the flamboyant courtroom performance of Göring, the bench attempted to limit the historical excurses of the defendants: "The Tribunal has allowed the Defendant Göring, who has proclaimed himself to be responsible as the second leader of Nazi Germany, to give his evidence without any interruption whatever, and he has covered the whole history of the Nazi regime from its inception to the defeat of Germany. The Tribunal does not propose to allow any of the other defendants to go over the same ground in their evidence except insofar as it is necessary for their own defense."[42] Such a narrow approach distressed some defendants, such as Alfred Rosenberg, who took the stand stating: "In order to comply with the wish of the Tribunal, I do not want to give a lengthy exposition of my views as evolved from my study of history. I do not at all mean the study of anti-Semitic writings but of Jewish historians themselves."[43] However, his testimony did move in the direction of lengthy, self-serving historical narratives, cut short eventually by his own attorney. Furious, "at the end of the day he rebuked his attorney for interrupting him, and his attorney tried to argue that the court was not interested in the history of philosophy. Rosenberg turned (. . .) and said: 'Well, if they just want to make it a criminal trial, why don't the prosecution stick to criminal acts instead of attacking my ideology?' "[44] Göring had less success among his codefendants when he was minimizing or justifying the crimes committed by the regime. Even loyalists like Baldur von Schirach commented on Auschwitz: "That is the greatest and most devilish mass murder of history."[45] Denying these crimes made Albert Speer confide to the prison psychiatrist: "It was the truth and that is all there is to it. I wouldn't have been so mad at Göring if he had not tried to falsify history by making a heroic legend out of this rotten business. (. . .) No, none of them must go down in history as the least bit worthy of respect. Let the whole damned Nazi system and all who participated in it, including myself, go down with the ignominy and disgrace it deserves!"[46]

In order to evoke history again, the defendants had to wait for the closing statements on the last day of August 1946. Some, as Albert Speer, used this opportunity to improve their position by showing regret and assuming a limited amount of responsibility and contempt for the rest of the Nazi leadership. Unrepentant defendants, such as Rudolf Hess, used this opportunity solely, as he stated, "for the sake of the future judgment of my people and of history." In his otherwise rambling closing statement, he expressed delight:

"[I] was permitted to work for many years of my life under the greatest son whom my people has brought forth in its thousand-year history. (. . .) I do not regret anything." Baldur von Schirach shared his views on Hitler: "To me he remains the man who made Greater Germany a fact in German history." Wilhelm Keitel's final statement was worded more neutrally, insisting on his innocence "in the interest of historical truth," and so was von Neurath's: "My life was consecrated to truth and honor, to the maintenance of peace and the reconciliation of nations, to humanity and justice. I stand with a clear conscience not only before myself, but before history and the German people." Franz von Papen even warned the judges: "Only if this High Tribunal recognizes and acknowledges the historic truth will the historical meaning of this Tribunal be fulfilled." Von Ribbentrop agreed that "this Trial was to be conducted for the purpose of discovering the historical truth," but continued: "From the point of view of German foreign policy I can only say: this Trial will go down in history as a model example of how, while appealing to hitherto unknown legal formulas and the spirit of fairness, one can evade the cardinal problems of 25 years of the gravest human history." The informal leader among the defendants, Hermann Göring, also attempted to influence posterity with a final appeal to history, evaluating the trial in his closing statement as an "erroneous conception which is entirely devoid of logic, and which will be rectified someday by history."[47] Listening to their exposés, Albert Speer expressed doubts about the political feasibility of the trial, which was in his view "adding another final chapter that gives some of the leaders a chance to make fine speeches and make a good appearance in history, and make people think there was something good in it after all."[48]

However, the prosecution was also in a position to evoke history in its closing remarks, starting with Jackson, who did not fail to characterize the exposés of the accused: "History will know that whatever could be said, they were allowed to say. They have been given the kind of trial which they, in the days of their pomp and power, never gave to any man." In his own closing statement he was equally concerned with history, as he proceeded to "outline with bold strokes the vitals of this trial's mad and melancholic record, which will live as the historical text of the twentieth century's shame and depravity."[49] His French colleague, M. Champetier de Ribes, used the same opportunity to remind the bench at the end of his case that "the chief concern of this trial is above all that of historical truth. Thanks to it, the historians of the future, as well as the chronicler of today, will know the truth of the political, diplomatic, and military events of the most tragic period in our history."[50] These words echoed the expectations of British Chief Prosecutor Hartley Shawcross, expressed at the opening of the case: "This Tribunal, acting, as we know it will act notwithstanding its appointment by the victorious powers, with complete and judicial objectivity, will provide a contemporary touchstone and an authoritative and impartial record to which future historians may turn for truth, and future politicians for warning."[51]

Figure 2.2 Judges of the International Military Tribunal in Nuremberg

The judges hardly needed such a reminder. By the end of August 1946 both sides were heard, and deliberations had begun between them. After 406 sessions during 216 courtroom days, eight men—four principal judges and four alternates—rendered the judgment. The British alternate, Norman Birkett, was well aware of the uniqueness of their role in "the greatest trial in history. The historians of the future will look back to it with fascinated eyes." He felt that reaching the judgment required "not only knowledge of law but a knowledge of history, particularly German history, a knowledge of men and worldly affairs."[52] Overwhelmed by the procedural aspects of the trials, as well as by the abundance of the evidence, the judges proceeded with caution, taking their time. "The judges were not keen to become the targets of historians," observed Telford Taylor.[53] Hence for nearly one month they scrutinized both applicable laws and evidence, reassembling on September 30, 1946, in a courtroom filled with journalists, reporters, visitors, and cameras.

As they began to read out the judgment, the judges summarized the statistics of the trial, emphasizing the extraordinary number of introduced documents. The judges were clearly much impressed by this documentary basis: "Much of the evidence presented to the Tribunal on behalf of the Prosecution was documentary evidence, captured by the Allied armies in German army headquarters, Government buildings, and elsewhere. The case, therefore, against the defendants rests in a large measure on documents of their own making, the authenticity of which has not been challenged except in one or two cases."[54] How did the judges wrestle with this abundance? Firstly, they took a historical step back: "For the purpose of showing the background of the aggressive war and war crimes charged in the Indictment, the Tribunal will begin by reviewing some of the events that followed the first World War, and in particular, by tracing the growth of the Nazi Party under Hitler's leadership to a position of supreme power from which it controlled the destiny of the whole German people, and paved the way for the alleged commission of all the crimes charged against the defendants." This review, starting with the section named, went on to carefully recount the sequence of events spanning the interwar period, in a lengthy account of *Machtergreifung*, followed by descriptions of sets of violations of international treaties by Germany, culminating in the waging of a series of wars of aggression characterized by war crimes and crimes against humanity.[55] However, this historical background did not follow the indictment blindly:

> The "Common Plan or Conspiracy" charged in the Indictment covers 25 years, from the formation of the Nazi Party in 1919 to the end of the war in 1945. The Party is spoken of as "the instrument of cohesion among the defendants" for carrying out the purposes of the conspiracy—the overthrowing of the Treaty of Versailles, acquiring territory lost by Germany in the last war and "Lebensraum" in Europe, by the use, if necessary, of armed force, of aggressive war. The "seizure of power" by the Nazis, the use of terror, the destruction of trade unions, the attack on Christian teaching and on Churches, the persecution of Jews, the regimentation of youth—all these are said to be steps deliberately taken to carry out the common plan. It found expression, so it is alleged, in secret rearmament, the withdrawal by Germany from the Disarmament Conference and the League of Nations, universal military service, and seizure of the Rhineland. Finally, according to the Indictment, aggressive action was planned and carried out against Austria and Czechoslovakia in 1936–1938, followed by the planning and waging of war against Poland, and, successively, against 10 other countries. The Prosecution says, in effect, that any significant participation in the affairs of the Nazi Party or Government is evidence of a participation in a conspiracy that is in itself criminal. Conspiracy is not defined in the Charter. But in the opinion of the Tribunal the conspiracy must be clearly outlined in its criminal purpose. It must not be too far removed from the time of decision and of action. The planning, to be criminal, must not rest merely on the declarations of a party program, such as are found in the 25 points of the Nazi Party, announced in 1920, or the political affirmations expressed in *Mein Kampf* in later years. The Tribunal must examine whether a concrete plan to wage war existed, and determine the participants in that concrete plan."
>
> In doing so, the judges reached the conclusion that "that plans were made to wage war, as early as 5 November 1937, and probably before that (. . .) but the evidence establishes with certainty the existence of many separate plans rather than a single conspiracy embracing them all.[56]

After this restrictive reading of the conspiracy charge, the court proceeded to review the "the evidence relating to war crimes," finding it "overwhelming in its volume and its detail." Equally detailed was the Tribunal's recounting of murder and ill-treatment of the civilian population and prisoners of war, pillaging of public and private property, slave labor policy, persecution of the Jews, concentration camps, and other criminal facets of the Nazi regime. Regarding the responsibility for established crimes, the judges found that four out of the seven indicted institutions—Gestapo, Sicherheitsdienst (SD), Schutzstaffel (SS), and the Leadership Corps of the Nazi Party—were used for criminal purposes.[57] They were therefore declared criminal organizations. In a dramatic touch, the assessment of responsibility of individual defendants was left for the day after.

On the last day of the trial the president of the Tribunal read out the lengthy review of the individual criminal responsibilities of the twenty-two accused. In assigning individual responsibility the court bundled the personal histories of the accused with the general historical narrative, the point of the intersection being either the ascent of the Nazi Party, the Nazi takeover of power, the beginning of the Second World War, or the commencement of war crimes and crimes against humanity.[58] Twelve death penalties were rendered (to Hermann Göring, Hans Frank, Wilhelm Frick, Alfred Jodl, Ernst Kaltenbrunner, Alfred Rosenberg, Fritz Sauckel, Wilhelm Keitel, Joachim von Ribbentrop, Arthur Seys-Inquart, Julius Streicher, and to Martin Bormann in absentia). Seven accused received life sentences (Erich Räder, Walther Funk, and Rudolf Hess) or long-term imprisonment (twenty years for Baldur von Schirach and Albert Speer, fifteen years for Konstantin von Neurath, and ten years for Karl Dönitz). Three (Hans Fritzsche, Franz von Papen, and Hjalmar Schacht) were acquitted on all charges.[59] As the reading of judgment was finished, on October 1, 1946, at 14.50h, many shared Rebecca West's belief, who, once her boredom stage was overcome, concluded that a message of significant global importance had been sent: "The Judgment of the Nuremberg Tribunal may be one of the most important events in the history of civilization."[60] Rendered in front of the 600 people who filled the courtroom, 250 of whom were journalists from all over the world, the judgment was immediately translated into numerous languages and circulated, hitting the headlines around the globe, expressly becoming a historical event in its own right. As many might have disagreed over the specifics of the judgments, particular sentences, or aspects of the proceedings, the agreement that history had been put on trial in Nuremberg still stands today.

Breaching the Incompatibility Presumption

"History alone can judge the success or failure of this historic trial!" exclaimed John Paulinus Kenny in the aftermath of Nuremberg.[61] There has been no lack of attempts to influence that judgment ever since. As the Nuremberg proceedings represent one of the crucial legal, historical, political, and even cultural references of the contemporary world, their contributions and effects as well as their relation to history are constantly being debated. Questions regarding the legal basis of the trial, whether it should have taken place, the frame of the indictment, and the choice of the accused, and debates about the verdicts and evidence they were based on, demonstrate that Nuremberg has constantly been "on trial" for the last sixty years.[62] One need not to be more postmodern than prosecutor Telford Taylor himself to realize that "today Nuremberg is both what actually happened there and what people think happened, and the second is more important than the first."[63]

One of the central issues of this debate boils down to a simple question: Did Nuremberg get history right? The opinions were divided even among its architects: "We are too close to a trial to apprise its long-term effects," wrote Jackson to President Truman in his final report. Accepting his resignation, Truman showed more confidence: "For my part I have no hesitancy in declaring that historic precedent set in Nuremberg justifies the expenditure of effort," he wrote in October 1946, accepting Jackson's resignation. Ultimately, Jackson found solace in the conviction that "no history of this era can be entitled to authority which fails to take into account the record of Nuremberg."[64]

What did Germans have to say about this? In his famous 1946 book on the question of guilt, Karl Jaspers compared the outcome of the two world wars and reached the following conclusion: "Unlike the case in World War I when the war-guilt question was not decided against one side by the historians of all nations, this war was begun by Hitler Germany. (. . .) And today we have something entirely new in world history. The victors are establishing a court. The Nuremberg trial deals with crimes."[65] Hannah Arendt was more cautious. Concerned with the scale of Nazi crimes, which, as she wrote to Jaspers, "explode the limits of the law," she publicly expressed her doubts: "Just as there is no political solution within human capacity for the crime of administrative state murder, so the human need for justice can find no satisfactory reply to the total mobilization of a people for that purpose. Where all are guilty, nobody in the last analysis can be judged."[66] Still, Jaspers maintained that "the answer to all arguments against the trial is that Nuremberg is something really new. (. . .) Contradictions in detail are to be overcome by acts designed to bring world order out of confusion. It is wrong, secondly, to strike an attitude of outraged aggressiveness and to say no from the start. What happens in Nuremberg, no matter how many objections it may invite, is a feeble, ambiguous harbinger of a world order, the need of which mankind is beginning to feel. This is the entirely new situation (. . .). So it is precisely the German who might become aware of the extraordinary import of this harbinger. Our own salvation in the world depends on the world order which—although not yet established in Nuremberg—is suggested by Nuremberg."[67]

However, his was hardly the prevailing mood in Germany. Rebecca West noted that "indeed it revolted many Germans who saw the trials or read the transcripts, even when they were strongly anti-Nazi. This was due to a real national difference, not to be wiped out by improvisation such as in the Nuremberg trial. The procedure adopted by the Tribunal was a compromise between the English and the American procedures, as the French and Russians claimed no concessions to their national practices."[68] She went on to enumerate a number of procedural reasons that would strike Germans as unfair, concluding that "truly the courtroom at Nuremberg was a tank filled to the brim with misapprehension." She even claimed that "for the rest the Nuremberg trial must be admitted as a betrayal of hopes that it engendered. Conducted by officials sick with the weariness left by a great war, attended by only a handful of spectators, inadequately reported, constantly misinterpreted, it was an unshapely event (. . .) stamping no clear image on the mind of the people it had been designed to impress."[69] Other accounts differed, as there was no shortage of perceptive observers in the public gallery of IMT, which hosted Ernest Hemingway, Erika Mann, Ilja Ehrenburg, Louis Aragon, John Steinbeck, and many other participants of what Steffen Radlmaier called the "Nuremberg learning process."[70]

Polarization, as one of the early traits of the Nuremberg venture, proved to be lasting. Among early criticism, accusations of partiality were seen as most damaging, even by the IMT judges, as Norman Birkett warned: "If it continues to apply only to the enemy, I think the verdict of history may be against Nuremberg. (. . .) The United Nations should build a code upon it that is applied not merely to the enemy but to all. And if that is done, then I believe that Nuremberg will stand the test of history."[71] Whatever its immediate impact on Germany might have been, the trial was also to exemplify a universal shift toward human rights, best expressed through a creation of the United Nations. This attempt was well reflected in a number of Resolutions of its General Assembly, which regulated the issues of war crimes, affirming the principles of international law as applied in the Charter of the Nuremberg Tribunal and setting the stage for the creation of a permanent international criminal court through the activity of the International Law Commission, which had by 1950 recommended a set of the *Principles of International Law Recognized in the Charter of the Nürnberg Tribunal and in the Judgment of the Tribunal.* Principles of universal human rights from the Charter of United Nations were also specified in the 1948 *Declaration of Universal Human Rights*. The operationalization of those principles was to be secured by the expansion of the Geneva Conventions and particularly through the *Convention on the Prevention and Punishment of the Crime of Genocide*, which was adopted by the General Assembly in December 1948 and came into effect in January 1951.[72]

Still, as the world was undergoing an abrupt transition toward bipolar tensions, it soon became clear that "waging a war to end all wars" amounted to utopia. The international atmosphere was steadily eroding, and it did not take long for the once allied powers that had crushed the Nazi project to openly collide. The fragile system of international relations soon came to a paralysis, as sets of crises such as those over Trieste or Berlin were on the verge of triggering a global confrontation. Disagreements between the United Nations Security Council member states over the nature of commitments taken, followed by mutual accusations on hypocrisy, were shrinking the space for the interiorization of ambitious legal devices. It became clear that what had been regarded as the dawn of the new era of stability was not much more than the beginning of a new, potentially even deadlier confrontation. The inability to reach political consensus had closed the doors for negotiating the creation of a permanent international criminal court. With the wartime coalition falling apart, Americans continued the practice through twelve subsequent trials in front of the Nuremberg Military Tribunal.[73] Other governments embarked on national war crime trial projects, with varying motivations and outcomes. Remaining a discontinued precedent in international criminal law, Nuremberg was the obvious target of criticism coming from different quarters. A steady stream of monographs quickly grew into battles over the interpretation of Nuremberg. Propaganda from the East directly accused Western democracies of shielding the remnants of the Nazi regime. In the West, theories of totalitarianism that compared Stalinism with Hitlerism emerged, allowing for extremists to go even further, treating the joint venture of the Nuremberg trials as a pact with the devil.[74] As an example of a joint undertaking of the victorious powers, its achievements could not have been untouched by the arising global confrontation of the Cold War. Consequently, many interpretations of Nuremberg in the East were critical of the leniency of the Western judges of the accused, whereas interpretations in the West tended to criticize the very idea of organizing a trial alongside the Soviets.[75]

The universalist appeal was to be tested further in the East, on the other side of the globe, where even more robust debate was forcefully launched in the aftermath of the capitulation of Japan. The basic matrix of legal reckoning with the defeated enemy was much the same as in Europe. Between 1945 and 1951 there had been around 2,200 trials held by the Allied powers, encompassing around 5,700 accused, of which 920 were condemned to death, and over 3,000 to prison sentences.[76] In the midst of this activity stood the International Military Tribunal for the Far East (IMTFE), known as the Tokyo Tribunal. Against General MacArthur's idea to organize a speedy military trial for General Tojo and others directly responsible for the Pearl Harbor attack, Washington insisted on a large-scale trial that would paint a broad historical canvas. Although, curiously enough, the decision was reached for the sake of the stability of the occupied zone not to put Emperor Hirohito on trial, twenty-eight persons from Japan's military, political, and diplomatic elite were indicted. The proceedings lasted for over two years (April 29, 1946–November 12, 1948), during which time 419 witnesses were heard, and 779 affidavits and altogether 4,836 documents were submitted, generating a transcript subsequently published in twenty-two volumes.[77] It is no wonder that the presiding judge, Sir William F. Webb, opened the proceedings with these words: "There has been no more important criminal trial in all history."[78]

This was not only a comment on the scope and importance of the case, but also an implicit homage to the Nuremberg trial, as IMTFE was in many ways modeled after it. Emulating Robert Jackson, Chief Prosecutor Joseph B. Keenen exclaimed: "This is no ordinary trial, for here we are waging a part of the determined battle of civilization to preserve the entire world from destruction."[79] Furthering the analogy with Nuremberg, the indictment traced the Japanese activity starting from the invasion of Manchuria in 1931, but also drew an ideological parallel between Japan and Germany: "The mind of the Japanese people was systematically poisoned with harmful ideas of the alleged racial superiority of Japan over other peoples of Asia and even of the whole world. Such parliamentary institutions as existed in Japan were used as implements for widespread aggression, and a system similar to those then established by Hitler and the Nazi Party in Germany and by the Fascist Party in Italy was introduced."[80]

However, this parallel had its limitations, and Tokyo was no Nuremberg. Chief Prosecutor Keenan lacked Justice Jackson's enthusiasm, and the international prosecutorial team he was heading had a much tougher time than their European counterparts locating the incriminating documents. The political decision not to put the emperor on trial also undercut the historical dimension of the trial, creating a huge hole right in the middle of the case against the Japanese power elite, including four prime ministers, four foreign ministers, four war ministers, three chiefs of general staff, and other officials, who stood accused of crimes against peace, war crimes, and crimes against humanity in front of a much more heterogeneous panel of judges from Australia, Canada, China, France, India, the Netherlands, New Zealand, Philippines, and the United Kingdom, as well as two from the U.S. and the Soviet Union.

The accused in Tokyo did not resemble the quarrelsome, unruly, and demoralized lot of the Nuremberg dock. According to the Dutch judge Bert Rölling, they "were mostly first-rate people. Not all of them, but the majority of them were prominent people (. . .). In Germany, people dissociated themselves as much as possible with Hitler, saying that what he had done was disgusting. Nobody wanted to defend Hitler. (. . .) It was quite different in Japan. The Japanese defended the action of Japan in this Asian land and in the world, to liberate Asia and to change the world. And they had a case, in this respect."[81] Unlike the accused Nazis, who distanced themselves from Himmler, and particularly from Hitler, the Japanese defendants were uneasy about evoking a superior orders defense, as they would not want to implicate their emperor as their senior. They offered no aggressive defense, challenging the legality of the Tribunal and pointing out the ex post facto character of incriminations of a crime against peace and crimes against humanity. The Dutch judge summarized their case as follows: "They had lost the war, and they realized their actions would be condemned. They just wanted to prove to the world that what they did, from a certain point of view, could be understood and perhaps justified. (. . .) Cowards? Not at all. None of them, I think. They were really very dignified fellows. (. . .) Certainly, if you were to put yourself in the Japanese mind, then you could understand that many of them were deeply respected by the population (. . .) the Japanese accused had no bad conscience at all! (. . .) Our accused were the leaders and they had never, at least as far as our evidence went, committed war crimes or ordered war crimes to be committed. (. . .) The Japanese were not real scoundrels. They had no regard for anybody in warfare, and if they had a purpose, a specific goal, they did everything to reach it. But they were no sadists, they were not out for killing."[82]

The majority of judges did not share his views, as the judgment, issued in November 1948, did not contain a single acquittal. Seven accused were sentenced to death and executed, and others got prison sentences, which were, for all but four, life sentences. The massive 1,770-page judgment also followed the Nuremberg model—after revisiting the applicable law, it opened with a historic excurse: "In dealing with the period of Japanese history with which this indictment is mainly concerned it is necessary to consider in the first place the domestic history of Japan during the same period. (. . .) Indeed, the answers to the questions: 'Why did these things happen?' and 'Who were responsible for their occurrence?' will often only be found if the contemporaneous history of Japanese domestic politics is known."[83] What followed was a book-length historical account, described by British prosecutor at the trial, Arthur Comyns-Car, in the following manner: "Never before has it been possible for the facts of a vital period of history to be so fully investigated. (. . .) The Judgment of the Tokyo Tribunal is most full and careful and makes fascinating reading." Much more reserved was the Presiding Judge, Sir William Webb: "A judgment may itself be historic, yet its content may be incomplete as history."[84] He had good reasons for this reservation, as no one else knew better how difficult a process it was to reach it. Out of eleven judges, no less than five, including Webb, submitted separate opinions. The dissents touched on fundamental issues. "It is well-nigh impossible to define the concept of initiating or waging a war of aggression both accurately and comprehensively," wrote Justice B. V. A. Röling of the Netherlands in his own dissent. "The majority judgment has dealt extensively with the factual history of Japan, and with the part which the accused played in this history. (. . .) It seems however, necessary to dissent on some issues, where a different interpretation should be given to the facts laid before the Tribunal."[85] He went on for over fifty pages to lay down his interpretation of the historical events. If this was destabilizing, the dissenting opinion of Justice Pal of India was devastating. Almost as long as the judgment, it questioned the applicable law, in particular the notion of aggressive war, and the historical narrative as well, contesting the existence of a conspiracy of the accused: "The statesmen, diplomats and politicians of Japan were perhaps wrong, and perhaps they misled themselves. But they were not conspirators. They did not conspire. To appreciate what happened, it is only just to see the events by putting them in their proper perspective."[86] Justice Pal continued to advocate his assessment that "the historic causes of the war simply defy legal judgment." During his 1952 visit to Japan he delivered a speech in Hiroshima: "It should become clear by reading of my judgment that the Western powers were the very ones that committed the detestable invasion of Asia. (. . .) I beg you to investigate thoroughly the truthful history from the Manchurian Incident throughout the outbreak of the Greater East Asia War by reading my judgment. I cannot let it pass when Japanese children are being burdened by a perverted sense of guilt and go down the road of servility and decadence. (. . .) Mistaken history must be rewritten."[87]

Researchers seemed to agree. The first detailed study on the Tokyo trial had an indicative title, *Victor's Justice*. Its author, Richard Minear, critically investigated IMTFE, but also opted to take "one step further and conclude that the processes of history are too complex to be subjected to the adjudication of any tribunal. (. . .) Historical process does not yield to adjudication; and to attempt to make history justiciable is doomed from the start." Hence, in his view, "there may be little connection between legal guilt and innocence on the one hand and historical verdict on the other."[88] Clearly, an incompatibility theory between legal and historical judgment was at work there.

A similar process was underway in Germany, where a steady stream of revisionist literature was growing, predictably resting on the argument that not individuals, but German history, was put to a trial set up by the victors and judged ex post facto.[89] Less predictably, similar tones could be heard in the House of Lords of the British Parliament in May 1949, by Maurice Pascal Alers, Baron Hankey, seasoned civil servant and wartime cabinet member, who advocated discontinuation of the war crimes trials in Germany. Nuremberg was in his view "imitated all over Europe, resulting in the judicial persecution and often death of countless and often innocent people. (. . .) In both Nuremberg and Tokyo, the victors tried and judged the vanquished."[90] Hankey was ever more critical about its historical account: "Contrary to general belief, the history on which the Nuremberg judgments and findings were based is not accurate. (. . .) Judgment was based entirely upon the evidence that they obtained from the Germans. They did not find out what was going on in the Allied countries. (. . .) That is equally true of the even more important introductory review of the rise of Hitler and his gang with which the Judgment opens for the purpose of showing the background of the aggressive war and the war crimes charged in the indictment (. . .)." He concluded: "I cannot see that we gained anything by the Nuremberg trials (. . .) the most urgent thing is to bring all these trials to an end."[91]

Probably no person in the House of Lords was more irritated with this approach than former presiding judge of IMT, Geoffrey Lawrence, who had been recently elevated to peerage as Lord Oaksey. He objected that "the tribunal had some years to cover in their judgments, and though they recited the rise of Hitler to power they could scarcely be expected to write a complete history of the period." The Earl of Perth came to his aid, agreeing that the judgment, "as Lord Oaksey said, does not purport to be a complete history of events in Germany and elsewhere between the two wars."[92] The motion to abolish the war crime trials did not pass, but the debate was a typical illustration of the fatigue of war crimes prosecutions, gradually stalled by the termination of occupation, the creation of the Federal Republic of Germany, and its transformation into a key Western ally in Europe. Interestingly, in his book Hankey concluded that the Nuremberg judgment "can hardly be described as fair or just. It certainly is not history. Yet, by staging legal trials was it not expected of lawyers to turn to historians?" He deplored that the proceedings lacked in historical expertise, as "at the time they had no expert assessors with them."[93] Equally stubborn remained Justice Lawrence: "Had it not been for the long drawn out and elaborate Trial, the production of German documents, the authenticity of which could not be and was not denied, and the actual evidence of several of the worst criminals themselves, no one would have believed what the Germans did. (. . .) One frequently meets ignorant or prejudiced people who do not believe it still."[94]

Despite the attacks, Nuremberg legacy had a number of guardians. Chief Prosecutor of the Tokyo Tribunal Joseph Keenen held that "Tokyo and Nuremberg war crimes trials were the manifestation of an intellectual and moral revolution which will have a profound and far reaching influence upon the future of world society. (. . .) The transitory features of the Tokyo trial are related to permanent values to be found in legal history and philosophy—values which are immutable and eternal."[95] A more eloquent defense of these principles was offered by Benjamin Ferenz, one of the prosecutors in the subsequent Nazi war crimes trials: "Who didn't know that it was illegal to murder a million innocent people, including hundreds of thousands of women and children, helpless people, because of their color, their race, or their religion? Who didn't know that such conduct was illegal? It was not ex post facto, but was putting into positive international law fundamental principles of humanity and of morality, and national law, and making them legally binding through international law."[96] Even a figure like Hans Kelsen, one of the most influential legal positivists, was ready to concede that "justice required the punishment of these men as Nuremberg defendants (. . .) to punish those who were morally responsible for the international crime of the Second World War may certainly be considered as more important than to comply with the rather relative rule against ex post facto law, open to so many exceptions."[97]

Interestingly, the Nuremberg judges and prosecutors were intuitively aware of the curious duality of their relation to the past. On the one hand, they relied on enormous historical documentation, transforming it into legal evidence, producing a sizable legal judgment that they expected to serve as a template for future history writing. On the other hand, they showed an awareness, as Judge Norman Birkett did, that "the final verdict upon Nuremberg will no doubt be passed in the distant future; it will be the verdict of history. What we can do in present time is, in quietude, to discuss some of the important matters upon which the verdict of history may finally rest."[98] Could more be done? One of the answers was obvious—the availability of trial records for future researchers was seen as the natural continuation of the stabilization of the legal legacy of the postwar trials. However, the very magnitude of the trials was complicating the task of their complete publication. The abridged transcripts of proceedings held in the British zone amounted to six thick volumes. Prefacing the first of these volumes, its editor-in-chief, none other than Nuremberg prosecutor David Maxwell Fyfe, suggested that "the need for a permanent record of examples of these trials has increased rather than diminished. It is doubtful whether there will ever be time to write, or whether humanity would have the tenacity and imagination to comprehend, a complete history of the atrocities perpetrated. Yet it is essential to-day and forever that mankind should have some idea of what tyranny harnessed to the modern scientific state can mean."[99] Birkett himself noted that this documentation "is to be regarded as much more than the account of a criminal trial (. . .). It is a valuable contribution to history of a highly specialized kind. (. . .) Future generations should know the facts (. . .) from the dispassionate record of a formal trial. (. . .) The books of the present kind preserve for the historians and the legislator the actual records of the facts and the law, the submissions and contentions, and thus help future generations to avoid the errors and evils of the past."[100]

The termination of the war crimes prosecution increased the zeal among the guardians of the Nuremberg legacy as an ethical, political, and historical watershed. As the complete transcripts and documentation of the International Military Tribunal, with its total of over fifty volumes, were about to be published in four languages, to substitute numerous abridged versions, Thomas J. Dodd, member of the U.S. prosecution team at IMT, exclaimed that the trial "was a detailed and exhaustive analysis, under judicial authority and through adversarial proceedings, of the historical facts and forces, before and during the worst war in history (. . .). The record itself, when completed, will exceed by considerable margin much more than fifteen thousand printed pages. In it will be found the substance for a thousand discussions, for innumerable analytical reviews, and, I expect, for hundreds of volumes. It is a vast reservoir of information, bearing the stamp of hard judicial examination. But it is more than a record; it is more than a reservoir of information; it is more than a library. It is the written history of the first postmortem on a catastrophe that cost millions upon millions of lives."[101] Legal scholar Herbert Wechsler, principal assistant to U.S. Nuremberg Judges Biddle and Parker, addressed the annual meeting of the

American Historical Association in December 1946: "One may say without impertinence to historians that the judgment that history will render upon a legal proceeding is not usually a matter of acute concern either to counsels or to the court. In this respect, at least, the Nuremberg trial was a highly exceptional affair; for the perspective of most of the participants, and even that of the defendants, was focused very much on the future, distant and problematical as it is. (. . .) The verdict of history will not be rendered for a long time, but we may be certain that the process of deliberation will be active and that the debate has already begun."[102]

Wechsler would probably be surprised to find out that seventy years later, the debate is still ongoing and the end of deliberation is not in sight. The gist of the controversy is neatly localized by Primiel and Stiller: "Historians have frequently criticized Nuremberg for failing to account for historical complexity and bring about adequate justice, while jurists are wary of the historical agenda of the trials."[103] It therefore comes as no surprise that even today there is still no clear answer to a seemingly easy question: Did Nuremberg get history right? For Mark Osiel, Nuremberg fixed the responsibility of a handful of accused top Nazi leaders, promoted a misguided, conspiratorial view on the past by an overemphasis on the conspiracy charge and the consequent downplaying of crimes against humanity, and also "appears to have been both boring and illiberal at once, on many accounts."[104] On the other hand, for Michael Marrus, Nuremberg was a turning point which "at its best moments, set an example for a kind of historical judgment—impartial, but not necessarily dispassionate; fair-minded, but not without moral compass; searching in quest of truth, while recognizing the formal limitations that attend to the endeavor in an adversarial proceeding."[105] Such disagreements, as well as the flood of literature on the occasion of its fiftieth and sixtieth anniversaries, undoubtedly show that "the internal conflicts and contradictions of the rule of law discourses and historical distortions which informed Nuremberg arose at some level between the legal functions of the process and the broader political, representational or metaphoric roles assigned to the Trials."[106] The lack of consensus on the content of that legacy is well captured in the title of a recent volume: *The Legacy of Nuremberg: Civilizing Influence or Institutionalized Vengeance?*[107] The opinions on the merits of Nuremberg are likely to remain divided as long as its legacy is seen in an unnecessarily holistic manner, whereas detailed scrutiny reveals a number of narratives and counter-narratives deployed during this judicial reckoning. Recognizing the existence of these multiple agencies and their confrontations, not only between the prosecution and the defense, but also between and even within the prosecution teams and among defendants themselves, would help us to understand its complex impact.

Whereas the legacy of Nuremberg remains open for debate, it is safe to assert the unique impact it had on the relationship between law and history. Whatever commentators might think about whether Nuremberg got its history right, nobody doubts that the incompatibility presumption was breached in its courtroom. This is vividly described by Shoshana Felman:

> Trials have always been contextualized in—and affected by—a general relation between history and justice. But they have not always been judicially concerned with this relationship. Until the middle of the twentieth century, a radical division between history and justice was in principle maintained. The law perceived itself either as ahistorical or expressing a specific stage in society's historical development. But law and history were separate. The courts sometimes acknowledged they were part of history, but they did not judge history as such. This state of affairs has changed since the constitution of the Nuremberg tribunal (. . .) which for the first time called history itself into a court of justice. In the wake of Nuremberg, a displacement has occurred in relationship between history and trials. Not only has it become thinkable to put history on trial, it has become judicially necessary to do so. Nuremberg did not intend, but has in fact produced, this conceptual evolution that implicitly affects all later trials, and not only the tradition of war crimes and of international criminal law. In the second half of the twentieth century, it has become part of the function of trials to repair judicially not only private but also collective historical injustices.[108]

Tipping off the sensitive balance between history and law did not simply overwrite the incompatibility presumption. In some ways, it even radicalized the problem: "The confluence of two distinct disciplines—history and justice—in the investigation and prosecution of Nazi war crimes and crimes against humanity has been the subject of controversy since Nuremberg International Military Tribunal," writes Erich Haberer.[109] However, this intervention significantly destabilized two traditional safeguards that had kept the disciplines apart. On the one hand, no statute of limitations was envisaged for the crimes adjudicated in Nuremberg, opening an epoch of their prosecution which was to last much longer than contemporaries ever supposed. The notion of historical distance, the other important pillar of incompatibility, also cracked under the weight of documentation accessible for scrutiny much sooner than usual. An abundance of historical documentation became available for scholarly scrutiny as it was seized, exhibited on trial, published, and widely circulated. History had indeed been brought to trial in a major reconfiguration of the relationship between history and law.

Notes

1 Cf. Lynn Hunt, *Inventing Human Rights: A History* (New York: Norton 2007); Lyal S. Sunga, *Individual Responsibility in International Law* (Dordrecht: M. Nijhoff, 1992), 16–17.

2 Signed by a number of states, the treaty originally conceived by U.S. Secretary of State Frank Kellogg and French Prime Minister Aristide Briand intended to

exclude aggressive war from international relations. Cf. Gerry Simpson, *Law, War and Crime* (Cambridge: Polity Press, 2007), 144–145.

3 "Commission of Responsibilities, Majority Report, March 29, 1919," in Michael Marrus, *The Nuremberg War Crimes Trial 1945–6: A Documentary History* (Boston: Bedford Books, 1997), 6.

4 *Der Vertrag von Versailles: Amtlicher Text der Entante und amtliche deutsche Ubersetzung* (Berlin: Auftrage des Auswartigen Amtes, 1924), 206–221.

5 The assessment of the effects of the trials are in Jürgen Matthäus, "The Lessons of Leipzig," in *Atrocities on Trial: Historical Perspectives on the Politics of Prosecuting War Crimes*, eds. Heberer Patricia and Jürgen Matthäus (Lincoln: University of Nebraska Press, 2008), 3–24. Detailed studies of Leipzig and Istanbul trials: Gerd Hankel, *Die Leipziger Prozesse: Deutsche Kriegsverbrechen und ihre strafrechtliche Verfolgung nach dem Ersten Weltkrieg* (Hamburg: Hamburger Edition, 2003); Vahakn N. Dadrian and Taner Akçam, *Judgment at Istanbul: The Armenian Genocide Trials* (New York: Bergham Books, 2011).

6 Shoshana Felman and Dori Laub, *Testimony: Crises of Witnessing in Literature, Psychoanalysis, and History* (New York: Routledge, 1992), xiv.

7 A comparative scrutiny of this reckoning is in Istvan Deak, Jan T. Gross, and Tony Judt, *The Politics of Retribution in Europe: World War II and Its Aftermath* (Princeton: Princeton University Press, 2000).

8 A seminal study on the decision to organize a trial is F. Smith Bradley's *The Road to Nuremberg: How the Allies Finally Agreed to Try the Nazi Leaders—Rather Than Summarily Shoot Them Down* (New York: Basic Books, 1981).

9 See Patricia Heberer and Matthäus, *Atrocities on Trial*, 25–102, 159–186. See also Claudia Kurtsidis-Haider and Winfried R. Garscha, eds. *Keine "Abrechnung" NS-Verbrechen, Justiz und Gesellschaft in Europa nach 1945* (Leipzig/Wien: Akademische Verlangsanstalt, 1998), 122–150.

10 In different phases, the Soviets, Americans, and British even preferred summary executions to prolonged trials. Those dilemmas are analyzed in detail in Arieh Kohavi, *Prelude to Nuremberg: Allied War Crimes Policy and the Question of Punishment* (Chapel Hill, NC: University of North Carolina Press, 1998), 63–89. See also the correspondence in Michael Marrus, *The Nuremberg War Crimes Trial 1945–6: A Documentary History* (Boston: Bedford Books, 1997), 22–34.

11 With a majority of the Nazi elite in their custody, Americans had the strongest say, but the other Great Powers had their interests. For example, the British objected to putting the Navy commanders on the stand, having in mind that naval combat was traditionally not the area of warfare Great Britain wanted to see being criminalized. The Soviets however insisted on indicting both Admirals Karl Dönitz and Erich Roeder, as they had them in custody. Telford Taylor, *The Anatomy of the Nuremberg Trials* (New York: Alfred A. Knopf, 1992), 8.

12 *Letter from Robert Jackson to Harry S. Truman* (6 June, 1945): 11, War Crimes File (WCF), Rosenman Papers, Harry S. Truman Presidential Museum & Library (HTPML), http://www.trumanlibrary.org/whistlestop/study_collections/nuremberg/documents/index.php?pagenumber=2&documentid=14-7&documentdate=1945-06-06&studycollectionid=nuremberg&groupid=, accessed on 21.2.2016.

13 Paraphrase is usually taken from Robert E. Connot, *Justice at Nuremberg* (New York: Carroll & Graf 1988), xiii. The original is in Robert Kempner, "The Nuremberg Trials as Sources of Recent German Political and Historical Materials," *American Political Science Review* XLIV.2 (June 1950): 448.

14 Quoted in Donald Bloxham, *Genocide on Trial: War Crimes Trials and the Formation of Holocaust History and Memory* (Oxford: Oxford University Press, 2001), 17.

15 Taylor, *The Anatomy of the Nuremberg Trials*, 51.
16 *Letter from Robert Jackson to Harry S. Truman* (6 June, 1945): 10–11. WCF, HTPML.
17 Judith Shklar, *Legalism: Law, Morals, and Political Trials* (Cambridge: Harvard University Press, 1986), 200.
18 Quoted in Ann Tusa and John Tusa, *The Nuremberg Trial* (London: BBC Books, 1995), 205.
19 The bargaining over the list of defendants is described in Taylor, *The Anatomy of the Nuremberg Trials*, 79–82, 86–95. The indictment of organizations was only one of the legal innovations applied by the prosecution in order to encompass the criminal nature of Hitler's regime. Cf. Stanislaw Pomorski, "Conspiracy and Criminal Organisation," in *The Nuremberg Trial and International Law*, eds. George Ginsburgs and V.N. Kudriavtsev (Dordrecht: Kluwer Academic Publishers, 1990), 213–248.
20 *Letter from Robert Jackson to Harry S. Truman* (6 June, 1945): 12–13, WCF, HTSPM.
21 "Indictment" in *The Trial of the Major War Criminals Before the International Military Tribunal* (Nuremberg: International Military Tribunal, 1947), vol. II, 29–94. Electronic version at the Yale Law School Avalon Project, *Nuremberg Trials Collection*, vol. 1, Indictment, http://avalon.law.yale.edu/imt/count.asp, accessed on 21.2.2016.
22 "Robert Jackson's Address" in *The Trial of the Major War Criminals*, vol.II, 98–99, 117.
23 Robert Jackson, "Full Faith and Credit." *Columbia Law Review* 1 (1945): 6.
24 Peter Calvocoresi, *Nuremberg: The Facts, the Law and the Consequences* (London: Chatto & Windus, 1947), 125.
25 Ann Tusa and John Tusa, *The Nuremberg Trial*, 96.
26 *Correspondence between Harry S. Truman and Robert Jackson* (17 October, 1946): 3, WCF, HTPML, http://www.trumanlibrary.org/whistlestop/study_collections/nuremberg/documents/index.php?pagenumber=3&documentid=2–7&documentdate=1946–10–17&studycollectionid=nuremberg&groupid=, accessed on 22.3.2016.
27 Lord Justice Lawrence, "The Nuremberg Trial" in *Perspectives on the Nuremberg Trial*, ed. Guénaël Mettraux (Oxford: Oxford University Press, 2008), 291.
28 Rebecca West, *A Train of Powder* (London: Virago Press, 1955), 3.
29 Taylor, *The Anatomy of the Nuremberg Trials*, 52.
30 *Letter from William Donovan to Robert Jackson* (27 November, 1945): 2. WCF, HSTPM, http://www.trumanlibrary.org/whistlestop/study_collections/nuremberg/documents/index.php?pagenumber=2&documentid=7–5&documentdate=1945–11–27&studycollectionid=nuremberg&groupid=, accessed on 21.2.2016.
31 Extensive documentation over this cooperation is in the Truman Presidential Museum, *Meeting of the World Jewish Congress with Robert H. Jackson*. Records of the World Jewish Congress (12 June, 1945): 2, WCF, HSTPM, http://www.trumanlibrary.org/whistlestop/study_collections/nuremberg/index.php?action=docs#1945, accessed on 21.2.2016. Cf. Michael Marrus, "Jewish Lobby at Nuremberg: Jacob Robinson and the Institute of Jewish Affairs, 1945–1946," *Cardozo Law Review* 27.4 (2006) 1651–1665.
32 Michael R. Marrus, *The Holocaust at Nuremberg*, 9. http://www1.yadvashem.org/download/about_holocaust/studies/marrus_full.pdf, accessed on 21.2.2016. Cf. Cohen Boaz, "Dr. Jacob Robinson, the Institute of Jewish Affairs and the Elusive Jewish Voice in Nuremberg," in *Holocaust and Justice: Representation and Historiography of the Holocaust in Post-War Trials*, eds. David Bankier and Dan Michman (Jerusalem: Yad Vashem and Berghahn Books, 2010), 85.

33 Jacob Robinson, *Some Basic Ideas with Regard to the Appearance of a Jewish Witness at the International Military Tribunal* (5 September, 1945): 2, WCF, HSTPM, http://www.trumanlibrary.org/whistlestop/study_collections/nuremberg/documents/index.php?pagenumber=2&documentid=C107–8–1&documentdate=1945–09–05&studycollectionid=nuremberg&groupid=, accessed on 21.2.2016.

34 "Report from Jacob Robinson to the World Jewish Congress, Decision of the Board of Review on the Problem of Approval of Jewish Experts" (6 December, 1945): 7, WCF, HSTPM, http://www.trumanlibrary.org/whistlestop/study_collections/nuremberg/documents/index.php?pagenumber=7&documentid=C14–16–1&documentdate=1945–12–06&studycollectionid=nuremberg&groupid=, accessed on 21.2.2016.

35 Ibid., 9–10.

36 Ibid., 6.

37 G. M. Gilbert, *Nuremberg Diary* (New York: Da Capo Press, 1995), 296.

38 Ibid., 86.

39 Leon Goldensohn, *The Nuremberg Interviews* (New York: Vintage Books, 2005), 15.

40 Göring's testimony and cross-examination in *Trial of the Major War Criminals*, vol. IX, 235–672.

41 Gilbert, *Nuremberg Diary*, 35, 150, 323.

42 *Trial of the Major War Criminals*, vol. IX, 673.

43 Ibid., vol. XI, 451.

44 Gilbert, *Nuremberg Diary*, 267.

45 *Trial of the Major War Criminals*, vol. XIV, 432.

46 Gilbert, *Nuremberg Diary*, 397, 211. The Speer case was, and still is, a matter of a lively debate, fueled by his memoirs. Albert Speer, *Erinnerungen* (Frankfurt am Mein: Propyläen Verlag, 1969), and furthered by Gitta Sereny, *Albert Speer: His Battle with Truth* (London: Picador, 1996).

47 *Trial of the Major War Criminals*, vol. XXII, 373, 406, 375, 408, 402, 367.

48 Gilbert, *Nuremberg Diary*, 240.

49 *Trial of the Major War Criminals*, vol. XIX, 397–399.

50 Ibid., vol. XIX, 530.

51 Ibid., vol. III.

52 Quoted in Robert E. Connot, *Justice at Nuremberg* (New York: Carroll & Graf, 1988), xi.

53 Taylor, *The Anatomy of the Nuremberg Trial*, 554. Details on their deliberation are in Bradley Smith, *Reaching Judgment at Nuremberg* (New York: Meridian Book, 1979).

54 "Judgment" in *Trial of the Major War Criminals*, vol. XXII, 413.

55 "The Nazi Regime in Germany: The Origin and Aims of the Nazi party," in: Ibid., vol. XXII, 415–458.

56 *Trial of Major War Criminals*, vol. XXII, 467–468.

57 Ibid., 469–523.

58 These intersections were singled out in Gilbert, *Nuremberg Diary*, 437–448.

59 *Trial of Major War Criminals*, vol. XXII, 524–589.

60 Ann Tusa and John Tusa, *The Nuremberg Trial*, 14.

61 John Kenny, *Moral Aspects of Nuremberg* (Washington: Pontifical Faculty of Theology, 1949), 46.

62 The seminal introductory account given by Telford Taylor, and the study by Ann and John Tusa, were written quite some time ago. Telford Taylor, *The Anatomy of the Nuremberg Trials: A Personal Memoir* (New York: Alfred A. Knopf, 1992); Ann Tusa and John Tusa, *The Nuremberg Trial* (London: BBC Books,

1995). However, it is an open question whether these books were as influential as the more popular digested accounts of the trials that mushroomed in the post-war period. See Cf. Joe Heydecker and Johhanes Leeb, *The Nuremberg Trial: A History of Nazi Germany as Revealed Through the Testimony at Nuremberg* (Westprot: Greenwood Press, 1962). Many accounts of participants are collected in Guénaël Mettraux, *Perspectives on the Nuremberg Trial* (Oxford: Oxford University Press, 2008).

63 Telford Taylor, *Nuremberg and Vietnam: An American Tragedy* (Toronto: Bantam, 1971), 13–14.

64 *Correspondence between Harry S. Truman and Robert Jackson* (17 October, 1946): 5, 8, WCF, HSTPLM, http://www.trumanlibrary.org/whistlestop/study_collections/nuremberg/documents/index.php?pagenumber=6&documentid=2–7&documentdate=1946–10–17&studycollectionid=nuremberg&groupid=, accessed on 21.2.2016.

65 Karl Jaspers, *Die Schuldfrage. Ein Beitrag zur Deutschen Frage* (Zurich: Artemis Verlag, 1946), 29–35.

66 Hannah Arendt, *Essays in Understanding, 1930–1954* (New York: Shocken, 1994), 130, 150. About her correspondence with Jaspers on the topic see Robert Fine, "Crimes against Humanity: Hannah Arendt and the Nuremberg Debates," *European Journal of Social Theory* 3 (2000): 296.

67 Jaspers, *Die Schuldfrage*, 30–35.

68 West, *A Train of Powder*, 257.

69 Ibid., 260, 262.

70 Steffen Radlmaier, *Den Nüremberger Lernprozess: Von Kriegsverbrechern und Starreportern* (Frankfurt am Mein: Eichborn, 2001).

71 Norman Birkett, "International Legal Theories Evolved at Nuremberg," in *Perspectives on the Nuremberg Trial*, ed. Guénaël Mettraux, 307.

72 See United Nations General Assembly Resolutions 3, 19, 20, 21 (1946), and particularly resolution 95 from December 14 entitled Affirmation of the Principles of International Law Recognized by the Charter of the Nuremberg Tribunal. http://www.un.org/documents/resga.htm, accessed on 21.2.2016. See also the 1950 ILC Report: *Principles of International Law Recognized in the Charter of the Nürnberg Tribunal and in the Judgment of the Tribunal*, http://untreaty.un.org/ilc/texts/instruments/english/draft%20articles/7_1_1950.pdf.

73 Cf. Kim C. Primiel and Alexa Stiller, *Reassessing the Nuremberg Military Tribunals: Transitional Justice, Trial Narratives and Historiography* (New York: Berghahn Books, 2012). See also Jonathan Friedman, "Law and Politics in the Subsequent Nuremberg Trials," in Heberer, *Atrocities on Trial*, 88–89.

74 See for example a pamphlet of the right-wing extremist British People's Party: "It is not fitting that after a war in which a continent has been devastated and a world brought near to starvation, such a tragic farce should be played." *Failure at Nuremberg. An Analysis of Trial, Evidence and Verdict* (London: Research Department of the British People's Party, s.a.), 42.

75 The shifting importance of Nuremberg in a wider context is problematized in Donald Bloxham, "Milestones and Mythologies: The Impact of Nuremberg," in *Atrocities on Trial*, ed. Patricia Heberer, 263–282. For the United States, this impact was analyzed by William J. Bosch, *Judgment on Nuremberg, American Attitudes Towards the Major German War Crimes Trials* (Durham, NC: North Carolina University Press, 1970). On the IMT and German environment see Christopher Burchard, "The Nuremberg Trial and its Impact on Germany," *Journal of International Criminal Justice* 4 (2006): 800–829.

76 See Philip R. Piccigallo, *The Japanese on Trial: Allied War Crimes Operations in the East 1945–1951* (Austin: University of Texas Press, 1979), 7–10.

77 *The Tokyo War Crimes Trial* (New York: Garland Publishing Co., 1981), vol. I-XXII. A selected collection is accessible at a digital exhibition of the University of Virginia Law Library, *The Tokyo War Crimes Trial*, http://lib.law.virginia.edu/imtfe/. Key documents and a selection of transcripts were recently published by Neil Boister and Robert Cryer (eds.), *Documents on the Tokyo International Military Tribunal* (Oxford: Oxford University Press, 2008).
78 Ibid., 16.
79 Ibid., 274.
80 Ibid., 16.
81 B.V.A. Rölling, *The Tokyo Trial and Beyond: Reflections of a Peace-Monger* (London: Polity Press, 1993), 32–33.
82 Ibid., 38, 46–47.
83 The majority judgment is in Boister and Cryer, *Documents on the Tokyo International Military Tribunal*, 110. Also in an online version: http://werle.rewi.hu-berlin.de/tokio.pdf.
84 The historical part of the judgment is in Ibid., 110–594.
85 "Opinion of the Member for the Netherlands," in Ibid., 709.
86 "Dissenting Opinion of the Member from India" in Ibid., 1299. Cf. *Dissenting Opinion of Justice Pal* (Tokyo: Kokusho-Kanokai, 1999), http://www.sdh-fact.com/CL02_1/65_S4.pdf.
87 Quoted in Yuma Totani, *The Tokyo War Crimes Trial* (Cambridge, MA: Harvard East Asian Monographs, 2008), 226.
88 Richard Minear, *Victor's Justice, The Tokyo War Crimes Trial* (Princeton: Princeton University Press, 1971), 150, 177. For more than three decades this was a commonly accepted verdict on IMTFR, and only in the last couple of years have new publications of documents and studies appeared reexamining the neglected "twin" of Nuremberg. Cf. Yuma Totani, *The Tokyo War Crimes Trial* (Cambridge, MA: Harvard East Asian Monographs, 2008). Also Neil Boister and Robert Cryer, *The Tokyo International Military Tribunal: A Reappraisal* (Oxford: Oxford University Press, 2008); Madoka Futamura, *War Crimes Tribunals and Transitional Justice: The Tokyo Trial and the Nuremberg Legacy* (New York: Routledge, 2007); Yuki Tanaka, Tim McCormack and Gerry Simpson (eds.), *Beyond Victor's Justice: The Tokyo War Crimes Trials Revisited* (Leiden/Boston: Martinus Nijhoff Publishers, 2011).
89 Such a view on the trial is to be found in the work of one of the defendants in the subsequent trials, Graf Schwerin von Krosigk, *Die grossen Schauprozesse: Politische Justiz vonder Antike bis zur Gegenwart* (München: Bastei Lübbe, 1981), 356–397. Defense attorneys also attempted at revision. Cf. Rudolf Aschenauer, *Zur Frage einer Revision der Kriegsverbrecherprozesse* (Nurnberg: s.n., 1949). Otto Kranzbühler, *Rückblick auf Nuernberg*, Hamburg 1949. Revision was by no means limited to Germany. One of its early cornerstones was Maurice Bardéche's book *Nuremberg or the Promised Land* (1947).
90 He published his exposé in Lord Hankey, *Politics, Trials and Errors* (Oxford: Penn-in-hand, 1950), 56.
91 House of Lords Debate 05 May 1949, vol. 162, 402–405, http://hansard.millbank systems.com/lords/1949/may/05/german-war-crimes-trials, accessed on 21.2.2016.
92 House of Lords Debate 19 May 1949, vol. 162, 876–879, http://hansard.mill banksystems.com/lords/1949/may/19/japanese-war-crime-trials, accessed on 21.2.2016.
93 Hankey, *Politics, Trials and Errors*, 68.
94 Geoffrey Lawrence, "The Nuremberg Trial," in *Perspectives on the Nuremberg Trial*, ed. Guénaël Mettraux, 292–293.
95 Joseph Keenan and Brendan Brown, *Crimes Against International Law* (Washington: Public Affair Press, 1950), vi.

96 Benjamin Ferencz, "The Experience of Nuremberg," in *International Crimes, Peace, and Human Rights: The Role of the International Criminal Court*, ed. Dinah Shelton (New York: Transnational Publishers, 2000), 8–9.
97 Hans Kelsen, "Will the Judgment in the Nuremberg Trial Constitute a Precedent in International Law?" *The International Law Quarterly* 2 (Summer 1947): 165.
98 Norman Birkett, "International Legal Theories Evolved at Nuremberg," in *Perspectives on the Nuremberg Trial*, ed. Guénaël Mettraux, 299.
99 David Maxwell Fyfe (gen. ed.) *War Crimes Trials* (London: William Hodge, 1948–9), vols. I–VI, xiii.
100 Norman Birkett, "Foreword," in *Trial of Nikolaus von Falkenhorst*, ed. E.H. Stevens (London: William Hodge, 1948), xiii, xx.
101 Thomas J. Dodd, "The Nuremberg Trials," in *Perspectives on the Nuremberg Trial*, ed. Guénaël Mettraux, 190–191.
102 Herbert Wechsler, "The Issues of the Nuremberg Trial," in *Perspectives on the Nuremberg Trial*, ed. Guénaël Mettraux, 308.
103 Primiel and Stiller, *Reassessing the Nuremberg Military Tribunals*, 4.
104 Mark Osiel, *Mass Atrocity, Collective Memory and the Law* (Brunswick and London: Transaction Publishers, 2000), 6–9, 91, 97–100. Reargued in Mark Osiel, "In Defense of Liberal Show Trials—Nuremberg and Beyond," in *Perspectives on the Nuremberg Trial*, ed. Guénaël Mettraux, 704–728.
105 Michael Marrus, "The Holocaust at Nuremberg," *Yad Vashem Studies* 26 (1998): 6.
106 David Fraser, *Law after Auschwitz: Towards a Jurisprudence of the Holocaust* (Durham: Carolina Academic Press, 2005), 123.
107 David A. Blumenthal and Timothy L.H. McCormack (eds.), *The Legacy of Nuremberg: Civilizing Influence or Institutionalized Vengeance?* (The Hague: Martinus Nihjhof, 2007).
108 Shoshana Felman, *The Juridical Unconscious: Trials and Traumas in the Twentieth Century* (Cambridge: Harvard University Press, 2002), 11–12.
109 Erich Haberer, "History and Justice: Paradigms of the Prosecution of Nazi Crimes," *Journal for Holocaust and Genocide Studies* 19.3 (2005): 487.

Bibliography

Arendt, Hannah. *Essays in Understanding, 1930–1954*. New York: Shocken, 1994.

Aschenauer, Rudolf. *Zur Frage einer Revision der Kriegsverbrecherprozesse*. Nurnberg: s.n., 1949.

Bankier, David and Dan Michman, eds. *Holocaust and Justice: Representation and Historiography of the Holocaust in Post-War Trials*. Jerusalem: Yad Vashem and Berghahn Books, 2010.

Berkowitz, Roger. "History and the Noble Art of Lying." *Rechtsgeschichte* 4 (2004): 22–27.

Bloxham, Donald. *Genocide on Trial: War Crimes Trials and the Formation of Holocaust History and Memory*. Oxford: Oxford University Press, 2001.

Blumenthal, David A. and Timothy L.H. McCormack, eds. *The Legacy of Nuremberg: Civilizing Influence or Institutionalized Vengeance?* The Hague: Martinus Nihjhof, 2007.

Boister, Neil and Cryer Robert, eds. *Documents on the Tokyo International Military Tribunal*. Oxford: Oxford University Press, 2008.

Boister, Neil and Cryer Robert. *The Tokyo International Military Tribunal: A Reappraisal*. Oxford: Oxford University Press, 2008.

Bosch, William J. *Judgment on Nuremberg, American Attitudes Towards the Major German War Crimes Trials*. Durham, NC: North Carolina University Press, 1970.

Bradley, F. Smith. *The Road to Nuremberg: How the Allies Finally Agreed to Try the Nazi Leaders—Rather Than Summarily Shoot Them Down*. New York: Basic Books, 1981.

Burchard, Christopher. "The Nuremberg Trial and its Impact on Germany." *Journal of International Criminal Justice* 4 (2006): 800–829.

Calvocoresi, Peter. *Nuremberg. The Facts, the Law and the Consequences*. London: Chatto and Windus, 1947.

Connot, Robert E. *Justice at Nuremberg*. New York: Carroll & Graf, 1988.

Dadrian, Vahakn N. and Taner Akçam. *Judgment at Istanbul: The Armenian Genocide Trials*. New York: Bergham Books, 2011.

Deak, Istvan, Jan T. Gross and Tony Judt. *The Politics of Retribution in Europe: World War II and Its Aftermath*. Princeton: Princeton University Press, 2000.

Der Vertrag von Versailles: Amtlicher Text der Entante und amtliche deutsche Ubersetzung. Berlin: Auftrage des Auswartigen Amtes, 1924.

Dissenting Opinion of Justice Pal. Tokyo: Kokusho-Kanokai, 1999. http://www.sdh-fact.com/CL02_1/65_S4.pdf (accessed on 21.2.2016).

Douglas, Lawrence. *The Memory of Judgment: Making Law and History in the Trials of the Holocaust*. New Haven: Yale University Press, 2005.

Failure at Nuremberg: An Analysis of Trial, Evidence and Verdict. London: Research Department of the British People's Party, s.a.

Felman, Shoshana. *The Juridical Unconscious: Trials and Traumas in the Twentieth Century*. Cambridge: Harvard University Press, 2002.

Ferencz, Benjamin. "The Experience of Nuremberg," in *International Crimes, Peace, and Human Rights. The role of the International Criminal Court*, ed. Dinah Shelton. New York: Transnational Publishers, 2000, 8–20.

Fine, Robert. "Crimes against Humanity: Hannah Arendt and the Nuremberg Debates." *European Journal of Social Theory*, 3 (2000): 296.

Fraser, David. *Law after Auschwitz: Towards a Jurisprudence of the Holocaust*. Durham: Carolina Academic Press, 2005.

Futamura, Madoka. *War Crimes Tribunals and Transitional Justice: The Tokyo Trial and the Nuremberg Legacy*. New York: Routledge, 2007.

Fyfe, David Maxwell, gen. ed. *War Crimes Trials*. London: William Hodge, 1948–1949.

Gilbert, G. M. *Nuremberg Diary*. New York: Da Capo Press, 1995.

Goldensohn, Leon. *The Nuremberg Interviews*. New York: Vintage Books, 2005.

Haberer, Erich. "History and Justice: Paradigms of the Prosecution of Nazi Crimes." *Journal for Holocaust and Genocide Studies* 19.3 (2005): 487–519.

Hankel, Gerd. *Die Leipziger Prozesse: Deutsche Kriegsverbrechen und ihre strafrechtliche Verfolgung nach dem Ersten Weltkrieg*. Hamburg: Hamburger Edition, 2003.

Hankey, Lord. *Politics, Trials and Errors*. Oxford: Penn-in-hand, 1950.

Harry S. Truman Presidential Museum and Library. http://www.trumanlibrary.org/whistlestop/study_collections/nuremberg/documents/ (accessed on 21.2.2016).

Heberer, Patricia and Jürgen Matthäus, eds. *Atrocities on Trial: Historical Perspectives on the Politics of Prosecuting War Crimes*. Lincoln: University of Nebraska Press, 2008.

Heydecker, Joe and Leeb, Johhanes. *The Nuremberg Trial: A History of Nazi Germany as Revealed through the Testimony at Nuremberg*. Westprot: Greenwood Press, 1962.

House of Lords Debate, 05 May 1949, vol. 162, 402–405, 876–879, accessed on 21.2.2016.

Hunt, Lynn. *Inventing Human Rights: A History*. New York: Norton 2007.

Jackson, Robert. "Full Faith and Credit: The Lawyer's Clause of the Constitution." *Columbia Law Review* 1 (1945): 1–34.

Jaspers, Karl. *Die Schuldfrage: Ein Beitrag zur Deutschen Frage*. Zurich: Artemis Verlag, 1946.

Keenan, Joseph and Brendan Brown. *Crimes Against International Law*. Washington: Public Affair Press, 1950.

Kelsen, Hans. "Will the Judgment in the Nuremberg Trial Constitute a Precedent in International Law?" *The International Law Quarterly* 2 (Summer 1947): 153–171.

Kempner, Robert. "The Nuremberg Trials as Sources of Recent German Political and Historical Materials." *American Political Science Review* XLIV.2 (June, 1950): 447–459.

Kenny, John. *Moral Aspects of Nuremberg*. Washington: Pontifical Faculty of Theology, 1949.

Kohavi, Arieh. *Prelude to Nuremberg: Allied War Crimes Policy and the Question of Punishment*. Chapel Hill, NC: University of North Carolina Press, 1998.

von Krosigk, Graf Schwerin. *Die grossen Schauprozesse: Politische Justiz vonder Antike bis zur Gegenwart*. München: Bastei Lübbe, 1981.

Kurtsidis-Haider, Claudia Winfried and R. Garscha, eds. *Keine "Abrechnung" NS-Verbrechen, Justiz und Gesellschaft in Europa nach 1945*. Leipzig/Wien: Akademische Verlangsanstalt, 1998.

Marrus, Michael. *The Nuremberg War Crimes Trial 1945–6: A Documentary History*. Boston: Bedford Books, 1997.

Marrus, Michael. "Jewish Lobby at Nuremberg: Jacob Robinson and the Institute of Jewish Affairs, 1945–1946." *Cardozo Law Review* 27.4 (2006): 1651–1665.

Marrus, Michael R. "The Holocaust at Nuremberg." *Yad Vashem Studies* 26 (1998). http://www1.yadvashem.org/download/about_holocaust/studies/marrus_full.pdf (accessed on 21.2.2016).

Mettraux, Guénaël. *Perspectives on the Nuremberg Trial*. Oxford: Oxford University Press, 2008.

Minear, Richard. *Victor's Justice, The Tokyo War Crimes Trial*. Princeton: Princeton University Press, 1971.

Osiel, Mark. *Mass Atrocity, Collective Memory and the Law*. Brunswick and London: Transaction Publishers, 2000.

Piccigallo, Philip R. *The Japanese on Trial: Allied War Crimes Operations in the East 1945–1951*. Austin: University of Texas Press, 1979.

Pomorski, Stanislaw. "Conspiracy and Criminal Organisation," in *The Nuremberg Trial and International Law*, eds. George Ginsburgs and V. N. Kudriavtsev. Dordrecht: Kluwer Academic Publishers, 1990, 213–248.

Posner, Richard A. "Past-Dependency, Pragmatism, and Critique of History in Adjudication and Legal Scholarship." *The University of Chicago Law Review*, 67 (2000): 573–605.

Primiel, Kim C. and Alexa Stiller. *Reassessing the Nuremberg Military Tribunals: Transitional Justice, Trial Narratives and Historiography*. New York: Berghahn Books, 2012.

Radlmaier, Steffen. *Den Nüremberger Lernprozess: Von Kriegsverbrechern und Starreportern*. Frankfurt am Mein: Eichborn, 2001.

Rölling, B.V.A. *The Tokyo Trial and Beyond: Reflections of a Peace-Monger*. London: Polity Press 1993.

Sereny, Gitta. *Albert Speer: His Battle with Truth*. London: Picador, 1996.

Shklar, Judith. *Legalism: Law, Morals, and Political Trials*. Cambridge: Harvard University Press, 1986.

Shoshana Felman and Dori Laub. *Testimony: Crises of Witnessing in Literature, Psychoanalysis, and History*. New York: Routledge, 1992.

Simpson, Gerry. *Law, War and Crime*. Cambridge: Polity Press, 2007.

Speer, Albert. *Erinnerungen*. Frankfurt am Mein: Propyläen Verlag, 1969.

Stevens, E.H., ed. *Trial of Nikolaus von Falkenhorst*. London: William Hodge, 1948.

Sunga, Lyal S. *Individual Responsibility in International Law*. Dordrecht: M. Nijhoff, 1992.

Tanaka Yuki, Tim McCormack and Gerry Simpson, eds. *Beyond Victor's Justice: The Tokyo War Crimes Trials Revisited*. Leiden: Martinus Nijhoff Publishers, 2011.

Taylor, Telford. *Nuremberg and Vietnam: An American Tragedy*. Toronto: Bantam, 1971.

Taylor, Telford. *The Anatomy of the Nuremberg Trials a Personal Memoir*. New York: Alfred A. Knopf, 1992.

The Tokyo War Crimes Trial. vol. I–XXII. New York: Garland Publishing Co., 1981.

Totani, Yuma. *The Tokyo War Crimes Trial*. Cambridge, MA: Harvard East Asian Monographs, 2008.

Trial of the Major War Criminals Before the International Military Tribunal. vol. I–XLII. Nuremberg: International Military Tribunal, 1947. Electronic version at The Yale Law School Avalon Project, *Nuremberg Trials Collection*. http://avalon.law.yale.edu/subject_menus/imt.asp (accessed on 21.2.2016).

Tusa, Ann and John Tusa. *The Nuremberg Trial*. London: BBC Books, 1995.

United Nations General Assembly Resolutions. http://www.un.org/documents/resga.htm (accessed on 21.2.2016).

West, Rebecca. *A Train of Powder*. London: Virago Press, 1955.

Part II

Improvisations

Experimenting with Historical Forensic Contribution

3 An Inquisitorial Paradigm Emerges

Historical Forensics and Nazi Crimes

But what of historians? How did they fit into the postwar landscape of the shifting relations between history and law? The Nuremberg trial, the greatest history lesson ever conveyed by a trial, was held in the absence of historians, except in an auxiliary role. They were partaking indirectly. Jakob Robinson was assisting occasionally in the preparation of the cases due to his language skills and familiarity with the archival material, whereas Peter Calvocoressi was rushing through the abundance of captured German papers, checking their authenticity and sorting the documents of evidentiary value for the trial. Only on extraordinary occasions were historians part of the larger forensic undertakings, such as the pursuit of Hitler's corps, conducted by British historian Hugh Trevor-Roper, who subsequently published an important book about the last days of Adolf Hitler, literally digging under the rubble of his regime.[1]

Under the Rubble: European Historiography After Nuremberg

Could historians have contributed more? The conventional answer would be no, given the lack of distance, the inaccessibility of the archives, and the quintessentially politicized topic. However, in light of the unprecedented horror of the Second World War, the responsibility of the historian was speedily redefined. The great collapse compelled prominent historians to write about the drama of their own times, such as Marc Bloch's *Strange Defeat* (1940). The tone of these writings was alarming, and the wording occasionally judgmental. Even Friedrich Meinecke, the pope of historicism, expressed the need to come to terms with the horrendous events of the most recent past in a book of a telling title—*German Catastrophe* (1946): "Many a German reader who agreed with me in condemning Hitlerism will (. . .) want to plead 'extenuating circumstances.' As if I had not always weighed such considerations in my mind!"[2] More importantly, the atrocities of the Second World War prompted a certain remoralization of historiography, particularly in the disputed area of contemporary history.[3] Historical distance was simply not what it used to be, as "under the intellectual shock induced by the events of the twentieth century, historians have rushed into paths along which their pre-1914 predecessors ventured only with caution."[4]

There were strong heuristic facilitators of this interest. The governmental practice of publishing selected sources, established during the course of the First World War and in its immediate aftermath, was continued with greater zeal, leading to large collections such as *Foreign Relations of the United States, Documents diplomatiques français*, and *Documents on British Foreign Policy*.[5] Additionally, substantial parts of the captured German archives soon became available in the holdings of the Public Record Office of Great Britain and in the U.S. National Archives. Last but not least, the documentation from the trials started pouring in. Hence "historians were provided an essentially unprecedented look at materials of the most recent past and were thereby enabled to take a new look at the 1930s and the war years much sooner than would otherwise have been the case."[6]

There was no shortage of such trials in the immediate postwar period. In addition to the Nuremberg trial of major war criminals, military tribunals were activated in all four occupying zones under the Control Council Law no. 10, and domestic courts started working as well.[7] Through a complementary process of denazification, the American zone alone combed through thirteen million people with questionnaires.[8] Additionally, the German courts started working in 1946, convicting 5,228 persons in the Western zones by 1950; however, only 228 were convicted for capital offenses, typically wartime crimes committed by Germans against Germans.[9] But trial records were not easily accessible. This was the case even with the highly publicized twelve trials of high-ranking Nazi perpetrators of the Military Tribunal in Nuremberg (NMT).[10] These trials were considered a necessary sequel to Nuremberg, of utmost importance for the reeducation of Germany. Some of this pedagogical zeal can be read in the judgment in the case against Fieldmarschal Erich Milch, written by Judge Michael Musmanno: "The present trial is one chapter in the book which will forever condemn *Mein Kampf* and offer to the new German nation a volume of proved fact, whose every page will tell of the sorrow awaiting any people which permit any man or men to hoist deceit above truth, power above justice, oppression above tolerance, war above peace and man above God."[11] Less bombastic, but certainly not less zealous, was NMT's Chief Prosecutor, Brigadier General Telford Taylor, for whom the trials were an opportunity "to promote the interest of historical truth and to aid in the reestablishment of democracy in Germany."[12]

As these trials were coming to an end, General Telford Taylor reasoned in his final report: "One thing we can do is to make the facts available to German historians, so that future generations of Germans will be able to grasp the full and malignant import of the Third Reich, and understand why it proved such a terrible engine of destruction for the world and for Germany herself."[13] He knew that the trials would have only limited impact on a definitive historical account: "As the years pass, the Nuremberg documentation

Figure 3.1 General Telford Taylor at the stand of the Nuremberg Military Tribunal

will be merged with other sources and will lose its unique historical value."[14] Therefore he acted with urgency. However, Taylor failed to secure funding for publishing of the complete trial transcripts and their translation to German. Only the abridged transcripts of these trials were published due to funding problems, a decision that Taylor considered "a failure to put the necessary 'ammunition' into the hands of those Germans who can make use of the documents presented and testimony given during the trials in reconstituting a democratic German society."[15] Coming to terms with the decision to print the abridged transcripts from the subsequent Nuremberg trials alongside the collection of exhibited documents, he made sure to circulate as much of that material as possible to universities and libraries around the world. "It is true, to be sure, that the reorientation of German thought along democratic lines must ultimately be accomplished by the Germans themselves. But the least we can do is to insure that the documents which expose the true nature of the Third Reich are circulated throughout Germany. The Nuremberg documents must be utilized to the full in writing German history, if the Germans of today are to grasp the truth about the past."[16] Such hopes would have probably proven unfounded, if the documents did not fall on already fertile ground. The idea that historians could legitimately explore their own epoch was preconditioned by the unprecedented availability of historical sources, disclosed by the Nuremberg trial, published in various government-sponsored editions, printed in memoirs of the protagonists, or seized and made available by the victorious Allied forces. There was much enthusiasm to use this situation: "To the cry 'we appeal to the verdict of history', the answer should and could be: Here is the verdict of history.", addressed Gavin Henderson Scotland Branch of the Historical Association in 1941: "Too long has the study of history condemned itself to sterility; and it is so to be hoped that more and more historians will follow the example of their founder Thucydides and labor in the difficult but fruitful field of contemporary history." Many, like Max Beloff, appreciated the risks of this leap: "Thus the historian must not enter lightly into the contemporary field, nor imagine that it is one wherein he will be recognized as possessing special authority. (. . .) The chief object of the historian in this field should be to make it plain that in history, at any rate, there can be a verdict without a trial."[17] Yet the temptation was irresistible.

One of the rising practitioners of contemporary history, Alan Bullock, founder of the Recent History Group at Oxford University, systematized this "combination of circumstances powerful enough to overcome these drawbacks and the doubts and inhibitions they create and to attract men and women, who could perfectly well have made a reputation in the study of other periods of history, to work in a field so full of pitfalls." All of those circumstances were related to the Second World War: "First, interest. The events through which we have lived since 1914 seem to me to exceed in sheer magnitude, pace and intensity those of all but a few periods of history (. . .). Second, a sense of urgency—a conviction that there were facts to be revealed (the facts about the concentration camps, for instance) and lessons to be drawn (such as the price of appeasing the Nazis) (. . .). Third, luck. The capture of the archives of the German Government and the evidence brought to light in the war crimes trials opened up, as never before so soon after the event, the secret history of twelve of the most dramatic years of European history (. . .). Fourth, experience. The war brought many academics out of their university environment and involved them, whether in the forces, in intelligence or propaganda work, government departments, or in the Resistance, in events which they have later gone back to study and write about (. . .). Fifth, demand (. . .) for accounts of the history of our own time and the events of which have powerfully influenced the lives of all of us."[18]

Hence, the immediate postwar years brought about an unprecedented change in the institutional setting, the methodology, the heuristics, and the basic sensibility on which historical studies were based. The creation of new historical institutions to support this interest provided the necessary infrastructure for the new role of historians. In France, this was the Committee for the History of the Second World War, with its *Revue d'histoire de la deuxieme guerre mondiale*.[19] In Italy, there was the Instituto italiano per gli studi storici "Benedetto Croce" (1947); in the Netherlands it was the State Institute for War Documentation (1945), currently the NIOD Institute for War, Holocaust and Genocide Studies. Cultural institutions also served such purposes, be they the Wiener Library in London (1933) or Yad Vashem in Jerusalem (1953). However, the most robust institutional development happened in Germany, where the Franco-German Agreement on Controversial Issues in European History from 1951 led to the creation of Georg Eckert Institut in Braunschweig. Similar motivations led to the creation of the Institut für Europäische Geschichte in Mainz (1950) and the Institut für Zeitgeschichte in Munich. The latter was founded in 1947, and its first name, Institut zur Erforschung der nationalsozialitischen Politik, addressed its purpose in researching the totalitarian experience of recent German history. The Institute was the most active among new institutions such as the Research Institute for the History of National Socialism at Hamburg, the Department for Recent History at Friedrich Meinecke Institute in Berlin, the Commission for the History of Parliamentary and Political Parties in Bonn, the Office for Research into Contemporary Military History in Freiburg, and others. The Institute's central publication, *Vierteljahrshefte für Zeitgeschichte* (1953), not only spearheaded research of the recent past, but also fostered methodological insights in this domain and hosted the first international conference on contemporary history in 1955, assembling sixty scholars from the entire Western hemisphere and dealing with topics such as the military in a totalitarian state, European states and the rise of the Third Reich, the theory and practice of the expansion of national-socialism, resistance, and collaboration.[20] Important steps were also taken to break free from the constraints of the framework of national historiographies, which were increasingly seen as straitjackets that prompt xenophobia and chauvinism. The International Committee of Historical Sciences quickly resumed its activity with the help of UNESCO, vested to integrate members from defeated nations as soon as their professional organizations reconstituted; its first postwar Congress was held in Paris in 1950, and the second one in Rome in 1955 included German historians as well.[21] "The years following the Second World War saw a return to forms of cooperation and communication between historians from countries previously at war with each other."[22] However, cooperation was not to be confused with forgetting. One might agree with Olivier Dumoulin that Europe was experiencing nothing less than the emergence of "a combatant historiography after 1945."[23]

Vergangenheitsbewältingung between Law and History

But was there any impact of this change for legal reckoning with the Nazi past? Occupied Germany, which was in the center of this effort, remained conspicuously silent during the first postwar years. In the words of *Newsweek*'s correspondent, "Probably there is no city in the world in which people on the street talk less about the trials than Nuremberg, and no country in the world in which less is known about the trials as Germany."[24] The hope that the mere appearance of Nazi leadership in the Nuremberg docks would trigger an immediate transformative process in German society proved too optimistic. "There in Nuremberg," wrote Rebecca West, "the Germans, pale among the rubble, were waiting for the punishment as a purification, after which they might regain their strength and rebuild their world." However, no sooner had the judgment been announced did dissent appear. "Of course," people said and still say, "it was right that the Nazis should have been punished for what they did to the Jews. To the Left Wing. To the religious dissidents. To the Poles. To the Czechs. To the French deportees.

To half Europe. But aggressive war, that was a new crime, invented for the occasion, which had never been written on the statute book."[25] In the face of such reactions, the occupiers were deeply engaged in the fortification of the truth, as British prosecutor in Nuremberg David Maxwell-Fyfe wrote:

> After exhausting wars men tend to suffer from certain weariness of mind. Thus lassitude can make men shrink from facing unpleasant facts. It exhibits itself in an easy-going skepticism as to how much was the truth, and how much propaganda. Escapism as to gas chambers to-day might let the gas chambers escape from history to-morrow. For it is more likely that in the future, defenders of Nazis and Japanese methods will arise. There have been no more skilled apologists in the past than German professors and historians. Such apologists may well return, but they will be confronted by the admissions of the many accused found guilty and by the mass of incriminating documents produced at the trials whose authenticity has been established by the very man who wrote them. I believe that the would-be apologist will be faced by an impregnable fortification of truth.[26]

The Allied strategy was vested in the hope that the documentary value of exhibited evidence would have a long-term effect. Robert Kempner was confident that "no scholars and student can analyze the recent past and the contemporary scene without looking into the Nuremberg records and document collections."[27] To that end, he convincingly summarized the historical importance of the IMT and NMT documenting effort:

> From July 1945 until July 1949, the Palace of Justice in Nuremberg housed the world's greatest research institute of European foreign relations and history, and of German government, military and business administration. (. . .) Expressed in figures, the Nuremberg material amounts to about 2,500 pages of judgments running to one million words. The Court transcripts total 134,765 mimeographed pages averaging 250 words in addition to 10,000 printed pages of the record of the International Military Tribunal. A very important part of the Nuremberg research material consists of 42,000 court exhibits of various sizes, mainly of German origin (. . .) the total of documents reproduced for the trials amounts to more than 750,000 mimeographed pages.[28]

Actually, it was precisely the size of this venture that was its curse. At the beginning of this process, the Allied enjoyed a clear advantage, their upper hand clearly visible through a photographic glimpse into documentation rooms of prosecution and defense in Nuremberg. However, as the trials subsided, the advantage was fading: "Anybody who now wants to learn the facts can, of course, obtain the transcript of the trial published by the Allied Governments," remarked Rebecca West. "This, as issued by Her Majesty's Stationery Office, is in twenty-two parts and costs just under

Figure 3.2 Document rooms of prosecution and defense at the Nuremberg War Crimes Trials

seven pounds. (. . .) The documents, which are about as bulky and costly, have been published in an incomplete and unsatisfactory form. Those who can afford to buy these publications will have to find eight feet of bookshelf for them. It is indeed a pity that this material is not accessible to the general reader." She shared Kempner's enthusiasm, but was still happy that the documents underwent legal scrutiny before becoming plain historical sources: “Though they are not now easily accessible to the general reader, they are there for the student; and the lawyers had to act with a haste that was all to the good. The historians would have taken them to their studies, shut the doors, and dealt with them at the slow pace of scholarship.”[29]

The architects of the Nuremberg trials were sharing hopes that increased availability of transcripts and evidence would confront the postwar German legal system and historians alike with the criminal legacy of its recent past. To that end, prosecutor Jackson optimistically prefaced one of the first studies of Nuremberg documentation:

> Never have the archives of a belligerent nation been so completely exposed as were those of Nazi Germany at the Nuremberg trial. (. . .) The result is a documentation unprecedented in history as to any major war. Lord Acton, in his inaugural lecture as a professor of history in Cambridge, said: ‘We are still at the beginning of the documentary age, which will tend to make history independent of historians . . .’ It may be doubted whether we are more independent of historians, however, when such an avalanche of documents descends upon the world that their meaning and import can be learned only from fair and intelligent arrangement, condensation, and interpretation. This, in a hurried and partisan way, both the prosecution and the defense attempted to do as part of the trial. But its record of forty two volumes is too vast, detailed, and disjointed for general study. Now, Professor Harris—by scholarship and experience admirably qualified—in the calm of intervening years has prepared a factual summary of the evidence that is objective, accurate, and comprehensive.[30]

Tellingly, this study was not written by a German. “The intellectual descendants of Ranke and Treitschke carefully concealed their thoughts regarding the most horrifying organization ever invented by Germans—they wrote no book on SS, no major work on Himmler’s Eastern policy, no study of National-Socialist police machine. The German historians left the field wide open to their foreign colleagues.”[31] Restructuring the academic life in a devastated country was a complex task. Beneath the declarative commitment to intellectually reorientate Germany and relink it with the West, continuities were looming, making this break seem less than clear.[32] No sooner was the Association of German Historians reestablished in September 1949 than its first chairman Gerhard Ritter defined the tasks of contemporary historiography as immense and comparable to “the battle over so-called Kriegsschuldfrage which eventually led to the worldwide success of the German basic positions.” He concluded that in light of the national catastrophe, “Today we need to deal with much more rubble”; thus he advocated the creation of specialized research institutions led by experienced experts, with the goal of saving whatever could be saved from the national heritage, tainted with the Nazi legacy.[33]

Such reasoning was echoing the restoring of German statehood in May 1949, spearheaded by the conservative elite personified by the Chancellor Konrad Adenauer, tasked with transforming the county from occupied enemy into military ally of the West. In the field of *Vergangenheitspolitik*, this change was expressed in the policies of clemency, which amounted to forgetting and moving on. Under the amnesty law for persons convicted on short sentences, from December 1949 until January 1951 an entire army of eight hundred thousand people benefited. Many of those, as well as many who lost their positions in the denazification process, could hope to re-enter public service or collect their pensions, in according to the law promulgated in May 1951.[34] Along these lines, the Institute for Contemporary History started acquiring small contributions on the basis of archival records of the Nazi period and collecting *Aussagen* (over twelve thousand depositions and affidavits from three thousand persons in the first two years) and combining them with documents to create short and dense, comprehensively footnoted reports *(Gutachten)*, mostly for the purposes of reparations or for reinstating previously lustrated persons in public service.[35] Prefacing the edition of selected contributions, the director Paul Kluke wrote about the "special task of the Institute, directed toward the immediate application of historical findings for decision-making in practical life. Government authorities and courts saw the need (. . .) to demand help from historians in clarifying difficult factual questions. So they turned (. . .) with requests for information on historical facts to the Institute for Contemporary History, which took on this new, originally unforeseen task. In the last years it issued approximately 150 reports." He was quick to express reservations: "The competence of the Institute entails neither making assessments of a juridical nature, nor in the same way anticipating such judgments, but only in finding the facts and presenting historical assessments, which are supposed to help create the preconditions for making legal judgments."[36] Still, the modesty of these statements was indicative—1949 is not a repetition of 1919; German contemporary historiography was to be rebuilt in a transnational intellectual environment and highly unlikely to embark on huge apologetic endeavors resembling the *Kriegsschuldfrage*.[37]

However, the readiness to process war crimes before German courts was dwindling, as the new tendencies were particularly quickly understood within the judiciary, which by and large belonged to the more conservative part of German society, burdened with a number of troubling personal continuities with the Nazi era and coupled with inertia, which hindered the investigation of wartime criminality.[38] The statistics of war crimes–related judgments in postwar Germany were telling: between 1945 and 1950, 5,228 persons were sentenced; this trend quickly spiraled downwards after the establishment of the Federal Republic of Germany (1949), whose courts convicted 259 persons in 1951, and 123 in 1952.[39] The number of investigations was dropping as well. Increasingly, trials held by the occupying powers were perceived as an exercise in "victor's justice."[40] A public opinion survey conducted in 1950 by the U.S. High Commission revealed that 38% of the population in Germany considered the IMT proceedings as fair, compared to 78% four years earlier.[41]

Nuremberg judgments were increasingly falling into oblivion or being evoked selectively. The expectation that the mere quantity and availability of sources would secure the historical narrative framed by the trial proved unfounded. It seems that the mere proliferation of piles of material acted as a discouraging factor. Even when engaging with such documents, German scholars had an agenda of their own. The documentation deriving from the postwar trials attracted attention in Göttingen, where Professor of International Law Herbert Kraus, who defended Hjalmar Schacht in Nuremberg, reestablished an Institute for International Law (Institut für Volkerrecht) as early as 1945.[42] The documentation from the Nuremberg trials therefore held an important place in the activity of this institution, and was partially published from 1949 in its series *Göttinger Beiträge für Gegenwartsfragen*. Kraus expressed the hope that the Institute would succeed in publishing all of the judgments of the Nuremberg Military Tribunal in German and English, with full annotations.[43] To that end he hired Hans-Günther Seraphim (1903–1992), twice-wounded former officer on the Eastern front, previous Ostforscher and relative of Nazi-affiliated scholar Peter Heinz Seraphim. After the war, he became a member of a commission assembled in 1946 to publish documents of the IMT. He also served as an advisor to the defense in the Nuremberg Medical Case Trial (U.S. v. Karl Brandt and others, 1946–7) and in the Einsatzgruppen case (U.S. v. Otto Ohlendorf and others, 1947–8).[44] Kraus brought him to Göttingen to oversee the indexation of the subsequent Nuremberg trials and to hold a seminar on the newest history and its methodology.[45] Eventually, in 1951 he entrusted him with the creation of the Department for Contemporary History of the Institute for International Law in Göttingen.

With such a strengthened voice, Seraphim could develop his conceptual ideas on the relationship between history and law. "What is history, and its youngest branch, contemporary history, doing in one such institute?" mused Seraphim in one of the first postwar reflections on the trials and history written in Germany, published in a *Festschrift* to his mentor Kraus: "This connection between legal and historical research which at first appears surprising, becomes understandable when we return to its starting point—the post-war trials." In his opinion, "these processes went beyond the usual goals of judicial proceedings (. . .). They were supposed to uphold the mirror toward the defeated population, in which their historical guilt, and the path they have taken, should be recognized. In this respect, it was part of the goal of the Nuremberg proceedings to paint a picture of German history beginning with the Nazis' seizure of power, and to keep it in a binding form." Seraphim disagreed with what he perceived as the extralegal purposes of these trials "as long as they serve or served the exploration of recent past, which belongs to the area of historical science."[46] He gave numerous examples of the use of documentation in the courtroom, with which interpretation he disagreed and which led him to the conclusion that "from the point of view of historical science, the question of whether we are to affirm or deny the historical picture created by Nuremberg, at this point the investigations are answering negatively." As a conservative member of the intellectual elite typical of his time, he dreaded the idea of German history being established in a courtroom and saw the identification of the entire German people with Nazism as unjust. Seraphim stepped forward not only as a strong critic of the Nuremberg proceedings, but also as a firm supporter of the theory of incompatibility between history and law, concluding that "legal method and historical method fundamentally differ, and therefore history cannot and must not be written by the juridical method."[47] Seraphim did not just theorize the relation between these methods, but did his best to rectify it. Diether Pohl rightfully noted that "it is difficult to establish the first *criminal* court case on Nazi crimes, in which a historian was asked to testify," yet in all probability he was the first postwar historian to take part in the criminal proceedings as an expert.[48]

The trial in question was held in Düsseldorf in March 1949. The town's former Gauleiter (Nazi party chief) and police leadership were charged with shooting German citizens who planned to surrender the city without a fight in April 1945 in the so-called Aktion Rheinland. The court acquitted the accused, reasoning inter alia that the defense of Düsseldorf was crucial for maintaining the evacuation lines for refugees from the East. The importance of these evacuation lines was confirmed by "Dr.S, research fellow of one of the recreated Institutes of the University of Göttingen, devoted to an analysis of Nuremberg documentary material, previously a historian in the Index section of the Nuremberg prosecution [sic]"[49] Actually, in Nuremberg Military Trials he was working for the defense. Although Seraphim's contribution was to forward the cause of the defendants, it would be an oversimplification to perceive him as an ordinary Nazi sympathizer. In a fair assessment, he is described as "belonging to those (. . .) who opposed the 'Nuremberg view of history,' which he wanted to overturn through scholarship."[50] He was in favor of domestically prosecuting the worst transgressions of the Nazi regime, as he perceived the individuation of their criminal liability as the only way of unburdening the German people of the stigma of collective responsibility. Such was the motivation which prompted him to lend his forensic contribution to the court. To that same end, he took part in the 1952 Remer trial as an expert.

The Remer trial was one of the first opportunities for wide reckoning with Nazism in German courtrooms. The *spiritus movens* behind it was Fritz Bauer (1903–1968), Jewish lawyer and prewar Social Democrat, who was disbarred in 1933 and who immigrated to Denmark after spending time in a concentration camp. Bauer was one of the early partisans of bringing war criminals on trial, authoring a book of the same title as early as 1944. In the book he bluntly stated that "the German people need a lesson in applicable international law."[51] He returned to Germany in 1949 to assume the role of public prosecutor in Braunschweig: "I came back, because I believed

I could bring (. . .) some of the spirit and determination of resistance in the emigration in their fight against governmental injustice with me. German democracy had already failed once because it had no democrats. I wanted to be one of them. The German judiciary had already failed once when it ought to have defended the democracy but had misused its power—and the crimes of the government had been endless between 1933 and 1945 (. . .) I wanted to be a lawyer who would not just pay lip service to the law and

Figure 3.3 Prosecutor Fritz Bauer

to justice, to humanity and peace."[52] However, soon upon his return he discovered that his views were quite atypical for his surroundings. "In the judiciary, I feel like I am living in exile."[53] Dissatisfied with a stalemate in legal reactions to the crimes against humanity committed in Nazi Germany, he singlehandedly launched a set of initiatives toward the prosecution of Nazi war criminals.

For a determined and imaginative prosecutor, such opportunities were many, as the postwar political scene of the young Federal Republic was filled with remnants of the ominous past. One such notorious comeback was certainly that of Major General Otto Ernst Remer (1912–1997), who infamously contributed to the crushing of the rebellion of July 20, 1944.[54] After the war, he continued to partake in political life, leading a Socialist Reich Party that seemed to do well in the early 1950s—in regional elections his party won 11% in Lower Saxony. He created an outrage at one of his party meetings in May 1951 in Braunschweig, publicly labeling leaders of the resistance he crushed as traitors on the foreign payroll: "These conspirators were in great part traitors of the country, paid from abroad. (. . .) The time will come when they will be shamefully silent about belonging to 20.July 1944."[55] Families and friends of executed resistance found such utterances both hurtful and threatening. Coming from the opposition circles himself, Federal Minister of Interior Robert Lehr filed a criminal complaint against Remer for slandering, which Fritz Bauer's office was quick to pursue under the article 186 of German Criminal Code (*übler Nachrede* – defamation).

Bauer's understanding of the case and its implications was clear—it was to be "a rehabilitation of the Resistance, and nothing else."[56] The motivation was even clearer—it was "an occasion to clarify the history and problematic of 20 July 1944."[57] Bauer understood that this was a topic on which it was possible to forge a unique consensus between large segments of German postwar society, from the left to the right of the political spectrum. He intended to use this case to draw public attention to the topic and to once and for all legally exonerate the German resistance. His choice of witnesses for the prosecution, resistance members and the relatives of the most prominent conspirators, reflected this intent. Furthermore, in his desire to both legitimize and contextualize the resistance, Bauer resorted to a rather unorthodox method. He planned on introducing the experts from the field of humanities to write reports *(Gutachten)* and to appear as experts *(Sachsverständige)*, along with eyewitnesses of the events. This was an unconventional choice, as until then the German judiciary had rather limited experience with experts coming from the humanities and social sciences. This was the realm of technical and medical experts, rarely with anything more exotic than psychiatry. Consciously striving to broaden that horizon, Bauer used legal options that allowed for the prosecutor to suggest experts to the court; he hoped the chamber would accept his unconventional choice of forensic disciplines, as well as his choice of experts who would not only provide forensic contributions, but also reflect a wide coalition on the issue of the rehabilitation of the July plotters.[58]

Therefore on March 7, 1952, the rather unusual proceedings started at the criminal court in Braunschweig. The first witnesses were expert theologians, Professors Rupert Angermair and Professor Hans Joachim Iwand, followed by a historian of the church, Professor Ernst Wolf. They testified about the moral and theological implications of the resistance according to Catholic and Lutheran creed.[59] On the next day retired Major General Helmut Friebe, one of the leaders of the Alliance of German Soldiers, firmly concluded that during the seven postwar years former soldiers had had their eyes opened by revelations that put resistance leaders in a favorable light. He ended his account depriving Remer of the support he might have expected from veterans:

> We, his former comrades, have deeply regretted that destiny confronted this young officer in July 1944 with a situation with consequences the bearing of which I should assume are beyond the powers of any human being. No judgment will be made here as to whether his decision on 20 July was right or wrong. But the consequences of his decision were so terrible, and have cost so much of the best German blood, that we old soldiers had expected that a man to whom destiny gave such a burden to carry until the end of his life would recognize this, and would thereafter live quietly and in seclusion. We, his former comrades, lack any sympathy for the fact that Herr Remer fails to summon up this attitude of self-effacement.[60]

Eventually, it was the historians' turn. Perhaps unexpectedly, but in accordance with his overall strategy, Bauer's choice fell on the more conservative segment of the craft. He initially contacted Hans Rothfels, who had just returned from exile to assume a chair at the University of Tübingen and who had become director of the newly founded Institute for Contemporary History in Munich. He authored one of the first comprehensive accounts of German resistance against Hitler, praising the fighters' resoluteness and courage.[61] Surprisingly, Rothfels was very reserved: "I assume it is well known that I hold the memory of the resistance fighters in very high esteem (. . .) as well as their deep seated patriotism, which was at the same time German and European. As a layman I cannot judge on the legal matter. But if I would be asked by the defense, as is to be expected, about the facts, I do not see how I could dispute that in the sense of positive law, the people of July 20 did not commit high treason, nor were they traitors of their country," he wrote to Bauer, who promptly replied on 18 December 1951: "You are not summoned as a legal expert on the question of whether the resistance was high treason or not. The prosecution considers itself sufficiently competent to determine that. (. . .) You, Herr Professor, are to be invited as an expert on contemporary history [Sachverständiger für Zeitgeshichte]. Your task would be, just as it was in your book, to reconstruct the story of July 20 on the basis of your source knowledge of sources. (. . .).

Under no circumstances are you expected to pronounce value judgments alien to historians or make legal conclusions." Still, Rothfels declined.[62]

The topic of resistance was apparently more controversial than Bauer had thought, but he continued to search for experts and eventually contacted Professor Percy Ernst Schramm, a well-known medievalist, and Dr. Hans-Günther Seraphim, both from the University of Göttingen. Schramm was hardly less conservative than Seraphim. He was a First World War veteran, and had volunteered in the Second World War, becoming a diarist of the German High Command. He was also a witness in the Nuremberg trial in the defense of General Alfred Jodl, and had lost tenure at Göttingen due to his Nazi affiliation.[63] Nonetheless, in the Remer case Schramm testified about the general military situation in the summer of 1944, in order to answer the question: "What was the military position on 20.July 1944?" He depicted the hopelessness of the German military position through a detailed overview of the situation in the front lines, and came to the conclusion that by that time "the war was inevitably lost." Hence, in his view, "the outcome of the war can be explained neither with sabotage nor with treason."[64] This was a highly relevant conclusion, as Bauer hoped that such a credible account would dispel the myth that the conspirators were stabbing Germany in the back and hence contributed to the military defeat in the Second World War.[65]

Equally interesting was Bauer's other choice—Seraphim, who testified about two subjects which were topics of his report: the motives of the resistance of July 20, 1944, and the description of the course of events on that day with special emphasis of the role Major Remer played. Immediately before the trial, in a letter to Seraphim, Bauer stressed the crucial character of his report, in which he emphasized that he "rejected all attempts to bypass this topic."[66] Once in court, Seraphim proceeded cautiously with his forensic contribution, emphasizing the difficulties of such a task for the historian, particularly stressing that the event was quite recent and that the all the sources were not by a long stretch available to researchers.[67] Still, he was able to reconstruct the events of the conspiracy by making full use of the legal material deposited over the last few years in Göttingen's Institut für Völkerrecht, including the Nuremberg trials documents, as well as the stenographic notes of the trial against Witzleben and others at the notorious Volksgerichthof (Nazi People's Court). The documentary approach was supplemented with the personal recollections of Ludwig Beck and Hennig von Tresckow from the military side, as well as Ulrich von Hassell and Carl Feierdrich Goerdeler. Seraphim concluded that although the German resistance was a heterogeneous phenomenon, the aspiration to remove the regime was by and large motivated by patriotic reasons, with "the intent to reestablish legal order in Germany and preserve the freedom and independence of the German people and state." He had no doubts that the event was "a German endeavor"; he also concluded that the conspirators were inspired by "the hope that the success of the act would show to the world that even under the most difficult circumstances they could affect change in the rule of law, morality and orderly relations of Germans. In the case of failure, this beacon of the other Germany was supposed to prove that the German people and National Socialism were two different things."[68] Similar views were echoed by a number of eyewitnesses of the resistance, like Countess Marion Yorck von Wartenburg, Alexander von Hasse, Dr. Otto John, Dr. Fabian von Schlabrendorff, and others. Their depositions were summarized in a spirited plaidoyer given by Fritz Bauer on the last day of the trial, March 11, 1952. He reiterated that the purpose of the trial was "to explain if the people of July the 20th were traitors of the country, or not." He did not shy away from the fact that the 1944 Criminal Code stipulated: "Treason within the meaning of this paragraph is committed by him who, with the aim of jeopardizing the well-being of the Reich, permits the passing of secrets of state to another person."[69] However, he concluded that in "legal terms this was not high treason" and that "a political regime embodying injustice such as the Third Reich cannot be the object of high treason at all." Therefore, "the task of the prosecution and the judges of the democratic state is to rehabilitate without reservations and reductions the heroes of 20 July, on the basis of facts which are now known to us, and on the basis of the binding law, both of today and of back then."[70]

The deliberation lasted for four days, a time filled with uncertainties. "It was highly symptomatic that after the prosecutor's speech the presiding judge said he was still in a conflict of conscience as to what had been said about treason. He himself, so he declared, had been taken prisoner by the Russians at Stalingrad and had experienced afterwards how a number of German Generals and other officers had joined the pro-Soviet committee 'Free Germany.' 'I could not approve of this conduct,' the judge said. And he added that it was extremely difficult for a German court of law to reach a decision on the question of treason in connection with July 20th. The Court adjourned."[71]

The judges reconvened on March 15 to read out their lengthy verdict, which offered a detailed scrutiny of the events of July 20 and the motivations of its participants. The judges opened with a great step back, describing the events from 1933 and the subsequent "development of suppression of all oppositional expression which opened the door and gate to the politically directed terror (. . .). Starting with the Reichstag fire, through June 30, 1934 and November 9, 1938, what German people had to go through was a screaming injustice [*schreiendes Unrecht*], whose purging is necessary. It is difficult and bitter for a German court to have to pronounce something like this."[72] This historical excurse was based on the accounts of eyewitnesses and expert witnesses, whose contribution the judges fully acknowledged: "The general knowledge of Professor Doctor Schramm is beyond any doubt," notes the judgment, which also incorporates the basic conclusions from "the detailed report of historian expert Dr. Seraphim on the motives of the resistance fighters of 20. July 1944."[73] On the basis of their findings and the statements of witnesses, they concluded that the conspirators "consistently acted out of burning patriotism, showing selfless sacrifice and a sense of responsibility towards their people."[74] Their convictions by the Volksgerichthof were dismissed as irrelevant and "irreconcilable with the legal thinking of today." That allowed the court to conclude that Otto Remer did indeed defame the resistance fighters. "He had proved himself to be a brave officer in war at the front. On the other hand, it was found that the accused was still was living in the worldview of 1944, and still had not rid himself of these notions even seven years after the war. What had then on 20 July been an understandable mistake, was to be seen today as incorrigible spite."[75]

As observed by Guenther Lewy, "The court in its verdict accepted the opinion of the prosecutor that the Third Reich represented a state devoid of justice (Unrechtsstaat), but it refused to deny the Nazi regime all lawful status. (. . .) The resisters were cleared of Remer's accusation of high treason on narrower grounds. The decisive question, declared the verdict, was the motives and intentions of the conspirators. (. . .) In a formal sense the plotters had committed high treason by taking up contact with Germany's enemies. Yet, this had been done not in order to harm their country but to serve it. (. . .) They had done all this for the sake of 'the preservation of the German people and state in freedom and independence.'"[76]

Not only was Remer sentenced, but the road was also cleared for his party to be banned. He fled the country to avoid prison. The resistance was fully vindicated, and Bauer came out triumphant. However, from Bauer's point of view, not only the judges, but also the audience needed to be convinced. Interest in the trial was undisputable. As reported by a contemporary journalist, "In front of the courthouse each morning, one hour before the opening of the courtroom, there was a long, human snake. The entrance tickets were in high demand. In the wide and bright courtroom, witnesses and experts were making their statements into the microphone."[77] To be sure, not all in the courtroom, or outside of it, were convinced of Remer's guilt. Press coverage was ambiguous. Some pointed out, such as Tilo Bode in *Frankfurter Allgemeine Zeitung*, that Remer remains a scapegoat, a marginal figure in this legal undertaking. Others tended to question the necessity of historical expertise and the very motivation of the judges, such as Josef Schmidt in an article entitled "A Tribunal is supposed to write History?"[78] His provocation was eloquently responded to by Ernst Friedländer: "This law-court struggled with Germany's recent history as the German people themselves are still struggling with their recent history. The dark years from 1933 to 1945 were the real issue at Brunswick. One might say that a criminal court is not the right place to teach or to re-teach history. But who else is there to do the job? Altogether too many Germans have been under the spell of Nazi propaganda during the war. They have their own history wrong."[79]

For Friedländer, this was "a case of dead men on trial. For those really accused and condemned in this Criminal Court were Hitler and the Nazi leaders. It was their lawlessness and their crimes that stood accused. And they were found guilty. In the struggle of the German people with their own history this trial was only one step. But it was a step in the right direction."[80] The role of experts in this enterprise did not go unnoticed: "There were among the witnesses for the prosecution theologians of both the Protestant and the Roman Catholic faith, a historian and a former general. These men were by no means eyewitnesses of what happened in 1944. They testified as experts, but not on slander. They explained the teachings of the Churches on resistance against tyranny. They spoke of the soldier's oath and of the limits of the soldier's allegiance to a ruthless ruler. They analysed Germany's military position in July, 1944. It all came down to expert opinion on the question whether the plotters had been heroes or traitors."[81]

Indeed, it seemed that historical, ethical, and theological experts acted more like witnesses for the prosecution, rather than experts of the court. Consequently, they came under increasing pressure. After the trial, Seraphim wrote to Bauer about "a whole series of letters he received, including some that reveal a shocking mentality of certain circles." His recommendation was that "one should as soon as possible attempt to educate as much as possible people who are open-minded on this issue (. . .) through as wide a distribution of an authentic account as feasible."[82] Bauer was of the same mind, and he negotiated with a number of publishers on a book containing the material from the trial. These negotiations ultimately failed, but Bundeszentrale für Heimatsdients published a special volume dedicated to the trial, and Seraphim's own institution, Institut für Völkerrecht, published the expert reports and the judgment.[83]

Bauer's temporary alliance with conservatives paid off. The director of the Institute, Herbert Kraus, who was defense counsel in Nuremberg and remained highly suspicious toward legal interventions into Germany's recent past, prefaced this volume, embracing the expert reports as "striving for objective scholarly knowledge" and expressing the hope that the book would "contribute to clarifying our assessment of the martyrs of July 20th and their ethos."[84] Certainly, dissenters still remained, contesting this development.[85] However, resistance was further vindicated through workshops convoked by Hermann von Witzleben, assembling historians, jurists, officers, and theologians convinced that objectivity is not "neutrality toward good and bad" and tasked to "investigate the history of military resistance against national socialist rule through available documents and the questioning of remaining witnesses."[86] The first volume was introduced by Helmut Krausnick, one of the key researchers at the Institute for Contemporary History, and prefaced by none other than the president of the Federal Republic, Theodor Heuss.[87] Not the least due to such endorsement, the vindication of the resistance survived the test of time. Along with it, historical forensics acquired a modest foothold in German courtrooms.

Historical Forensic Contribution: Searching for Intent from Nuremberg to Ludwigsburg

The success of the Remer trial was more an exception than the rule for the Federal Republic. In the year of this trial only 123 persons were convicted for a crime of the Nazi period; exactly the same the year after, and the number continued to drop—44 in 1954, and only 21 in 1955.[88] With only a handful of new cases down the legal tube and the upcoming pardons to war criminals serving their time in German prisons, there was a growing conviction that war crimes investigations were on their way out. The subject matter of processed crimes was also specific: "Of the over 450 trials that took place in West Germany for war crimes between the end of the war and the Ulm trial in 1958, over 75% concerned crimes in Germany proper and nearly 65% with Germans as the primary target group of these crimes."[89] These statistics reflected the notion that Germans were the prime victims of Nazism. Some of the most gruesome transgressions of the Nazi regime were prosecuted, such as the project to exterminate the sick in the Nazi program of euthanasia. As early as 1953, a trial was held in Göttingen against two doctors who took part in the murders, characterized with thickly contextualized judgment, containing information on the development of the extermination policies. The judges credited "historical expert Dr. S.," none other than Hans-Günther Seraphim, whose previous experience made him an expert of high demand.[90]

In the absence of any central authority over the criminal investigations of the Nazi regime, such endeavors were largely left to the local prosecutor's offices, which pursued them with uneven élan. The judges also showed uneven enthusiasm in contacting historians, whereas historians showed similar reluctance. Bohum judge Herbert Froesse contacted Percy Shramm in 1953 to act as expert in the case against the wartime commander of the concentration camp Stutthof, who was accused of organizing the gassing of hundreds of Jewish inmates and killing them through injection of gasoline. Schramm refused, but recommended Seraphim, who indeed lent his expertise in this case. This case helped Seraphim assert his authority over the documents; he procured material from the Nuremberg Military Tribunal related to the "euthanasia" program, and concluded that Stutthof was originally not intended to be the site of the execution of the program, but was only involved later, with its commander deciding who lived and who died in the program beginning in autumn 1944. Interestingly, in this case Seraphim asked for documentation on the camp Stutthof from the Institute for Contemporary History in Munich, but without a positive answer.[91] Nonetheless, Seraphim continued submitting forensic contributions in other euthanasia trials.[92]

There was much less success in legally tackling Nazi crimes against non-Germans, primarily the Jews. Initial attempts to contextualize such cases had limited success, although there were historians ready to commit. Even Hans Rothfels, at the helm of the Institute for Contemporary History, overcame his distaste for testifying and joined the attempt to retry Gerhard Peters, former general manager of the company Degesch, whose procurement of Zyklon B for the SS was deemed by the prosecution as an accessory to murder. However, although Rothfels' opinion on the authenticity of the famous Gerstein report was accepted into evidence, Peters was acquitted after a long and complex legal battle, including a repeated review of the case and a full retrial.[93] The very scale of the extermination project challenged the legal system: "In other words, the German courts, in confronting the Holocaust, were caught in the horns of a dilemma. To omit history from the trial altogether was an impossibility, given the nature of the crimes involved, but to construct that history in the normative vocabulary of German law was to distort the events of the Holocaust in ways that profoundly minimized its radicality and socio-structural scope," wrote Devin Pendas.[94]

It was not until 1958 that the more ambitious legal undertakings occurred, giving prominence and further impetus to the Nazi criminality complex. Some progress was also made in the wider investigation of Nazi policies toward the Jews in the East. It was again Seraphim who broke the ice, as "in the following years Seraphim appeared several times as an expert in NS trials, strengthening the idea of calling upon historical expertise in such processes."[95] His status of expert was particularly reinforced with more ambitious background testimonies, such as the one on "the history of labor deployment of Jews in Generaalgouvernment 1939–1942," accepted by the Hamburg court in early 1958.[96] It was therefore no surprise when he was contacted to partake in the process that would decisively move legal reckoning with the Nazi regime toward deeper acknowledgment of its crimes against non-Germans.

The case, which came to be known as the Ulm Einsatzkommando trial, involved the wartime activity of Memel police commander Bernhard Fischer-Schweder and his associates.[97] His postwar career epitomized the depths of the problems besetting the *Vergangenheitsbewältingung* process. Fischer-Schweder had spent the postwar years under an assumed identity, but had resurfaced under his real name and applied for re-entry into civil service under Article 131, becoming the head of the refugee camp in Ulm in early 1954. However, his high profile led to an investigation which soon uncovered that he had been an SA member from 1925, and SS member and director of the Memel police in 1941. Forced to resign, he went as far as to sue the government for reinstatement in 1955. This brought him to the attention of the Chief Prosecutor in Ulm, Rudolf Mettler. Mounting evidence depicted the Memel police chief as a brutal personality, who supervised the mass execution of the Jews in the Tilsit region from the beginning of the invasion by the USSR in late June 1941, at the helm of one of the infamous Einsatzgruppen. He was arrested on May 3, 1956. By that time, a proactive prosecutor from Ludwigsburg, Erwin Schüle, had been sent to Stuttgart, bringing a new dimension to the case. He maintained that Fischer-Schweder's actions needed to be understood within the wider context of the "crime complex."[98] Within this attempt to broaden the scope and depth of the case, the quest for witnesses and documentation started anew. While Schüle was researching at the Berlin Documentation Center, Rudolf Mettler conducted research at the Institute for Contemporary History in Munich, whose experts, particularly Helmut Krausnick and Hans Buichheim, provided help. The quest also went beyond the borders of Germany—documents were sought from Yad Vashem and the Wiener library in London. Evidence from the Nuremberg trials related to the Einsatzgruppen was analyzed as well. The outcome of these efforts was a 212-page indictment for murder against Fischer-Schweder and his nine wartime colleagues, made public June 25, 1957. It contained a lengthy elaboration of the organization of the mass murders, labeling Hitler, Himmler, and Heydrich as chief perpetrators, analyzing the structure of the *Einsatzkommandos*, scaling from the macro level to the field of responsibilities of the accused. Fischer-Schweder and the others were alleged to have killed over five thousand Jews in the region from June to August 1941.[99]

The trial, which eventually started in Ulm on April 25, 1958, attracted considerable attention. As prosecutor Mettler noted in the days following the arrest, "It especially comes down to what would have happened to the accused if they had not followed orders."[100] Under German law, clear intent was needed in order for the killing to be labeled as murder, defined by the 1871 German criminal code as "killing another person from thirst of blood, satisfaction of his sexual desires, avarice or other base motive in a malicious and brutal manner."[101] In the absence of the intent, be it blood lust or political motivation, the killer would still be held liable, but likely only as an accessory to murder. Clinging on this distinction, the strategy of the defense was to present defendants as insignificant cogs in the machine of the regime, obeying orders not only with little enthusiasm, but also under extreme duress *(Befehlsnotstand)*.[102] This issue was raised most forcefully by defense attorney Rudolf Aschenauer, one of the defense attorneys in the trial. He maintained that "If an SS-man, especially in times of war, did not carry out a superior's order he put his life in immediate danger." The concept of obeying orders under duress resonated well with the idea that the responsible are found on top, and fit into the German postwar policy of gradual reintegration of members of the former regime. In connection to this defense line, the court required an expert opinion to the question of "whether SS leaders or SS men who refused participation in 'cleansing actions' or other 'annihilation measures' that were ordered by the rulers of the Third Reich could expect harm or damage to life and limb."[103] The defense attorneys unprecedentedly proposed their colleague Aschenauer, former attorney in the Nuremberg Einsatzgruppen trials, as an expert, which the judges predictably ruled out. Less predictably, they accepted a historical expert in the area of motivation and intent of the accused. It was Hans-Günther Seraphim.

As a former defense consultant in the NMT case against Otto Ohlendorf and other members of the Einsatzgruppen, Seraphim was exceptionally well placed to write a report on the topic concerned with the risk their members faced in disobeying orders in the Third Reich. Or at least so he claimed in a letter to the Ulm prosecutors in February 1958: "I am ready to act for the said question as an expert witness in the proceedings referred to. In the last twelve years I have dealt almost exclusively with the relevant issues of documentation of the Nazi period, both as a member of the editorial committee of the 'Blue Edition' of the IMT and since 1949 as head of the Contemporary History Department of the Institute of International Law, which I myself have built, as well as lecturer at the University. In my research among other things my attention was turned to the said question. (. . .) I would be grateful for timely notification about the timetable."[104] Seraphim was most probably in a hurry to secure his presence upon realizing that the Institute for Contemporary History was getting involved in the case. Therefore he proved very helpful to the prosecution, quickly submitting a twenty-six-page report and taking the stand on July 18, 1958. His general conclusion was clear: "In more than ten years of research focused particularly on the history of the SS and related police organizations, this expert witness has not found a single case that resulted in 'damage to life and limb' when an SS officer refused to carry out an 'annihilation order.'" He even went further to conclude that "these men did not live in fear; they themselves spread it across the land through their activities." According to Seraphim, the worst that could happen to such a person would be reassignment to the front, but "transfer to the front or anywhere else cannot be seen as danger to life and limb.'"[105] He based his findings on Himmler's statements and speeches, concluding that "a refusal to obey an order to exterminate inmates was not regarded by Himmler as disloyalty in the context of the SS Weltanschauung and therefore was not deemed to be a capital crime. Rather, a refusal was considered 'character weakness.' This explains why it was not followed by any punishment."[106]

On the same day, another historian took the stand. It was the deputy director of the Institut für Zeitgeschichte, Helmut Krausnick, who had gotten in touch with the prosecution already during the investigation period, assisting Prosecutor Mettler in finding the Einsatzkommando reports. The collaboration of the prosecutors with the fellows of the Institute for Contemporary History during the investigation led to an invitation to write an expert report about obeying orders under duress for the trial. "Ulm investigators actually intended to engage Herman Krauscnick, deputy head of Institute for Contemporary History or another fellow of the Institute as experts for the trial." Krausnick expressed general readiness in November 1957, but he declined in January 1958. The reason was interesting. As one of the editors of a collection of primary sources—Einsatzgruppen reports—he was concerned that as a witness he might be "rejected as biased or a priori determined.'"[107] Krausnick instead set to prepare a report on a more general matter, on the genesis of the Final Solution, a condensed history of discriminatory measures against the Jews. Krausnick's testimony was much broader in scope then Seraphim's, detailing the escalation of anti-Jewish policies after 1933 and their intensification with the outbreak of the Second World War, leading to the policy of mass murder.[108] The two experts did not coordinate their activity, which was an early signal of historiographic tensions over the interpretation of the recent past.[109]

The trial lasted until the end of August 1958. It involved 172 witnesses, including a number of experts, coming from different disciplines besides historical science. However, once the verdict against Bernhard Fischer-Schweder and the nine others was read, finding them guilty for assisting to murder, and convicting them to prison sentences ranging between three and fifteen years, the role that historical forensic contribution played became obvious. The verdict in the Ulm trial significantly contained a long description of the historical context, entitled *Entwicklung der Judenfrage* (Development of the Jewish Question), which tracked the anti-Jewish measures from 1933 until the formulation of the extermination policies. The actions of the accused were put into this wider historical context in which Hitler, Himmler, Heydrich, and the other dignitaries of the Reich figured as *Taturheber* and *Haupttäter* (originators, initiators of criminal deed) whose accomplices Bernhard Fischer-Schweder and the others eventually became. The background to the verdict was largely taken from Krausnick's and Seraphim's reports: "On the basis of his years of studies, expert Dr. Kra. has convincingly shown in his report, which was endorsed by the court, that the extermination orders trace back to Hitler (. . .). Once the main perpetrators decided to destroy the entire Jewish race in Europe, they were from the beginning searching for the way this destruction was to be given the pretense of legitimacy, as convincingly concluded by expert dr. Ser.," read the verdict.[110] It seems that the newspapers got it right when reporting the day after the testimony of both historians: "This time, the historians had the floor."[111]

The legal framing of historical events set up in the Ulm trial would have a huge impact on subsequent Holocaust-related cases in Germany, much to the engagement of Schüle, who was convinced of the necessity of the centralization of Holocaust-related criminality research. Under his influence, exactly such an institution was formed by the end of 1958, named the Zentrale Stelle der Landesjustiz verwaltungen zur Aufklärungen nationalsozialistischer Gewaltberbrechen (Central Office of the State Justice Ministries for the Investigation of National Socialist Crimes of Violence). According to Diether Pohl, "This investigative unit paved the way for a new kind of cooperation between historians and prosecutors. During the first days of 1959, the newly appointed prosecutors in Ludwigsburg, under the leadership of the Ulm chief investigator Schüle, started systematic investigations on all Nazi crimes, an enormous task with very little information available."[112] Historians were seen as possible interpreters of documentation that was shedding additional light on the particular cases: "Since the late 1950s, the majority of German documents which had been captured by the Western Allies were transferred to the Bundesarchiv and its military branch." As the documents were amassing, "more and more historians made their way to Ludwigsburg, which is now common practice in the field."[113] The number of investigations opened by Ludwigsburg rose from 488 (in 1958) to 1,075 (in 1959) and 1,326 (in 1960). One could notice a similar trend in the number of indictments (from 28 in 1958 to 32 in 1959 and 48 in 1960) and convictions within the general jurisdiction, which meant that the legal system was responsive to this intervention.[114] There was a similar turn in the use of historical expertise: "Consultation of the archives or historical institutions by investigative authorities or court in criminal proceedings against NS perpetrators was at first not the rule in the '50s. They grew in importance because due to the frequent denials by the accused, the lack of witnesses and the holes in their memories, documentation in many NS proceedings came to carry a special weight. At first, investigators as well as historians were facing a problem with sources. From the middle of the '50s (. . .) they increasingly started consulting the Institute for Contemporary History and other information centres."[115] Norbert Frei highlighted important milestones of this thorny evolution toward wider cooperation between the legal system and contemporary history, which Erich Haberer calls "the Ludwigsburg paradigm."[116]

Although long-term synergic aspects of this inquisitorial paradigm were recently scrutinized by Dieter Pohl and Mathew Turner, it is important to emphasize that in this early stage its future was all but certain.[117] It was embedded in the wider context of the policy of *Vergangenheitsbewältigung* in West Germany, criticized in 1959 by Theodor Adorno as "a modish slogan that has become highly suspect during the last few years," as it "does not mean seriously working upon past. (. . .) On the contrary, its intention is to close the books on the past and, if possible, even remove it from memory. The attitude that everything should be forgotten und forgiven, which would be proper for those who suffered injustice, is practiced by those party supporters who committed the injustice. (. . .) Criminology in Germany is not yet up to modern standards at all," he stated bluntly.[118]

Juicy scandals seemed to prove him right. No sooner did one Georg Heuser become chief of Rheinland-Pfalz criminal police, in 1958, than he was arrested, in June 1959, under suspicion that he commanded the Einsatzgruppe in murderous operations in Belarus in 1942.[119] The very prosecutor assigned to this case, Wilhelm Foge, was revealed to be a military special prosecutor in Minsk in 1942.[120] Embarrassing examples were reaching toward the top of the security apparatus. Hans Globke, Chancellor Adenauer's security advisor, director of the Chancery, and seasoned civil servant, although never a party member, coauthored a number of Nazi legislative acts, the most infamous being the Nuremberg Laws, as he once was a deputy director of the Nazi Ministry of Interior.[121] What could be done about that? Wider public involvement in addressing these matters started with the so-called *Verjährungsdebatte*—the debate on the application of the statute of limitations for prosecution for crimes of the Nazi period.

This debate was sparked in 1960, with the twenty-year expiration date for charging murder approaching, rendering the worst atrocities committed during the Third Reich unprosecutable by 1965. The awareness that this severely limited and almost extinguished the possibility of legal reckoning with the crimes committed between 1933 and 1945 led to strong reactions. With increased vigor and stronger voice, the victims and their representatives demanded the erasure of the statute of limitations and pointed to deficiencies of the project of legally dealing with the past in German courtrooms. Major cultural figures, like philosopher Karl Jaspers or prosecutor Fritz Bauer, argued for the abolition of the statute of limitations.[122] However, others, like Otto Kircheimer, author of the influential book *Political Justice*, argued that "German authorities had a full decade to get busy, and, official assertions to the contrary, could have undertaken many more prosecutions than they managed to do. At best, uncertain shifts in public appreciation were not good enough reason to withdraw from anybody the benefits of the statute of limitations."[123]

Kircheimer was doubting both the readiness of German authorities and the very ability of the inquisitorial paradigm grounded in continental law to wrestle with such cases: "But what about the continental procedure? While under Anglo-American procedure the prosecution tries to establish proof of the contentions made in the indictment, with the defense trying to do the same, in continental European practice the act of accusation only offers the court a preliminary version of historical happenings. It is the job of the court to find the reconstruction of historical incident which will serve as an adequate basis for the verdict. In this job of reconstruction the judge is not bound by the assertion and offering of either party; rather, both prosecution and defense, although given a number of procedural prerogatives, among them to call witnesses and experts, remain auxiliaries of the court."[124] In his view, inquisitorial procedure was pushing a judge into a position of pseudohistorian: "The continental judge, though, will have made a painstaking study of the whole file of the case transmitted to him by the prosecutor. It will contain everything which has transpired so far, including police reports, pretrial depositions of defendants and witnesses, and defense motions to the criminal record of the defendant. As he has perforce formed some opinion on the case, he is tempted to make reality conform to the file."[125]

His fellow émigré from Germany, Hans W. Baade of Duke University, shared this notion, noting that "the German courts have lately placed increasing reliance on expert opinions of historians when faced with intricate problems of recent political history, and in spite of this reliance on experts, their determinations of historical fact have been open to substantially the same objections that were raised against historical fact finding by the Federal Constitutional Court." For him, "the lesson seems clear: judicial pronouncements on political history are fraught with unusually grave dangers and should be avoided wherever possible."[126] This lesson he deemed important in the light of "professional and even to some extent judicial criticism of decisions of the U.S. Supreme Court (. . .) especially strong where the Court (. . .) sought to base its decision in part on an attempt to reconstruct the meaning of a constitutional provision in the light of contemporary political history."[127] Reflecting their understanding of incompatibility between history and law, and outlining the problems facing the inquisitorial process typical for continental law, Kircheimer and Baade also foresaw the challenge posed to the courts of adversarial procedure, which was just about to be confronted with the adjudication of historical injustice.

Notes

1 Important preliminary research for the Nuremberg trial was conducted by Colonel Tommy Thomson, Librarian at the British Foreign Office, and Dr. W.R. Perkins from the State Department, editor of *Foreign Relations of the United States*. Particularly important in this respect were the young experts on Germany from Anglo-Saxon countries. Some of them were professionally influenced by the Nuremberg experience, like Peter Calvocoressi. *Nuremberg: The Facts, the Law and the Consequences* (New York: MacMillan, 1948); Hugh Trevor-Roper, *The Last Days of Hitler* (London: Pan Books, 2002).

2 Friedrich Meinecke, *Die Deutsche Katastrophe: Betrachtungen und Erinnerungen* (Wiesbaden: Eberhard Brockhaus Verlag, 1949), 6–7.

3 This change was announced in Chester McArthur Destler, "Some Observations on Contemporary Historical Theory," *The American Historical Review* 55.3 (April, 1950): 503–529.

4 Roland Mousnier and Rene Pillorget, "Contemporary History and Historians of the Sixteenth and Seventeenth Centuries," *Journal of Contemporary History* 3.2 (1968): 107.

5 The chief benefactor of this process was diplomatic history, thoroughly reshaped into interdisciplinary and comparative history of international relations by Pierre Renouvin and his disciples, but also enriched with the panoramic insights of Lewis Namier, which were boldly grasping toward the most recent period (*Diplomatic Prelude*—1948, *Europe in Decay*—1950, *In the Nazi Era*—1952). This trend dates back to the wartime period, during which Namier started publishing works on contemporary history. Cf. Lewis Namier, *Conflicts: Studies in Contemporary History* (London: Macmillan, 1942).

6 Gerhard L. Weinberg, "Setting and Significance of the Nuremberg Tribunal," in *Nazi Crimes and the Law*, eds. Nathan Stoltzfus and Henry Friedlander (German Historical Institute: Washington, 2008), 37.

7 Until 1949, the French courts convicted 2,107 persons, issuing 104 death sentences; the British convicted 1,085 persons, 240 to death; Americans convicted 1,814 persons, 450 to death. The scope of retribution in the Soviet zone, although unclear, might have exceeded 13,000 convictions. Data is provided by David Cohen, "Transitional Justice in Divided Germany after 1945," in *Retribution and Reparation in the Transition to Democracy*, ed. Jon Elster (Cambridge: Cambridge University Press, 2006) 63. Slightly different numbers for the American zone (1,941 processed, 1,517 convicted, 324 death penalties) came from official German data. Cf. Rolf Vogel (ed.), *Ein Weg aus der Vergangenheit: Eine Dokumentation zur Verjährung und zu den NS-Prozessen* (Frankfurt: Ullstein

Verlag, 1969), 9–10. Regarding the ambigious, but still much more vigorous than expected, record of German courts see Edith Raim, *Nazi Crimes against Jews and German Post-War Justice, The West German Judicial System during Allied Occupation (1945–1949)* (Oldenbourg: De Gruyter, 2015).

8 Of these, only 930,000 were actually examined by denazification tribunals: 1,549 were classified as major offenders, 21,000 as offenders, 104,000 as lesser offenders, 475,000 as followers. Fines were imposed in 569,600 cases, employment restrictions were enacted in 124,400 cases, 23,100 persons were found ineligible for public office, 25,900 were subject to property confiscation, 30,500 were assigned to labor without imprisonment, and 9,600 went to labor camps. Cf. Cohen, *Transitional Jutice in Divided Germany*, 75.

9 Adalbert Rückerl, *NS-Verbrechen vor Gericht* (Heidelberg: Müller Verlag, 1982), 121.

10 Of the indicted 185 persons, 177 stood trial in separate proceedings against Nazi industrials, jurists, military commanders, SS officials, and doctors. In the following years, 142 were convicted: 23 were sentenced to death, 20 to life sentences, and the rest to prison terms. Jonathan Friedman, "Law and Politics in the Subsequent Nuremberg Trials," in *Atrocities on Trial*, ed. Patricia Heberer, 88–89.

11 "The Milch Case: Judgment," in *Trials of War Criminals before the Nuernberg Military Tribunals Under Control Council Law No. 10* (Washington, D.C.: United States Government Printing Office, 1950), vol. II, 859.

12 Telford Taylor, *Final Report to the Secretary of the Army on the Nuremberg War Crimes Trials Under Control Council Law No. 19* (Washington, D.C.: Department of the Army, 1949), 101.

13 Taylor, *Final Report*, 102. Nuremberg Military Tribunal trial records were only partially published in 14 volumes of *Trials of War Criminals before the Nurnberg Military Tribunals Under Control Council Law No. 10* (Washington, D.C.: United States Government Printing Office, 1950). They are known as "the green series." Documents from the trials were also physically removed and returned to the International Court of Justice at The Hague, with complete or partial sets of the mimeographs sent to the National Archives in Washington, D.C., and to more than a number of academic institutions. One of these, Harvard Law School, recently started a project at the Harvard Law School Library: *Nuremberg Trials Project: A Digital Document Collection. The Thirteen Nuremberg Trials*, http://nuremberg.law.harvard.edu/php/docs_swi.php?DI=1&text=nur_13tr, accessed on 21.2.2016.

Subsequent Nuremberg trials have recently attracted substantive attention. About the historical impact of subsequent trials see Kim C. Priemel and Alexa Stiller, *Reassessing the Nuremberg Military Tribunals. Transitional Justice, Trial Narratives and Historiography*, (New York: Berghahn Books, 2012). Their legal importance is also emphasized in Kevin Jon Heller, *The Nuremberg Military Tribunals and the Origins of International Criminal Law* (Oxford: Oxford University Press, 2012).

14 Telford Taylor, *The Nuremberg Trials*, in *Mettraux, Perspectives on the Nuremberg Trial*, ed. Guénaël (Oxford: Oxford University Press, 2008), 404.

15 Taylor, *Final Report*, 101–102.

16 Ibid., 106.

17 Gavin B.Henderson, "A Plea for the Study of Contemporary History", History, 26.101 (June 1941): 53-55. Max Beloff, "The Study of Contemporary History: Some further reflections", History, 30.111 (March 1945): 83-84.

18 Alan Bullock, "Introduction," in *Contemporary History in Europe*, ed. Donald Cameron Watt (London: George Allen and Unwin Ltd., 1969), 11–13.

19 In 1978 it transformed into the Institut d'histoire du temps present.

20 About its foundation: John Gimbel, "The Origins of the Institut für Zeitgeschichte: Scholarship, Politics, and the American Occupation, 1945–1949," *The American Historical Review* 70.3 (April, 1965): 714–731. Mission stated in Hans Rothfels, "Zeitgeschichte als Aufgabe," *Vierteljahrshefte für Zeitgeschichte* 1 (1955): 1–8; Thilo Vogelsang, "Die Zeitgeschichte und ihre Hilfsmittel," *Vierteljahrshefte für Zeitgeschichte* 3 (1955): 211–222. More in Gabriele Metzler, *Einführung in das Studium der Zeitgeschichte* (Paderborn: Ferdinand Schöning 2004), 22–24.

21 Karl Dietrich Erdmann, *Toward a Global Community of Historians: The International Historical Congresses and the International Committee of Historical Sciences 1898–2000* (New York: Berghahn Books, 2005), 188–192.

22 Martina Cattaruzza and Sacha Zala, "Negotiated History? Bilateral Historical Commission in the 20th Century Europe," in *Contemporary History on Trial: Europe since 1989 and the Role of the Expert Historian*, eds. Harriet Jones, Kjell Östberg and Nico Randeraad, 125.

23 Dumoulin, *Le rôle social de l'historien*, 306–312.

24 Heike Kroesche, "Der Nurnberger Prozess gegen die Hauptkriegsverbrecher 1945/46 im Spannungsfeld von veröffentlichter Meinung und Bevölkerung," *Juristische Zeitgeschicte*, Band 16 (2008): 134.

25 West, A Train of Powder, 53–54.

26 David Maxwell Fyfe (ed.), "Introduction," *War Crimes Trials* (London: William Hodge, 1948–9), vol. I–VI, xiii.

27 Robert Kempner, "The Nuremberg Trials as Sources of Recent German Political and Historical Materials," *American Political Science Review* XLIV.2 (June, 1950): 448.

28 Ibid., 447.

29 West, A Train of Powder, 254, 261–262.

30 Robert H. Jackson, "Introduction," in *Tyranny on Trial: The Evidence at Nuremberg*, ed. W.R. Harris (New York: Barnes and Noble, 1954), ii.

31 Heinz Höhne, *The Order of the Death's Head: The Story of Hitler's SS* (London: Penguin Books, 2000), 7.

32 On the connection between German historians and Nazism see Konrad Jaraussch and Rüdiger Hohls, *Versäumte Fragen* (Stuttgart: Deutsche Verlags-Anstalt, 2000). Also Konrad Jarausch, "Unasked Questions: The Controversy About Nazi Collaboration Among German Historians," in *Lessons and Legacies*, ed. Jeffry M. Diefendorf (Evanston, Ill: Northwestern University Press, 2004), vol. VI, 190–208. A short overview of the most sensitive period in Winfried Schulze: "German Historiography from the 1930s to the 1950s," in *Paths of Continuity: Central European Historiography from the 1930s to the 1950s*, eds. Hartmut Lehmann and James Van Horn Melton (Cambridge: Cambridge University Press, 2003), 19–42.

33 Gerhard Ritter, "Gegenwärtige Lage und Zukunftsaufgaben deutscher Geschichtswissenschaft," *Historische Zeitschrift* 170 (1950), 16–18.

34 Gesetz zur Regelung der Rechtsverhältnisse der unter Artikel 131 des Grundgesetzes fallenden Personen, *Bundesgesetzblatt*, teil I, 58 (1953): 1287–1310. Detailed overview in Norbert Frei, *Adenauer's Germany and the Nazi Past: The Politics of Amnesty and Integration* (New York: Columbia University Press, 2002), 41–66.

35 The Institute produced short studies about different topics (e.g., was the Catholic church an organization persecuted by the Nazi regime; deportations of the Gypsies in May 1940; the program of euthanasia), or memos about the structure of different pillars of the regime. The shortness of reports is a misleading indicator about an amount of work invested in them, as seen from over five hundred pages of preparatory material for just one topic. Cf. Hans Buchheim,

"Materialsammlung zur Verfolgung der 'Zigeuner' in der NS-Zeit," Institut für Zeitgeschichte, Archivdatenbank MS 410, http://www.ifz-muenchen.de/archiv/Ms_0410_0000_0000.pdf. Made between 1953 and 1957 by the Institute's researchers, Martin Broszat, Hans Buchheim, Helmut Heiber, and doctoral candidates Hellmuth Auerbach and Hermnman Graml, the reports were occasionally forwarded for usage in criminal trials as well, such as proceeding against Erich von dem Bach-Zelewski and Josef Sepp Dietrich for their role in the murders during the Night of Long Knives. These cases dragged on in Landgericht München, leading to mild prison sentences. For the Sepp Dietrich case the Institute for Contemporary History organized the entire team and started assembling the documentation. Institut für Zeitgeschichte, Archivdatenbank ZS 450, http://www.ifz-muenchen.de/archiv/zs/zs-0450.pdf. Cf. Andreas Eichmüller, *Keine Generalamnestie: Die Strafverfolgungvon NS-Verbrechen in der frühenBundesrepublik* (München: Oldenburg Verlag, 2012), 369.

36 Paul Kluke, "Vorwort," In *Gutachten des Instituts für Zeitgeschichte* (München: Institut für Zeitgeschichte, 1958), 9, 10.

37 Astrid M. Eckert, "The Transnational Beginnings of West German Zeitgeschichte in the 1950s," *Central European History* 40.1 (March, 2007): 63–87.

38 This reversal was researched by Edith Raim, *Nazi Crimes against Jews and German Post-War Justice, The West German Judicial System during Allied Occupation (1945–1949)* (Oldenbourg: De Gruyter, 2015), 290–310. An overview of the state of the postwar German Judiciary is in Rebecca Witmann, *Tainted Law: The West German Judiciary and the Prosecution of War Crimes*, in *Atrocities on Trial*, ed. Patricia Heberer, 211–217.

39 Adalbert Rückerl, *NS-Verbrechen vor Gericht* (Heidelberg: Müller Juristicher Verlag, 1982), 329–332. More recent statistics differ slightly in numbers but not in tendencies. Andreas Eichmüller, "Die Strafverfolgung von NS-Verbrechen durch westdeutsche Justizbehörden seit 1945: Eine Zahlenbilanz," *Vierteljahrshefte für Zeitgeschichte* 56.4 (2008): 621–640.

40 Rudolf Aschenauer, *Zur Frage einer Revision der Kriegsverbrecherprozesse* (Nurnberg, s.n., 1949). Otto Kranzbühler, *Rückblick auf Nürnberg* (Hamburg: Zeit-Verlag, 1949).

41 See Kroesche, *Der Nurnberger Prozess . . .*, 133–145.

42 Cf. *Völkerrechtliche Forschung—25 Jahre Institut für Völkerrecht der Universität Göttingen* (1930–1955) (Göttingen: *Institut für Völkerrecht*, 1955). Cf. Kai Arne Linnemann, *Das Erbe des Ostforschung: Zur Rolel Göttignens in der Gescgihtswissechaft der Nachkriegszeit* (Marburg: Tectum Verlag, 2002), 14.

43 Herbet Kraus, "Geleitwort," in *Die Rechtprechung der Nürenberger Militärtribunale. Sammlung der Rechthesen der Urteile und gesonderten Urteilsbegründungen der dreizehn Nuremberg Prozesse* (Bonn: Girardet, 1952), iii.

44 Rebecca Wittmann. *Beyond Justice* (Cambridge: Harvard University Press, 2005), 80. Cf. Hilary Earl, *The Nuremberg SS-Einsatzgruppen Trial, 1945–1958: Atrocity, Law and History* (Cambridge: Cambridge University Press 2009).

45 Hans-Günther Seraphim (ed.), *Indices zu den zwölf Nürnberger U.S.-Militärgerichtsprozesse* (Göttingen: Institut für Völkerrecht, 1950–6), I–IV. See also Hans-Günther Seraphim, "*Die Erschließung der Nürnberger Prozeßakten*," *Der Archivar* 28, (1975): 417–422; Hans-Günther Serpahim, "*Quellen zur Erforschung des Dritten Reiches*," *Politisches Archiv* 17 (1950): 3307–3310.

46 Hans-Günther Seraphim, "Nachkriegsprozesse und zeitgeschichtliche Forschung," in *Mensch und Staat in Recht und Geschichte: Festschrift fur Herbert Kraus*, eds. Hans Kruse and Hans-Gunther Seraphim (Kitzingen/Main: Holzner-Verlag, 1954), 436.

47 Seraphim, "Nachkriegsprozesse und zeitgeschichtliche Forschung," 454–455.

48 Diether Pohl, *Prosecutors and Historians: Holocaust Investigations and Historiography in the Federal Republic 1955-1975*, conference paper "Justice and the Holocaust," Yad Vashem, Jerusalem in December 2006, 1. There is no centralized witness database in Germany. However, courtesy of Dick de Mildt, editor of the database Justiz und NS Verbrechen, who compiled a report on historical expertise in Nazi-related crimes: *List of Historians (Expert Witnesses) Mentioned in the German Trial Judgments Series Justiz und NS-Verbrechen: Sammlung deutscher Starfurteile wegen nationalsozialistischer Tötungsverbrechen, 1945–2012* (Amsterdam: Ex Post Facto, 2013).

49 Landsgericht (LG) Düsseldorf (5.3.1949) 8 Ks 1/49, in *Justiz und NS Verbrechen, Samlung Deutscher Strafurteile wegen nationalsozialistischer tötungsverbrechen*, eds. C.M. Rüter en dr. D.W. de Mildt (Justiz und NS Verbrechen) (Amsterdam: University Press Amsterdam, 1970), lfd 125, vol. 4, 209.

50 Eichmüller, *Keine Generalamnestie*, 366.

51 Fritz Bauer, *Die Kriegsverbrecher vor Gericht* (Zürich/New York: Europa Verlgag, 1945), 211.

52 Irmtrud Wojak, *Fritz Bauer 1903–1968: Eine Biographie* (München: C.H. Beck, 2009), 363.

53 Ibid., 232.

54 He was the person ordered to arrest Josef Goebbels, but he reversed against the conspirators, contributing to their downfall. After the war he published his account on the events of the fateful day: Otto Remer, *20. Juli 1944* (Hamburg-Neuhausen: Verlag Deutsche Opposition, 1951).

55 "Frankfurter Allgemeine Zeitung," 5.5.1951.

56 Wojak, *Fritz Bauer . . .*, 267.

57 Claudia Fröhlich, "Der Braunschweiger Remer-Prozess 1952. Zum Umgang mit dem Widerstand gegen den NS-Staat in der frühen Bundesrepublik," in *Schuldig. NS-Verbrechen vor deutschen Gerichten. Beiträge zur Geschichte der nationalsozialistischen Verfolgung in Norddeutschland*, Heft 9 (2005): 20. More about the case in Wojak, *Fritz Bauer . . .*, 265–279. More critical interpretation of Bauer's role by Boris Burghardt, "Vor 60 Jahren: Fritz Bauer und der Braunschweiger Remer-Prozess. Ein Strafverfahren als Vehikel der Geschichtspolitik," *Journal der Juristischen Zeitgeschichte* 2 (2012): 47–92.

58 On the role of experts in the German criminal system see the detailed analysis by Karlhans Dippel, *Die Stellung des Sachverständingen im Strafprozess* (Heidelberg: Dekker, 1986).

59 "Urteil des Landgerichts Braunschweig vom 15. März 1952 in der Stragsache engen Generalmajor a.D Remer wegen übler Nachrede," in *Die im Braunschweiger Remerprozess erstatteten moraltheologischen und historischen Gutachten nebst Urteil*, ed. Herbert Kraus (Hamburg: Girardet Co., 1953), 9–40.

60 Generalleutnat Friebe, "Gutachten überdie Stellung des Offizierkorps zum 20. Juli," in Ibid., 85, 103.

61 Hans Rothfels, *The German Opposition to Hitler, An Appraisal* (Chicago: Henry Regnery Company, 1948); published in Germany as *Die deutsche Opposition gegen Hitler* (Krefeld: Scherpe, 1949).

62 Their correspondence is deposited in Niedersächische Staatsarchiv and is explored and quoted at length by Claudia Froehlich, "*Wider die Tabuisierung des Ungehorsams": Fritz Bauers Widerstandsbegriff und die Aufarbeitung von NS-Verbrechen* (Frankfurt: Campus Verlag, 2006), 47–48.

63 He soon rejoined the faculty and even developed a methodological interest in contemporary history: Percy E. Schramm, "Probleme der neueren und neuesten Geschichte," *Deutsche Universitäts Zeitung* XI.11 (1956): 6–8.

64 Percy Ernst Schram, *Historisches Gutachten über die Kriegslage in Sommer 1944*, in *Die im Braunschweiger Remerprozess . . .*, ed. Herbert Kraus, 80. In

his case a problem evolved clearly of distinguishing between an eyewitness and an expert. Further underpinnings of this division in German criminal law can be found in Friedrich Toepel, *Grundstrukturen . . .*, 264–284.

65 The press related that "treason did not play a significant role in their defeat. The expert therefore refuted the stab-in-the-back legend propagated by the party of the extreme right." *Frankfurter Allgemeine Zeitung*, March 10, 1952.

66 Cf. Fröhlich, *Wider die Tabuisierung des Ungehorsams*, 65.

67 Dr. Hans Günther Seraphim, *Entwurf zu einem Gutachten*, in *Die im Braunschweiger Remerprozess . . .*, ed. Herbert Kraus, 49.

68 Ibid., 55–56. The content of both historical forensic contributions is scrutinized at length by Timo Metzner, *Das Öffentliche Bild Vom Deutschen Widerstand Gegen Den Nationalsozialismus: Deutschland 1945–1952* (Nordenstedt: Grin Verlag, 2007), 88–93.

69 Guenter Lewy, "Resistance to Tyranny: Treason, Right or Duty?" *The Western Political Quarterly* 13.3 (1960): 581.

70 „Eine Grenze hat Tyrannenmacht. Plaedoyer im Remer-Prozess", in Fritz Bauer, *Die Humanitaet der Rechtsordnung* (Frankfurt/New York: Camopus, 1998), 169–179. Also available at http://www.braunschweiger-zeitung.de/media/755236-2695/Plaedoyer-Fritz-Bauer-Remer-Prozess-1952.pdf, accessed on 21.2.2016.

71 Ernst Friedländer, "Dead Men on Trial," *The Spectator*, March 28, 1952, 6.

72 "Urteil des Landgerichts Braunschweig vom 15. März 1952 in der Strafsache engen Generalmajor Remer wegen übler Nachrede," in *Die im Braunschweiger Remerprozess . . .*, ed. Herbert Kraus, 122.

73 Ibid., 112. 125. Importantly, they explicated the necessity of differentiating between expert witnesses *(sachverständige Zeuge)* and experts *(Sachsverständige)*. Whereas the expert provides the court expertise on the basis of experience and knowledge of things about which the professional judges have no knowledge, an expert witness reports on perceptions that he was able to make only because of its special expertise—for example, DNA testing (Civil Procedure: § 414 ZPO). Ibid., 124. In contrast, the judges declined the application by the defendant's attorneys to call former fieldmarshals Alfred von Kesselring and Erich von Manstein, Admiral Doenitz, and General Guderian, and other military figures as expert witnesses on "the scope and meaning of the soldier's oath," claiming that the issue was covered by expert reports. Ibid., 112.

74 Ibid., 128.

75 Ibid., 136.

76 Guenter Lewy, "Resistance to Tyranny: Treason, Right or Duty?" *The Western Political Quarterly* 13.3 (September, 1960): 581–582.

77 Quoted in Fröhlich, "Der Braunschweiger Remer-Prozess 1952 . . .," 17.

78 Thilo Bode, "Remer wird zur Randfigur des Prozesses," *Frankfurter Allgemeine Zeitung*, March 10, 1952; Josef Schmidt, "Ein Landgericht soll Geschichte schreiben. Der 20. Juli 1944 als eigentlicher Gegenstand des Beleidigungsprozesses gegen Remer in Braunschweig," *Frankfurter Allgemeine Zeitung*, March 11, 1952.

79 Ernst Friedländer, "Dead Men on Trial," *The Spectator*, March 28, 1952, 6.

80 Ibid., 7.

81 Ibid., 6.

82 Quoted in Fröhlich, "Der Braunschweiger Remer-Prozess 1952 . . .," 126.

83 *Die Wahrheit über den 20. Juli 1944* (Bonn: Bundeszentrale für Heimatsdients, 1954).

84 Kraus, *Die im Braunschweiger Remerprozess . . .*, 8.

85 See Albert Mirgeler, "Geschichte aus der Distanz"; Michael Freund, "Geschichte ohne Distanz"; and Ernst Forsthoff, "Die Rückkehr zum Rechtstaat" in *Deutscher Geist zwischen Gestern und Morgen*, ed. Joachim Moras (Stuttgart: Deutsche Verlags Anstalt, 1954), 298–348.

86 Heinrich von Witzleben (ed.), *Vollmacht des Gewissens* (Frankfurt am Mein/ Berlin, *Europäischen Puublikation*, 1956), 9.

87 Helmut Krausnick, "Vorgeschichte und Beginn des militaärischen Widerstandes gegen Hitler," in Ibid., 177–384.

88 Adalbert Rückerl, *NS-Verbrechen vor Gericht* (Heidelberg: Müller Juristicher Verlag, 1982), 329–332. More recent statistics differ slightly in numbers but not in tendencies. Andreas Eichmüller, "Die Strafverfolgung von NS-Verbrechen durch westdeutsche Justizbehörden seit 1945: Eine Zahlenbilanz," *Vierteljahrshefte für Zeitgeschichte* 56.4 (2008): 621–640.

89 Patrick Tobin, *Crossroads at Ulm: Postwar Germany and the 1958 Ulm Einsatzkommandotrial.* Ph.D Dissertation (Chapel Hill: University of North Carolina, 2013), 27.

90 LG Göttingen (2.12.1953), 6 Ks1/53, *Justiz und NS Verbrechen*, vol. 11, 744.

91 This might have been an institutional competitivness, as the Institute was developing its own courtroom expertise. Eichmüller, *Keine Generalamnestie* . . ., 365–367.

92 LG Bochum (16.12.1955) 17 Ks 1/55, *Justiz und NS Verbrechen*, lfd.446, vol. 14, 206. Similar crimes were the subject of his testimony in the trial of a doctor from a concentration camp. Flossenburg LG Weiden (29.5.1956), Ks 2/55, *Justiz und NS Verbrechen*, vol.13, 750, 755–757. In both cases the accused were sentenced to imprisonment. It is particularly interesting that Seraphim took part in "euthanasia" proceedings, having in mind that his cousin Peter Heinz Seraphim was one of the vocal proponents of the practice. Cf. Benno Mueller-Hill, *Tödliche Wissenschaft: Die Aussonderung von Juden, Zigeunern und Geisteskranken 1933–1945* (Hamburg: Rowohlt, 1984), 48. On the cases see Dick De Mildt, *In the Name of the People: Perpetrators of Genocide in the Reflection of Their Post-War Prosecution in West Germany* (The Hague: Martinus Nijhoff, 1996), 132–148 and Michael Bryant, *Confronting the "Good Death": Nazi Euthanasia on Trial, 1945–1953* (Boulder: University Press of Colorado, 2005).

93 Rothfels published the famous Gerstein report, whose author, a repentant SS officer, was no longer alive. Dr. Hans Rothfels, "Augenzeugenbericht zu den Massenvergasungen," *Vierteljahrshefte für Zeitgeschichte* 1 (1953): 177–194. The report was evoked in the judgment. Cg LG Frankfurt am Mein (27.5.1955), 4a Ks 1/55, *Justiz und NS Verbrechen*, lfd.415, vol. 13,112, 123, 125.

94 Devin Pendas, *Frankfurt Auschwitz Trial, 1963–1965: Genocide, History, and the Limits of the Law* (New York: Cambridge University Press, 2006), 300.

95 Eichmüller, *Keine Generalamnestie* . . ., 367.

96 LG Hamburg 13/57 (NS-Gewaltverbrechen in Lagern, Petrikau), LG Düsseldorf (5.3.1949) 8 Ks 1/49 (Verbrechen der Endphase, Düsseldorf), in: *Justiz und NS Verbrechen*, lfd 125, vol. 4, 209; vol. XIV, 748–749.

97 On the trial see Claudia Fröhlich, "Der 'Ulmer Einsatzgruppenprozess' 1958: Wahrnehmung und Wirkung des ersten großen Holocaust-Prozesses," in *NS-Prozesse und Deutsche Öffentlichkeit: Besatzungszeit, frühe Bundesrepublik und DDR*, eds. Jörg Osterloh and Clemens Vollnhals (Vandenhoeck & Ruprecht, 2011), 233–261, and in particular a recent disseration of Patrick Tobin, *Crossroads at Ulm: Postwar Germany and the 1958 Ulm Einsatzkommando trial.* PhD Dissertation (Chapel Hill: University of North Carolina, 2013).

98 Ibid., 179.

99 The indictment of June 25, 1957 is analyzed in Ibid., 179–245.

100 Patrick Tobin, *No Country for Old Fighters, Postwar Germany and the Origins of the Ulm Einsatzkommando Trial.* MA Thesis (Chapel Hill: University of North Carolina, 2009), 42.

101 Strafgesetzbuch (StGB), § 211.
102 More in Kurt Hinrichsen, "Befehlsnotstand," in *NS Prozesse*, ed. Adalbert Rückerl (Karlsruhe: Verlag C.F. Mueller, 1971), 131–161.
103 Rebecca Wittmann, *Beyond Justice: The Auschwitz Trial* (Cambridge: Harvard University Press, 2005), 80.
104 Hans-Günther Seraphim to Staatsanwaltschaft beim Landgericht Ulm (12.2.1958); text of letter reproduced courtesy of Patrick Tobin.
105 Quoted here from Wittmann, *Beyond Justice*, 80–81.
106 Hermann Langbein, *People in Auschwitz* (Chapel Hill: University of North Carolina Press, 2004), 509.
107 Eichmüller, *Keine Generalamnestie* . . ., 368. He also notes the correspondence between Mettler and Krauscnik on the matter.
108 The original of Krausnick's *Gutachten* is not located in his collection of expert reports at the Institut für Zeitgeschichte, Archivdatenbank ED 419; bd.10–12. Interestingly enough, Krausnick did not include it in the second volume of the Institute for Contemporary History's *Gutachten* (Stuttgart: Deutsche Verlags-Anstalt, 1966). Perhaps the reason was that in its developed form it was published around the same time with other reports from the Frankfurt Auschwitz trial. Krausnick eventually published much of his findings in Helmut Krausnick and Hans-Heinrich Wilhelm, *Die Truppe des Weltanschaungskrieges: Die Einsatzgruppen der Sicherheitspolizeiund des SD 1938–1942* (Stuttgart: Deutsche Verlags-Anstalt, 1981).
109 It seems that there was a certain tension between Seraphim and IfZ researchers, expressed in previous years when the former asked for documentation from the Institute for Contemporary History. He might have seen their growing involvement in the trials as trespassing on his territory and might have retaliated with attempts to undermine the scholarly authority of other potential experts, for instance by negatively commenting on Gerald Reitlinger's synthesis on the Final Solution as he did to Erich Schüle. Eichmüller, *Keine Generalamnestie* . . ., 363, 367.
110 LG Ulm (29.8.1958), Ks 2/57 (Litauen), in *Justiz und NS Verbrechen*, 1945–1966, vol. 15. 66, 68. It is a custom in German judgments to abbreviate the surnames of witnesses. The gist of the historical context is on pages 27–36.
111 *Ulmer Nachrichten*, 19.7.1958.
112 Pohl, *Prosecutors and Historians* . . ., 3. On the history of Central Station see an account by a long-standing director: Adalbert Rückerl, *NS-Verbrechen vor Gericht* (Heidelberg: C. F. Müller Juristischer Verlag 1982), 329–332.
113 Pohl, *Prosecutors and Historians*, 3, 10.
114 Andreas Eichmüller, "Die Strafverfolgung von NS-Verbrechen durch westdeutsche Justizbehörden seit 1945. Eine Zahlenbilanz," *Vierteljahrshefte für Zeitgeschichte* 56.4 (2008): 621–640.
115 Eichmüller, *Keine Generalamnestie* . . ., 369.
116 Erich Haberer, "History and Justice: Paradigms of the Prosecution of Nazi Crimes," *Holocaust and Genocide Studies* 19 (2005): 487–488. Cf. Norbert Frei, "Die Rückkehr des Rechts: Justiz und Zeitgeschichte nach dem Holocaust: eine Zwischenbilanz," in *1945 und Wir: Das Dritte Reich in Bewusstsein der Deutchen*, ed. Norbert Frei (München: C.H. Beck, 2005), 63–82.
117 Dieter Pohl, "Prosecutors and Historians: Holocaust Investigations and Historiography in the Federal Republic 1955–1975," in *Holocaust and Justice: Representation and Historiography of the Holocaust in Post-War Trials*, eds. David Bankier and Dan Michman (Jerusalem: Yad Vashem, in Association with Berghahn Books, 2010), 117–129. Mathew Turner. "Historians as Expert Witnesses: How do Holocaust Perpetrator Trials Shape Historiography?" *Alfred Deakin Research Institute*, Working Paper, 22 November, 2011, 3–12.

118 Adorno lectured on the topic for the first time in 1959. The final version of the essay appeared in 1963, entitled *Was bedeutet: Aufarbeitung der Vergangenheit*, here taken from Theodor Adorno, "The Meaning of Working through the Past," in *Critical Models and Catchwords* (New York: Columbia University Press, 1998), 89, 100.

119 LG Koblenz (6.12.1961) (Massenvernichtungsverbrechen durch Einsatzgruppen), Lfd.512, in C.M. Rüter en dr. D.W. de Mildt, *Justiz und NS Verbrechen . . .* (Amsterdam: University Press Amsterdam, 1970), lfd 512, vol. 523. In this trial both Krausnick and Seraphim testified again.

120 JTA. Judge Testifies on Nazi killings of 3500 Jewish Children in Minsk, November 15, 1962. http://www.jta.org/1962/11/15/archive/judge-testifies-on-nazi-killing-of-3500-jewish-children-in-minsk.

121 Detailing on the Globke affair, John P.Teschke. *Hitler's Legacy: West Germany Confronts the Aftermath of the Third Reich* (New York: Peter Lang Publishing, 1999), 173–220. Globke was show trialed in absentia in the DDR, but was to step down from the office in honorable retirement together with Adenauer in October 1963.

122 Karl Jaspers, "Für Völkermord gibt es keine Verjährung," in *Provokationen*, ed. Karl Jaspers (Pieper Verlag: München, 1969), 122–145. Fritz Bauer, "Die Verjährung der nazistischen Massenverbrechen," in *Die Humanität der Rechtsordnung. Ausgewählte Schriften* (Frankfurt am Main: Campus Verlag, 1998), 149–156.

123 Otto Kircheimer, *Political Justice* (Princeton: Princeton University Press, 1961), 336, f.49.

124 Ibid., 345.

125 Ibid., 346.

126 Hans W. Baade, "Social Science Evidence and the Federal Constitutional Court of West Germany," *The Journal of Politics* 23.3 (1961):456, 468.

127 Ibid., 457.

Bibliography

Adorno, Theodor. *Critical Models and Catchwords*. New York: Columbia University Press, 1998.

Bauer, Fritz. *Die Kriegsverbrecher vor Gericht*. Zürich and New York: Europa Verlgag, 1945.

Bauer, Fritz. *Die Humanität der Rechtsordnung*. Frankfurt and New York: Camopus, 1998.

Beloff, Max. "The Study of Contemporary History: Some further reflections", History, 30.111 (March 1945): 75-84.

Bode, Thilo. "Remer wird zur Randfigur des Prozesses," *Frankfurter Allgemeine Zeitung*, 10 March, 1952.

Bryant, Michael. *Confronting the "Good Death": Nazi Euthanasia on Trial, 1945–1953*. Boulder: University Press of Colorado, 2005.

Buchheim, Hans. "Materialsammlung zur Verfolgung der 'Zigeuner' in der NS-Zeit," Institut für Zeitgeschichte, Archivdatenbank MS 410. http://www.ifz-muenchen.de/archiv/Ms_0410_0000_0000.pdf.

Burghardt, Boris. "Vor 60 Jahren: Fritz Bauer und der Braunschweiger Remer-Prozess: Ein Strafverfahren als Vehikel der Geschichtspolitik." *Journal der Juristischen Zeitgeschichte* 2 (2012): 47–92.

Calvocoressi, Peter. *Nuremberg: The Facts, the Law and the Consequences*. New York: MacMillan, 1948.

Cohen, David. "Transitional Justice in Divided Germany after 1945," in *Retribution and Reparation in the Transition to Democracy*, ed. Jon Elster. Cambridge: Cambridge University Press, 2006.

Destler, Chester McArthur. "Some Observations on Contemporary Historical Theory." *The American Historical Review* 55.3 (1950): 503–529.

Die Wahrheit über den 20.Juli 1944. Bonn: Bundeszentrale für Heimatsdients, 1954.

Dippel, Karlhans. *Die Stellung des Sachverständingen im Strafprozess*. Heidelberg: Dekker 1986.

Dumoulin, Olivier. *Le rôle social de l'historien: De la chaire au prétoire*. Paris: Albin Michel, 2003.

Earl, Hilary. *The Nuremberg SS-Einsatzgruppen Trial, 1945–1958: Atrocity, Law and History*. Cambridge: Cambridge University Press, 2009.

Eckert, Astrid M. "The Transnational Beginnings of West German Zeitgeschichte in the 1950s." *Central European History* 40.1 (2007): 63–87.

Eichmüller, Andreas. "Die Strafverfolgung von NS-Verbrechen durch westdeutsche Justizbehörden seit 1945: Eine Zahlenbilanz." *Vierteljahrshefte fürZeitgeschichte* 56.4 2008: 621–640.

Eichmüller, Andreas. *Keine Generalamnestie: Die Strafverfolgungvon NS-Verbrechen in der frühen Bundesrepublik*. München: Oldenburg Verlag, 2013.

Erdmann, Karl Dietrich. *Toward a Global Community of Historians: The International Historical Congresses and the International Committee of Historical Sciences 1898–2000*. New York: Berghahn Books, 2005.

Frei, Norbert. *Adenauer's Germany and the Nazi Past: The Politics of Amnesty and Integration*. New York: Columbia University Press, 2002.

Frei, Norbert. *1945 un Wir: Das Dritte Reich in Bewusstsein der Deutchen*. München: C.H. Beck, 2005.

Friedländer, Ernst. "Dead Men on Trial," *The Spectator*, 28 March, 1952, 6.

Fröhlich, Claudia. "Der Braunschweiger Remer-Prozess 1952: Zum Umgang mit dem Widerstand gegen den NS-Staat in der frühen Bundesrepublik," *Beiträge zur Geschichte der nationalsozialistischen Verfolgung in Norddeutschland* 9, Heft (2005): 17–28.

Fröhlich, Clauida. *"Wider die Tabuisierung des Ungehorsams": Fritz Bauers Widerstandsbegriff und die Aufarbeitung von NS-Verbrechen*. Frankfurt: Campus Verlag, 2006.

Fröhlich, Claudia. "Der 'Ulmer Einsatzgruppenprozess' 1958: Wahrnehmung und Wirkung des ersten großen Holocaust-Prozesses," in *NS-Prozesse und Deutsche Öffentlichkeit: Besatzungszeit, frühe Bundesrepublik und DDR*, eds. Jörg Osterloh and Clemens Vollnhals. Vandenhoeck & Ruprecht, 2011, 233–261.

Gesetz zur Regelung der Rechtsverhältnisse der unter Artikel 131 des Grundgesetzes fallenden Personen, *Bundesgesetzblatt*, I, 58 (1953): 1287–1310.

Gimbel, John. "The Origins of the Institut für Zeitgeschichte: Scholarship, Politics, and the American Occupation, 1945–1949." *The American Historical Review* 70.3 (1965): 714–731.

Gutachten des Institut für Zeitgeschichte, Band I–II, München/Stuttgart: Institut für Zeitgeschichte/Deutsche Verlags-Anstalt, 1958, 1966.

Harvard Law School Library. *Nuremberg Trials Project: A Digital Document Collection. The Thirteen Nuremberg Trials*. http://nuremberg.law.harvard.edu/php/docs_swi.php?DI=1&text=nur_13tr (accessed on 21.2.2016).

Heller, Kevin Jon. *The Nuremberg Military Tribunals and the Origins of International Criminal Law*. Oxford: Oxford University Press, 2012.

Henderson, Gavin B. "A Plea for the Study of Contemporary History", History, 26.101 (June 1941): 51-55.

Hinrichsen, Kurt. "Befehlsnotstand," in *NS Prozesse*, ed. Adalbert Rückerl, Karlsruhe: Verlag C.F. Mueller, 1971, 131–161.

Höhne, Heinz. *The Order of the Death's Head: The Story of Hitler's SS*. London: Penguin, 2000.

Jackson, Robert H. "Introduction," in *Tyrrany on Trial: The Evidence at Nuremberg*, ed. W.R. Harris. New York: Barnes and Noble, 1954, i–xii.

Jarausch, Konrad. "Unasked Questions: The Controversy about Nazi Collaboration Among German Historians," in *Lessons and Legacies*, vol. VI, ed. Jeffry M. Diefendorf. Evanston, IL: Northwestern University Press, 2004, 190–208.

Jarausch, Konrad and Rüdiger Hohls. *Versäumte Fragen*. Stuttgart: Deutsche Verlags-Anstalt, 2000.

Jaspers, Karl. *Provokationen*. Pieper Verlag: München, 1969, 122–145.

Jones, Harriet, Kjell Östberg and Nico Randeraad, eds. *Contemporary History on Trial: Europe since 1989 and the Role of the Expert Historian*. Manchester: Manchester University Press, 2007.

Kempner, Robert. "The Nuremberg Trials as Sources of Recent German Political and Historical Materials." *American Political Science Review* 44.2 (1950): 447–459.

Kircheimer, Otto. *Political Justice*. Princeton: Princeton University Press, 1961.

Kraus, Herbet. "Geleitwort," in *Die Rechtprechung der Nürenberger Militaertribunale: Sammlung der Rechthesen der Urteile und gesonderten Urteilsbegruendungen der dreizehn Nuremberg Prozesse*. Bonn: Girardet & Co, 1952.

Kraus, Herbert. *Die im Braunschweiger Remerprozess erstatteten moraltheologischen und historischen Gutachten nebst Urteil*. Hamburg: Girardet Co., 1953.

Krausnick, Helmut and Hans-Heinrich Wilhelm. *Die Truppe des Weltanschaungskrieges: Die Einsatzgruppen der Sicherheitspolizei und des SD 1938–1942*. Stuttgart: Deutsche Verlags-Anstalt, 1981.

Kroesche, Heike. "Der Nurnberger Prozess gegen die Hauptkriegsverbrecher 1945/46 im Spannungsfeld von veröffentlichter Meinung und Bevölkerung," *Juristische Zeitgeschicte*, Band 16 (2008): 122–138.

Langbein, Hermann. *In Namen des deutschen Volkes*. Wien: Europa Verlag, 1960.

Langbein, Hermann. *People in Auschwitz*. Chapel Hill: University of North Carolina Press, 2004.

Linnemann, Kai Arne. *Das Erbe des Ostforschung: Zur Role Goettignens in der Gesccihtswissechaft der Nachkriegszeit*. Marburg: Tectum Verlag, 2002.

Maxwell Fyfe, David, ed. *War Crimes Trials*. London: William Hodge, 1948–1949.

Meinecke, Friedrich. *Die Deutsche Katastrophe: Betrachtungen und Erinnerungen*. Wiesbaden: Eberhard Brockhaus Verlag, 1949.

Metzler, Gabriele. *Einführung in das Studium der Zeitgeschichte*. Paderborn: Ferdinand Schöning, 2004. *Deutschland 1945–1952*. Nordenstedt: Grin Verlag, 2007.

Metzner, Timo. *Das Öffentliche Bild Vom Deutschen Widerstand Gegen Den Nationalsozialismus: Deutschland 1945–1952*. Nordenstedt: Grin Verlag, 2007.

De Mildt, Dick. *In the Name of the People: Perpetrators of Genocide in the Reflection of Their Post-War Prosecution in West Germany*. The Hague: Martinus Nijhoff, 1996.

De Mildt, Dick. *List of Historians Expert Witnesses Mentioned in the German Trial Judgments Series Justiz und NS-Verbrechen: Sammlung deutscher Starfurteile wegen nationalsozialistischer Tötungsverbrechen, 1945–2012*. Ex Post Facto: Amsterdam, 2013.

Mousnier Roland and Rene Pillorget. "Contemporary History and Historians of the Sixteenth and Seventeenth Centuries." *Journal of Contemporary History* 3.2 (1968): 93–109.

Mueller-Hill, Benno. *Tödliche Wissenschaft: Die Aussonderung von Juden, Zigeunern und Geisteskranken 1933–1945.* Hamburg: Rowohlt, 1984.

Namier, Lewis. *Conflicts: Studies in Contemporary History.* London: Macmillan, 1942.

Pendas, Devin. *Frankfurt Auschwitz Trial, 1963–1965: Genocide, History, and the Limits of the Law.* New York: Cambridge University Press, 2006.

Pohl, Dieter. *Prosecutors and Historians: Holocaust Investigations and Historiography in the Federal Republic 1955-1975*, conference paper "Justice and the Holocaust," Yad Vashem, Jerusalem in December 2006.

Pohl, Dieter. "Prosecutors and Historians: Holocaust Investigations and Historiography in the Federal Republic 1955–1975," in *Holocaust and Justice: Representation and Historiography of the Holocaust in Post-War Trials*, eds. David Bankier and Dan Michman. Jerusalem: Yad Vashem, in Association with Berghahn Books, 2010, 117–129.

Priemel, Kim C. and Alexa Stiller, eds. *Reassessing the Nuremberg Military Tribunals: Transitional Justice, Trial Narratives and Historiography.* New York: Bergham Books, 2012.

Raim, Edith. *Nazi Crimes against Jews and German Post-War Justice, The West German Judicial System during Allied Occupation (1945–1949).* Oldenbourg: De Gruyter, 2015.

Remer, Otto. *20. Juli 1944.* Hamburg-Neuhausen: Verlag Deutsche Opposition, 1951.

Ritter, Gerhard. "Gegenwärtige Lage und Zukunftsaufgaben deutscher Geschichtswissenschaft." *Historische Zeitschrift* 170 (1950): 16–18.

Rothfels, Hans. *The German Opposition to Hitler, An Appraisal.* Chicago: Henry Regnery Company, 1948.

Rothfels, Hans. *Die deutsche Opposition gegen Hitler.* Krefeld: Scherpe, 1949.

Rothfels, Hans. "Augenzeugenbericht zu den Massenvergasungen." *Vierteljahrshefte für Zeitgeschichte* 1 (1953): 177–194.

Rothfels, Hans. "Zeitgeschichte als Aufgabe." *Vierteljahrshefte für Zeitheschichte 1* (1953): 1–8.

Rückerl, Adalbert. *NS-Verbrechen vor Gericht.* Heidelberg: Müller Juristischer Verlag, 1982.

Rüter, C.M. and D.W. de Mildt. *Justiz und NS Verbrechen, Samlung Deutscher Strafurteile wegen nationalsozialistischer tötungsverbrechen.* Justiz und NS Verbrechen. Amsterdam: University Press Amsterdam, 1970.

Schmidt, Josef. "Ein Landgericht soll Geschichte schreiben: Der 20. Juli 1944 als eigentlicher Gegenstand des Beleidigungsprozesses gegen Remer in Braunschweig," *Frankfurter Allgemeine Zeitung*, 11 March, 1952.

Schulze, Winfried. "German Historiography from the 1930s to the 1950s," in *Paths of Continuity: Central European Historiography from the 1930s to the 1950s*, eds. Hartmut Lehmann and James Van Horn Melton. Cambridge: Cambridge University Press, 2003, 19–42.

Seraphim, Hans-Günther, ed. *Indices zu den zwölf Nürnberger U.S.-Militärgerichtsprozesse.* Göttingen: Institut für Völkerrecht, 1950–1956.

Serpahim, Hans-Günther. "Quellen zur Erforschung des Dritten Reiches." *Politisches Archiv* 17 (1950): 3307–3310.

Seraphim, Hans-Günther. "*Die Erschließung der Nürnberger Prozeßakten.*" *Der Archivar* 28 (1975): 417–422.

Seraphim, Hans-Günther and Hans Kruse. *Mensch und Staat in Recht und Geschichte: Festschrift fur Herbert Kraus*. Kitzingen/Main: Holzner-Verlag, 1954.

Taylor, Telford. Final Report to the Secretary of the Army on the Nuremberg War Crimes Trials Under Control Council Law No. 19. Washington, D.C.: s.n., 1949.

Taylor, Telford. "The Nuremberg Trials," in *Perspectives on the Nuremberg Trial*, ed. Guénaël Mettraux. Oxford: Oxford University Press, 2008.

Teschke, John P. *Hitler's Legacy: West Germany Confronts the Aftermath of the Third Reich*. New York: Peter Lang Publishing, 1999.

Tobin, Patrick. *No Country for Old Fighters, Postwar Germany and the Origins of the Ulm Einsatzkommando Trial*. MA Thesis, Chapel Hill: University of North Carolina, 2009.

Tobin, Patrick. *Crossroads at Ulm: Postwar Germany and the 1958 Ulm Einsatzkommandotrial*. PhD Dissertation, Chapel Hill: University of North Carolina, 2013.

Trevor-Roper, Hugh. *The Last Days of Hitler*. London: Pan Books, 2002.

Trials of War Criminals before the Nuernberg Military Tribunals Under Control Council Law No. 10. Washington: United States Government Printing Office, 1950.

Turner, Mathew. "Historians as Expert Witnesses: How do Holocaust Perpetrator Trials Shape Historiography?" in *Alfred Deakin Research Institute*, Working Paper 22, November 2011, 3–12.

Ulmer Nachrichten, 19 July, 1958.

Vogel, Rolf, ed. *Ein Weg auis der Vergangenheit: Eine Dokumentation zur Verjährung und zu den NS-Prozessen*. Frankfurt: Ullstein Verlag, 1969.

Vogelsang, Thilo. "Die Zeitgeschichte und ihre Hilfsmittel." *Vierteljahrshefte für Zeitgeschichte* 3 (1955): 211–222.

Völkerrechtliche Forschung—25 Jahre Institut für Völkerrecht der Universität Göttingen 1930–1955. Göttingen: Institut für Völkerrecht, 1955.

Watt, Donald Cameron, ed. *Contemporary History in Europe*. London: George Allen and Unwin, 1969.

Weinberg, Gerhard L. "Setting and Significance of the Nuremberg Tribunal," in *Nazi Crimes and the Law*, eds. Nathan Stoltzfus and Henry Friedlander. German Historical Institute: Washington, 2008.

Wittmann, Rebecca. *Beyond Justice: The Auschwitz Trial*. Cambridge: Harvard University Press, 2005.

Wojak, Irmtrud. *Fritz Bauer 1903–1968: Eine Biographie*. München: C.H. Beck, 2009.

4 An Adversarial Paradigm Emerges
Historical Forensics and Racial Discrimination

The path that brought historians to courtrooms on the other side of the Atlantic was no less complicated. Significantly different in outlook, it did ride on the same postwar wave, sharing a similar motivation—to account for historical injustices based on racial prejudice. Attempts to put such a bad past on trial were met with similarly stiff resistance, influenced by the adversarial character of the common law system. American legal scholar Ben Palmer, addressing the American Bar Association in 1946, stated that "lawyers and historians face common problems: The analysis of documents and of evidence, the choice and arrangements of material to make a convincing case. The lawyer's purpose is frankly partisan; the historian's professedly impartial." However, his address, which was otherwise praise to the incompatibility between history and law, also contained an almost prophetic corollary: "And yet there is a ceaseless drift as unperceived without history as the movements of the stars to the naked eye. And we cannot contribute, however humbly, to that vision without which the people perish unless we are aware of the drift and, if possible, can determine its direction. But alas, many of us (. . .) are oblivious of the distant drum."[1] The distant drum that undermined the incompatibility theory in the U.S. was the issue of racially motivated discrimination.

Solving an "American Dilemma": Desegregation between Law and Social Science

At the time of Palmer's writing, over half a million Black soldiers served in the U.S. military in a global war against the blatantly racist regimes of the Axis.[2] They were to return home, where in many a state they were treated as second-class citizens. Segregation was cutting deep into every aspect of everyday life of the Southern states:

> The state of Texas did not allow interracial boxing matches. Florida did not permit white and black students to use the same editions of some textbooks. In Arkansas, white and black voters could not enter a polling place in the company of one another. North Carolina required racially

> separate washrooms in its factories. South Carolina required them in cotton mills. Four states required them in their mines. In six states, white and black prisoners could not be chained together. In seven states, tuberculosis patients were separated by race. In eight states, parks, playgrounds, bathing and fishing facilities, amusement parks, racetracks, pool halls, circuses, theaters and public halls were all segregated. Ten states required separate waiting rooms for bus and train travelers. Eleven states required Negro passengers to ride in the back of the buses and streetcars. Eleven states operated separate schools for blind. Fourteen states segregated railroad passengers on trains within their borders. Fourteen states segregated mental patients. Seventeen states required segregation of public schools, four others permitted the practice if the local communities wished it, and in the District of Columbia the custom has prevailed for nearly ninety years.[3]

It took a global shift induced by the Second World War to provide an adequate momentum for change, which had been on the agenda for decades. Black Americans were drafted into the military alongside the whites, they were dying alongside the whites, and they could rightfully expect to be treated like whites. Not coincidentally, the first attempts at desegregation started in the armed forces in the immediate postwar period, with the executive branch of government taking the lead during the presidency of Harry S. Truman.[4] His administration also addressed the issue in wider context by establishing a Committee on Civil Rights in 1946.[5] Its final report framed segregation both as a burning moral issue and a dire economic problem. With the onset of the Cold War, it was also seen as an international embarrassment, best expressed by the Secretary of the State, Dean Acheson: "The existence of discrimination against minority groups in this country has an adverse effect on our relations with other countries."[6] However, translating these recommendations into comprehensive federal legislation proved difficult, in the light of stiff resistance from the Southern states and their representatives. This cleavage presented a fruitful field for activism, drawing attention to paradoxes: during the war, in some Southern states, German prisoners of war were allowed in pubs from which Black people were barred. Meanwhile, the American Red Cross was still segregating the blood of Black and white people, in order not to mix it through transfusions. Dubbing the war aim as "Double V"—victory over racism abroad and home—the National Association for the Advancement of Colored People (NAACP) gave this campaign a nationwide profile.[7]

Still, the NAACP remained focused on its prime goal—it was challenging discriminatory legislation, and increasingly focusing on the issue of public schooling. Education was one of the strongholds of Southern segregation, grounded in the "separate but equal" doctrine, ensuring that the states provided for equality of segregated schooling.[8] However, reality was far from it—Black teachers were generally receiving half the salaries of their white colleagues; expenditures on Black children in South Carolina, for example, were four times less than on white children; and schools for Black children were not only fewer, but also understaffed, underfurnished, and overcrowded, claimed the NAACP, which is why its Legal Defense and Education Fund under Thurgood Marshall, its leading strategist, particularly stimulated the filing of claims in this area.[9]

How to substantiate these cases? Among others, Thurgood Marshall opted for a legal avenue through which the results of scholarly research could be conveyed to the courts—expert witnessing. Tellingly, one of the first disciplines that came to his mind was history. "In 1947 Thurgood Marshall of the NAACP Legal Defense Fund asked me to assist him in a case that had arisen in Kentucky," remembered John Hope Franklin (1915–2009), Harvard graduate and a history professor at Howard University, author of the widely acclaimed book *From Slavery to Freedom* (1947). The case had to do with a colleague historian: "Lyman Johnson, a history teacher in the public schools of Louisville, had applied to pursue graduate studies at the University of Kentucky. He was denied admission (. . .) so Marshall sued the University of Kentucky, demanding Johnson's admission. In preparing his argument, Marshall asked me to make a study of the two institutions, comparing the library facilities, the offerings in the respective departments of history, and the qualifications of the teaching personnel. I was only too happy to do so."[10] Black himself, living and working in Washington, D.C., Franklin knew all too well what segregation was: "While working at the Library of Congress, one of my closest friends, a white historian, came by my study room one Friday afternoon and asked me to lunch with him the following day. I reminded him that since the following day would be a Saturday, the Supreme Court restaurant would be closed, and there was no other place in the vicinity where we could eat together."[11] Therefore he conducted the analysis with both academic rigor and activist zeal. However, the judge made a summary ruling in Johnson's favor. "Everyone was delighted with the verdict except, perhaps, me, who had worked assiduously to make the case for Johnson and wished, more than anything else, to testify against the university."[12] Marshall's deputy, Robert Carter, wrote to him: "I can't say that I am sorry that we didn't have to use your testimony, but I must confess that there is a tinge of regret that we were not permitted to parade you in the courtroom. However, we may have another chance on some other occasion." Franklin responded: "If the opportunity arises again, I shall be pleased to do whatever I can to aid in your significant work."[13]

Actually, there was no shortage of such opportunities. Successes in higher education cases encouraged the NAACP to approach the true crux of the matter—segregation in public primary and secondary education. It supported such cases in Kansas, Delaware, the District of Columbia, Virginia, and South Carolina. These cases featured unprecedented mobilization of social scientists, triggering expert reports, collective briefs, and individual testimonies compiled by academics, social scientists, psychologists, and educationalists on the disastrous effects of the segregated educational system upon the self-esteem of young Black Americans.[14] By the end of the Second World War, NAACP litigants could use "the benefit of a half-century evolution in the social sciences that declared segregation to be both a cause and a result of the victimization of black America."[15] Already, Ashley Montagu's voluminous debunking of racial theory, *Man's Most Dangerous Myth* (1942), and Gunnar Myrdal's book *An American Dilemma* (1944), which clearly outlined the disastrous effects of the subordinated status of the Black people in the U.S., particularly in the area of education, were advocating legal remedies: "The whole system of discrimination in education in the South is not only tremendously harmful to the Negroes, but it is flagrantly illegal, and can easily be so proven in the courts."[16] "Race" became a suspect word, both as a political concept and as an analytical tool, and its debunking became part of the scholarly mainstream. Such an agenda was strongly promoted in UNESCO's statement "The Race Question," signed by authorities such as Claude Levi-Strauss, Morris Ginsberg, Ashley Montagu, Franklin Frazier, Otto Klineberg, and others. The statement called for "[dropping] the term 'race' altogether and [speaking] of ethnic groups."[17] This new creed was promoted in the U.S. by a generation of social scientists prone to social action and ready to organize to such an end: the Society for the Psychological Study of Social Issues (SPSSI), formed in 1936; the Commission on Community Interrelations (CCI), formed in 1944 by the American Jewish Congress, as well as the Commission on Law and Social Action (CLSA), joined ranks and started preparing surveys among scholars, solidifying the consensus on the detrimental effects of segregation and using them as amicus curiae briefs in related trials.[18]

Meanwhile, the *Briggs* v. *Elliott* case from Clarendon County in South Carolina featured educationalists like Matthew Whitehead and Ellis Knox of Howard University, Harold McNally of Teacher's College, Columbia, and social psychologists Kenneth and Mamie Clark of City College of New York, whose experiments with dolls, children, and the interiorization of racist attitudes aroused considerable interest and attracted Marshall's deputy Robert Carter; but they still were not persuasive enough for the judges to reach a decision favoring desegregation.[19] Even more experts appeared in Kansas, in the case of Oliver Brown and alia v. Board of Education of Topeka. Brown was the father of a Black girl, Linda, who was unable to enroll in the public school just around the corner, and was forced to attend an all-Black school over a mile away. The case was filed by the NAACP with the District Court of Kansas on February 28, 1951. In line with the general strategy, Robert Carter attempted to mobilize many reputed experts from the field of the social sciences. Some of the leading figures, such as Harvard Professor Gordon Allport, head of the American Psychological Association, or Otto Klineberg, the Canadian psychologist from Columbia who debunked the racial bias of standard IQ tests and co-coauthored the

UNESCO statement, refused to testify—sympathetic to the cause, they were nonetheless unable to act on short notice.[20] Less known but more willing scholars agreed and ultimately appeared as experts in front of the Kansas court. The bellicose and antagonistic nature of the cross-examination was not deprived of entertaining moments accompanying this introduction of the social sciences into the courtroom. For instance, Professor Hugh Speer of the Department of Education at the University of Kansas City was forced to explain to the judges that "in professional circles we have a term called the great 'gestalt' which means the sum is greater than the whole," causing Judge Mellot's reaction:

Judge Mellot: "What was that word?"
The witness: (spelling) "G-e-s-t-a-l-t."[21]

It is interesting that, although the NAACP did not consider engaging historians as experts, history did appear in the courtroom during the cross-examination of Horace English, professor of psychology at the Ohio State University:

Q: You are familiar, of course, as an educator, with the experience that was had back in the reconstruction days, sometimes referred to as the carpet-bagger days in the south. (. . .)
A: I am not here as an expert on history, but I read history that way, yes.
Q: Surely. Don't you realize that the experience of that period was that they had a tremendous amount of trouble, tremendous amount of emotional outburst and that it caused 'a great deal of strife between the races' and didn't work at all.
A: Well, if the Court wants a layman's opinion on history, I will answer that question to the best of my knowledge as a layman on history; I am not here as a historian.

Judge Huxman: It seems to me the question is going far afield.[22]

However, the impact of social scientists on the Justices in the first instance was all but decisive. Judges were exasperated with the succession of experts:

Judge Mellott: You have had several (. . .) so-called expert testimony; how many will there be?
Mr. Greenberg: We have three or four more, Your Honor, and they are all different.
Judge Huxman: Well, now, we are not disposed to be critical, but it's my opinion from having listened to this testimony, the last four witnesses—that it's all cumulative. I can see no difference, substantial difference, between any of the testimony of the last three or four witnesses.[23]

On August 3, 1951 the District Court ruled in favor of the Board of Education, claiming that although convinced that segregation in public education has a detrimental effect upon Black children, the schooling system of Topeka was satisfying the "separate but equal" standard set by the U.S. Supreme Court in 1896, and that therefore neither the board nor the state were in constitutional violation, as in the system of separate schools "there is no willful, intentional or material discrimination."[24]

This standard was most staunchly defended in Virginia, in *Davis v. County School Board of Prince Edward County*, where expert witnesses were subjected to hostile cross-examinations about their own racial backgrounds by the opposing attorney.[25] This case also featured social scientists recruited as experts on the other side. As Virginian psychiatrists expressed a concern that the local population was not ready for the change desegregation would bring, Henry E. Garrett (1904–1973), former president of the American Psychological Association and the head of the Psychology Department at Columbia University, who was on Kenneth Clark's PhD committee, also testified for the state. This result was predictable: "The expert witnesses, the court declared, canceled each other out—both sides offered equally cogent arguments."[26] On the other hand, in a court in Delaware, the *Gebhard v. Belton* case featured fourteen expert witnesses, most prominently Otto Klineberg, a Canadian psychologist who taught social psychology at Columbia University. Klineberg convinced the courts that public schooling in the state did not adhere to the principle, but the court could not and would not challenge the constitutionality of the "separate but equal" principle expressed in the Plessy vs. Ferguson case.

Losing in four out of five states, the NAACP sponsored and coordinated the plaintiffs' appeal on all five judgments to the Supreme Court of the United States. Cases were merged and went down in history as Oliver Brown, et al. v. Board of Education of Topeka, et al., or simply as *Brown v. Board*. The claim binding the cases was that the leading doctrine in the educational systems of the American Southern states, condensed in the phrase "separate but equal," was leading to segregation and the de facto unequal treatment of Black children, influencing their self-esteem and keeping them at the margins of society; therefore, they argued, it was in breach of the Fourteenth Amendment of the U.S. Constitution from 1868, which secured that "no state shall (. . .) deny to any person (. . .) the equal protection of the laws." Hence the appellees went in front of the Supreme Court with a question: "Does the segregation of children in public schools solely on the basis of race deprive the minority children of equal protection under the laws guaranteed by the Fourteenth Amendment?"[27]

The case did not fall on deaf ears in the Supreme Court. For quite some time after the Second World War it had been gathering momentum to hear a case regarding segregation. Some of the Supreme Court Justices, like Hugo Black, privately referred to segregation as "Hitler's creed."[28] Justice Robert Jackson was of a similar mind. During the negotiations that had led to the foundation of the International Military Tribunal, Justice Robert Jackson was visibly embarrassed with this state of affairs: "We have some regrettable circumstances at times in our own country in which minorities are unfairly treated," he said, thinking of segregation and realizing that while it existed, the U.S. would be vulnerable to accusations of maintaining double standards.[29] One can only assume what his thoughts were in the IMT courtroom during the opening address of his French colleague, Francois de Menthon, who spoke about "the original sin of National Socialism from which all crimes spring, this monstrous doctrine of racism."[30] Returning from Nuremberg to resume his post in the Supreme Court, Jackson wrote to a friend: "You and I have seen the terrible consequences of racial hatred in Germany. We can have no sympathy for racial conceits which underlie segregation policies."[31]

However, the case was not about the morality of segregation in public schooling, but of its constitutionality. Before the case was initially argued in front of the Supreme Court the judges had an opportunity to scrutinize the briefs submitted by the parties. The NAACP legal team continued to rely heavily on the evidence provided by social scientists, presented to the Supreme Court in an annex to the brief condensed by Kenneth Clark, Stuart Cook, and Isidor Chein and undersigned by thirty-two leading social science experts.[32] The states, represented by skillful attorneys, the most prominent being John W. Davis, former Democrat candidate for the presidency, remained unimpressed with such evidence: "I think I have never read

Figure 4.1 U.S. Supreme Court Justice Robert Jackson as Chief Prosecutor in Nuremberg

a drearier lot of testimony than that furnished by the so-called educational and psychological experts," concluded Davis. His brief stated that "there is a large body of respectable expert opinion to the effect that separate schools, particularly in the South, are in the best interest of children of both races as well as of the community at large."[33] However, Davis did not even bother to specify further, determined to argue primarily for the constitutionality of separate public education under the "separate but equal" doctrine, nicknamed the South's Magna Carta.

This strategy seemed more promising than one would have imagined. Insofar as the relation between Brown and the Fourteenth Amendment and the issue of segregation was concerned, even Justice Jackson could only lament: "Nothing in the text says it's unconstitutional. Nothing in the opinions of the courts that says it's unconstitutional. Nothing in the history of the 14th amendment (. . .) on the basis of precedent segregation is ok (. . .) Marshall's brief starts and ends in sociology."[34] Nonetheless, the case was heard on December 9, 1952 in front of the nine judges of the Supreme Court, presided by Fred Vinson. During this oral argument, the parties restated their basic claims.[35] The Justices were inquisitive but cryptic, and when the court adjourned on December 11, there were no hints on their standpoints.

Fearing that divided opinions could aggravate the already heated atmosphere, in June 1953 the Supreme Court accepted the proposal of Justice Felix Frankfurter to ask for additional evidence from the parties. His reasoning was blunt: "However passionately any of us may hold egalitarian views, however fiercely any of us may believe that such a policy of segregation as undoubtedly expresses the tenacious convictions of the Southern States is both unjust and shortsighted, he travels outside his judicial authority if for this private reason alone he declares unconstitutional policy of segregation."[36] On June 8 the Supreme Court therefore asked the parties in litigation to reargue the cases by answering "the following questions insofar as they are relevant to the respective cases: "What evidence is there that the Congress which submitted and the state legislatures and conventions which ratified the Fourteenth Amendment contemplated or did not contemplate, understood or did not understand, that it would abolish segregation in public schools?" The Justices also wanted to hear the opinions on whether it was "within the judicial power, in construing the Amendment, to abolish segregation in the public schools."[37] Consequently, both sides were asked to take a close look at the history of the Fourteenth Amendment (1868), discern the intent of its creators, draw the conclusions relevant for their case, and present them to the Supreme Court by the end of 1953.

Brown and History in the U.S. Supreme Court and Outside

This request came unexpected, as historical interpretation of intent was typically seen as the prerogative of the court. "Constitutional review fora have a tendency to rely on references to history and traditions," notes Renara Uitz;

the U.S. Supreme Court had the longest record of decisions grounded in the quest for the original meaning of constitutional texts through a historical analysis of the intent of its creators.[38] Justice Harold H. Burton observed that he readily went back to colonial times in a quest for historical facts of relevance to the case: "The Justices of the Supreme Court do take judicial notice of historical facts. We usually go back to original sources for our information rather than looking into secondary historical writings."[39] Surely, some of the Justices, like Robert Jackson, doubted this method. He was "not confident that the effort of Justices to restate the early law as it appeared to the forefathers is either complete or accurate. Judges often are not thorough or objective historians."[40] On the other pole was Justice Felix Frankfurter, "undoubtedly the most history-minded Justice ever to sit on the Supreme Court."[41] Although it remained unclear why the Justices felt the need to outsource the historical investigation, the parties had many reasons to take their request very seriously.

There were several possible venues for providing an answer. Senior legal advisors to the NAACP (Milton Konvitz, William Robert Ming, John Frank) differed over the ways to provide this historical input. "Robert Ming (. . .) argued forcibly that the particularistic historical evidence favorable to the NAACP case was either so scanty or so unconvincing that sound strategy called for the abandonment of any attempt to make an argument based on the framers' immediate historical intent. Dangerous as it was, he said, the Court's request ought to be by-passed and the case argued in terms of the overall spirit of humanitarianism, racial equalitarianism and social idealism which had dominated the rise of the abolitionist movement." However, the others were mostly of the opinion noted, that such approach would "run the risk of incurring the Court's direct censure and loss of the case."[42] Consequently, a decision was reached to compose a detailed brief, not only based on the sources from the mid-nineteenth century, but also consulting secondary historical literature. Such approach was much in line with a famed case, *Communist party v. Commonwealth*, argued in 1951 in front of the High Court of Australia, where Judge Dixon stated that "courts may use the general facts of history as ascertained or ascertainable from the accepted writings of serious historians."[43] However, the problem was that the established historical works of the interwar period were hardly advancing their case. Indeed, as early as 1935, W.E.B. Du Bois, one of the founders of the NAACP, wrote off much of such literature as supremacist "propagation of history," warning that "the treatment of the period of Reconstruction reflects small credit upon American historians as scientists. We have too often a deliberate attempt so to change the facts of history that the story will make pleasant reading for Americans."[44] Against such background, the Legal Defense Fund did not have much choice—the decision was made to turn to historians to produce new material. There was no evidence that the NAACP leadership heard for historians in the Dreyfus case or the appearance of historians in the German courts, not even for Fritz

Bauer's experiments in the Remer case. However, in the light of successful forensic usage of social science evidence, the NAACP did not hesitate to call upon historians of the postwar generation ready to challenge the orthodoxy.

Initially, NAACP lawyers were pragmatic. Their thinking was expressed bluntly by Robert Carter: "We wanted historians to look at the whole thing from the perspective of the blacks and their aspirations, not from some cloud. All history is a distortion of sorts, depending on the historian's myopia and precepts."[45] Hence they started with a historian versed in the topic of emancipation of slaves, familiar with the period of Reconstruction and sympathetic to the case—John Hope Franklin: "I received a telephone call from Thurgood Marshall inquiring about my plans for the autumn of 1953. I responded that I would be returning to the only regular job that I had, the one at Howard University. He told me that I would be also working for him, and if I did not agree to do so, he would regret the fate that the gods would dispense on me. I replied that under the circumstances there was nothing I could do but bow to his command."[46] Further, encouraged by the successes of the NAACP in mobilizing social scientists, Marshall decided to engage in similar brinkmanship. To that end, he appointed John A. Davis, professor of political science from Lincoln University, to coordinate an academic research task force on this subject. At first, Davis was quite optimistic. The president of his own Lincoln University, famed historian of education Horace Mann Bond, readily agreed. He concluded that on the basis of the process of Congressional readmission of the Southern states, "not a single one was admitted, or readmitted, to the union with any phrase in the constitution (. . .) that sanctioned segregation, or mentioned race, in connection with the public education system. (. . .) What better proof do you want of the intent of the 39th Congress?"[47]

Building on this assumption, Davis decided to hit straight to the top. In the postwar period the implicit racism that was informing the work of many interwar historians was gradually sidetracked by the historiography of liberal consensus, so he contacted his former mentor, famous historian Henry Steely Commager, hoping he might take the lead. However, in a striking parallel with the case of Hans Rothfels in the Remer trial, Commager, although sympathetic to the cause, refused. "The framers of the amendment did not, so far as we know, intend that it should be used to end segregation in schools." Therefore, Commager suggested: "I strongly urge that you consider dropping this particular argument, as I think it tends to weaken your case."[48] Finding out through further consultations that this was a mainstream opinion among historians, Jack Greenberg of the NAACP felt that "the rejection of our position was a real blow—it put us right down on the ground."[49]

Overcoming disappointment, the NAACP kept searching for scholars willing to support their position. "The Court order immediately produced a wild scramble on both sides for the services of constitutional historians, Reconstruction scholars, experts on public law and so on. The questions the Court had asked were not the kind that lawyers ordinarily deal with, and on the face of them, the NAACP lawyers confessed themselves, to the self-satisfied amusement of a number of historians and political scientists, to be substantially helpless."[50] On the advice of influential historian of Reconstruction Howard Beally, Davis contacted his former student, C. Vann Woodward of Johns Hopkins University, author of the highly praised *Origins of the New South 1877–1913;* Woodward conditioned his acceptance: "I should feel constrained by the limitations of my craft (. . .). I would stick to what happened and account for it as intelligently as I could (. . .). You see, I do not want to be in a position of delivering a gratuitous history lecture to the Court. And at the same time I do not want to get out of my role as historian." The overall coordinator, Davis was assuring him: "Your conclusions are your own. If they do not help our side of the case, in all probability the lawyers will not use them. If they do help our argument, the present plan is to include them in the overall summary argument and to file the whole work as a brief in the appendix. No matter what happens, your work will be of real educational value to the men who must argue before the court."[51] Similar scruples were expressed by a constitutional historian from Wayne State University, Alfred Kelly, who also joined a team, having been contacted directly by Marshall by letter in early July 1953.[52] To this core group (Franklin, Woodward, Kelly, Bond) were added other contributors, such as Howard Jay Graham, bibliographer of Los Angeles County Law Library, and Jacobus ten Broek, professor of political science from Berkeley. Rayford Logan of Howard University and Herbert Gutman of the University of Rochester joined, as well as a number of social scientists (Clark, Klineberg, William Penrose) already familiar with the case. By mid-July 1953, Thurgood Marshall was able to report to the NAACP Board of Directors that his team had found "social scientists and political scientists, as well as lawyers, who are willing to work through the summer (. . .). We have been fortunate enough," he bragged, "in getting men and women who are absolutely tops in their respective fields to work with us."[53] In honesty, he was still making last-minute calls. Graham, for example, was contacted exactly around that time: "On June 16, 1953, I received a telegram from Mr. Thurgood Marshall (. . .). Would I join in preparation of working papers on the history and adoption of the Fourteenth Amendment for use of counsel engaged in the requested rebriefings? (. . .) A paper was needed which would (. . .) relate the drafts and the Amendment to the broader streams of constitutional theory and history."[54]

Even if Marshall was overstating the readiness of the team, at least a number of historians were on board. Their activity was under the overall coordination of Davis, within a plan he presented to Marshall in early September. The plan was

> to engage specialists (. . .) to write specific monographs (. . .) to develop material which will be of aid in preparing the final briefs. This kind of

> work is tedious, expensive and often unrewarding (. . .). It is a very fruitless thing to attempt to determine the intent of politicians (. . .) for they seldom say what they intend. Hence the wider use of historian's discipline can explain much of the politician's behavior. (. . .) The method for developing this research was to set a general course (. . .) in the hope that their collective efforts will result in a total argument. A conference of outstanding scholars has been called for September 26–8 to test and criticize the results of the research.[55]

In anticipation of the conference, the bulk of the work was conducted in late summer, as lawyers and historians learned about each other's methodological approaches and disciplinary requirements. "Thurgood and his colleagues turned to historians to assist them in finding the answers," remembered Franklin. "This was an exciting experience for the nonlegal scholars, as they saw how eager the legal luminaries were to hear what they had to say."[56] Robert Carter, Marshall's deputy, recollected this learning experience: "We had worked during the summer on the issues involved and had engaged educators, historians, and political and social scientists to undertake research on specific issues and to provide us with monographs setting forth their conclusions."[57] Howard Jay Graham wrote a lengthy ninety-eight-page paper on the overall purpose of the Thirteenth and Fourteenth Amendments, covering the "broad perspective of anti-slavery movement of which they were the consummation," and Van Woodward also wrote a twenty-seven-page paper on the pace and ultimate failure of the Reconstruction, "The Background of the Abandonment of Reconstruction."[58] Meanwhile, Horace Mann Bond coordinated a Committee for Historical Development (including John Frank, Mabel Smyth, and Roel Gallagher), which was wrestling with a particularly thorny issue—how could it be that the same Congress that had framed the Fourteenth Amendment had also allocated funding for segregated schools in the very District of Columbia?[59] As papers started coming in, it became apparent that both the evidence and its possible interpretations were ambiguous and inconclusive. Therefore, the work on historical input was soon transformed into a classical model of a scholarly workshop, as evidenced by John Hope Franklin:

> At Thurgood's request I wrote a paper on a history of segregation in the public schools. I read it to him and his colleagues at one of our sessions. It was called "Jim Crow Goes to School: The Genesis of Legal Segregation in Southern Schools," and was later published in South Atlantic Quarterly. The piece elicited many comments from the historians and the lawyers, who said that they could use some of my findings in the brief they were preparing. The historians added to my findings by citing from their own research, while the lawyers seemed to be in the awe of what we were able to dig up. In the discussions that followed the reading of my paper and in other discussions, one of them would say: "Let's

> hear what Vann has to say," while another would ask "Al" Kelly, the great constitutional historian, what he thought of my findings. (. . .) As for me—and I suspect the same was true for the other scholars—it was exhilarating.[60]

Franklin was also "impressed with the way in which our work was appreciated by the lawyers. They spoke with precision about what transpired in the House of Representatives (. . .). They were remarkably familiar with what transpired in both houses of the Congress from day to day (. . .). The lawyers seemed to have no difficulty in juxtaposing past with the present, because they had become legal historians. I could not have asked for a greater transformation. (. . .) I was quite confident that they would have no difficulty in presenting their arguments, even the historical arguments, to the United States Supreme Court."[61] Carter was equally satisfied with the cooperation, as "a formidable group of the most brilliant scholars in their respective fields gathered in New York on September 14, and most did not leave until the end. They included John Hope Franklin, Rayford Logan, C. Vann Woodward, and Alfred Kelly (. . .). At the meeting scholars who had undertaken specific assignments for us presented their papers to the group. Suggestions and possible alternative approaches were proposed. We adhered to a time limit for discussion of each paper. The lawyers, particularly those scheduled to argue, were getting a valuable preparatory education. Beginning the next day and for several days thereafter we met in smaller groups for intense discussion centered on each of the presentations at the plenary session."[62] Jack Greenberg had an impression that "our massive effort culminated in a meeting of more than one hundred participants at the Overseas Press Club on West Fortieth Street in September. It divided into seminars to consider all the major problems and made recommendation for the final product."[63]

The last stage was the actual production of the brief. Its principal drafter, Alfred Kelly, described the thorny process:

> I left the September conference expecting to have no more to do with the segregation cases beyond what I might read in the newspapers. Ten days later, early in October, however, I was supposed to receive a phone call from Thurgood Marshall. (. . .) My help, he said with careful flattery, was needed very badly on the brief. My vanity thus touched to the quick, I came (. . .) to sit down and hammer out a draft of a brief for the Supreme Court. To this end he locked us up, so to speak, in an isolated suite of offices (. . .). Ming and I spent the next three days there, with no one present but a stenographer, walking up and down, dictating, arguing, and orating to one another. The brief drafting was mostly Ming and comparatively little Kelly, in the first place Ming knew how to draft a brief and I didn't. (. . .) At the end of three days we had a brief. Ming said it would do (. . .). But early in November, Marshall called

> me, informed me (. . .) to come down to New York for another five days. (. . .) we were joined by John Frank of the Yale Law School (. . .) Marshall informed the two of us that Ming's draft was fine as far as it went, but that it didn't go far enough (. . .) to get involved in specific historical detail. (. . .) Thurgood said: "and if I try this approach, those fellows will shoot me down in flames."[64]

Jack Greenberg describes these final touches: "In October, Thurgood, Bob, Connie, Spotts, Lou Redding, Bob Ming, and I met with Alfred Kelly over a period of five days to struggle with the history, which concluded in a drafting session between Ming and Kelly. Finally, that draft was redone in November by Kelly and John Frank. Our battle with history was finished and nothing could be gained by rehearsing the contending positions."[65] Robert Carter was also satisfied: "This had been for me, and I believe for most of the staff, one of the most exhilarating intellectual experiences we ever had. As a result, our brief was an outstanding document (. . .) the first part of the brief, written by me; the rest of the brief, written by Thurgood and Spottswood."[66]

Historians themselves had mixed feelings when confronted with the brief. "It was in early November that the draft of the Legal Defense Fund's brief began to take shape. We were all invited to comment on it, to offer suggestions, corrections, criticisms, or whatever observations came to mind. It was at this point that the tables were turned. While a few weeks earlier we historians had regarded ourselves as authorities on Reconstruction and the legislative history of the Fourteenth Amendment, we were now awed by the very appearance of the brief, its formality, its legalistic wording, and its deference to the Court," wrote Franklin.[67] Although among the principle drafters, Alfred Kelly was concerned with the final product of the collective work, which he regarded as a "law-office history. It presented, indeed, a great deal of perfectly valid constitutional history. But it also manipulated history in the best tradition of American advocacy, carefully marshaling every possible scrap of evidence in favor of the desired interpretation and just as carefully doctoring all the evidence on the contrary, either by suppressing it when that seemed plausible, or by distorting it when suppression was not possible. The brief submitted for the respondent Southern school boards was no less law-office history. It, too doctored, distorted, twisted, and suppressed historical evidence in as competent a fashion as did the NAACP." Kelly adds: "I did not understand the relationship between advocacy and history at that point. I was trying to be both advocate and historian within the same paper."[68] Jack Greenberg agreed: "He seemed to be unaware of the nature of legal advocacy, in which the other side is given both the opportunity and responsibility for presenting the conflicting view, and for pointing out errors, omissions, and misinterpretations, if any, in the first side's presentation."[69] Other historians were not so concerned. Howard Graham concluded that " 'law office history' of course, early became a pejorative term, but only for excess, and excess was not the problem here. 'Law office history' as such can educate and liberate as well as direct and constrain. And lately it has."[70]

The brief of the NAACP was a massive 256-page-long document of complex structure and equally complex authorship.[71] It was comprised of three parts. The first one tracked a history of the application of the Fourteenth Amendment. It clearly rested on papers written by John Hope Franklin and C. Vann Woodward. The second part, edited predominantly by Kelly with wide usage of the work of Howard Graham, Bond, and Jacobus ten Broek, dealt with the original intent of the framers of the Amendment, and the third part contained recommendations to the court on the remedies, devised by Spotswood Robinson. The final draft was composed by Franklin, Ming and Kelly, and then redrafted by Kelly and the legal team of the NAACP, which had a final say in its composition. Condensing the argument in a paragraph, the brief stated:

> The evidence, both in Congress and in legislatures of the ratifying states, reflects the substantial intent of the Amendment's proponents and the substantial understanding of its opponents that the Fourteenth Amendment would, on its own force, proscribe all forms of state-imposed racial distinction, thus necessarily including all racial segregation in public education. The Fourteenth Amendment was actually a culmination of the determined efforts of the Radical Republican majority in Congress to incorporate into our fundamental law the well-defined equalitarian principle of complete equality for all without regard to race or color. The debates in the 39th Congress and succeeding Congresses clearly reveal the intentions that the Fourteenth Amendment would work a revolutionary change in our state-federal relationship by denying to the states the power to distinguish on the basis of race.[72]

Hence, when the Supreme Court reconvened on December 7, 1953, the Justices were confronted with sets of historical findings that diverged completely. On the first hearing, summarizing the historical evidence for the NAACP, attorney Spotswood Robinson argued that "the historical evidence which we submit demonstrates that the Congress that submitted it and the legislatures and conventions that ratified the Fourteenth Amendment contemplated and understood that it would abolish segregation in public schools."[73] He noted "considerable evidence of the intention of the framers to broadly provide for the complete legal equality of all men, irrespective of race" and "abundant evidence demonstrating that radical Republicans of the 39th Congress desired and intended that the Fourteenth Amendment would affect both the invalidation of the existing Black Codes and any and all future attempts to impose governmental caste distinctions predicated upon race."[74] The NAACP was arguing a loose, overall intent of the legislators to end the segregation, prompring Justice Frankfurter to ask about "individual utterances of this, that or other congressman or senator?"[75] Robinson had no choice but to repeat his conclusion: "We do not claim that every state in the Union understood the Fourteenth Amendment as abolishing school segregation. But we do submit that, considering the evidence overall, there was substantial understanding (. . .) that the Fourteenth Amendment would have the scope that we attribute to it, and that consequently school segregation laws would be invalidated."[76]

This argument was met head on by John Davis, representative for the appellees, who presented the argument that "the overwhelming preponderance of the evidence demonstrates that the Congress (. . .) did not contemplate and did not understand that it would abolish segregation in public schools." He stressed that "our friends the appellants take an entirely contrary view, and they take it, in part, on the same historical testimony; certain fallacies underlie, I think, their course in reaching that conclusion (. . .) in their recounting of history, is the assumption that the anti-slavery pre-Civil war crusade, the abolitionist crusade, was directed not only against slavery, but against segregation in schools. I do not think that this thesis can be sustained, for the thrust and movement of the abolitionists was directed toward one thing and one thing only: the abolition of slavery, and from that nothing can be deduced which is helpful to the Court in its study of this section of history. (. . .) Now if I gather my friend's position both in brief and argument, they hope from the debates of such a congress to distill clear, specific evidence of congressional intent. I do not think that is possible; but there is a source from which congressional intent can be gathered, far more reliable (. . .). What did the Congress do?"[77] As a strong argument he used the fact that the same Congress actually introduced segregated schooling within the very city of Washington, asking, "Is it conceivable to any man that Congress should submit to the states an amendment destroying their right to segregated schools and should contemporaneously and continuously institute a regime of segregated schools in the District of Columbia?"[78] He summed up with a dose of humor: "Now, your Honors then are presented with this: We say there is no warrant for the assertion that the Fourteenth Amendment dealt with the school question. The appellants say from the debates in Congress it is perfectly clear that the Congress wanted to deal with the school question; and the Attorney General, as a friend of the Court, says he does not know which is correct. So your Honors are afforded the reasonable field for selection."[79] And indeed, "Reading the two briefs in succession, a moderately astute Martian would have concluded that each side had examined totally different historical evidence," notes Richard Kluger.[80] Yet, the Justices were reserved, occasionally asking for clarifications, but without much interest. As they withdrew to deliberate, remembers Jack Greenberg, "it all seemed rather curious. They had turned our world upside down with a demand for the most exhaustive historical research ever conducted for a Supreme Court case. (. . .) Did they, perhaps, not care about the history? Or were the questions at oral argument just a game the Justices play?"[81]

He was not far from the mark. The Court actually anticipated such disagreement between the parties. Between the hearings, Justice Frankfurter assigned court clerk Alexander Bickel to look at the Congressional records. His report, circulated between the judges prior to reargument, was clear. Despite his personal beliefs on racial relations, Bickel was forced to report: "It is impossible to conclude that the 39th Congress intended that segregation be abolished; impossible also to conclude that they foresaw it might be, under the language they were adopting."[82] The Justices also reached the same conclusion. Jackson argued that among the legislators of the time "may be found a few who hoped that it would bring about complete social equality and early assimilation of the liberated Negro into an amalgamated population. But I am unable to find any indication that their support was decisive, and certainly their view had no support from the great Emancipator himself." Justice Clark was even blunter, saying that "he always thought that the Fourteenth Amendment covered the matter and outlawed segregation. But the history shows different."[83] Actually, even to the judges most inclined to strike down segregation, historical evidence could at best appear to be inconclusive regarding the matter at stake. It seemed impossible to overturn previous Supreme Court opinions on the basis of historical evidence. However, it turned out that this historical detour served an important purpose. Chief Justice Frederick Vinson suddenly died in September 1953, between the argument and reargument of Brown. Earl Warren became the new Chief Justice of the Supreme Court. He helped bridge the gap between the desire for judicial activism promoted by Justices Black and Douglas, and the theory of judicial restraint argued by Justices Frankfurter and Jackson, bluntly stating to his colleagues that he saw no other logic for maintaining segregation in public facilities unless they subscribed to the "logic of inherent inferiority of the colored race."[84]

Warren worked tirelessly throughout January and February in order to secure the unanimous support of his colleagues for outlawing segregation. In a memorandum from early 1954, Justice Jackson noted that "a profound change through awful consequences of racial prejudice by the Nazi regime caused a revulsion against the kind of racial feeling."[85] By the end of the month all nine Justices voted in favor of the NAACP. What remained was for Warren himself to draft an opinion, which was made public on May 17, 1954. Signed by Justice Warren, the majority opinion reminded that "in each of the cases, minors of the Negro race, through their legal representatives, seek the aid of the courts in obtaining admission to the public schools of their community on a nonsegregated basis. In each instance, they had been denied admission to schools attended by white children under laws requiring or permitting segregation according to race. This segregation was alleged to deprive the plaintiffs of the equal protection of the laws under the Fourteenth Amendment." Turning on history, the Justices concluded: "Reargument was largely devoted to the circumstances surrounding the adoption of the Fourteenth Amendment in 1868. It covered exhaustively consideration of the Amendment in Congress, ratification by the states, then existing practices in racial segregation, and the views of proponents and opponents of the Amendment. This discussion and our own investigation convinced us that, although these sources cast some light, it is not enough to resolve the problem with which we are faced. *At best, they are inconclusive.* (. . .) What others in Congress and the state legislatures had in mind cannot be determined with any degree of certainty." With this observation, the Court famously concluded:

> In approaching this problem, we cannot turn the clock back to 1868, when the Amendment was adopted, or even to 1896, when Plessy v. Ferguson was written. We must consider public education in the light of its full development and its present place in American life throughout the Nation. Only in this way can it be determined if segregation in public schools deprives these plaintiffs of the equal protection of the laws. Today, education is perhaps the most important function of state and local governments (. . .). Such an opportunity where the state has undertaken to provide it, is a right which must be made available to all on equal terms (. . .). To separate them from others solely because of their race generates a feeling of inferiority as to their status in the community that may affect their hearts and minds in a way unlikely ever to be undone. (. . .) We conclude that, in the field of public education, the doctrine of "separate but equal" has no place. Separate educational facilities are inherently unequal. Therefore, we hold that the plaintiffs and others similarly situated for whom the actions have been brought are, by reason of the segregation complained of, deprived of the equal protection of the laws guaranteed by the Fourteenth Amendment.[86]

The NAACP team was jubilant. The wider reactions were abundant and loud, both positive and negative. "What was the Warren Supreme Court to do? It did something unprecedented in our history. It threw out the window the Constitution and all previous court interpretations, and arrogated to itself a function reserved only for our representatives in Congress (. . .). It wrote a law—a law based on the very doubtful psycho-sociological precept that if the races went to separate schools, it would retard the development of the Negro children," wrote Rosalie Gordon.[87] Conservative parts of American society accused the Supreme Court of "basing the decision on sociology rather than on law, of rejecting the intent of the framers of the Fourteenth Amendment and the established precedents in favor of science fiction."[88] Less venomous critics pointed out that relying on social and behavioral sciences evidence in the courtroom was a dangerous path: "Today the social psychologists (. . .) are liberal and egalitarian in basic approach. Suppose (. . .) they were to present us with a collection of racist notions and label them 'science.' What then would be the state of our constitutional rights?" asked Edmond Cahn.[89] The Justices were attacked for plunging into judicial activism. One of the key points of the initial controversy was the impact of expert opinions on the Justices and their opinion, which stated that "this finding is amply supported by modern authority." Those modern authorities were quoted in a footnote to the judgment, labeled afterwards as "the most dispute-laden footnote in American constitutional law," which contained the works of social science on the issue of the effects of segregation, including the sociological and pedagogical briefs submitted to the Supreme Court in the case.[90]

With a public focused on the impact of social sciences, historians were initially shielded due to the low profile their contribution had in the courtroom. This ruling earned its place in constitutional history exactly as "it was able to avoid the dilemma because the record of history, properly understood, left the way open to, in fact invited, a decision based on the moral and material state of the Union in 1954, not 1866," wrote Alexander Bickel.[91] It was acknowledged that "there are times when both judge and historian should recognize that history is simply beside the point. (. . .) In such a case, the judge must transcend history, as the Supreme Court did in Brown v. Board of Education."[92] It seemed that "the Justices flirted rather seriously with a resort to history as a precedent-breaking device. At the last moment, however, they drew back," as Kelly wrote, also giving his interpretation of the Court's logic:

> It would seem likely that the evident difficulties presented by the various histories precipitated a serious difference of opinion among the Justices themselves, in a situation where unanimity was essential and even concurring opinions might damage the prestige of the decision. (. . .) Equipped with an impressive mass of historical evidence with which it might well have rewritten the history of the amendment's purpose, the Court reneged. As though in embarrassment, Mr. Chief Justice Warren's opinion declared the historical evidence with respect to the Fourteenth Amendment's intent concerning state segregation laws to be inconclusive. (. . .) In other words, the Court rejected history in favor of sociology.[93]

However, this was hardly a reason for historians to feel disappointed. "While any graduate student might shudder at being told his or her research was 'at best (. . .) inconclusive,' this was exactly the comment these scholars wanted to hear. 'Inconclusive' was a huge victory against the white supremacist view of Reconstruction that had so long dominated American historiography."[94] Historical briefs came as a great help to the Justices of the Supreme Court, torn between their personal convictions and a conservative, precedent-driven constitutional review. Historians convinced them that there was no conclusive interpretation of the original intent of the amendment regarding segregated public education. Social scientists filled this gap with the data that helped the Supreme Court to reach a unanimous verdict that overturned the precedents and made segregated schooling unconstitutional, opening the way for further revolution in civil rights.

Historical Forensic Contribution: From the Antechamber into the Adversarial Arena

As courtrooms became perceived as places in which scholarship could legitimately serve a public function, the confidence of social scientists and historians alike was boosted in regard to the legal relevance of their findings. The way for rethinking the relations between history and law was also opened. "All lawyers are, of course, in some sense students of legal history," wrote Justice Warren, introducing the first issue of the journal *American Legal History* (1957), "but legal history as history has generally been neglected by a profession too busy with the work at hand to be self-conscious about itself, its traditions, its past."[95] This was about to change, as further incentive in this direction came from "litigation involving Indian tribes. In no other field of public law does history play so decisive a role," wrote Charles Miller, one of the foremost legal historians of the new generation of the early 1960s.[96] That was hardly a coincidence; as Renata Uitz reminds us: "Very few domains of law are as entangled with the ghosts of the repressive past and the postmodern language of constitutionalism and rights as indigenous law.".[97]

In the U.S., the starting point of tackling the legacy of institutionalized mistreatment of the native Indian population also belonged to the aftereffects of the Second World War, with the creation of the Indians Claims Commission (1946), a judicial panel with a mandate to reexamine relations between Indian tribes and the federal government.[98] As the ensuing scramble began, over six hundred applications regarding land claims were submitted by 1951. "The job of an expert, at this point in a land case, was critical for the claimant (. . .). To qualify for occupancy, land use must have been consistent, either continual or seasonal, and the use must have been of vital importance in the economy of the people constituting the group."[99] It was no surprise that claimants largely turned to historians, as "during the 1930s and 1940s, most professional historians who surveyed the record weighed in largely on the side of Native Americans (. . .). They made of the story no simple morality play, but their ultimate conclusions decisively shifted the moral balance of historical research from a celebration of white conquest to a requiem for the values of equity and decency in American democracy."[100]

A number of historians testified for the plaintiffs in Otoe and Missouria vs. United States, decided in March 1953, in the successful claim in which over $1 million was awarded to the tribe: "The eminent historian and researcher, Dr. Waldo Wedel and his wife, Mrs. Wedel, and B.B. Chapman, Professor of History at Oklahoma A&M College, all confirm the exclusive use and occupancy by the plaintiff of the tract involved herein (. . .) evidence of value consists of the testimony and research of Dr. Thomas LeDuc, Research

Professor, Department of History, University of Nebraska, a witness for the plaintiff. (. . .) Dr. Le Duc contends that the land should be valued at $1.50 per acre as of the date of the cession."[101] Among these testimonies, a particularly comprehensive role belonged to Berlin Basil Chapman (1900–1994) from Oklahoma A&M College.[102] Luther Bohanon, who represented the plaintiffs, was full of praise for his historical contribution: "No man to my knowledge has tendered to the Otoe and Missouria Tribe a higher and more worthy service than that rendered by Dr. Chapman in his historical research, and the giving of his testimony before the Indian Claims Commission. It is significant and should be stated that in his research he transgressed the usual type of service in that he produced all the data available, whether it be at the moment for the best interest of the Otoe and Missouria claim, or at the moment for the best interest of the Government in denying the claim. (. . .) His manuscript was so documented and footnoted that no one, not even opposing counsel, chose to disagree with the findings or the conclusions he made."[103] Chapman was equally enthusiastic: "One of my finest seminar experiences was in October, 1950, when Bohanon called me as a witness before the Indian Claims Commission in Washington. There for three days I reviewed a study in an effort to give a fair and impartial presentation of the history of the lands of the Otoes and Missourias.[104] Chapman was not the only, and probably not even the first expert to take the stand in this case. In January 1948 at the beginning of this case. The Indian Claims Commission held a hearing on the terrain, in Oklahoma City and also at Otoe Council House near Red Rock, Dr Morris L. Wardell, Professor of History in in the University of Oklahoma, testified for Otoes.[105] Still, when this case was argued in Washington, Berlin Chapman delivered his expert report for the Otoes, and Mildred Mott Wedel, anthropologist and archeologist, appeared as an expert for the Department of Justice on October 4 1950.[106] When on December 11, 1953, Indian Claims Commission awarded 1,156,000$ of compensation to the tribe, Department of Justice unsuccessfully appealed to the United States Court of Claims in May 1955. With the Supreme Court denying certiorari in October 1955, the last legal obstacle was removed and the compensation begun.[107]

However, not all cases were as successful, in part because the state started using expert testimony of historians and anthropologists as well. This action prompted institutional development, as "anthropological and historical reports used as evidence in Native American claims against the U.S. Government were brought together for the first Ohio Valley Historic Indian Conference, precursors of the American Society for Ethnohistory."[108] The first issues of its journal, *Ethnohistory*, were devoted to the introduction of anthropological and ethnohistorical evidence into the combatant courtroom of the adversarial legal system. In it, Julian Stewart expressed concern that "the Indian claims cases present challenge to anthropology that seem to me more fundamental than is generally recognized." He warned: "If anthropology is to maintain a scientific standing in these cases it must recognize that

Figure 4.2 Berlin B. Chapman (second row, second from the left) with the Otoes and Missourias officials and their legal team

Source: Berlin B. Chapman, *The Otoes and Missourias. A Study of Indian Removal and the Legal Aftermath*. (Oklahoma City, Okla.: Times Journal Pub 1965), 286.

it would be truly embarrassing were persons holding identical theoretical views to interpret the same body of evidence in opposite ways because they happened to be witnesses for opposing sides in a particular case. Sympathy for the Indians or the taxpayer, monetary considerations, and other factors perhaps subtly influence the witness, but I would like to think that they are insignificant."[109] Historians were seen as less biased, and hence more acceptable experts. Newcomers to the field of expert witnessing, such as Helen Hornbeck Tanner, were surprised to find legals "to be remarkably lax concerning any rules for being an historical expert witness. The simple fact that I had recently obtained my Ph.D from the University of Michigan seemed to qualify me to discuss and offer opinion about a broad range of history and about many Indian tribes. It did not seem to matter that my field of specialization was Latin American History or that I had never had a course in any branch of Anthropology. In fact, the lack of exposure to formal training in Anthropology probably was a positive factor. The lawyers appearing at the Indian Claims Commission seemed ambivalent about anthropologists."[110]

Land claims continued pouring in before the Indian Claims Commission, along with historical expert testimony supporting them. By 1960 over $42 million was awarded, in 1961 the commission's mandate was prolonged, and in 1962 Congress even recommended financing the experts who would appear, as Chief Commissioner Arthur V. Watkins observed: "Most of the claims before the commission had their origin more than 100 years ago (. . .). In order to establish their claims the Indian tribes or bands require the service of expert witnesses (. . .) the Commission will be hearing and passing upon the testimony of literally hundreds of expert witnesses, historians, anthropologists, ethnologists, archeologists, appraisers, and so forth."[111] Indians were increasingly getting "their day in court," in the words of a semi-official account of ICC activity.[112] Gradually and with shortcomings, their plight was receiving national attention, crowned with a steady stream of Supreme Court verdicts, starting in 1973, confirming tribal sovereignty over reservations. A number of these opinions were written by none other than Justice of the Supreme Court Thurgood Marshall.[113]

This astonishing development was hardly imaginable only two decades earlier, when the U.S. was struggling to implement *Brown v. Board of Education*. In the years after *Brown*, the first attempts to include Black children in the "integrated" schooling system in the South were met with strong and violent resistance. Well after Brown, of almost three million Black children in Southern states, only 2% went to school with whites. The sluggish pace even led to a second Brown decision, a year later, calling for the desegregation of public schools "with all deliberate speed."[114] People as familiar with the situation in the South as Vann Woodward drew their own conclusion: "Of course, I was very much involved and I knew what had gone into the preparation of the case and the amicus curae brief prepared by the NAACP, and all of that. And the court showed signs of welcoming interest and I can't say it caught me off guard. I was of course enormously pleased, though I admit that I heard phrase they put in there about "all deliberate speed," and I thought, "Well, how many decades does that mean?"[115] Although racial discrimination in public education was rendered unconstitutional, its enforcement in the Southern states amounted to a state of emergency. In October 1962 the University of Mississippi was desegregated, with James Meredith attending his first class in American history, but this came after a riot leading to two persons killed, 375 injured, and 30,000 troops deployed to suppress what Vann Woodward characterized as "the most serious challenge to the Union since the Civil War."[116]

In such an atmosphere, historians who worked for the NAACP also became targets of criticism: "They produced a 235-page brief. It must stand as a pathetic monument to what happens when historians cease to be historians and take up the unlicensed practice of the law," wrote one of the vocal proponents of segregation, James Kilpatrick.[117] Without even knowing it, he had hit upon the uncertainties of one of the leading historians behind the brief, Alfred Kelly, who worried that he and his colleagues were engaged in creation of a "law-office history" for the NAACP: "I suppose if a man is without a scruple, this matter will not bother him, but I am frank to say that it bothered me terribly." He shared his concerns at the annual convention of the American Historical Association in 1961, where his short exposé garnered quite a bit of attention.[118] In a very candid way, he disclosed many informal details about the complex context in which historians were working.

> I was facing for the first time in my own career the deadly opposition between my professional integrity as a historian and my wishes and hopes with respect to a contemporary question of values, of ideals, of policy, of partisanship, and of political objectives. (. . .) I am very much afraid that for the next few days I ceased to function as a historian and instead took up the practice of law without a license. (. . .) Never has there been, for me at least, a more dramatic illustration of the difference in function, technique and outlook between lawyer and historian. It's not that we were formulating lies, there was nothing as crude and naive as that. But we were using facts, emphasizing facts, bearing down on facts, sliding-off facts, quietly ignoring facts, and above all interpreting facts in a way to do what Marshall said we had to do—'get by those boys down there.'[119]

Fascinated by Marshall's flamboyant personality, Kelly wrote: "Sometimes Marshall could reveal a mood of sudden savagery and bitterness." He recalled his strong sense of humor: " 'Alfred, you are one of us here and I like you. But'—and this in voice of terrible intensity—'I want you to understand that when us colored folks takes over, every time a white man draws a breath, he'll have to pay a fine.' A moment later, the good humor and charm returned."[120]

Marshall's frankness came with a price soon enough, during the congressional confirmation of Marshall's appointment as federal judge. The segregationist minority used every opportunity to challenge his credentials. So Congressman Strom Thurmond demanded Kelly's exposé to be reprinted in the Congressional Records in 1962 in order to block Marshall's appointment as federal judge, claiming it demonstrated his bias and racist notions. At the hearing, Marshall himself claimed to have been misquoted in the paper: "I don't know where under the sun Dr. Kelly got that from." Yet the Senate's subcommittee dealing with judicial appointments felt compelled to call Kelly himself to testify. He insisted on reading the statement, which expressed his "firm belief in the integrity, honor and decency of Judge Thurgood Marshall." He was subsequently questioned.

Senator Johnston:	Dr. Kelly, I believe you are a historian; is that true?
Kelly:	Yes, sir; a historian and perhaps a constitutional expert.
Senator Johnston:	And when you write, you try to write the truth; isn't that true?
Kelly:	Yes, sir; history consists of both fact and interpretation, however.

Kelly emphasized that the paper he delivered to the AHA was published by the *Washington Star* without authorization. All the potentially embarrassing recollections from the "incriminating" paper Kelly attributed to Marshall's peculiar sense of humor. He explained Marshall's alleged bias by insisting that in the Brown case Marshall "was functioning as an advocate, not as a historian."[121] On September 11, 1962, Marshall was confirmed as a federal judge with forty-four senators for and sixteen against, but historians who took part in the legal process discovered that they could be summoned to testify as well. Kelly's experience was the first in a long row of challenges faced by expert historians as a consequence of their public exposure.

The antagonistic nature of these exchanges was not only a consequence of political differences. Much of it was built into the adversarial nature of the legal procedure. Dr. Helen Hornbeck Tanner, historian from the Newberry Library, Chicago, who served as an expert witness in Indian claims from early 1960s, reflected frankly: "My experience has taught me that the law is opposed to history; that history and the law are in a state of perpetual warfare in the court of law. As a historian, I feel that every time I have gone into a courtroom, I have been flung into an arena where I might be chewed up by the legal lions before I can get out alive." Among the greatest obstacles in her work were the "absolutely irrational rules of evidence for using historical information. (. . .) The whole process was very anti-historical and showed no respect for my profession," and "it has become an endless challenge to try to arrange historical information so it can be processed by the legal system." She was proposing radical interventions into the institution of expert witnessing to enable creation of a more balanced historical forensic contribution: "I think it would be a mark of progress if historians working on opposed sides of the same legal case were allowed to have discussions and come to agreements on the basic facts of the case. (. . .) So, I feel that the historian should be in the 'third corner.'" However, she expressed serious doubts about the possibility of such improvement: "I really believe that Anglo-Saxon law, because of its embedded value system, is fundamentally incapable of reaching decisions that achieve justice in Indian terms."[122]

On a theoretical level, corresponding views were expressed by Carl Friedrich, who around the same time finally explicated the theory of incompatibility. He promptly admitted the close connection between the two disciplines, considering their "tie too intimate and to obvious too need laboring. Law is frozen history. In an elementary sense, everything we study when we study law is the report of an event in history, and all history consists of such records or reports." Praising the importance of both realms for the existence of Western civilization, he strongly advised keeping them separate: "To put it hortatively: the dogmatic and conceptual foundation of the law needs the softening impact of an inquiry into the past in order to free itself for the future. But such historical 'softening' must not be carried too far, or the legal fabric is dissolved and with it the society which it sustains." Friedrich emphasized that "the jurist is not concerned with the same dimension of interpretation as is the historian," and therefore argued for the necessity to "go a step further now and to advance the argument that the specific task of the student of law, of the jurist, is antithetical to that of the historian. By the very nature of his enterprise he is dragged into an ahistorical position."[123]

Structural implications of this incompatibility for expert witnessing were drawn by the seminal study *Political Justice* by Otto Kircheimer, who also reached the conclusion that the Anglo-American and continental trial organizations rest on two radically different assumptions:

> The Anglo-American trial remains essentially at the disposal of the parties, while the continental trial revolves around judge's own responsibility to search for the truth. Anglo-American adversary procedure organizes the trial as a battle of wits between the prosecution and defense, with the judge acting as their referee (. . .). May parity be restored by the judge's intervention? Many authorities will answer unhesitatingly in the affirmative, upholding the judicial practice not only to put the witness additional questions that are liable to clarify an issue, but also to call additional witnesses, even expert witnesses, if need be; the latter the judge may do on his own. The proposition sounds excellent on paper, but how would it fit into the system of adversary proceedings?[124]

However, at the time of his writing, an astonishing chain of events was set in motion which would test these theories in practice, bringing historians of both adversarial and inquisitorial systems toward a dramatic intersection.

Notes

1 Ben Palmer, "The Historian and the Lawyer," *American Bar Association Journal* 32 (1946): 530, 535.
2 Neil A. Wynn, *The Afro-American and the Second World War* (London: Paul Eleck, 1976), 19, 24. With around 13 million Black people, amounting to 10% of the U.S. population, the number of Black American soldiers was quickly increasing from around 97,000 at end of 1941 to 467,883 by end of 1942.
3 Richard Kluger, *Simple Justice: The History of Brown v. Board of Education and Black America's Struggle for Equality* (New York: Vintage, 2004), 327.
4 Harry S. Truman Library and Museum, Collection on Desegregation of the Armed Forces, http://www.trumanlibrary.org/whistlestop/study_collections/desegregation/large/index.php?action=chronology.
5 Harry S. Truman Library and Museum, *Records on the President's Committee on Civil Rights*, http://www.trumanlibrary.org/hstpaper/pccr.htm.
6 *To Secure these Rights: The Report of the President's Committee on Civil Rights* (Washington: GPO, 1947), 143.
7 James Rown, *The Double V: How Wars, Protest, and Harry Truman Desegregated America's Military* (New York: Bloomsbery, 2013), 197–231.
8 Constitutionally recognized through *Plessy v. Ferguson* (1896), this principle was translated to education through *Cumming v. School Board (1899)*. Cf. Morgan Kousser, "Separate But Not Equal? The Supreme Court's First Decision on Racial Discrimination in Schools," *The Journal of Southern History* 44 (1980): 17–44.
9 For more on the general strategy of the NAACP see Mark V. Tushnet, *The NAACP's Legal Strategy against Segregated Education, 1925–1950* (Chapel Hill, London: The University of North Carolina, 2004). On the role played by Marshall in the postwar change of strategy see Juan Williams, *Thurgood*

Marshall: American Revolutionary (New York: Random House, 1998), 143–194.

10 *Mirror to America, The Autobiography of John Hope Franklin* (New York: Farrar, Straus and Giroux, 2005), 143. "Invitation to testify from NAACP to John Hope Franklin," 24 March 1949, in John Hope Franklin Papers, Box S/15 Rubenstein Library, Duke University. Detailed instructions about the scope of his expert testimony were transmitted to Hope by Marshall's deputy Robert Carter: Proquest History Vault, *Papers of the NAACP*, Part 03: The Campaign for Educational Equality, Series B: Legal Department and Central Office Records, 1940–1950 (NAACP 3B), *Desegregation lawsuit at University of Kentucky*, 92–93.

11 John Hope Franklin, "The Dilemma of the American Negro Scholar," in *Soon, One Morning: New Writing by American Negroes, 1940–1962*, ed. Herbert Hill (New York: Knopf, 1963), 72.

12 Franklin, *Mirror to America*, 143.

13 Proquest History Vault, *Papers of the NAACP*, Part3B, Desegregation lawsuit at University of Kentucky, 133–134.

14 Details of the strategy are outlined in Mark Chesler, Joseph Sanders, Debra Kalmuss, *Social Science in Court: Mobilizing Experts in the School Desegregation Cases* (Madison: University of Wisconsin Press, 1989) and John P. Jackson, *Social Scientists for Social Justice: Making the Case Against Segregation* (New York: New York University Press, 2001).

15 Kluger, *Simple Justice*, 314.

16 Gunnar Myrdal, *An American Dilemma: The Negro Problem and Modern Democracy* (New York: Harper, 1944), vol. I, 342.

17 UNESCO, *The Race Question*, 3–6, 31, http://unesdoc.unesco.org/images/0012/001282/128291eo.pdf. Expert reports on the issue commissioned by UNESCO from 1950, 1951, 1964, and 1967 are assembled in *Four Statements on the Race Question* (Paris: UNESCO, 1969).

18 Jackson, *Social Scientists for Social Justice*, 62–78.

19 Kenneth Clark became a liaison between the social science community and the NAACP; Jackson, *Social Scientists for Social Justice* 110, 114–117.

20 Ibid., 114–117; Kluger, *Simple Justice*, 336–337.

21 University of Michigan Law School, The Civil Rights Litigation Clearinghouse, *Brown v. Board of Education*, Topeka, United States District Court District of Kansas. Transcript of Proceedings, 35, http://www.clearinghouse.net/chDocs/public/SD-KS-0001-0002.pdf.

22 Ibid., 161–162.

23 Ibid., 174.

24 *Brown v. Board of Education*, 96 F. Supp. 797 (D. Ks. 1951).

25 Professor Isidor Chein of New York City College was asked by attorney Justin Moore: "Are you 100% Jewish? (. . .) That answers my question. I simply wanted to find out what was the story about that." Quoted in Kluger, *Simple Justice*, 493.

26 Jackson, *Social Scientists for Social Justice*, 151.

27 U.S. Supreme Court, *Brown v. Board of Education*, 347 U.S. 483 (1954), http://laws.findlaw.com/us/347/483.html.

28 Michael J. Klarman, *From Jim Crow to Civil Rights: The Supreme Court and the Struggle for Racial Equality* (Oxford: Oxford University Press, 2004), 303. Not without a reason: "I have studied with great interest the laws of several American states concerning prevention of reproduction of people whose progeny would, in all the probability, be of no value or injurious to the racial stock," confided Adolf Hitler to Otto Wagener, SA Chief of Staff. According to Niall Ferguson, "it was the Southern states whose legal prohibitions on interracial

sex and marriage provided the Nazis with templates when they sought to ban relationships between 'Aryans' and Jews." Niall Ferguson, *War of the World, Twentieth-Century Conflict and the Descent of the West* (London: Allen Lane, 2006), 221.
29 The minutes of the London Conference for the preparation of the trial, in Michael Marrus, *The Nuremberg War Crimes Trial 1945–6: A Documentary History* (Boston: Bedford Books, 1997), 45.
30 G.M. Gilbert, *Nuremberg Diary* (New York: Da Capo Press, 1995), 123.
31 Michael J. Klarman, "Brown v. Board 50 Years Later," *Humanities* 3 (2004): 2.
32 Named *The Effects of Segregation and the Consequences of Desegregation*, this text was republished as "Social Science Statement in the Brown v. Board of Education of Topeka Supreme Court Case," *American Psychologist* 59.6 (2004): 495–501.
33 Kluger, *Simple Justice*, 543, 545.
34 Klarman, *From Jim Crow to Civil Rights*, 296.
35 See Philip B. Kurland and Gerhard Casper (eds.), *Landmark Briefs and Arguments of the Supreme Court of the United States: Constitutional Law, Vol.49A: Brown vs. Board of Education* (Arlington, VA: University Publications of America, 1976), 1. Also in Electronic form in The University of Michigan Library, Digital Archive Brown v. Board of Education, *Oral Arguments*, http://www.lib.umich.edu/brown-versus-board-education/oralarguments.htm.
36 Klarman, *From Jim Crow to Civil Rights*, 304.
37 The entire document is reproduced in Kluger, *Simple Justice*, 615–616.
38 Renata Uitz, *Constitutions, Courts and History, Historical Narratives in Constitutional Adjudication* (Budapest: CEU Press Budapest, 2005), i.
39 John J. Daly, *The Use of History in the Decisions of the Supreme Court: 1900–1930* (Washington, D.C.: Catholic University of America, 1954), ix. The special relationship between the U.S. Supreme Court and history is analyzed in Charles Miller, *The Supreme Court and the Uses of History* (Cambridge, MA: Harvard University Press, 1969).
40 Robert Jackson, "Full Faith and Credit," *Columbia Law Review* 45 (1945): 6.
41 Alfred H. Kelly, "Clio and the Court: An Illicit Love Affair," *The Supreme Court Review* (1965): 130.
42 Alfred H. Kelly, "An Inside View of Brown v. Board," in *Removing a Badge of Slavery: The record of Brown v. Board of Education*, ed. Mark Whitman (Princeton and New York: Markus Wiener Publishing, 1993), 222–223.
43 High Court of Australia, Communist Party v. Commonwealth HCA 5; (1951) 83 CLR 1 (9 March 1951) para. 38.
44 W.E.B. Du Bois, *Black Reconstruction in America 1860–1880* (New York: Harcourt Brace, 1935), 713.
45 Kluger, *Simple Justice*, 623–624.
46 John Hope Franklin, "My Life and Times with Thurgood Marshall," in *Remembering Brown at Fifty*, eds. Orvile Vernon Burton and David O'Brien (Urbana and Chicago: University of Illinois Press, 2009), 199. See Also NAACP Legal Defense and Educational Fund, 1953–1954 Brown vs. Board of Education case. John Hope Franklin Papers, Box S/15 Rubenstein Library, Duke University.
47 Wayne J. Urban, *Black Scholar: Horace Mann Bond, 1904–1972* (Athens: University of Georgia, 1992), 172.
48 Neil Jumonville, *Henry Steele Commager: Midcentury Liberalism and the History of the Present* (Chapel Hill: University of North Carolina Press, 1999), 151.
49 Jack Greenberg, *Crusaders in the Courts: Legal Battles of the Civil Right Movement* (New York: Twelve Tables Press, 2004), 181.
50 H. Kelly, "An Inside View of Brown v. Board," 220.

51 Kluger, *Simple Justice*, 623–624. Woodward's correspondence regarding Brown is kept at Yale University Library, Manuscripts and Archives, C. Vann Woodward Papers, Series II, 78/39.
52 Kelly, "An Inside View of Brown v. Board," 219.
53 Memorandum from Thurgood Marshall to the Board of Directors of the NAACP from July 16, 1953, is quoted in Felicia Kornbluh, "Disability, Civil Rights, and Law: Jacobus enBroek, Howard Jay Graham, and the New Politics of Equality in the Middle Twentieth Century," Presentation at Center for the Study of Law and Society Boalt Hall School of Law Berkeley, CA, January 30, 2012.
54 Howard J. Graham, *Everyman's Constitution* (Madison: State Historical Society of Wisconsin, 1968), 268–269.
55 Proquest History Vault, *Papers of the NAACP*, Part 03: The Campaign for Educational Equality, Series C: Legal Department and Central Office Records, 1951–1955, (NAACP 3C) *The Nature of the Non-Legal Research*, 1–2.
56 Franklin, "My Life and Times with Thurgood Marshall," 200–201.
57 Robert Carter, *A Matter of Law: A Memoir of Struggle on the Cause of Equal Rights* (New York and London: The New Press, 2012), 125.
58 C. Van Woodward, "The Background of the Abandonment of Reconstruction," Yale University Library Manuscript and Archives, C. Vann Woodward Papers, Box 78/39.
59 Drafts in different stages of preparation are accessible at Proquest History Vault, Papers of the NAACP, Part 3C, State report to the 14th Amendment; *Supplements to the Brief.*
60 Franklin, "My Life and Times with Thurgood Marshall." 201.
61 Ibid., 203.
62 Carter, *A Matter of Law*, 125–126. An extract of the program is reproduced in Proquest History Vault, Papers of the NAACP, Part 01: Supplement, 1951–1955, Legal Defense and Educational Fund report, including cases on education, housing, and recreation, September 15, 1953–June 15, 1954.
63 Greenberg, *Crusaders in Courts*, 195. It is worth reproducing a report from this gathering: "On September 25, 26, 27 and 28, a nation-wide conference was held in New York City of lawyers, historians, educators and psychologists working on the segregated school cases which have been set for re-argument in the United States Supreme Court on December 7, 1953. The conference began with an explanation of the objectives of the conference by the Director-Counsel, Thurgood Marshall. His opening remarks were followed by an explanation of the objectives of each of the four seminars by the chairmen. The first seminar, on the Post Reconstruction Era, was chaired by William Coleman, Esq., of Philadelphia. The discussion at this seminar centered around a monograph prepared by Professor C. Vann Woodward of John Hopkins University, Baltimore, Maryland, entitled: 'The Background of the Abandonment of Reconstruction,' and a monograph prepared by Professor John Hope Franklin entitled: Howard University, 'The Genesis of Segregation in the New South with Special Reference to-Separate Schools for Negroes.' Participants in this seminar were: John Hope Franklin, Howard Beale, Frank D. Reeves, C. Vann Woodward, James Nabrit, Rayford Logan and Robert L. Carter. The second seminar was chaired by Loren Miller, Esq., of Los Angeles, California. This seminar concerned itself with the History of the Fourteenth Amendment. The basis of the discussion in this seminar was a monograph prepared by Howard Jay Graham, Esq., Law Librarian, Los Angeles County Bar Association, entitled: 'The Purpose and Meaning of Sections One and Five of the Fourteenth Amendment: The Historical Evidence Reexamined,' legal memoranda prepared by Staff Attorney Constance Baker Motley and Professor Howard Jenkins of Howard University School of Law;

and a monograph prepared by Professor Alfred H. Kelly of Wayne State University, Detroit, Michigan, entitled: 'Congress, the Fourteenth Amendment and School Segregation statutes.' Participants in this seminar were: Alfred Kelly, U. S. Tate, Harvey Mansfield, Robert Ming, Robert Cushman, Jr., Robert F. Carr, Roward Jenkins, Marvin Karnatkin, Louis Pedding, Wallace Sayre, Constance Baker Motley, John Davis and Thurgood Marshall. The third seminar, chaired by John Frank, Professor of Law, Yale University, concerned itself with the history of public education for Negroes and the impact of the Fourteenth Amendment on Negro education. Dr. Horace Mann Bond, of Lincoln University, a monograph on this subject which was the basis of discussion in this seminar. Dr. Bond's monograph dealt with the contemporary understanding of the impact of the Fourteenth Amendment on segregated schools and with the intent of the framers of the Fourteenth Amendment with respect to segregated schools; the understanding of the Congress which ratified the Fourteenth Amendment with respect to segregated schools and the understanding of the state legislatures that ratified the Fourteenth Amendment with respect to segregated schools. Participants in this seminar were: Horace T. Bond, Louis Pollack, George Johnson, Albert Blum, Charles Thompson, Charles Wright, Lillian Chisoim, Charles Dabney, Rabel Smythe, Elwood Duncan and Smith Haynes." The fourth seminar, chaired by Professor Jack Weinstein of Columbia University School of Law, concerned itself with the type of decree or order which should be issued by the Supreme Court or the original trial court as a result of the Supreme Court's decision in these cases. Legal memoranda prepared by staff attorneys Jack Greenberg, David Pinsky, and Spottswood Robinson III were the basis of discussion in this group. Proquest History Vault, Papers of the NAACP, Part 01: Supplement, 1951–1955, Monthly Report, September 15–October 9, 1953.

64 Kelly, "An Inside View of Brown v. Board," 223–224.

65 Greenberg, *Crusaders in Courts*, 195.

66 Carter, *A Matter of Law*, 127.

67 Franklin, "My Life and Times with Thurgood Marshall," 202.

68 Kelly, *Clio and the Court*, 144; Kluger, *Simple Justice*, 640.

69 Greenberg, *Crusaders in Courts*, 201.

70 Graham, *Everyman's Constitution*, 268.

71 See Philip B. Kurland and Gerhard Casper (eds.), *Landmark Briefs and Arguments of the Supreme Court of the United States: Constitutional Law*, Vol.49A: Brown vs. Board of Education (Arlington, VA: University Publications of America, 1976), 160–393. This endeavor was costly as well. Marshall calculated that it took $40,000 to finance research, travel, and printing costs. Williams and Marshall, *American Revolutionary*, 222.

72 Brief for Appellants in Nos 1, 2, and 4 and for Respondents in no. 10 on Reargument, 17–18, in Kurland and Casper, *Landmark Briefs and Arguments*, 530–531.

73 The electronic form can be found in The University of Michigan Library, Digital Archive Brown v. Board of Education, *Oral Arguments*, http://www.lib.umich.edu/brown-versus-board-education/oralarguments.htm.

74 Ibid., 3–4.

75 Ibid., 10.

76 Ibid., 16.

77 Ibid., 33–34.

78 Ibid., 38.

79 Argument of John W. Davis, Ibid., 35.

80 Kluger, *Simple Justice*, 648. The representatives for the states also prepared a brief, as they were unable to find "a scintilla of evidence to the effect that the framers intended the amendment to outlaw segregated schools." "All available

evidence points to the conclusion that a majority of the Congress which submitted the Fourteenth Amendment did not contemplate or understand that it would abolish segregation in the public schools," confidently stated one of the briefs. "Brief for the state of Kansas on Reargument," Kurland and Casper, *Landmark Briefs and Arguments of the Supreme Court of the United States*, vol. 49, 774. On the making of the brief see Sydnor Thompson, "John W. Davis and His Role in the Public School Segregation Cases—A Personal Memoir," *Washington and Lee Law Review* 52 (1996), 1679–1695. Interestingly, the General Attorneys' Office submitted a brief of over five hundred pages for the U.S. as amicus curia. It also used the works of historians (including Woodward and Graham) and reached this conclusion: "The congressional history of the Fourteenth Amendment shows that the Amendment was proposed and debated as a part of a broad and continuing program to establish full freedom and legal equality for Negroes." Kurland and Casper, *Landmark Briefs and Arguments* of the Supreme Court of the United States, vol. 49, 978.

81 Greenberg, *Crusaders in the Courts*, 206.

82 Alexander Bickel, "Letter to Justice Frankfurter, 22 August, 1953," in *Removing a Badge of Slavery: The Record of Brown v. Board of Education*, ed. Mark Whitman (Princeton and New York: Markus Wiener Publishing, 1993), 235. Bickel's recollections on the drafting can be found in Alexander Bickel, "The Original Understanding of the Segregation," *Harvard Law Review* 69 (1955): 1–65.

83 Klarman, *From Jim Crow to Civil Rights*, 212–214.

84 Ibid., 292.

85 Kluger, *Simple Justice*, 690.

86 U.S. Supreme Court, *Brown v. Board of Education*, 347 U.S. 483 (1954), accessed at "Brown v. Board of Education (I)," *The Oyez Project at IIT Chicago-Kent College of Law*, http://www.oyez.org/cases/1950–1959/1952/1952_1, accessed on 10.5.2015.

87 Rosalie M. Gordon, *Nine Men Against America, The Supreme Court and Its Attack on Our Liberties* (New York: The Devin Adair Company 1958), 85–86.

88 Herbert Garfinkel, "Social Science Evidence and the School Segregation Cases," *The Journal of Politics* 21 (1959): 37.

89 Edmund Cahn, "Jurisprudence," *New York University Law Review* 30 (1955): 150–167.

90 The famous footnote eleven of the U.S. Supreme Court was compiled by Warren's law clerk, consistent of some of the works mentioned during the proceedings (B. Clark and G. Myrdal), supplemented by some additional readings. This is commented on at length by Sanjay Mody, "Brown Footnote Eleven in Historical Context: Social Science and the Supreme Court's Quest for Legitimacy," *Stanford Law Review* 54 (2002): 793–830 and Michael Heise, Brown v. Board of Education, Footnote 11, and Multidisciplinarity 90 Cornell L. Rev. 279 (2005).

91 Alexander Bickel, *The Original Understanding and the Segregation Decision, in Politics and the Warren Court* (New York: De Capo Press 1973), 261.

92 William M. Wiecek, "Clio as Hostage: The United States Supreme Court and the Uses of History," *California Western Law Review* 24 (1987): 234–235.

93 Kelly, *Clio and the Court*, 148.

94 Paul Finkelman, "John Hope Franklin," in *Clio's Favorites: Leading Historians of the United States 1945–2000*, ed. Robert Allen Rutland (Columbia and London: University of Missouri Press, 2000), 66–67.

95 Earl Warren, "Introduction," *American Journal for Legal History* 1 (1957): 1.

96 Charles Miller, *The Supreme Court and the Uses of History* (Cambridge, MA: The Belkap Press, 1969), 24.

97 Uitz, *Constitutions, Courts and History*, 268.

98 Nancy Oestreich Lurie, "The Indian Claims Commission Act," *The Annals of the American Academy of Political and Social Science* 311 (1957): 60. Cases before the Indian Claims Commission are electronically stored in the Digital Library of Oklahoma State University: http://digital.library.okstate.edu/icc. See also Index to Indian Claims Commission Decisions, Native American Rights Fund, Boulder, Col., 1976, http://www.narf.org/nill/documents/ICC/index_to_icc.pdf. Norman A. Ross (ed.), *Index to the Expert Testimony before the Indian Claims Commission* (New York: Congressional Informational Service New York Clearwater Pub. Co., 1973), http://cisupa.proquest.com/ksc_assets/catalog/504.pdf. A more recent appraisal is in David E. Wilkins, *Hollow Justice, A History of Indigenous Claims in United States* (New Haven, CT: Yale University Press, 2013).

99 See *United States Indian Claims Commission Final Report*, 8–10, http://www.narf.org/nill/documents/icc_final_report.pdf, accessed on 21.2.2016.

100 Ellen Fitzpatrick, *History's Memory: Writing America's Past 1880–1980* (Cambridge, MA: Harvard University Press, 2002), 120.

101 Ottoe and Missouria Tribe vs. United States (1953), http://digital.library.okstate.edu/icc/v02/iccv02p335.pdf. Cf. Thomas Le Duc, "The Work of the Indian Claims Commission under the Act of 1946," *Pacific Historical Review* 26.1 (February, 1957): 1–16.

102 After attending and teaching at public schools in Marion County, West Virginia, he received a bachelor's degree from the University of West Virginia in 1924 and a master's degree in history from Harvard University in 1927. From 1927 to 1930 he served on the history faculty at Oklahoma A&M College (now OSU) and then attended the University of Wisconsin, where he earned a doctorate in history in 1931. See Bob L. Blackburn, "Chapman, Berlin Basil," *Encyclopedia of Oklahoma History and Culture*, www.okhistory.org, accessed on 28.3.2016. His personal papers are available at Western History Collections of University of Oklahoma Libraries, Dr. Berlin Basil Chapman Collection, expert report and related material contained in boxes C42, C58, and C59.

103 Luther Bohanon, "Foreword," in *The Otoes and Missourias. A Study of Indian Removal and the Legal Aftermath*, ed. Berlin B. Chapman (Oklahoma City, OK: Times Journal Pub 1965), iv.

104 Ibid., vi. In this expanded form of the initial report, he also reflects on his testifying. Ibid., 241–287.

105 B.B.Chapman, *The Otoes and Missourias*, 239

106 For her it was a learning experience, as she appeared in another case on December 1954 and Fenruary 1955: "Do I have to stand by exactly what I said in that case?", she asked the judges: "I have come across more references."Ibid, 275

107 Ibid., 245.

108 *The American Society for Ethnohistory*, http://www.ethnohistory.org/sections/about_ase.

109 Julian H. Steward, "Theory and Application in a Social Science," *Ethnohistory* 2 (1955): 292.

110 Helen Hornbeck Tanner, "History vs. the Law: Processing Indians in the American Legal System," *University of Detroit Mercy Law Review* 76 (1999): 699–700. Cf. Helen Tanner, American Indian Collection, Darcy Library of Beulah, http://www.darcylibraryofbeulah.org/special-collections/helen-tanner-american-indian-history-collection, accessed on 21.2.2016.

111 House of Representatives, Subcommittee on Indian Affairs, June 19, 1962, 3–4, 24. HRG-1963-IIA-0039 Decision to Finance the Testimony of Expert Witnesses Before the Indian Claims Commission, 02 May, 1963.

112 A semi-official account on the ICC activity: Harvey D. Rosenthal, *Their Day in Court: A History of the Indian Claims Commission* (New York: Garland, 1990).
113 Cf. Rebecca Tsosie, “Separate Sovereigns, Civil Rights, and the Sacred Text: The Legacy of Justice Thurgood Marshall’s Indian Law Jurisprudence,” *Arizona State Law Journal* 27 (1994): 495–533.
114 The gradual implementation of this decision is the subject of Charles J. Ogletree’s *All Deliberate Speed: Reflection on the First Half Century of Brown v. Board of Education* (New York: W. W. Norton, 2004.)
115 Civil Rights Digital Library, http://crdl.usg.edu/. Oral history interview with C. Vann Woodward, January 12, 1991, 25–26, http://docsouth.unc.edu/sohp/A-0341/A-0341.html.
116 C. Vann Woodward, *Strange Career of Jim Crow* (Oxford: Oxford University Press, 2001), 173.
117 James Kilpatrick, *The Southern Case for School Segregation* (New York: Crowell-Collier Press, 1962), 133.
118 Alfred H. Kelly, “An Inside View of Brown v. Board,” paper delivered to the American Historical Association, December 28, 1961. Quoted here from Mark Whitman (ed.), *Removing a Badge of Slavery: The Record of Brown v. Board of Education* (Princeton and New York: Markus Wiener Publishing, 1993), 219–227.
119 Ibid., 222, 224–225.
120 Ibid., 226.
121 *Nomination of Thurgood Marshall: Hearings Before a Subcommittee of the Committee on the Judiciary, United States Senate, Eighty-Seventh Congress, Second Session, on Nomination of Thurgood Marshall, of New York, to be United States Circuit Judge for the Second Circuit* (Washington, D.C.: U.S. Government Printing Office, 1962), 163–189.
122 Tanner, History vs. the Law: Processing Indians in the American Legal System 693, 698, 708.
123 Carl Ioachim Friedrich, “Law and History,” *Vanderbilt Law Review* 63 (1961): 220, 249.
124 Otto Kirchheimer, *Political Justice: The Use of Legal Procedure for Political Ends* (Princeton: Princeton University Press, 1961), 342–343.

Bibliography

Bickel, Alexander. “The Original Understanding of the Segregation.” *Harvard Law Review* 69 (1955): 1–65.

Carter, Robert. *A Matter of Law: A Memoir of Struggle on the Cause of Equal Rights*. New York/London: The New Press, 2012.

Chapman, B. Chapman. *The Otoes and Missourias: A Study of Indian Removal and the Legal Aftermath*. Oklahoma City, OK: Times Journal Pub, 1965.

Chesler, Mark, Joseph Sanders and Debra Kalmuss. *Social Science in Court: Mobilizing Experts in the School Desegregation Cases*. Madison: University of Wisconsin Press, 1989.

Civil Rights Digital Library. http://crdl.usg.edu/ Oral history interview with C. Vann Woodward, 12 January, 1991, 25–26. http://docsouth.unc.edu/sohp/A-0341/A-0341.html.

Clark, Kenneth B., Isidor Chein and Stuart W. Cook. *The Effects of Segregation and the Consequences of Desegregation*, published as “Social Science Statement in the Brown v. Board of Education of Topeka Supreme Court Case," republished in *American Psychologist* 59.6 (September, 2004): 495–501.

Daly, John J. *The Use of History in the Decisions of the Supreme Court: 1900–1930.* Washington, D.C.: Catholic University of America Press, 1954.

Digital Library of the Oklahoma State University. http://digital.library.okstate.edu/icc.

Du Bois, W.E.B. *Black Reconstruction in America 1860–1880.* New York: Harcourt Brace, 1935.

Ellen Fitzpatrick. *History's Memory: Writing America's Past 1880–1980.* Cambridge: Harvard University Press, 2002.

Ferguson, Niall. *War of the World: Twentieth-Century Conflict and the Descent of the West.* London: Allen Lane, 2006.

Finkelman, Paul. "John Hope Franklin," in *Clio's Favorites: Leading Historians of the United States 1945–2000*, ed. Robert Allen Rutland. Columbia, MS and London: University of Missouri Press, 2000.

Four Statements on the Race Question. Paris: UNESCO, 1969.

Franklin, John Hope. *From Slavery to Freedom: A History of African Americans.* New York: Knopf, 1947.

Franklin, John Hope. John Hope Franklin Papers, Box S/15, 24 March 1949, NAACP Legal Defense and Educational Fund, 1949: University of Kentucky Segregation Case, Rubenstein Library, Duke University.

Franklin, John Hope. "The Dilemma of the American Negro Scholar," in *Soon, One Morning: New Writing by American Negroes, 1940–1962*, ed. Herbert Hill. New York: Knopf, 1963.

Franklin, John Hope. *Mirror to America, The Autobiography of John Hope Franklin.* New York: Farrar, Straus and Giroux, 2005.

Franklin, John Hope. "My Life and Times with Thurgood Marshall," in *Remembering Brown at Fifty*, eds. Orvile Vernon Burton and David O'Brien. Urbana and Chicago: University of Illinois Press, 2009.

Garfinkel, Herbert. "Social Science Evidence and the School Segregation Cases." *The Journal of Politics* 21 (1959), 37–59.

Gilbert, G.M. *Nuremberg Diary.* New York: Da Capo Press, 1995.

Gordon, Rosalie M. *Nine Men against America, The Supreme Court and Its Attack on Our Liberties.* New York: The Dvin Adair Company, 1958.

Greenberg, Jack. *Crusaders in the Courts: Legal Battles of the Civil Right Movement.* New York: Twelve Tables Press, 2004.

Harry S. Truman Library and Museum. Records on the President's Committee on Civil Rights. http://www.trumanlibrary.org/hstpaper/pccr.htm.

Hearings before a Subcommittee of the Committee on the Judiciary, United States Senate, Eighty-Seventh Congress, Second Session, on Nomination of Thurgood Marshall, of New York, to be United States Circuit Judge for the Second Circuit. Washington: U.S. Government Printing Office, 1962.

High Court of Australia, Communist Party v Commonwealth HCA 5; (1951) 83 CLR 1, 9 March 1951, para. 38.

House of Representatives, Subcommittee on Indian Affairs, June 19, 1962, HRG-1963-IIA-0039 Decision to Finance the Testimony of Expert Witnesses Before the Indian Claims Commission, 2 May, 1963.

Index to Indian Claims Commission Decisions, Native American Rights Fund, Boulder, Col., 1976. http://www.narf.org/nill/documents/ICC/index_to_icc.pdf.

Jackson, John. *Social Scientists for Social Justice: Making the Case Against Segregation*. New York: New York University Press, 2001.
Jackson, Robert. "Full Faith and Credit." *Columbia Law Review* 45 (1945): 1–34.
Jumonville, Neil. *Henry Steele Commager: Midcentury Liberalism and the History of the Present*. Chapel Hill: University of North Carolina Press, 1999.
Kelly, Alfred H. "Clio and the Court: An Illicit Love Affair." *The Supreme Court Review* (1965): 119–158.
Kilpatrick, James. *The Southern Case for School Segregation*. New York: Crowell-Collier Press, 1962.
Kircheimer, Otto *Political Justice: The Use of Legal Procedure for Political Ends*. Princeton: Princeton University Press, 1961.
Klarman, Michael J. "Brown v Board 50 Years Later." *Humanities* 3 (2004): 1–20.
Klarman, Michael J. *From Jim Crow to Civil Rights: The Supreme Court and the Struggle for Racial Equality*. Oxford: Oxford University Press, 2004.
Kluger, Richard. *Simple Justice, The History of Brown v. Board of Education and Black America's Struggle for Equality*. New York: Vintage, 2004.
Kornbluh, Felicia. "Disability, Civil Rights, and Law: Jacobus TenBroek, Howard Jay Graham, and the New Politics of Equality in the Middle Twentieth Century," Presentation at Center for the Study of Law and Society Boalt Hall School of Law Berkeley, CA, January 30, 2012.
Kousser, Morgan. "Separate But Not Equal? The Supreme Court's First Decision on Racial Discrimination in Schools." *The Journal of Southern History* 44 (1980): 17–44.
Kurland, Philip B. and Gerhard Casper, eds. *Landmark Briefs and Arguments of the Supreme Court of the United States: Constitutional Law*, vol. 49A: Brown vs Board of Education. Arlington, VA: University Publications of America, 1976.
Le Duc, Thomas. "The Work of the Indian Claims Commission under the Act of 1946." *Pacific Historical Review* 26.1 (February, 1957): 1–16.
Lurie, Nancy Oestreich. "The Indian Claims Commission Act." *The Annals of the American Academy of Political and Social Science* 311 (1957): 56–70.
Marrus, Michael. *The Nuremberg War Crimes Trial 1945–6: A Documentary History*. Boston: Bedford Books, 1997.
Miller, Charles. *The Supreme Court and the Uses of History*. Cambridge, MA: Harvard University Press, 1969.
Mody, Sanjay. "Brown Footnote Eleven in Historical Context: Social Science and the Supreme Court's Quest for Legitimacy." *Stanford Law Review* 54 (2002): 793–830.
Myrdal, Gunnar. *An American Dilemma: The Negro Problem and Modern Democracy*. New York: Harper, 1944.
Ogletree, Charles J. *All Deliberate Speed: Reflection on the First Half Century of Brown v. Board of Education*. New York: W.W. Norton, 2004.
Palmer, Ben. "The Historian and the Lawyer." *American Bar Association Journal* 32 (1946): 530–536.
Proquest History Vault. *Papers of the NAACP*, Part 03: The Campaign for Educational Equality, Series B: Legal Department and Central Office Records, 1940–1950.
Rosenthal, Harvey D. *Their Day in Court: A History of the Indian Claims Commission*. New York: Garland, 1990.

Ross, Norman A., ed. *Index to the Expert Testimony before the Indian Claims Commission Congressional Informational Service*. New York: Clearwater Pub. Co., 1973.
Rown, James. *The Double V: How Wars, Protest, and Harry Truman Desegregated America's Military*. New York, Bloomsbery, 2013.
Steward, Julian H. "Theory and Application in a Social Science." *Ethnohistory* 2 (1955): 292–302.
Tanner, Helen. American Indian Collection, Darcy Library of Beulah, http://www.darcylibraryofbeulah.org/special-collections/helen-tanner-american-indian-history-collection (accessed on 21.2.2016).
Tanner, Helen Hornbeck. "History vs. the Law: Processing Indians in the American Legal System." *University of Detroit Mercy Law Review* 76 (1999): 693–712.
Thompson, Sydnor. "John W. Davis and His Role in the Public School Segregation Cases—A Personal Memoir." *Washington and Lee Law Review* 52 (1996) 1679–1695.
To Secure These Rights: The Report of the President's Committee on Civil Rights. Washington: GPO, 1947.
Tsosie, Rebecca. "Separate Sovereigns, Civil Rights, and the Sacred Text: The Legacy of Justice Thurgood Marshall's Indian Law Jurisprudence." *Arizona State Law Journal* 27 (1994): 495–533.
Tushnet, Mark V. *The NAACP's Legal Strategy against Segregated Education, 1925–1950*. Chapel Hill, London: The University of North Carolina, 2004.
Uitz, Renata. *Constitutions, Courts and History, Historical Narratives in Constitutional Adjudication*. Budapest: CEU Press Budapest, 2005.
UNESCO. *The Race Question*. http://unesdoc.unesco.org/images/0012/001282/128291eo.pdf.
United States Indian Claims Commission Final Report. http://www.narf.org/nill/documents/icc_final_report.pdf.
University of Michigan Law School, The Civil Rights Litigation Clearinghouse, Brown v. Board of Education Topeka and United States District Court District of Kansas. Transcript of Proceedings, 35. http://www.clearinghouse.net/chDocs/public/SD-KS-0001–0002.pdf.
Urban, Wayne J. *Black Scholar: Horace Mann Bond, 1904–1972*. Athens, GA: University of Georgia, 1992.
Warren, Earl. "Introduction." *American Journal for Legal History* 1 (1957): 1–34.
Western History Collections of University of Oklahoma Libraries, Dr. Berlin Basil Chapman Collection, Boxes C42, C58 and C59.
Whitman, Mark, ed. *Removing a Badge of Slavery: The Record of Brown v. Board of Education*. Princeton and New York: Markus Wiener Publishing, 1993.
Wiecek, William M. "Clio as Hostage: The United States Supreme Court and the Uses of History." *California Western Law Review* 24 (1987): 227–267.
Wilkins, David E. *Hollow Justice, A History of Indigenous Claims in United States*. New Haven, CT: Yale University Press, 2013.
Williams, Juan. *Thurgood Marshall: American Revolutionary*. New York: Random House, 1998.
Woodward, C. Vann. "The Background of the Abandonment of Reconstruction," in Yale University Library Manuscript and Archives, C. Vann Woodward Papers, Box 78/39.
Woodward, C. Vann. *Origins of the New South, 1877–1913*. Baton Rouge: Louisiana State University Press, 1951.

Woodward, C. Vann. *Reunion and Reaction: The Compromise of 1877 and the End of the Reconstruction*. Boston, MA: Little, Brown and Company, 1951.
Woodward, C. Vann. *Thinking Back: The Perils of Writing History*. Louisiana State University Press, Baton Rouge, 1986.
Woodward, C. Vann. *Strange Career of Jim Crow*. Oxford: Oxford University Press, 2001.
Wynn, Neil A. *The Afro-American and the Second World War*. London: Paul Eleck, 1976.

Part III

Intersections

The Institutionalization of Historical Forensic Expertise

5 Clio Takes the Stand

A Turning Point

"I have to inform the Knesset that a short time ago one of the greatest of the Nazi war criminals, Adolf Eichmann (. . .) is under arrest in Israel and will shortly be placed on trial in Israel under the terms of the law for trial of Nazis and their collaborators," announced Israeli Prime Minister Ben Gurion on May 23, 1960. This short and dry statement was to mark a revival of interest in the prosecution of Nazi crimes, unprecedented since the Nuremberg. "Perhaps no other event of the post-World War II period elicited so much interest in the tragedy that befell European Jewry as the capture and trial of Adolf Eichmann," writes Randolph Braham about the trial. Robert Kempner was enthused: "Historical scenes of the Final solution, which I here attempted to describe through documents and statements of witnesses, are now finding their juridical expression. (. . .) Eichmann did not escape earthly justice."[1]

The Eichmann Case: The Quest for Historical Context in an Adversarial Setting

The forthcoming trial of a man who in the public eye was responsible for organizing and overseeing the extermination of European Jewry was raising expectations both in a country in which a quarter of its population, around half a million, were Holocaust survivors, and outside its borders. "The Eichmann trial will tell us as other historians have tried, that anti-Semitism was not a byproduct of National Socialism, as the record of the Nuremberg trials might indicate," wrote Harry Golden, whereas Ben Gurion himself considered the trial an indispensable opportunity to ensure "that our youth remember what happened to the Jewish people."[2] Some authors like Victor Golanz were troubled with such an approach: "I think of Ben-Gurion with the greatest respect, but his reasons for bringing Eichmann to trial show a fundamental misconception. (. . .) He wants young Jewry to know beyond question what their people have suffered. Dear God, don't they not know already? (. . .) To show the whole world that what 'anti-Semitism through history' could result in (. . .) increasing, rather than diminishing anti-Semitism."[3] Ben Gurion thought just the opposite. In another interview on the eve of the trial, he stated that "the world should be faced with the potentials of anti-Semitism. (. . .) Eichmann's personal fate is unimportant. It is the unveiling of the entire extermination program against the Jews that matters."[4] In his view, this quintessential example of bringing history to trial was supposed to repeat the Nuremberg judicial memory-making venture, but also to revise much of it by stressing the uniqueness of the Holocaust as the crime of crimes of the Nazi regime. Eichmann stood accused under the Nazi and Nazi Collaborator Punishment Law, which incorporated the wording of the Nuremberg Charter, but specifically emphasized crimes against Jewish people among crimes against humanity, war crimes, and other offenses stipulated by the law.[5]

Now, after a decade during which the law was applied to process a handful of alleged Jewish collaborators, Israeli authorities had at their disposal a man described in Nuremberg and afterwards as "shipping agent of Holocaust" and "chief organizer of the Final Solution." And so the Israeli legal system was tasked with this unprecedented mission. Article 14 of the Nazi and Nazi Collaborator Punishment Law provided that "prosecution for an offense under this Law may only be instituted by the Attorney General or his representative." That was not unusual. Modeled after English common law, Israel's criminal procedure was "accusatory and adversarial. It is for the parties and not for the court to submit all the relevant evidence at their disposal."[6] In criminal cases, "in Israel [the] prosecutor acts at his discretion. The Attorney General has to report to the Minister of Justice and to the Government on his actions and ought to consult them particularly on matters of political, security or other public significance. However, his ultimate decisions are his own."[7] Therefore the architecture of the case was largely in the hands of Attorney General Gideon Hausner. His views on the purpose of the criminal trial were suitably broad: "In any criminal proceedings, the proof of guilt and the imposition of a penalty, although all-important, are not exclusive objects. Every trial also has a correctional and educational aspect. It attracts people's attention, tells a story and conveys a moral."[8] Applying them to the Eichmann case, his strategy echoed Ben Gurion's motivation to "bring the youth closer to the nation's past."[9] What better stage to do this than at a trial which attracted global attention before it had even begun?

The unprecedented event was followed by an unprecedented investigation. The large task of revealing the development of the anti-Semitic policies in Germany and the mechanism of the annihilation of the Jews was conducted by the newly founded unit of the Israeli police, "Bureau 06." They were at the same time investigating Eichmann's wartime activity and the entire process of the destruction of European Jewry. This investigation lasted for almost a year, yielding impressive results, as at the time factual knowledge on the Holocaust was in scratches and fragments, with synthetic overviews being almost absent, just in the making, or just out of print, like Raul Hilberg's *Destruction of the European Jews* or Wolfgang Scheflller's

Judenverfolgung im Dritten Reich.[10] Eventually, alongside interrogating Eichmann, police investigators were doing thorough historical research, working with the materials produced at the postwar trials, finding new documents, and identifying prospective witnesses. By the beginning of the trial, an impressive documentary basis was gathered.

During case preparation, the prosecution concluded that the material gathered by Bureau 06 needed to be presented in court in a comprehensive way. Moshe Praeger, one of the first Israeli Holocaust scholars, was acquainted with the investigation and wrote to Ben Gurion that "the police have no idea of the land mines lying in their path, they have no concept of the historical background." As early as September 1, he concluded that even though "the investigative work, along with the amassing of documentation, is mostly praiseworthy (. . .) what they lack is a measure of its *depth*. (. . .) They need the help and cooperation of experts in Holocaust research." He suggested that "in light of the Prime Minister's public declarations regarding the historical significance of the Eichmann trial (. . .) the unmistakable conclusion is that the scope of the trial must not be narrowed by presenting only incriminating material that relates personally and directly to the accused Eichmann, but rather, the Nazi campaign of annihilation against the Jewish Nation must be unfolded in detail."[11] With Ben Gurion and Hausner reaching the same conclusion, the quest began for appropriate experts, simultaneously with the selection of eyewitnesses, 110 of whom ultimately appeared.

In contrast, only one historian would do, but finding him was easier said than done. Both personal and institutional academic interest in the Holocaust was still in the cradle, including the famed Yad Vashem Memorial (established in 1953).[12] At a meeting of the police and prosecutors in the office of Yad Vashem chairman Arieh Kubovy, presided by Hausner in August 1960, the conclusion was reached that "all that was required was the presentation of compilation of speeches, articles, books and other publications," but locating an appropriate person to deploy this overview was much harder. A long list of Israeli scholars was rejected - Dr. Shauel Esh was seen as too young, Dr. Moshe Praeger as too self-confident, Dr. Marion Mushkat and Dr. Joseph Kermish from Yad Vashem were out aside as insiders On the other hand, Ota Kraus and Erich Kulka, Auschwitz survivors and publicists, were also taken out of consideration, along with all the foreign experts. "If we do invite a witness to give a general testimony on the Holocaust, it should be a Jewish witness of suitable stature," concluded Hausner.[13] Therefore the necessity to balance proximity and distance from the subject matter narrowed the choice to Dr. Jacob Robinson and to Salo Wittmayer Baron (1895–1989), professor of Jewish History at Columbia University, in effect the founder of Jewish studies in the U.S.[14] Robinson refused. Although he had been fixated on Eichmann since the Nuremberg Tribunals, naming him "probably more directly responsible for the destruction of the Jews than any other Nazi," he preferred acting as an overall historical consultant to the prosecutor.[15]

The final call was made in consultations with Ben Gurion, foreign minister Golda Meir, and other high-ranking government officials, which is indicative of the importance attached to the role. Ben Gurion had reservations about Baron, as he preferred his candidate, minister of education Zalman Shazar, but Baron nonetheless prevailed as Hausner's choice. In his view, given the international significance of the trial, the concept of an internationally recognized authority of Jewish descent would be the more appropriate choice.[16] Therefore on December 26, 1960, the Israeli Minister of Justice, Pinchas Rosen, wrote in confidence to the Israeli consul in New York:

> In a conference which took place with the participation of the Prime Minister, the Foreign Minister, the Government's Legal Councilor, the directors General of the Prime Minister's office and the Foreign Office and of Dr. Jacob Robinson, adviser to the prosecution at the Eichmann trial, it was decided to ask you to contact Professor S. Baron and to ask him whether he would be prepared to serve as witness for the prosecution at that trial. Professor Baron's testimony would have to include a general description of the status of European Jewry on the eve of the Catastrophe, its importance, and national as well as cultural quality, a general description of the human and national potential contained in it, as well as the description of the remnants of the culture which remained after the Catastrophe when the holocaust ended. (. . .) This testimony, as we have indicated, should be the historic testimony at that trial and we see in Professor Baron a man with the competence and qualification needed for offering such a testimony on the Catastrophe of the Jewish people.[17]

On being contacted at the end of 1960, Baron accepted, undoubtedly flattered. He was interested and well informed on the topic, as during the late interwar period and wartime, he had coordinated the efforts of the Jewish Cultural Reconstruction, an organization that documented the scope of the damage to the European Jewish communities, and hence was well placed.[18] The idea of testifying did not strike him as odd, perhaps also because, working at one of the hubs of U.S. academia, it is difficult to imagine that he failed to observe the role played by American historians in antidiscrimination cases.

Upon acceptance, Baron was advised to compile in secrecy nothing less than a report on the state of European Jewry before and after the Second World War. Hausner wrote to him, explaining that for the prosecution "it is important to prove the Nazi intention to annihilate the Jewish people, and therefore it is vital for the trial to present documentation that will expose the national and cultural value of the Jewish centers that were destroyed in the Holocaust."[19] Baron understood his task, and immediately started drafting and redrafting his testimony. Interestingly, one of the early versions begins with observations about an enormous change in contemporary history since the Second World War: "I believe I ought to begin with a reservation: usually historians of contemporary problems face the standard objections that a) they necessarily lack historical perspective; and b) that most pertinent documents are still hidden away in archives. In this particular case, however, the tremendous changes during the last fifteen years place the period before 1945 at such a relative distance that perspectives almost resemble those relating to previous ages. The capture and publication of millions of German secret documents and the great articulateness of most leading participants in the events have made an enormous amount of material available which, while still partially incomplete, allows for certain tentative conclusions."[20]

Baron came to Jerusalem on March 30, 1961 from his university in an equally secretive manner, waiting for the trial to commence. During this time, he was receiving further instructions about finalizing his testimony, both by Hausner and Robinson, who feared his presentation might turn boring. Baron snapped under pressure: "Boredom is relative and very often depends on the manner in which the facts are presented. Anyway, nothing was more boring than the testimony of the Yad Vashem representative regarding the validity of certificates and documents, and yet you accepted this testimony as being essential to the trial." Hausner was quick to withdraw: "You will, of course, express your opinion on historical issues as you

Figure 5.1 The opening of the Eichmann trial

see fit. Your unique standing and your publications are sufficient guarantee that the picture you present will be accurate and enthralling."[21] However, if Baron thought that he was free from pressure, on the eve of the trial he received an invitation he could not refuse. On April 10, he was invited to a meeting with Prime Minister Ben Gurion, who suggested the insertion of some details, mostly the names of prominent Jews. Baron integrated these changes, and included the name of Ben Gurion himself among notables, giving final touches to the testimony. Still, the prime minister remained concerned, confiding to his diary: "Concerned about his testimony. I told him that it is important to show to the younger generation (and also to the rest of the world) how great was the qualitative loss in the destruction of six millions, and therefore, he must describe the spiritual character of Judaism that was destroyed, illustrated by great personalities: Einstein, Bialik, Dubnow and others."[22] The next day the trial began.

History Examined and Cross-Examined in the Eichmann Trial

On April 11, 1961, seated in a booth of bulletproof glass in a Jerusalem courtroom, Adolf Eichmann was read fifteen counts of indictment, including crimes against the Jewish people, crimes against humanity and membership in criminal Nazi organizations. In the midst of enormous public attention, with full video broadcast from the equally full courtroom, Gideon Hausner delivered his opening speech.[23] He was followed by the first witnesses for the prosecution, among them Professor Salo Baron, who was finalizing his exposé in this heated atmosphere.[24] Finally Baron appeared on the stand, testifying through two lengthy sessions on April 24, 1961. After being questioned about his qualifications, which included three doctorates (in philosophy, law, and political science), he started by apologizing for his poor Hebrew. Aware of the uniqueness of his role, he began his testimony upon being examined about his credentials with a methodological justification of his position, particularly emphasizing the unusual situation regarding the early availability of sources, which made historical analysis possible:

> I appear here as a witness, not an eye-witness or a jurist, but as a historian. It is known that a historian who studies contemporary history is always confronted with a double problem. The first problem is: Does one already have a historical perspective? Generally, one does not, until the passing of several decades, at least. The second problem is: Does one have documents? These are usually locked away and not available and one does not know about events that happened until 50 years later or more. It seems to me that precisely in this regard, there is a difference. The period before the Second World War is so remote from this generation, and sometimes so forgotten even by people who lived through it, that already, it seems to me, we have a historic perspective which

> usually is lacking in such cases. And with regard to documents, perhaps we are fortunate in that many of the German archives were captured by the Allies and many of them have already been published. Also many of the participants in these events wrote diaries, autobiographies and so on and the material accumulated at such a pace that there is perhaps need for a vast bibliography, merely to have on record the large number of these manifestations.[25]

This statement of methodological optimism regarding both the heuristic problems and the issue of scholarly distance was followed by the first session of his testimony, dedicated to the milieu in which the interwar European Jewry lived. Baron testified with respect to the economic conditions, demographical tendencies, cultural contributions, and political diversity of various Jewish communities in Europe, underlining "the exceptionally vital and creative force of the Jewish world in Europe of that time."[26] He showed keen preparedness, as he was testifying from memory, consulting his draft statement only occasionally.[27] According to spectator Haim Guri,

> Hour after hour, Professor Salo Baron, of Columbia University, stood discussing "European Jewry," which I know more about now than I did when it was still alive. A Jew, now an American, around sixty, balding, dressed in a dark suit. He spoke softly, in professorial tones, as if lecturing his students. In measured tones, he painted a broad picture of the life that was, from the beginning of the Common era to the time of Eichmann. In his methodical way, the professor developed a historical, demographic and cultural picture, and it made me dizzy. (. . .) A very long lecture, so full of facts and figures that I felt I was drowning. (. . .) Eichmann took notes and listened. It fascinated him. He learned from Professor Baron that, had he not done what he had done, there would now be twelve million Jews living in Europe. (. . .) The morning session was devoted to marvelous panorama of European Jewish life as it had been. The afternoon session was devoted to ashes.[28]

Baron went on to testify about the pressure on European Jewry at the time, providing historical examples of the development of anti-Semitism in Europe, with special emphasis on the extreme emanations of hatred in Germany in the thirties. He emphasized the continuity of anti-Semitic sentiments in European culture, but stressed the murderous novelties brought about by Nazism. In the second session, Baron contrasted the previous account with the chilling description of the destruction of the European Jewish communities. Baron calculated both the factual and the demographic loss during the course of the Holocaust, dramatically reminding the courtroom that "the Jewish people would have now totaled about 20,000,000 souls or more. Instead of 20,000,000 there are 12,000,000."[29] He concluded the testimony by tracking the dynamics of the Nazi conquest of much of Europe and the

Figure 5.2 Professor Salo Baron on the stand

consequent spillover of their policy of extermination. He also warned in a dramatic tone that if Hitler's movement had appeared during the age of Bismarck, before the great Jewish migration, "the genocide of the Jewish people would have been almost total."[30] He gave a personal observation about his hometown Tarnów in Poland, which he visited in 1937 to find a thriving community of twenty thousand Jews. Upon his next visit, he found no more than twenty. "This observation, encapsulated the tragedy more profoundly than the hours of Baron's erudite scholarship," summarized Deborah Lipstadt.[31]

Baron finished his exposé without mentioning Eichmann's name a single time. Telford Taylor, who observed the trial for the *Spectator*, reacted:

> The impression that the prosecution was taking the whole temporal and geographical reach of anti-Semitism as the province of accusation was heightened when the first major witness took the stand. The enormously erudite Dr. Salo Baron, Professor of Jewish history and literature at Columbia University, lectured for several hours (. . .). All this was most enlightening, but had little enough to do with the guilt or innocence of Adolf Eichmann. However, the outer limits had not yet been reached, for in conclusion Dr. Baron ruminated aloud on how much worse it would all have been had Hitler come to power at the time of Bismarck, when the Jews were still concentrated in central Europe and before the great tide of emigration to America. Astrally remote as this speculation was from the issues of the trial, the court did nothing to cut the witness short, and it was subsequently learned that this particular might-have-been was one of Premier Ben Gurion's favorite topics, and that he had discussed it with Dr. Baron a few days before the latter testified.[32]

Half a century later, Stephen Landsman was equally puzzled: "The troublingly inflammatory nature of such testimony, which dwells not on the defendant's deeds but on the merits of suffering of the victims and the irrevocable loss to the Jewish people, was not remarked by either defense council or the court. It was central to the Holocaust story the prosecution set out to tell and had been laid at Eichmann's door whether it was his responsibility or not."[33] However, when Eichmann's experienced attorney, veteran of the Nuremberg trial defenses Dr. Robert Servatius, stood to cross-examine Baron, he was careful enough not to press the issue, although the Israeli criminal procedure treated cross-examination "as an invaluable tool for the discovery of the truth (. . .) in the criminal trial (. . .) viewed as one of the fundamental rights of a defendant."[34] It was an opportunity for the defendant to challenge not only the content of the testimony, but also the credentials and credibility of the witness himself. Servatius did neither. Instead, building on Baron's own approach of broad contextualization, he embarked on a protracted conversation with Baron, not deprived of philosophical overtones, filled with references to authors such as Hegel, Spengler, Marx, and others. "The two fell into a philosophical argument—Eichmann was still listening and taking notes,—about Hegel and Spengler and the 'spirit of history' and determinism and freedom. The court was elevated to the heights of intellectual and legal discourse."[35] Moving the examination in the direction of the subject of agency in history, Servatius unexpectedly opened a venue for unpleasant lines of questioning, asking Baron to provide the reasons for the widespread hatred of Jewish people. Servatius was proposing that large historical events such as the Second World War or genocide could not be seen exclusively through the lenses of human agency. He was trying to suggest that, in phenomena such as anti-Semitism, "irrational motives are at the root of the fate of this people, something beyond the understanding of a human being."[36]

Baron, probably the first historian ever to be cross-examined on the stand, was taken by surprise, although he had been warned from the beginning that he was "likely to be subjected to a cross examination by the defense which may try to trip him up on details and concrete data."[37] What he did not expect was Servatius' interpretative challenge, boiling down to the reasoning that no single human (and certainly not Eichmann) could bear full responsibility for such dramatic, all-comprising events which are best seen as history at work. Only then did Baron retract his assertion that "every individual person in his own way—and every human grouping, in my opinion, is responsible for its actions and cannot say that it merely executes the demands of history. Because, if so, anyone could interpret history specially for himself and the world would be chaotic. (. . .) This is not a historical question, but more a legal question. To what extent an individual person who is not a leader is also responsible in the historical sense—there is no doubt that sometimes insignificant people have much more influence on the course of history than their importance to the state warrants."[38] Baron's attempt to distinguish between legal and historical notions of responsibility seems to have tilted the sensitive division of labor between the judges and historians, causing the bench to react:

Presiding Judge: Why do you refer to this as a legal problem? This is not clear to me.
Witness Baron: I thought that here there was a question whether there is a distinction between a leader and an ordinary person as to whether he is responsible for changes in history or not.
Presiding Judge: Let us perhaps leave that to the jurists.
Witness Baron: Quite right.[39]

This was an early manifestation of the general reluctance of Eichmann's judges to allow history to enter their courtroom. They seemed much relieved once Baron finished his appearance, turning to the more conventional job of questioning the eyewitnesses. Many spectators were perplexed by the deposition of historical narratives in the courtroom, and were particularly troubled by the testimony of a professional historian, Salo Baron. For the majority of the audience, the content of his expert testimony was too abstract. Many found his bad Hebrew too distant, making the experience of testifying excruciating for him.[40] One of the observers of the trial, the Dutch writer Hary Mulisch, commented: "It was longwinded and interesting and professor-like, but I fail to see what does it have to do with Eichmann."[41] Even more critical was Jacob Robinson, founder and director of the Institute of Jewish Affairs, special consultant to Robert Jackson before Nuremberg, then legal advisor to the Israeli delegation to the UN and advisor to the prosecutor in the Eichmann case. He reviewed Baron's testimony in an internal document, finding it "incidental in content and form, fragmentary and inaccurate."[42] Particularly adamant was Ben Gurion himself, who confided to his diary: "Just as I feared (. . .) he embarrassed us. He spoke with me, and I knew at once that we had failed miserably. I was against it."[43] When Eichmann prosecutor Gideon Hausner later praised "the authoritative presentation by Professor Salo Baron of Columbia University, who painted a comprehensive picture of the Jewish scene in the last generations, reviewing what we had had and what we had lost," one could sense the tone of justification for his choices: "We used this technique since it was impossible to prove in detail the fate of over fifteen hundred Jewish centers and many thousands of Jewish localities that had been wiped out. Professor Baron's evidence filled in the gaps. He gave the court the general picture in each European state immediately after the catastrophe. We could then ask the court to infer that what had been proved in regard to the fate of one Jewish community had also befallen other Jews in the same country."[44] Baron himself was not publicly speaking about his experience, but was occasionally venting his own discontent in private correspondence with colleagues, and was adamantly clipping the newspaper articles regarding his testimony.[45] It does not seem that he shared the discontent about the testimony, as upon return to New York he prepared an article based on it, entitled "European Jewry Before and After Hitler: Responses at the Eichmann Trial."[46]

Meanwhile in Jerusalem, as eyewitness after eyewitness was taking the stand in a very dramatic atmosphere, the prosecution's decisiveness to introduce historical evidence was far from satisfied. At some point, prosecutor Hausner attempted to strengthen the case by calling no other but Hans-Gunther Seraphim, veteran expert from the Remer case and Ulm trial: "I can already tell the Court that I would like to submit a document, an expert opinion of Professor Serafim [sic.] of Göttingen University, which (. . .) concerns the possibility for SS officers to be released from duties which involved bloodshed, without thereby incurring damage, whether bodily or materially. We are trying to find out whether Professor Serafim [sic.] can appear here in person. He could appear, since according to our information, his past is unblemished. But he fell ill and is now recovering from his illness. If we shall be able to bring him here, we shall do so. If we shall not be able to do so, we shall wish to submit the written opinion, and then Defense Counsel will naturally be able to cross-examine him, if he so wishes."[47]

Being unable to secure Seraphim's presence, Hausner attempted to tender his expert report from the 1958 Ulm trial as evidence, leading to an interesting exchange, in which the judges aggressively disputed the admittance of the evidence:

Presiding Judge:	Was it presented as a legal authority?
Attorney General:	Yes, in the preliminary argument. On page five infra, six supra, of the judgment, the Court will find that this opinion is part of the material upon which the court in Ulm relied. This matter is significant, since Dr. Hans Guenther-Serafim [sic.], a lecturer in history at Göttingen University, was asked the following question by the court in Ulm, which also tried persons for offences involving executions in wartime: "Were rank-and-file SS men, or their leaders, who were active in purge or extermination operations, able to refuse to carry out such orders without suffering bodily harm or endangering their own lives?"
Presiding Judge:	In what field is this professor an expert?
Attorney General:	He is a professor of history who specializes in the Nazi period. He collected material, precedents, which he lists, and on which the court subsequently relied.
Presiding Judge:	What kind of precedents?
Attorney General:	Precedents of cases in which, to his knowledge, persons refused to execute orders of this kind or requested to be released from duties which entailed bloodshed, and what happened to them.
Judge Raveh:	Does this mean that he conducted investigations and took evidence?
Attorney General:	He collected historical material, and he recorded the details of each case.
Judge Raveh:	Does this mean that he interrogated witnesses?
Attorney General:	No, he examined documents and people. But, in the main, he was engaged in historical research based on documents and on material which was before various courts, including international tribunals. He collected all the available material. To the best of our knowledge, this is perhaps the most exhaustive expert opinion, anyhow within our knowledge, on this subject. The German court also required expert opinion in regard to this question, since it was difficult for it to refer to the evidence which is spread over a wide field.

Presiding Judge: But there they are much freer in regard to the acceptance of expert opinions than in our Courts.

Attorney General: I assume so, Sir. In any event, I request that this expert opinion be accepted as an exhibit. (. . .)

Presiding Judge: Again, as to the content of his expert opinion: He is not going to testify, as far as I can see, about anything which he himself heard from other SS personnel, only about his documentary research. Why not present to us the documents which he researched?

Attorney General: Not all of those are in our hands, Sir. He has collected them.

Presiding Judge: Really, we are straying far indeed from the source itself, from the best evidence, which we, after all, always strive to secure.

Judge Raveh: You said he also took evidence.

Attorney General: He spoke with people.

Judge Raveh: Does he remember the names of the persons with whom he spoke?

Attorney General: I believe so.

Judge Raveh: Are they living or deceased? Where can they be found?

Attorney General: I must say that, at this stage, I wished to ask the Court to accept this expert opinion; if Defence Counsel has any reservations or doubts about this, let us hear him.

Presiding Judge: I suggest that our rules of evidence not be forgotten completely. Not completely. (. . .) All right, let us hear Dr. Servatius, please, in regard to this question.

Dr. Servatius: Your Honour, the judges have already given expression to the objections to the acceptance of the document, and I concur with this view. However, there is an additional consideration concerning the qualifications of this specialist. He is described merely as a lecturer; he is, therefore, not a professor or any type of competent member of a university (. . .)

Attorney General: I understand that Serafim [sic.] is a serious researcher. Obviously, there can be differences of opinion in regard to this, but I understand that he has received awards for studies which he has carried out.

Presiding Judge: That will certainly not influence the decision of the Court.

Attorney General: If, however, a German court turns to him as an expert, perhaps, all things being considered, this gives him recognition as an expert in a matter concerning which he is requested to give an opinion.

Presiding Judge: We shall study this matter and will give a ruling.[48]

The panel of judges, presided by Moshe Landau, was very cautious about admitting a contested expert. When the attorney general tendered documents used by Seraphim, the judges compared it to the other documents they had. After considering the submitted material, the judges decided to dismiss Seraphim's expert report, which is one of the first decisions of this kind. It ruled that the findings of the expert were too general and gave preference to direct access to the documents he visited:

> The opinion includes excerpts from testimonies given in various trials, the cases of Ohlendorf and Pohl in Nuremberg and others, and from Hitler's speeches, and the conclusions which the expert drew from that material concerning the question put to him by the court in Ulm, viz.: Were SS officers or men exposed to the risk of death or to other serious bodily injury in case of a refusal to obey orders? The expert also says that, in the course of his protracted investigations, he did not find even one case where an SS officer suffered bodily injury owing to his refusal to fulfill an order. As far as the expert's conclusions are concerned, we will not admit it in evidence, for the drawing of such conclusions is a matter for the Court itself. With regard to the material on which the expert relied, we are not prepared to admit it in this indirect manner. We are ready to consider any application to submit the material itself, or portions thereof, which may be made to us. With regard to the material which the expert did not find in his investigations, we are of the opinion that the remarks of the expert on this subject are general, and too vague to be able to serve as evidence before us. Accordingly, we reject the application of the Attorney General.[49]

Deeming the expert evidence inadmissible, the Jerusalem court opened up a topic that would become the main trait of historical expert witnessing in the adversarial paradigm. As one side was proposing a witness, the other one was likely to object. To make the situation even more confusing, in the subsequent hearings it was the defense which asked for additional evidence to be introduced, including the Seraphim expert report, giving Hausner an opportunity to remind the court that he himself intended to "hear Dr. Serafim [sic.] as a witness on Eichmann's possibilities of being relieved of his duties (. . .) at the time Counsel for the Defence objected to this, inter alia, arguing that Serafim [sic.] was only a lecturer, and not a university professor."[50] Faced with this reversal, the judges brushed aside Seraphim's report entirely, as they were generally not comfortable with the novelty of historical expert witnessing invading their courtroom. The judges showed quite a bit of understanding about the tense junction between history and law, which was expressed in the judgment, rendered on December 12, 1961. The court sentenced Eichmann to death, but took a very reserved view on the historical and pedagogical aspects of the trial. Only small parts of Baron's testimony, mostly related to the demographic losses, entered the lengthy judgment.[51] Much of the judges' effort was directed toward the delineation of historical expertise from hearsay, and the demarcation between the conclusion of the historical report and the court's right to reach its findings. These considerations triggered some general and quite lucid remarks about the relationship between history and law:

> This is not the first time that the Holocaust has been discussed in court proceedings. It was dealt with extensively at the International Military Tribunal at Nuremberg (. . .) and also at several of the trials which followed; but this time it has occupied the central place in the Court proceedings, and it is this fact which has distinguished this trial from those which preceded it. Hence also the trend noticed during and around the trial, to widen its range. The desire was felt—understandable in itself—to give, within the trial, a comprehensive and exhaustive historical description of events which occurred during the Holocaust, and in so doing, to emphasize also the inconceivable feats of heroism performed by ghetto-fighters, by those who mutinied in the camps, and by Jewish partisans. (. . .) How could this happen in the light of day, and why was it just the German people from which this great evil sprang? Could the Nazis have carried out their evil designs without the help given them by other peoples in whose midst the Jews dwelt? Would it have been possible to avert the Holocaust, at least in part, if the Allies had displayed a greater will to assist the persecuted Jews? Did the Jewish People in the lands of freedom do all in its power to rally to the rescue of its brethren and to sound the alarm for help? What are the psychological and social causes of the group-hatred which is known as anti-Semitism? Can this ancient disease be cured, and by what means? What is the lesson which the Jews and other nations must draw from all this, as well as every person in his relationship to others? There are many other questions of various kinds which cannot even all be listed. In this maze of insistent questions, the path of the Court was and remains clear. It cannot allow itself to be enticed into provinces which are outside its sphere. The judicial process has ways of its own, laid down by law, and which do not change, whatever the subject of the trial may be. Otherwise, the processes of law and of court procedure are bound to be impaired, whereas they must be adhered to punctiliously, since they are in themselves of considerable social and educational significance, and the trial would otherwise resemble a rudderless ship tossed about by the waves. It is the purpose of every criminal trial to clarify whether the charges in the prosecution's indictment against the accused who is on trial are true, and if the accused is convicted, to mete out due punishment to him. Everything which requires clarification in order that these purposes may be achieved, must be determined at the trial, and everything which is foreign to these purposes must be

> entirely eliminated from the court procedure. Not only is any pretension to overstep these limits forbidden to the court—it would certainly end in complete failure (. . .) its ability to describe general events is inevitably limited. As for questions of principle which are outside the realm of law, no one has made us judges of them, and therefore no greater weight is to be attached to our opinion on them than to that of any person devoting study and thought to these questions. These prefatory remarks do not mean that we are unaware of the great educational value, implicit in the very holding of this trial, for those who live in Israel as well as for those beyond the confines of this state (. . .) but as far as this Court is concerned, they are to be regarded as by-products of the trial.[52]

In Jerusalem the judges showed keen awareness about the historical nature of their work, but also about the inherent tensions between legal and historical judgment, and did what they could to maintain the distinction between the two, reserving for themselves the right to judge Eichmann, and pronouncing all other aspects of their verdict incidental.

Despite judicial reservation, the extralegal effects of the trial were highly visible. Regardless of whether the judges saw it as by-product or not, it is difficult not to agree with Lawrence Douglas that "the prosecution did not use the law simply to pursue extralegal ends. Instead, by interrogating the standard conception of law, the Eichmann prosecution pushed the trial and a reluctant court to become a powerful forum for understanding and commemorating traumatic history." He concludes that "in terms of the trial's effect upon its observers, the success of Hausner's approach receives provocative confirmation from the many contemporaneous accounts and histories on trial."[53] And indeed, despite the toned-down engagement of historians as expert witnesses, recent research identifies this trial as a major forger of collective identity, not only among the community of Holocaust survivors and their relatives, but within the entire new generation of young Israelis, as its results and findings reached educational curricula.[54] It was an international turning point as well: "The capture, trial and execution of Adolf Eichmann were sensational events that for short periods dominated the news media of the time and changed forever perceptions of the Nazi persecution and mass murder of the Jews," writes David Cesarani in an edited volume dedicated to the international impact of the Eichmann trial on collective memory. He emphasized the importance of "the evidence and testimony amassed by the prosecution, as well as the way it was shaped and delivered in the courtroom," and stressed that "most historians and commentators do agree that the trial marked a turning point in perceptions of the recent past, (. . .) The trial had a brief, potent initial impact and then a longer term and more subtle influence on the formation of memory and historical consciousness."[55]

A Transnational Connection: From Jerusalem to Frankfurt

Nowhere did the Eichmann case resonate more strongly than in Germany. One of its keen observers was none other than Fritz Bauer, by that time Attorney General of Hesse. Bauer was even included in the hunt for Eichmann, providing the Israeli government with information on his whereabouts, even visiting Israel to protest against the inactivity of Israeli authorities. After the arrest, he requested that the German government demand Eichmann's extradition to Germany.[56] Undeterred by the restrictive approach of Jerusalem judges, he did not shy away from asking wider questions: "In the face of all the ghastly and appalling things that the Eichmann trial has once again revealed to us and to the entire world, everyone asks, we ask ourselves, how these things were possible?"[57] Bauer openly lamented the inability of the German judiciary to produce a satisfying answer. Since the return of its state prerogatives, the Federal Republic of Germany approached the issue of Nazi criminality (which Bauer called *altpolitische Prozessen*) with visible lenience. Proactive prosecutors like Bauer were using every opportunity to rock that boat. He understood that one of the reasons for the sidelining of the Holocaust in Germany lay in its juridical fragmentation: "The courts tried to divide the total event, e.g. the mass murder of millions in the extermination camps, into episodes (. . .) but this approach was a rape of what had happened, which was not a sum of individual events."[58]

As Bauer searched for a chance to address this problem, through a set of coincidences, his office in Frankfurt was assigned with investigating and prosecuting Auschwitz-related crimes.[59] The chief suspect was Richard Baer, one of the last commanders of Auschwitz, identified and arrested in October 1960. Alongside Baer, another twenty-three members of the Auschwitz SS personnel were put under arrest. A team working under his supervision completed the investigations and presented a seven-hundred-page-long indictment against twenty-two officers and guards of the infamous Auschwitz concentration camp, constructing a case that came to be known as the Frankfurt Auschwitz trial.[60] Much to the chagrin of Bauer's colleagues, Joachim Kügler and Georg Friedrich Vogel, who represented the prosecution in the case under prosecutor Dr. Hanns Großmann, Baer died in June 1963, leaving twenty members of Auschwitz personnel on the dock, with Robert Mulka, adjutant of the camp commander, being the most highly ranked. Bauer was not discouraged by the setback, and remained a driving force behind the case. It is difficult not to agree with Nuremberg prosecutor Robert Kempner: "I believe there would be no first large Frankfurt Auschwitz trial without the Hessian state prosecutor Fritz Bauer."[61] "Bauer's intentions were not strictly judicial but more broadly historical as well. Quite explicitly, beyond his concern with individual cases, Bauer wanted to bring to task a whole era, an entire ideology," comments Rebecca Wittmann, quoting Bauer: "One of the most important tasks of this trial is not only to present the horrendous facts, but also actually to teach ourselves something, that we here in Germany have completely forgotten in the course of the last one hundred years."[62]

Broad historical intentions, similar to Ben Gurion's and Hausner's in the Eichmann case, brought about similar results—the prosecution contemplated the wider commissioning historical expert reports. Bauer was successfully experimenting with historians as experts from the 1952 Remer trial, and he surely took notice of the role they played both in the Ulm trial and in the Eichmann case. Convinced about the indispensability of historians for providing a wider context in which crimes occurred, he initially entertained the idea of engaging experts from abroad—Yad Vashem or the Polish Auschwitz Museum. However, perhaps influenced by the under-effective performance of Salo Baron, a lone outsider giving a macro-level overview of the Holocaust, he soon turned to the idea of collective historical contributions from a closer and more obvious source—the Munich Institute for Contemporary History.

In April 1961, prosecutor Großman contacted the Institute for Contemporary History in Munich, where he met Hans Buchheim, one of the principal fellows who was extensively researching Nazi crimes. Buchheim was among the authors of previous reports done for the court, but expressed reservations in 1955 about the forensic role of the "historian, who has other tasks than judge and prosecutor. Not only that he is not allowed, but he has to renounce the position of defendant and prosecution."[63] However, at this meeting he "expressed principle readiness" of the Institute for Contemporary History to partake in a forthcoming trial.[64] This readiness reflected his own transformation, but also the evolution in the Institute. Ever since the director, Helmut Krausnick, testified as an expert in the 1958 Ulm trial, the contact resumed, particularly as prosecutor Schüle chaired Zentrale Stelle Ludwigsburg. "Cooperation with the justice was for the Institute not only an annoying duty, but the process from which they could gain knowledge on the history of national-socialism in return, adding documentation from legal investigation to other documents obtained differently in the archival holdings of the Institute."[65] There was a "clear coincidence of interests between the historians from the Institute and Fritz Bauer, in that both were hoping to use this historical testimony for broader, public pedagogical purposes," concluded Devin Pendas.[66]

Bauer readily grasped this opportunity for the normalization of historical expert testimony and was eager to maximize its impact in the courtroom. This led to a sequence of meetings between historians and prosecutors, dedicated to the division of labor. The most extensive of these such meetings was held on November 7, 1962, in the presence of the prosecutors from Frankfurt and Wiesbaden, representatives of Ludwigsburg Central Station, and the leadership of the Institute for Contemporary History—director Helmut Krausnick, his deputy Hans Buchheim, Martin Broszat, and Helmut Heiber. Speaking for the prosecution, Bauer "stressed that the findings of the newest history are presumed to be judicially notoriously recognized facts, but are actually not usable if not introduced in every proceeding. The purpose of old political trials—the overcoming of the past—cannot be achieved without the clarification of the background in which the crimes happened." He was clearly impressed with the way "the Eichmann trial through the richness of documents enabled bulletproof clarification of political events in the Third Reich in regard of Jewish policy." His conclusion was blunt: "The prosecution has to call experts. In this way we could avoid that the court dismiss this historical material out of ignorance or laziness."[67]

As "the need to introduce experts in *altpolitische* criminal trials was recognized from all present," it was agreed that "reports should present only the so-called 'background.'" Rather than concerning themselves with particular defendants, the overall task of historians was "to establish when the decisive actions of narrow circle of creators had spread to other persons, in particular to the lower levels of the services."[68] To that end, Bauer outlined seven fields which needed to be covered. It was agreed that Krausnick would cover the policy of persecution of the Jews 1933–1945, and Broszat would write about the Polish policy of the Nazis. Buchheim took on the project of writing about the creation of the SS hierarchy, the creation of concentration camps, and the *Befehlsnotstand* (obeying orders under extreme duress). On the treatment of Soviet prisoners of war, and the creation and activity of the Einsatzgruppen, the idea arose to contact two docents from the Free University of Berlin, Wolfgang Scheffler and Friedrich Zipfel.[69]

The pedagogical effect of the engagement of historians was also given full consideration: "The lecture of a recognized expert the process might provide an orderly contextualization of political events," claimed Bauer, insisting that "reports should be written and submitted orally. Written reports, which if possible should already serve in writing of the indictment, should be all encompassing. In particular they must emphasize the most important documents and, as to be expected in scholarly reports, they must quote them. (. . .) The scope of the oral reports depends on the scope of the process. They can differ in scope from the written reports, and they should be lively. They have to be understandable to a wider audience. Academic exposés should be avoided. Important documents, and, eventually photos, should be projected on the wall." It was also concluded that "expert reports should be published if possible, perhaps by Fischer Verlag."[70] This being agreed, historians went about to construct the reports, and Bauer's team to finalize the indictment.

Bauer wasted no time in preparing the legal ground. He took part in a debate about the reform of the German penal process and in January 1963 contributed the piece *The Rule of Experts*, in which he passionately argued that "experts, regarded in our legal system with simplification as 'help for the judges' are indispensable. (. . .) To bring out one example, the anti-Nazi trials of our times have shown, that we cannot by any means assume a sufficient knowledge about our history can be provided anywhere. Therefore reports of historians should be commissioned. The same goes for chemical, physical and technical questions."[71] Behind closed doors, he was equally vocal. On the meetings of the prosecutorial commissions in October of the same year, he claimed: "There is a further problem—in previous trials, the defense has succeeded in dismembering the proceedings into small pieces, so that neither the jurors, trial observers, nor the general public can get a general picture." Announcing to his colleagues commission of expert reports as a solution to this problem, he emphasized that "the meaning and purpose of the expert reports should be to make the true intentions of the Nazi regime accessible to the court and the German public in the form of scholarly presentations."[72] Therefore, besides the 252 eyewitnesses that the prosecution suggested for the upcoming trial, the list also contained no fewer than nine experts. Among them one was a graphologist, one was legal, and three were doctors. Four were historians.[73]

The trial commenced on December 20, 1963, with the reading of the indictment, a substantial part of which, almost a third of its seven hundred pages, was dedicated to the historical context. It addressed the development of the policy of extermination, with a description of the role concentration camps played in it, as well as a brief history of SS. Then it turned to the foundation of Auschwitz, the horrendous conditions of this camp, and the role it had in the implementation of the "final solution." The bulk of the indictment dealt with the individual responsibility of the accused, but the emphasis on the contextual part was clearly a consequence of close collaboration between prosecutors and historians, resulting in "a dual document,

Figure 5.3 The session of the Frankfurt Auschwitz trial

both historiographical and juridical in character."[74] After the indictment was read and the accused was identified, the time came for the evidentiary segment of the trial. Bauer rightfully anticipated that the judges might feel uncomfortable with this charge of historians into the courtroom. There were slim chances that the judges would automatically accept the historians' reports. Traces of suspicion toward this unorthodox approach could be found in a note from the substitute judge Werner Hummerich from January 26, 1964, entitled *Expert Reports on Structure and Development of SS and Concentration Camps?* The judge wrote:

> The issue of the structure and development (. . .) and the conclusions that stem out of it for or against the accused, is in the competence of the court in the first place. Expert could consequently be heard if there is such a need. But the reports would here in any case be worthless, contemporary history cannot be introduced in the trial, which is to be judged on the basis of concrete facts alone. General reports are more likely to blur than to clarify them. It can be further remarked that every general report leads the court toward widening of the subject which could be historically interesting, but dangerous. Contemporary historians as experts actively evaluate the past with their own scientific methods, but the court has to adhere to the rules of the German code of criminal procedure. Therefore, without a doubt, historians bring further uncertainties into the process, with findings which are completely meaningless in the framework of a trial, but once introduced could create reasonable doubts. In such situations, counter-reports and supra-reports seem inevitable. The controversy inevitably appears—which historians are to be taken as serious scientists, and which are not (historians from the Eastern bloc, who see Auschwitz as the outgrowth of monopolistic capitalism, or racially fanatical historians of western background!!!).[75]

Instead of bringing them to the court, suggested the judge, the prosecution should have used "objective historians, in order to assemble the documents (. . .) and relevant information on each defendant and their superiors. (. . .) The degree to which the prosecution was internally using experts for this purpose has no relevance for the court, as long as they appear in front of it."[76] Such an opinion of the judge was grounded in an inquisitorial German criminal procedure in which experts were primarily appointed by the court, with limited participation of the parties, which could propose experts or challenge their reports, but the judges were to make that decision.[77] However, Article 245 obliged the judges "to extend the taking of evidence to the witnesses and experts who appeared upon being summoned by the defendant or the public prosecution office, as well as to other evidence produced. The application shall be rejected if the taking of evidence is inadmissible. It may otherwise be rejected only if the fact for which evidence is to be furnished has already been proved or is common knowledge, if there is no connection between the fact and the matter being adjudicated, if the evidence is completely unsuitable, or if the application has been filed for the purpose of protracting the proceedings."[78] This was exactly the loophole used by the prosecution to override potential resistance of the judges. The prosecution informed the court on January 29, 1964 about its intention "to present four experts in accordance with §245 of the code of criminal procedure during several working days in the beginning of recording of evidence."[79] Unacquainted with the exact content of their expert reports, the judges were left no choice but to allow the exposés of the historians in the courtroom and to reach the decision on their admissibility only after hearing their oral presentations. Following this legal exchange, the historians were among the first witnesses for the prosecution.

Historical Forensic Contribution in Frankfurt

Although historical reports were dealing with different topics, they bore an important similarity, observes Dieter Pohl: "Historians were not investigating individual crimes or individual defendants, but were asked to demonstrate the background of mass murder, the development of Nazi ideology, the measures of anti-Jewish persecution, the structure and function of German institutions in the Third Reich."[80] The first one to take the stand was Hans Buchheim, who on February 8, 1964 testified on the *Organization of SS and Police Under Nazi Rule* during the sixteenth session of the trial. Helmut Krausnick's exposé on the *Persecution of the Jews* followed ten days later, and Martin Broszat testified during the seventeenth, eighteenth, and twenty-first sessions (until February 28) on both topics he took on: *The Concentration Camps, 1933–1945*, and *National-socialist Policy towards the Poles*. Their reports were based on detailed analysis of the sources, providing a scaled presentation of the layered context of events that led to the establishment of the extermination program in Auschwitz. Krausnick's report outlined the scope, extent, and uniqueness of the Nazi extermination campaign against the Jews. It was a short but chilling scrutiny of the gradual development of anti-Semitism, beginning with the mid-nineteenth century: "History has seen many instances of persecution of the Jews—but never a State-inspired persecution planned with such a diabolical consistency and carried through so cold-bloodedly and systematically, and on such a scale and with such terrible consequences, as that persecution set in motion by the National Socialist regime, with all the administrative and technical resources at its command, in the territories it controlled. In any study of the subject the German historian has a duty, now more than ever, to keep firmly in mind that this was no chance development and that even Hitler was no mere 'accident' of German history."[81] Quickly passing through the stages of the persecution after the Nazi takeover to the evolution of the extermination plan during the Second World War, his description ended with an account of Auschwitz: "Operations in Auschwitz were rounded off by the liquidation of hundreds of thousands of Hungarian Jews in the most systematic and comprehensive 'action' that had hitherto been taken—since when the name of the camp has become a symbol of the greatest massacre known to history."[82] This exposé set the stage for a more detailed scrutiny of the development of the mechanism of the concentration camps provided by Broszat. Historians understood well the role meant by Bauer, and their generalized topics were delivered with the clear purpose of providing the context deemed necessary by the prosecution in order to determine the individual criminal guilt of the accused.

However, not all went according to the Bauer's plan, as the Frankfurt Auschwitz trial was a huge event that played a role in German Cold War politics. Karl Kaul, lawyer and political figure from the DDR, represented the victims from East Germany in court, and he insisted on including the expertise of Jürgen Kuczynski, notable economic historian from Humboldt University, member of the East German Academy of Sciences, with an expert report entitled *The Integration of the Security Police and the Economic Interests in the Establishment and Operations of KZ Auschwitz and Its Sub-Camps*.[83] He was to testify on the economic basis of the camps in the gist of dogmatic Marxism. Performing the same trick as the prosecution, Kaul succeeded in putting him on the stand during the twenty-eighth session, on March 19, 1964. The defense attorneys protested against his testimony, claiming that he was not an independent expert, but a political agitator from the DDR. And indeed, Kuczynski maintained in the courtroom that it was "a historical fact that the wrong defendants are on trial. The monopoly capitalists and their helpers who now put atomic bombs in place of gas ovens are the truly guilty ones."[84] The contextualization provided in his report differed very much from the one provided by the experts of the prosecution. His inferences were much more general: "For thousands of years the state and the economic decision-makers have been in the closest collaboration."[85] He not only testified to the presence of the I. G. Farben facilities in Auschwitz, but reached the conclusion that the interests of this company in slave labor were the main reason for the existence of the camp, with the clear purpose of demonstrating, inter alia, that fascism was the last and the most deadly stage of capitalism.[86] Judge Hummerich took the lead:

Hummerich: So I may say that for you Mr. Ranke or Mr. Treitschke are not models?

Kuczynski: I would say for sure that Treitschke is not a model. Ranke is in some respects an outstanding model. (. . .)

Hummerich: Yes. But in terms of modern history, which must be seen politically, your role models are surely rather Engels, Marx and above all Lenin. When I say Lenin, in this special case of ours, I refer to his work "Imperialism, the Highest Stage of Capitalism."

Kuczynsky: Yes, certainly. (. . .)

Hummerich: That is something completely different from the way the gentlemen from Munchen were examining the problem.

Kuczynsku: Completely different. (. . .)

Attorney Laternser: Yes, yes. You are a Communist?

Kuczyncky: Yes, all the members of the Socialist Unity Party are Communists. (. . .)

Attorney Laternser: Who gave you the honorarium for this report? (. . .) I am saying that this is not an expert in a legal sense. The term expert implies that he is in the position to make independent judgments. Professor Kuczynsky is not independent.[87]

Eventually, convinced mostly by his shaky handling of the material, the court denied the status of expert to Kuczynski, expressing "distrust toward the impartiality of the expert."[88] Other contingencies followed. Dr. Heinrich Ulrich, initially commissioned to write a report on the mass execution of Soviet prisoners of war and the Kommisarbefehl, passed away on February 11, 1964. Deciding not to leave out this topic, the prosecution ordered another report from Dr. Hans Adolf Jacobsen on the same topic although the trial was well underway.[89] On July 2, 1964, Hans Buchheim reappeared to testify on the problem of the *Befehlsnotstands*. In his definite showdown with the issue of the Führer's orders, he separated obedience to the laws and orders from unconditional loyalty to Hitler, which was a part of the SS mentality. He stated that "it is the wrong perception that all of the Fuhrer's orders stemmed from the legal order and had a legislative effect."[90] Finally, Jacobsen took the stand on August 14, 1964, finalizing the historical part of the prosecution's case. Soon after the oral presentations, the experts submitted full written reports to the prosecution, which turned them into evidence to court.[91]

It remained to be seen how the court would evaluate them, but it was already clear that they caught the public's eye. Some of the reports crushed the entrenched myths of postwar German society. If Jacobsen's report tracked the practice of killing prisoners of war by the Wehrmacht as well as by the SS, the other Buchheim report delivered the decisive blow to the "obeying orders" defense, evoked by all the defendants in an attempt to minimize their responsibility, by stressing the readiness of soldiers to comply with criminal commands. In the absence of stenographic notes and audiovisual recordings, it is difficult to know exactly what was said in the courtroom, but their effect is seen in telling headlines in the press: "The Führer's Orders Were Not Binding," "They Knew They Were Committing Injustice," "Expert: There Is No Obeying Orders Defense For Camp Guards."[92]

For the very same reason, the presence of historians was particularly annoying for the defense, which attempted to deploy their choice of expert historian, Hans Günther Seraphim, only to be met with the court decision that "the knowledge of the expert who offered facts in the Mulka case holds no relevance for the decision."[93] So they continued to attempt to delegitimize the practice of historical expertise altogether. The most vicious attack came from Hans Laternser, the attorney who represented five defendants at the trial. In a book published immediately after the process, Laternser outlined the traditional role performed by experts in German criminal procedure and concluded that "it was very different in the Auschwitz trial." He described the expert reports as "useless" and the testimonies as "killing time." "Why then these reports?" he asked. "These general reports are superfluous and without any significance for the decision in the proceedings."[94] However, the extent of historical forensic contribution remained for the judges to discern, as the largest German trial on Nazi atrocities was coming to a close in summer 1965, after 193 trial sessions wherein they heard 356 witnesses and eight experts, five of them historians.

The Frankfurt Auschwitz Trial: The Quest for a Historical Context in an Inquisitorial Setting

It is remarkable how oral justification for the judgment, read by Judge Hans Hofmayer on August 20, 1965, structurally mirrors many of the reservations toward historical background stressed in the Jerusalem judgment to Eichmann. The judges emphasized their primary duty to render justice to the individual perpetrators:

> It is understandable that there was a desire to have this trial serve as a basis for broad, comprehensive historical presentation of events, to unravel the background leading up to this catastrophe, to depict and try to understand the political developments after World War I that led up to Auschwitz. (. . .) However, the court did not give in to the temptation and did not permit itself to be led astray from the path staked out by law and venture into regions closed to it. (. . .) The court has no right to pursue any other goal. (. . .) Although the trial has attracted attention beyond the borders of this country and been given the name 'Auschwitz Trial', as far as the court is concerned, it is the proceedings against Mulka and others. That is to say, as far as the court is concerned, the only consideration was the guilt of the accused men. The court was not convened for the purposes of overcoming the past. (. . .) This was an ordinary criminal trial, regardless of its background.[95]

However, these reservations faded away in the actual judgment. The presiding judge surely showed a lack of enthusiasm for dwelling on the background of the case. However, "as much as Judge Hofmeyer's instinct told him to leave history and politics to others, he could not help but recognize the need to situate the crimes of the Auschwitz Trial defendants in their historical context, or at least the juridical version of that context," concludes

Devin Pendas.[96] The degree of the responsibility of the individual accused was assessed in light of evidence and the testimonies of eyewitnesses. Six defendants were sentenced to imprisonment for life, three were released, and twelve were given sentences between four and fourteen years of imprisonment. The majority of the accused were treated as accomplices to murder (in thousands of cases), as the court took the view that that the "main perpetrators of extermination actions were Hitler as the author of the orders on 'the final solution of the Jewish question' and Himmler (. . .) as well as other persons of the narrow Führer's circle as Göring, Heydrich and others (. . .) for all the defendants convicted of aiding and abetting murder, the instigation came from the highest level of state leadership."[97]

Substantiation of this assertion called for historical contextualization. It might be argued, and indeed it was argued, that the court could have reached a similar verdict without this historical detour. "One could argue that the entire historical background given in the indictment was irrelevant to the charges, and in many ways, it was; however, it makes sense that the courts decided that some form of explanatory overview was necessary for trying crimes of this nature."[98] Approximately one-tenth of the judgment (forty of four hundred pages) was dedicated to this context, and it was mostly built on the content of reports of historical expert witnesses: "Findings about the creation and development of the Konzentrationslagern im NS-Staat rest on detailed and competent reports of experts Dr. Broszat, Dr. Buchheim and relevant laws and orders from that time." The court went on to determine the individual responsibility of the accused, duly crediting all the historical experts, "whose convincing and grounded presentations the court has entirely endorsed."[99] This was a great victory, not only for prosecutor Bauer, but also for the concept of historical forensic expertise in an inquisitorial setting.

The Institute for Contemporary History surely knew how to make the best of this momentum. It continued its project of assisting the courts with new *Gutachten* (expert reports) as well as publishing old ones. Such a second volume appeared in 1966, containing reports made after 1958. Its editor, new director Helmut Krausnick, explained that a number of requests for historical expertise increased significantly, due to "the great trials, which had been conducted or prepared from 1958 in particular against the personnel of Nazi concentration camps or Einsatzgruppen."[100] However, this volume did not contain the expert reports from the Frankfurt Auschwitz trial. These reports were to be published in their entirety, as submitted to the court, under the catchy title *Anatomy of the SS State*. With a print run of fifty thousand copies to this day, it became a formative work of German historiography in this field.[101] Reports were printed as submitted; the only insertion was the introduction, worthy of extensive quotation as it provided the experts with an opportunity to elaborate on their own position:

> Concentration camps crimes and the mass murder of Jews were essential features of National Socialist tyranny. Many people for various

> reasons forget this fact. (. . .) In the numerous trials of national Socialist criminals now being conducted in Germany, the question of the connection between political tyranny and ideological crimes is inevitably a relevant issue. The importance of these trials lies more in the fact that they pose the necessity of finding an answer to this question, than in their ostensible task of meting out justice for wrongs committed. The case of an accused who took part in these crimes can only be judged rightly if the whole moral, political and organizational background leading to his actions is surveyed. The task of the historical expert is to assist the Court by painting as clearly as possible a picture of this background. He is not there to concern himself with the case of any particular accused. Investigation into the circumstances of each individual case and pronouncement of guilt and innocence is exclusively the prerogative of the Court. It is for the expert to provide a picture of the historical and political landscape in which each individual occurrence took place.

The experts were also keenly aware of the extrajudicial importance of their work for wider reckoning with the Nazi past:

> Many Germans, for instance, wrestling with their own conscience are apt to allow their sense of communal political and moral guilt to overshadow the specific crimes of specific individuals; this is a widespread tendency to which the Court must not give way. A man may reproach himself for having been politically mistaken or having shown himself a coward, but between him and the man who actively and wholeheartedly participated in the regime's dirty business there is a difference not of degree but of kind. (. . .) No right-thinking person whose sense of right and wrong has not been warped can declare a man innocent if he has murdered thousands of defenseless human beings, no matter whether or not he can cite an order binding him to do so. (. . .) When presenting the history of the National Socialist period to the Court of Justice, a special effort must be made to do so rationally and dispassionately, for the facts presented are not merely the subject of an historical analysis which commits no one, but may have a decisive influence on the fate of the accused. Those taking part in public discussions before the court are in duty bound to weigh their words, and this is to the good that it constitutes an effective counterweight to the widespread habit of painting a highly emotional picture of the past in order to highlight certain major truths, but at the price of historical exactitude regarding facts and circumstances. Since Hitler's dictatorship is so obviously to be condemned from all points of view people are tempted to think too little about it. This is why, despite an immense mass of literature about the Third Reich, so little intelligent use has been made of it. The superficiality of many words on the subject is no more than a reflection of popular tendency; people prefer vivid writing (and it is difficult not to write vividly

> about Auschwitz); people try to evade the rationalism of the historian and prefer moralistic emotional theorizing. The current phrase is "conscience awakening." But a sleepy conscience is like a sleepy man: if a man is shaken hard enough he will wake up—and then after one or two half-waking moments will quickly go asleep again. That which man's intellect once grasps however will remain and will not disappear. So in order to come to terms intellectually with National Socialism and its era, the Germans have need not of emotionalism or some moral evangelistic movement but of sober work combined with intelligence and common sense. Otherwise we run the risk of drawing the wrong lessons from the past. The strict rules of the judicial proceeding point the way to a standard of rationalism of which we are in dire need. This was the standard which the authors of these submissions strove to maintain.[102]

With the Frankfurt Auschwitz trial historians definitely entered a courtroom, not through the back door, but through the main entrance. This endorsement, according to Devin Pendas, "also gave them the status of an 'official history.' This was not just another history of the Nazi regime and its atrocities. This was a history produced by the Institute for Contemporary History, a governmentally sanctioned historical institute, and read into evidence at a state trial; this was as close as a democratic society ever comes to having a historiographical party line."[103] Its growing centrality in research of recent history, as well as importance of expert functions in its ascent, was described by Hans Herzfeld: "The Munich Institute of Contemporary History, after a hesitant start, has come to occupy a central position in research; its library and archives in particular have been of great and growing service to international historical research. Although drawn in more and more as experts and authorities for the denazification and war-crimes trials, it has been able to expand the scope of its research to include the period since 1945. The *Vierteljahrshefte fur Zeitgeschichte* published by the Institute under the direction of Hans Rothfels, has become one of the leading international periodicals in the field. Although the Institute is mainly concerned with the analysis of the source material, it can not be said that the work sponsored by the Institute has tried to avoid the more controversial issues of the present, which at one time were dealt with more quickly and more thoroughly abroad. Thus, for example, the two-volume study, *Die Anatomie des SS- Staates*, based on the extensive evidence of four specialists, probably represents the most thorough treatment of such burning questions as the ultimate responsibility for the giving and obeying of orders in the SS; the running of concentration camps, the execution of the Kommissarbefehl, and the extermination of the Jews."[104] However, the impact of these testimonies went beyond this institution. After a number of experiments of limited success in the Remer, Ulm, and Eichmann cases, a combination of prosecutorial initiative and readiness of historians to reexamine the ethical and methodological purposes of their work brought about a historical forensic contribution into the German courtrooms to reckon with the thorniest issues imaginable. Unlike Salo Baron, who was contacted in secrecy and flown to Jerusalem with huge expectations, but without much preparation or consultation, historians in Frankfurt benefited both from institutional support and previous experiences.

On this intersection, historical forensic contribution evolved to be seen as indispensable "in establishing context. His expertise is needed because the narrow judicial conception of case-specific circumstances is insufficient for, and usually not applicable to crimes committed many years or even decades prior to their investigation. What is required instead is a broader conception of both the context of the crime itself and the larger historical framework that informs on the culpability of the defendants. In short, expert opinion (the historian) is called upon to provide the historical context that will meet these novel 'legal' requirements. Thus, in the post-World War Two war crimes trials, history was reintroduced into what was supposed to be a purely legal sphere of activity," observes Erich Haberer.[105]

With all the differences posed by the disciplinary requirements, this important synergic effect came to represent a setting typical for the inquisitorial processing of criminal cases, presenting a powerful breach into the theory of incompatibility between history and law and offering a stable paradigm of historical expertise in court. More sources were becoming available or were being generated by the courts and by historians, and a new generation of specialists, both of historians and lawyers, grew versed in the highly specific area of mass atrocities. However, in light of the forthcoming expiration date that was to make most of the crimes of the Nazi period unprosecutable in the Federal Republic of Germany after 1965, it was unclear whether the Frankfurt Auschwitz trial would be recorded by history as the end of the era of the prosecution of Nazi crimes or its new beginning. Historians took the stand in the courtroom, but now it was their time to take a standpoint, joining the other disciplines in a lively debate concerning the renegotiation of the relations between history and law.

Acknowledgments

Parts of this chapter were originally published in Vladimir Petrović, "The Role of Expert Witnesses in First Holocaust-related Trials," *Istorija 20.veka*, 1 (2007), 129–145.

Notes

1 Robert M.W. Kempner. *Eichmann und Komplizen* (Zurich: Europa Verlag, 1961), 444; Randolph L. Braham. *The Eichmann Case: A Source Book* (New York: World Federation of Hungarian Jews, 1969), iii. Braham's bibliography contains 1,173 entries from the 1960s alone. It stands as a testimony of worldwide interest in Eichmann's kidnapping, the nature of his crimes, the right of Israel to put him on trial, etc.

2 Harry Golden. "Foreword," in *The Case against Adolf Eichmann*, ed. Henry A. Zeiger (New York: Signet Books, 1960), vii. Ben Gurion quoted in Hannah Arendt, *Eichmann in Jerusalem, A Report on the Banality of Evil* (London: Faber and Faber, 1963), 8. Pedagogical and theatrical aspects of the Eichmann trial are discussed in Shoshana Felman, "Theaters of Justice: Arendt in Jerusalem, the Eichmann Trial, and the Redefinition of Legal Meaning in the Wake of the Holocaust," *Critical Inquiry* 27 (2001): 201–240. Cf. Lawrence Douglas, *The Memory of Judgment, Making Law and History in the Trials of the Holocaust* (New Haven: Yale University Press, 2005), 96–182.

3 Victor Golancz, *The Case of Adolf Eichmann* (London: Camelot Press, 1961), 16, 18–19.

4 JTA, "Ben Gurion Emphasizes Significance of Eichmann Trial to World," 4 April, 1961.

5 Nazi and Nazi Collaborator Punishment Law, https://www.jewishvirtuallibrary.org/jsource/Politics/nazilaw.html, accessed on 21.2.2016. Exclusively covering the period between 1933 and 1945, during which the state of Israel did not exist, this law was clearly meant to be applied retroactively. During its adoption debate in the Knesset brought in August 1950, it was loaded with historical references, prompting Attorney General Haim Cohen to address the deputies: "I beg your pardon if from the noble heights of history, I must bring you down to earth and to the dry reality of the legal debate." Quoted in Hanna Yablonka, *The State of Israel vs Adolf Eichmann* (New York: Shocken Books, 2004), 10.

6 Eliahu Harnon,"Criminal Procedure in Israel—Some Comparative Aspects," *University of Pennsylvania Law Review* 115.7 (1967): 1093.

7 Ibid., 1096–1097.

8 Gideon Hausner. *Justice in Jerusalem* (New York: Harper & Row, 1966), 292.

9 Hausner quoted in Douglas, *The Memory of Judgment*, 3.

10 The general overview that the police were using as a point of departure was Gerald Reutlinger's *The Final Solution: The Attempt to Exterminate the Jews of Europe* (New York: Beechhurst Press, 1953).

11 Yablonka, *The State of Israel vs Adolf Eichmann*, 68, 71.

12 Joseph Kermish, "Yad Vashem Contribution to the Trial," *Yad Vashem Bulletin* (April–May, 1962): 37–45.

13 Yablonka, *The State of Israel vs Adolf Eichmann*, 100.

14 Salo Wittmayer Baron, (1895, Tarnów–1989, New York City), originally from Galicia and of Polish, German, and Jewish descent, was one of the founders of Jewish studies in the U.S. Polyglot and interdisciplinarian, he defended doctorates in philosophy in 1917, in political science in 1922, and in law in 1924, also receiving a rabbinical ordination. Moving to the U.S. in 1929 and eventually settling as a historian, the author of the voluminous *Religious and Social History of the Jewish People* taught at Columbia University from 1930 until his retirement in 1963. He was famed for opposing "the lachrymose conception of Jewish history" and for integrating the entirety of Jewish history into the study of Jewish culture. More on Baron's life in Robert Liberles, *Salo Wittmayer Baron: Architect of Jewish History* (New York: New York University Press, 1995).

15 HSTML, Letter from Jacob Robinson to Robert H. Jackson, July 27, 1945 Records of the World Jewish Congress, http://www.trumanlibrary.org/whistlestop/study_collections/nuremberg/documents/index.php?documentdate=1945-07-27&documentid=C106-16-2&studycollectionid=&pagenumber=1, accessed on 22.2.2016.

16 Debates are elaborated in Yablonka, *The State of Israel vs Adolf Eichmann*, 100–101.

17 "Pinchas Rosen to Benjamin Eliav, Re Eichmann trial. December 26, 1960." Translation from Hebrew, Stanford University, Manuscripts Division, Salo W. Baron Papers, 1900–1980, Box 65/1.
18 Liberles, *Salo Wittmayer Baron*, 318–323.
19 Yablonka, *The State of Israel vs Adolf Eichmann*, 102.
20 Salo W. Baron, "Tentative Summary of Testimony," Stanford University, Manuscripts Division, Salo W. Baron Papers, 1900–1980, Box 65/1. Different versions of the testimony are also in Box 226/9, 406/2, 406/3, and 406/7.
21 Yablonka, *The State of Israel vs Adolf Eichmann*, 103.
22 Quoted in Liberles, *Salo Wittmayer Baron*, 330.
23 The defense was against filming the trial, but the prosecution was adamant about bringing it to public attention, as wide as possible. Eventually, with some constraints, filming was permitted. Still, the trial was shown on a TV screen in a nearby hall as there was still no television in Israel. Needless to say, radio and newspapers devoted full attention to the trial. Yablonka, *The State of Israel vs Adolf Eichmann*, 56–62.
24 "Memorandum for testimony, April 24, 1961." Salo W. Baron, Tentative Summary of Testimony, Stanford University, Manuscripts Division, Salo W. Baron Papers, 1900–1980, Box406/2.
25 Transcripts of Baron's testimony are available at *The Trial of Adolf Eichmann: Record of Proceedings in the District Court of Jerusalem* (Jerusalem: State of Israel, Ministry of Justice, 1992), vol. I, 169–190. Also available at The Nizkor Project, The Trial of Adolf Eichmann, Session 12 and Session 13, http://www.nizkor.org/hweb/people/e/eichmann-adolf/transcripts/Sessions/Session-012–03.html, accessed on 26.6.2006.
26 *The Trial of Adolf Eichmann*, vol. I, 170.
27 Parts of Baron's testimony visuals are also available at Eichmann trial, Sessions 12 and 13, http://www.youtube.com/watch?v=GFZ29SzRVq0.
28 Haim Gouri, *Facing the Glass Booth: The Jerusalem Trial of Adolf Eichmann* (Detroit: Wayne State University Press, 2004), 23.
29 *The Trial of Adolf Eichmann*, vol. I, 184. The demographics of the Holocaust were a particular problem for the investigation. During the investigation stage, the prosecution consulted a number of assessments ranging between four and seven million, but was not able to discern between them. Eventually Hausner took the attitude which Baron apparently adopted: "In the event of the question arising at the trial, we try to find the appropriate way of explaining that it does not really matter how many Jews the Germans killed directly and how many died in bombings and how many died as a direct result of the annihilation decision, but that millions did die. And if the general prosecution can prove many millions, whether four, six or seven, it makes no difference. The fact remains that were it not for Hitler, the Jewish nation would today number between 19 and 21 million people and we have only 11 million. So if he annihilated directly or indirectly or by the way of biological loss, it makes no difference whether the number is four, five or six million." Quoted in Yablonka, The State of Israel vs Adolf Eichmann., 83.
30 *The Trial of Adolf Eichmann*, vol. I, 189.
31 Deborah E. Lipstadt, *The Eichmann Trial* (New York: Schocken Books, 2011), 68.
32 Telford Taylor, *Adolf Eichmann's Third Life, The Spectator*, 21.4.1961, 10; Telford Taylor, *Mirror, Mirror on the Wall, The Spectator*, 19 May 1961, 6.
33 Stephan Landsman. *Crimes of the Holocaust: The Law Confronts Hard Cases* (Philadelphia: University of Pennsylvania Press, 2005), 75.
34 Harnon, *Criminal Procedure in Israel . . .*, 604.

35 Gouri, *Facing the Glass Booth*, 25.
36 *The Trial of Adolf Eichmann*, vol. I, 188.
37 "Pinchas Rosen to Benjamin Eliav, Re Eichmann trial. December 26, 1960." Translation from the Hebrew, Stanford University, Manuscripts Division, Salo W. Baron Papers, 1900–1980, Box 65/1.
38 *The Trial of Adolf Eichmann*, vol. I, 188–189.
39 Ibid.
40 Arthur Hertzberg reported Baron coming back "absolutely drained." Liberles, *Salo Wittmayer Baron*, 323.
41 Harry Mulisch, *Criminal Case 40/61, The Trial of Adolf Eichmann: An Eyewitness Account* (Philadelphia: University of Pennsylvania Press, 2005), 63–64.
42 Yablonka, *The State of Israel vs Adolf Eichmann*, 105.
43 Ibid., 103–104.
44 Gideon Hausner. *Justice in Jerusalem* (New York: Harper & Row, 1966), 326.
45 His collection of paper clippings is available at Stanford University, Manuscripts Division, Salo W. Baron Papers, 1900–1980, box 227, 1–4 and his correspondence in boxes 83/1 and 85/8.
46 Salo W. Baron, "European Jewry Before and After Hitler, Responses at the Eichmann Trial," *American Jewish Yearbook* 63 (1962): 3–49. It was reprinted as a book entitled *From a Historian's Notebook: European Jewry Before and After Hitler* (New York: American Jewish Committee, 1970).
47 *The Trial of Adolf Eichmann*, Vol. III, 1025.
48 Ibid., 1040–1041.
49 Ibid., 1135.
50 Ibid., vol. V, 2328, 2359. It is not clear why Hausner lost interest in hearing Seraphim before the court. It might be that the news had reached him that Seraphim changed his theory of duress. Testifying in the case of an SS block leader, he still maintained that objectively there was no danger for life and limb if perpetrators refused to obey criminal orders, but he emphasized the relevance of their subjective feeling of the possibility of such a danger. Cf. Hermann Langbein, *Im namen des deutschen Volkers: Zwischenbilanz der Prozesse wegen nationalsozialistischer Verbrechen* (Wien: Europa Verlag, 1963), 60–61.
51 The judges concluded that "the statistical data before us [is] far from being complete. Therefore, we shall not attempt to give specific figures even approximately but confine ourselves to a general finding, that the extermination of millions has been proved, and that, according to demographic calculations made by Professor Baron, in his evidence before us, on the basis of the sources mentioned in his testimony, there is no doubt that the total number of victims of the Final Solution was about six million (Session 13, Vol. I, pp. 183–185). Professor Baron also gave particulars of the destruction in various countries." *The Trial of Adolf Eichmann*, vol. V, 2172.
52 *The Trial of Adolf Eichmann*, vol. V, 2082. See also The Nizkor Project, The Trial of Adolf Eichmann, *Judgment*, http://www.nizkor.org/hweb/people/e/eichmann-adolf/transcripts/Judgment/Judgment-001.html.
53 Douglas, *The Memory of Judgment*, 182, 106.
54 Yablonka, *The State of Israel vs Adolf Eichmann*, 155–183.
55 David Cesarani. *After Eichmann: Collective Memory and the Holocaust Since 1961* (London: Routledge, 2005), 1, 3.
56 See Irmtrud Wojak, *Fritz Bauer 1903–1968: Eine Biographie* (München: C.H. Beck, 2009), 363. Bauer's own recollections are gathered in Fritz Bauer, *Die Humanität der Rechtsordnung: Ausgewählte Schriften* (Frankfurt am Main: Campus Verlag, 1998). More on Bauer: Matthias Meusch, *Von der Diktatur zur Demokratie: Fritz Bauer und die Aufarbeitung der NS-Verbrechen in Hessen (1956–1968)* (Wiesbaden: Historische Kommission für Nassau, 2001).

57 Quoted in Devin Pendas, *Frankfurt Auschwitz Trial, 1963–1965: Genocide, History, and the Limits of the Law* (New York: Cambridge University Press, 2006), 52.

58 Bauer, *Die Humanität der Rechtsordnung*, 83.

59 Circumstances which triggered the case are explored in Werner Renz, "Der 1 Frankfurter Auschwitz-Prozess: Zwei Vorgeschichten," *Zeitschrift für Geschichtswissenschaft* 7 (2002): 622–641.

60 Full records of the trial hearings were not kept, but partial transcripts are available on DVD: Fritz Bauer Institut und Staatliches Museum Auschwitz-Birkenau (eds.), *Der Auschwitz-Prozess: Tonbandmitschnitte, Protokolle und Dokumente* (Berlin: Digitale Bibliothek, 2004). Substantial parts are available online: *Tonbandmitschnitt des 1.Frankfurter Auschwitz-Prozesses*, http://www.auschwitz-prozess.de/. Detailed excerpts are also provided by Bernd Naumann, *Auschwitz, A Report on the Proceedings Against Robert Karl Ludwig Mulka and the Others Before the Court at Frankfurt* (New York: Frederick Praeger, 1965), and Hermann Langbein, *Der Auschwitz-Prozess: Eine Dokumentation* (Wien: Europa Verlag, 1965), vol. I–II. Seminal studies on the trial: Devin Pendas, *Frankfurt Auschwitz Trial, 1963–1965: Genocide, History, and the Limits of the Law* (New York: Cambridge University Press, 2006); Rebecca Wittmann, *Beyond Justice: The Auschwitz Trial* (Cambridge, MA: Harvard University Press, 2005); Werner Renz, "Auschwitz vor Gericht," *Hefte von Auschwitz* 24 (2009): 191–299.

61 Robert M.W. Kempner, *Ankläger einer Epoche, Lebenserinnerungen* (Frankfurt am Mein: Ullstein, 1983), 442.

62 Wittmann, *Beyond Justice: The Auschwitz Trial*, 64–65.

63 Hans Buchheim, "Die SS in der Verfassung des Dritten Reiches," *Vierteljahrshefte für Zeitgeschichte* 3 (1955): 127. This stance, however, was not irreconcilable with the professional assistance that he provided with success, such as the report "Deportations of the Gypsies in May 1940," described in 1956 by the president of the Bremen court as "especially precious." Hans Buchheim, "Materialsammlung zur Verfolgung der 'Zigeuner' in der NS-Zeit," Institut für Zeitgeschichte, Archivdatenbank MS 410/17, http://www.ifz-muenchen.de/archiv/Ms_0410_0000_0000.pdf.

64 The documentation related to the Auschwitz trial is mainly deposited in Hessisches Haputarchiv. However, the Fritz Bauer Institut (FBI) in its collection Sammlung Auschwitz-Prozess (SAP) holds the most relevant segments. FBI, SAP, *Vermerk von Dr.Grossman*, 3.5.1961.

65 Eichmüller, Keine Generalamnestie, 378–379.

66 Devin Pendas, "The Historiography of Horror: The Frankfurt Auschwitz Trial and the German Historical Imagination," in *Nazi Crimes and the Law*, eds. Nathan Stoltzfus and Henry Friedlander (Washington: German Historical Institute, 2008), 211–212. On historians' contributions to the Auschwitz trial: Irmtrud Wojak, "Die Verschmelzung von Geschichte und Kriminologie: Historische Gutachten im ersten Frankfurter Auschwitz-Prozess," in *Geschichte vor Gericht*, ed. Norbert Frei, 29–45; Norbert Frei, "Der Frankfurter Auschwitz-Prozess und die deutsche Zeitgeschichtsforschung," in *Auschwitz. Geschichte, Rezeption, Wirkung* (Frankfurt am Mein: Campus Verlag, 1996), 123–138; Irmtrud Wojak, "Herrshaft der Sachverständigen? Zum ersten Franfurter Auschwitz Prozess," *Kritische Justiz* 32 (1999): 605–615.

67 "Vermerk über eine Besprechung der altpolitischen Dezernenten der Staatsanwaltschaft bei dem Oberlandesgericht und der Staatanwaltschaften Frankfurt (M.) und Wiesbaden am 7. November 1962 bei herrn Generalstaatsanwalt Dr Bauer," 2. Fritz Bauer Institut (FBI), SAP (Sammlung Auschwitz-Prozess), *Vermerk . . .*

68 Ibid., 3.

69 Ibid., 4–5.
70 Ibid., 4–6, 8.
71 Fritz Bauer. "Herrschaft der Sachverständigen." *Frankfurter Rundschau* 10.01.1963.
72 The Minutes from the Fourth Meetings of the Leaders of the Special Commission for Working Through the Nazi Crimes from October 10, 1963 are quoted in Pendas, *Frankfurt Auschwitz Trial, 1963–1965*, 144.
73 The full list of the judges, prosecutors, advocates, the accused, and the witnesses is in Fritz Bauer Institute, Register zum Frankfurter Auschwitz-Prozess, http://www.fritz-bauer-institut.de/auschwitz-prozess/pdf/auschwitz-prozess.pdf, accessed on 26.6.2006.
74 Pendas, *Frankfurt Auschwitz Trial, 1963–1965*, 106–119.
75 "Nachlass Werner Hummerich, Sachverstandigengutachten ueber Gliederung und Aufbau von SS und KZ?" 1. Fritz Bauer Institut (FBI), SAP (Sammlung Auschwitz-Prozess).
76 Ibid., 1–2.
77 The English translation of the Code of Criminal Procedure of the Federal Republic of Germany is accessible at Legislationonline, http://legislationline.org/documents/section/criminal-codes. See §71, 74, 219, 244 of CCP.
78 Legislationonline, http://legislationline.org/documents/section/criminal-codes, Art 245 (2).
79 FBI, SAP, 29.1.1964.
80 Pohl, *Prosecutors and Historians*, 5.
81 Helmut Krausnick et al. (eds.), *Anatomy of the SS State* (London: Paladin, 1970), 121.
82 Ibid., 139.
83 The report is published in Jürgen Kuczynski, "Die Verflechtung von sicherheitspolizeilichen und wirtschaftlichen Interessen bei der Einrichtung und im Betrieb des KZ Auschwitz und seiner Nebenlager," in *Auschwitz—ein Prozess. Geschichte—Fragen—Wirkungen*, ed. Ulrich Schneider (Köln: Pappy Rossa Verlag: 1994), 33–59. Details in Pendas, *Frankfurt Auschwitz Trial, 1963–1965*, 147–153.
84 Pendas, *Frankfurt Auschwitz Trial, 1963–1965*, 151.
85 Schneider, *Auschwitz—ein Prozess*, 35.
86 Interestingly, during a court recess, Martin Broszat approached Kaul to tell him that he understood the purpose of the report to be "the typical Marxist view that National Socialism was merely the last chance for capitalism." Kaul retorted that Broszat's own report was limiting the responsibility to "a few dead Nazis." Pendas, *Frankfurt Auschwitz Trial, 1963–1965*, 148.
87 FAP, 28. Verhandlungstag, 19.3.1964. Anhörung des Sachverständigen Kuczynski, http://www.auschwitz-prozess.de/.
88 Pendas, *Frankfurt Auschwitz Trial, 1963–1965*, 154.
89 FBI, SAP, Grossman to Jacobsen, 24.6.1964.
90 Bernd Naumann, *Auschwitz*, 243–249.
91 FBI, SAP, Broszat to Grossman, 10.4.1964.
92 Press reports are analyzed by Irmtrud Wojak, "Herrschaft der Sachverstandigen? Zum ersten Frankfurter Auschwitz-Prozess in Kritische," *Justiz* 32 (1999): 605.
93 LG Frankfurt (19/20.8.1965) 4 KS 2/63 (Massenvernichtungsverbrechen in lagern, KZ Auschwitz)," *Justiz und NS Verbrechen*. Lfd. 695, vol. XXI, 453. Seraphim's report is accesible at Institut für Zeitgeschichte, Archivdatenbank GF 03.16 Erster Frankfurter Auschwitz-Prozess, band 38, Gutachten Hans-Günther Seraphim vom 01. Juli 1960; Bl. 5047–5067.
94 Hans Laternser, *Die andere Seite im Auschwitz-prozess, 1963–1965: Reden eines Verteidigers* (Stuttgart: Seewald Verlag, 1966), 82–84. He delighted in disclosing

sensitive information, from honoraria of reports (between 2020 to 6543 DM) to the NSDAP affiliation of Helmut Krausnick.

95 Die Urteilsbegründung, in Bernd Naumann, *Auschwitz: Bericht über die Strafsache gegen Mulka u.a. vor dem Schwurgericht Frankfurt* (Frankfurt am Mein: Athenaeum 1965), 521.

96 Pendas, *Frankfurt Auschwitz Trial*, 299–300.

97 LG Frankfurt (19/20.8.1965) 4 KS 2/63, *Justiz und NS Verbrechen*. Lfd.695, vol. XXI, 442, 454.

98 Wittmann, *Auschwitz on Trial*, 108.

99 LG Frankfurt (19/20.8.1965) 4 KS 2/63, *Justiz und NS Verbrechen*. Lfd.695, vol. XXI, 442, 454421–454422.

100 Helmut Krausnick, "Vorwort," in Gutachten des Instituts für Zeitgeschichte (Stuttgart: DVA, 1966), II, 9.

101 Reports were firstly published together in Hans Bucheim, Martin Broszat, Hans-Adolf Jacobsen and Helmut Krausnick, *Anatomie des SS Staates, Gutachten des Instituts fuer Zeitgeschichte* (Olten: Walter-Verlag, 1965), I–II, but also as *Gutachten des Instituts für Zeitgeschichte* (Stuttgart: Verlags Anstalt 1966) and soon reprinted in Hans Buchheim et al., *Anatomie des SS-Staates*, I–II (München: Deutscher Taschenbuch Verlag, 1967). This volume, which was reprinted many times thereafter, contains all the reports except Broszat's contribution on Nazi occupation policy in Poland. Quotations are taken from the English version: Helmut Krausnick et al., *Anatomy of the SS State* (New York: Walker, 1968). The other English translation: Helmut Krausnick et al. (eds.), *Anatomy of the SS State* (London: Paladin, 1970). Report of Martin Broszat, which was deployed in the court but not included in the volume: Martin Broszat, "Nationalsozialistische Polenpolitik," Institut für Zeitgeschichte, Archivdatenbank MS 244.

102 Helmut Krausnick et al., eds., *Anatomy of the SS State* (New York: Walker and Company, 1968), xiii–xv.

103 Pendas, *Frankfurt Auschwitz Trial*, 223–224.

104 Hans Herzfeld, "Germany: After the Catastrophe," *Journal of Contemporary History* 2.1, Historians on the Twentieth Century (January, 1967): 83.

105 Erich Haberer, "History and Justice: Paradigms of the Prosecution of Nazi Crimes," *Holocaust and Genocide Studies* 19 (2005): 487–488.

Bibliography

Arendt, Hannah. *Eichmann in Jerusalem: A Report on the Banality of Evil*. London Faber and Faber, 1963.

Baron, Salo W. "European Jewry before and after Hitler, Responses at the Eichmann Trial." *American Jewish Yearbook* 63 (1962): 3–49.

Baron, Salo. *From a Historian's Notebook: European Jewry before and after Hitler*. New York: American Jewish Committee, 1970.

Bauer, Fritz. "Herrschaft der Sachverständigen." *Frankfurter Rundschau*, 10 January, 1963.

Bauer, Fritz. *Die Humanität der Rechtsordnung. Ausgewählte Schriften*. Frankfurt am Main: Campus Verlag, 1998.

Braham, Randolph L. *The Eichmann Case: A Source Book*. New York: World Federation of Hungarian Jews, 1969.

Bucheim, Hans, Martin Broszat, Hans-Adolf Jacobsen, and Helmut Krausnick. *Anatomie des SS Staates, Gutachten des Instituts fur Zeitgeschichte*. Olten: Walter-Verlag, 1965, I–II.

Buchheim, Hans. "Die SS in der Verfassung des Dritten Reiches." *Vierteljahrshefte fur Zeitgeschichte* 3 (1955): 124–157.
Buchheim, Hans, et al. *Anatomie des SS-Staates*, I–II. München: Deutscher Taschenbuch Verlag 1967.
Cesarani, David. *After Eichmann: Collective Memory and the Holocaust since 1961*. London: Routledge, 2005.
Douglas, Lawrence. *The Memory of Judgment: Making Law and History in the Trials of the Holocaust*. New Haven, CT: Yale University Press, 2005.
Felman, Shoshana. "Theaters of Justice: Arendt in Jerusalem, the Eichmann Trial, and the Redefinition of Legal Meaning in the Wake of the Holocaust." *Critical Inquiry* 27 (2001): 201–240.
Frei, Norbert. "Der Frankfurter Auschwitz-Prozess und die deutsche Zeitgeschichtsforschung," In *Auschwitz. Geschichte, Rezeption, Wirkung*. Frankfurt am Mein: Campus Verlag, 1996, 123–138.
Frei, Norbert, Dirk van Laak and Michael Stolleis, ed. *Geschichte vor Gericht: Historiker, Richter und suche nach Gerechtigkeit*. München: Verlag C.H. Beck, 2000.
Fritz Bauer Institut. *Register zum Frankfurter Auschwitz-Prozess*. http://www.fritz-bauer-institut.de/auschwitz-prozess/pdf/auschwitz-prozess.pdf (accessed on 26.6.2006).
Fritz Bauer Institut. Sammlung Auschwitz-Prozess (SAP).
Fritz Bauer Institut. *Tonbandmitschnitt des 1. Frankfurter Auschwitz-Prozesses*. http://www.auschwitz-prozess.de.
Fritz Bauer Institut and Staatliches Museum Auschwitz-Birkenau, eds. *Der Auschwitz-Prozess: Tonbandmitschnitte, Protokolle und Dokumente*. Berlin: Digitale Bibliothek, 2004.
Golancz, Victor. *The Case of Adolf Eichmann*. London: Camelot Press, 1961.
Gouri, Haim. *Facing the Glass Booth: The Jerusalem trial of Adolf Eichmann*. Detroit: Wayne State University Press, 2004.
Gutachten des Instituts für Zeitgeschichte. Stuttgart: DAV, 1966.
Harnon, Eliahu. "Criminal Procedure in Israel—Some Comparative Aspects." *University of Pennsylvania Law Review* 115.7 (May, 1967): 1091–1108.
Harry S. Truman Presidential Museum and Library, Letter from Jacob Robinson to Robert H. Jackson, 27 July, 1945, Records of the World Jewish Congress. http://www.trumanlibrary.org/whistlestop/study_collections/nuremberg/documents/index.php?documentdate=1945-07-27&documentid=C106-16-2&studycollectionid=&pagenumber=1 (accessed on 21.2.2016).
Hausner, Gideon. *Justice in Jerusalem*. New York: Schocken Books, 1968.
Herzfeld, Hans. "Germany: After the Catastrophe." *Journal of Contemporary History* 2.1, Historians on the Twentieth Century (1967):79–91.
Institut für Zeitgeschichte, Archivdatenbank. http://www.ifz-muenchen.de/archiv/Ms_0410_0000_0000.pdf.
JTA, Ben Gurion Emphasizes Significance of Eichmann Trial to World, 4 April, 1961.
Kempner, Robert M.W. *Eichmann und Komplizen*. Zurich: Europa Verlag, 1961.
Kempner, Robert. *Ankläger einer Epoche, Lebenserinnerungen*. Frankfurt am Mein: Ullstein, 1983.
Kermish, Joseph. "Yad Vashem Contribution to the Trial." *Yad Vashem Bulletin* (April–May, 1962): 37–45.
Krausnick, Helmut et al. *Anatomy of the SS State*. New York: Walker, 1968.
Krausnick, Helmut et al., ed. *Anatomy of the SS State*. London: Paladin, 1970.

Kuczynski, Jürgen. "Die Verflechtung von sicherheitspolizeilichen und wirtschaftlichen Interessen bei der Einrichtung und im Betrieb des KZ Auschwitz und seiner Nebenlager." in *Auschwitz–ein Prozess. Geschichte–Fragen–Wirkungen*, ed. Ulrich Schneider. PappyRossa Verlag: Köln, 1994, 33–59.

Landsman, Stephan. *Crimes of the Holocaust: The Law Confronts Hard Cases*. Philadelphia: University of Pennsylvania Press, 2005.

Langbein, Hermann. *Im Namen des deutschen Volkers: Zwischenbilanz der Prozesse wegen nationalsozialistischer Verbrechen*. Wien: Europa Verlag, 1963.

Langbein, Hermann. *Der Auschwitz-Prozess: Eine Dokumentation*. Wien: Europa Verlag, 1965.

Laternser, Hans. *Die andere Seite im Auschwitz-prozess 1963–1965: Reden eines Verteidigers*. Stuttgart: Seewald Verlag, 1966.

LG Frankfurt, 19/20 August, 1965, 4 KS 2/63, *Justiz und NS Verbrechen*. Lfd.695, vol. XXI.

Liberles, Robert. *Salo Wittmayer Baron: Architect of Jewish History*. New York: New York University Press, 1995.

Lipstadt, Deborah E. *The Eichmann Trial*. New York: Schocken Books, 2011.

Meusch, Matthias. *Von der Diktatur zur Demokratie: Fritz Bauer und die Aufarbeitung der NS-Verbrechen in Hessen* (1956–1968). Wiesbaden: Historische Kommission für Nassau, 2001.

Mulisch, Harry. *Criminal Case 40/61, The Trial of Adolf Eichmann: An Eyewitness Account*. Philadelphia: University of Pennsylvania Press, 2005.

Naumann, Bernd. *Auschwitz, A Report on the Proceedings against Robert Karl Ludwing Mulka and the Others before the Court at Frankfurt*. New York: Frederick Praeger, 1965.

Nazi and Nazi Collaborator Punishment Law. https://www.jewishvirtuallibrary.org/jsource/Politics/nazilaw.html (accessed on 21.2.2016).

The Nizkor Project, The Trial of Adolf Eichmann, Session 12 and Session 13. http://www.nizkor.org/hweb/people/e/eichmann-adolf/transcripts/Sessions/Session-012–03.html.

Pendas, Devin. *Frankfurt Auschwitz Trial, 1963–1965: Genocide, History, and the Limits of the Law*. New York: Cambridge University Press, 2006.

Pohl, Dieter. *Prosecutors and Historians: Holocaust Investigations and Historiography in the Federal Republic 1955-1975*, conference paper "Justice and the Holocaust," Yad Vashem, Jerusalem in December 2006.

Renz, Werner. "Der 1. Frankfurter Auschwitz-Prozess: Zwei Vorgeschichten." *Zeitschrift für Geschichtswissenschaft* 7 (2002): 622–641.

Renz, Werner. "Auschwitz vor Gericht." *Hefte von Auschwitz* 24 (2009): 191–299.

Reutlinger, Gerald. *The Final Solution: The Attempt to Exterminate the Jews of Europe*. New York: Beechhurst Press, 1953.

Stanford University Manuscripts Division. Guide to the Salo W. Baron Papers, 1900–1980. http://www.oac.cdlib.org/findaid/ark:/13030/ft509nb07b/ Online Archives of California.

Stoltzfus Nathan and Henry Friedlander, eds. *Nazi Crimes and the Law*. Washington: German Historical Institute, 2008.

Taylor, Telford. "Adolf Eichmann's Third Life," *Spectator*, 21 April, 1961.

Taylor, Telford. "Mirror, Mirror on the Wall," *Spectator*, 19 May, 1961.

The Trial of Adolf Eichmann: Record of proceedings in the District Court of Jerusalem. Jerusalem: State of Israel, Ministry of Justice, 1992.

Wittmann, Rebecca. *Beyond Justice: The Auschwitz Trial.* Cambridge, MA: Harvard University Press, 2005.
Wojak, Irmtrud. "Herrshaft der Sachverständigen? Zum ersten Frankfurter Auschwitz Prozess." *Kritische Justiz* 32 (1999): 605–615.
Wojak, Irmtrud. *Fritz Bauer 1903–1968: Eine Biographie.* München: C.H. Beck, 2009.
Yablonka, Hanna. *The State of Israel vs. Adolf Eichmann.* New York: Shocken Books, 2004.
Zeiger, Henry, ed. *The Case against Adolf Eichmann.* New York: Signet Books, 1960.

6 Clio Takes a Stand

From the Turning Point to the Point of No Return

The growing involvement of historians in legal proceedings aimed to address past wrongs was bound to have a wider social impact, the more so as they appeared in trials that had such huge transformative potential. However, for this potential to materialize, no less than full-blown reconceptualization of disciplinary relations was needed. Carl Friedrich, one of the leading proponents of their incompatibility, felt that change was in the air: "It would seem that any reconsideration of 'law and history' is apt to be a string of commonplaces or the beating of the dead horse. Yet, both 'What is law?' and 'What is history' are questions which have not ceased to trouble the reflective students of both fields."[1] Furthermore, these questions were posed with a new urgency, in the context of contribution of these disciplines to social change.

Bonn to Königstein: Building the Bridge

Wider social in unlikely voice to confront such a trend was none other than Hannah Arendt's. Ever since Nuremberg, she remained consistently reserved about the possibilities of the courts to confront systemic injustices which "explode the limits of the law."[2] Consistently, she extended that skepticism to the U.S. Supreme Court *Brown* decision, which she saw "to burden children, black and white, with the working out of a problem which adults for generations have confessed themselves unable to solve." In her view, the court "can do no more than abolish the laws enforcing discrimination: it cannot abolish discrimination and force equality upon society."[3] However, her most systematic intervention in this direction came with her famed coverage of the Eichmann trial, which was rich with reflections on history and law. Attending over half of a four-month-long trial, she grew weary of the prosecution's attempt to utilize the trial to enhance Jewish national consciousness. Arendt was appalled with what she perceived as Ben Gurion's concept of trial as public lesson. In her very first reportage, she called him "the invisible stage manager of the proceedings" who "does not attend a single one of the sessions" and "speaks with the voice of the Attorney General," who "does his best—his very best—to obey his master."

Consequently, "it was history that, as far as the prosecution was concerned, stood in the center of the trial. 'It is not an individual that is at the dock at this historic trial, and not even the Nazi regime alone,' Ben-Gurion said, 'but anti-Semitism throughout history.' The tone set by Ben-Gurion was faithfully followed by Hausner. He began his opening statement with Pharaoh in Egypt (. . .). It was bad history and cheap rhetoric. Worse, it was clearly at cross-purposes with putting Eichmann on trial at all, since it suggested that perhaps he was only an innocent executor of some mysteriously foreordained destiny." Postulating her famous theory on the banality of evil, she embraced and famously formulated a rigid theory of incompatibility between history and law: "Justice demands that the accused be prosecuted, defended and judged, and that all the other questions of seemingly greater import—of 'How could it happen?' and 'Why did it happen?', of 'Why the Jews?' and 'Why the Germans?', of 'What was the role of other nations?' (. . .) be left in abeyance."[4]

In Arendt's view, it was exactly this broad historical approach to prosecution that opened a Pandora's box: "A few sessions later, when Professor Salo W. Baron of Columbia University had testified to the more recent history of Eastern European Jewry, Dr. Servatius could no longer resist the temptation and asked the obvious questions: 'Why did all this bad luck fall upon the Jewish people?' and 'Don't you think that irrational motives are at the basis of the fate of this people? Beyond the understanding of a human being?' "[5] In her view, this approach redirected attention from Eichmann's individual responsibility to the murky issues of the philosophy of history. Arendt did not directly criticize Baron, her senior colleague and long-time friend who had helped her intellectual socialization in the United States.[6] She implied that the prosecution had misused the academic, and instead praised the judges for their resistance to similar attempts to descend into a show trial. She condensed her conclusion in wording meant to become the new incompatibility dictum: "the purpose of the trial is to render justice, and nothing else; even the noblest of ulterior purposes—'the making of a record of the Hitler regime which would withstand the test of history' can only detract from the law's main business: to weigh the charges brought against the accused, to render judgment, and to mete out punishment."[7]

Powerful as it was, this statement did not go unchallenged in a vicious debate over Arendt's coverage of the Eichmann trial. The debate hardly focused on her critique of bringing history to trial, but mostly revolved around her portrayal of Eichmann, her controversial account of the role of the Jewish councils and the issue of the Jewish resistance, and her liberal borrowing from the work of other authors. One of her harshest critics was Jacob Robinson, who dedicated an entire book to prove that "Miss Arendt does not convey reliable information (. . .) the facts show up the historical falsities of Miss Arendt's narrative. Her errors demand correction."[8] Robinson labeled her dictum the product of laymen's theory of law. "Laws are not narratives of past history," he concluded, criticizing her "extreme reluctance

(. . .) to break fresh ground."[9] He emphasized that Arendt disregarded the adversarial nature of the criminal system in Israel, which assigns different roles to the prosecution and the judges. He countered Arendt's main argument, concluding that trials always have meta-juridical purposes, such as deterrence, sanction, reform, and restraint, as well as the by-products that do not taint the immediate purpose of doing justice. Therefore, he saw no problem in the fact that "one of the by-products of the trial was the mass education of the citizens of the State of Israel in the history of the dreadful catastrophe which befell the Jewish people."[10] Arendt retorted, challenging Robinson's credentials: "Prior to 1963 Mr. Robinson was not a historian—the Israeli trial authorities correctly mention his training as a lawyer." She saw his work as "a book written by a lawyer and meant to restate a prosecutor's case. To anyone willing and able to read, the result of Mr. Robinson's long labors will look like a prime example of a non-book. (. . .) The methods used in the pursuit of historical truth are not the methods of the prosecutor, and the men who stand guard over facts are not the officers of interest groups—*no matter how legitimate their claims*—but the reporters, the historians, and finally the poets."[11]

The debate, which started out as a set of exchanges between Arendt and people who conducted the Eichmann prosecution, soon spilled into a wider intellectual space.[12] Arendt further developed her concept of the inability of criminal trials to deal with mass state-sponsored violence. Her prime example was none other than "the Frankfurt trial, which in many respects reads like a much-needed supplement to the Jerusalem trial." The Frankfurt proceedings were equally disappointing to her as "the court tried hard to exclude all political questions (. . .) and to conduct the truly extraordinary proceedings as 'an ordinary criminal trial', regardless of its background. But the political background of both past and present (. . .) made itself factually and judicially present. (. . .) As the prosecution had indicted for mass murder, the assumption of the court (. . .) simply did not square with the facts." Unimpressed, she concluded: "The verdict here is not deemed to be the last word of either history or justice."[13] She was not a lone voice. Eugen Kogon, for one, commented on the Frankfurt judgment as an example of the lack of readiness to plunge into the contemporary history of Germany: "I have never before heard such a sovereign judicial self-restriction, which does not come from ignorance or from neglect of the historical-political circumstances, but is a direct result of knowledge of them."[14]

If for Arendt and Kogon incompatibility meant that neither the court nor the historians in Frankfurt went far enough, they most definitely did go too far for Ernst Forsthoff, legal scholar and jurist from Heidelberg, author of the book *Total State* (1934), who got disenchanted with Nazism but remained on the conservative side of the spectrum in the postwar period. He had strongly pushed forward his own version of the incompatibility theory: "There are sciences which focus on results, such as the natural sciences. This also goes for the legal sciences, so far as they are based on positive law. (. . .)

As far as philosophy is concerned, things are different, and the same goes for historical science." Evoking Ranke, he asserted that historians should not strive to the same sort of explanation as scientists, which in his view occurred when "contemporary historians came to testify as experts in organizations and the power relation within the SS. This opens up the question of what it means for contemporary historical research that they are taken as forensic experts." He expressed concern that as the historiography is subject to changes introduced by new research, it is unsuitable for courtroom purposes, constantly transplanted to the legal process, "alien and foreign to historical research"; transformed into expert reports, "it becomes apodictic, which spells the death for all humanities." He predicted nothing less than "the abolishment of contemporary historical research." On the other hand, he also saw this trend as a threat to the legal process: "The advent of historians as experts at trial triggers different questions, such as: what is to be done when a historical report which was very relevant for the trial gets refuted through subsequent research? Nova reperta? Retrial? That would mean that court and contemporary historiography are entering into a state of symbiosis." By no means friendly toward this development, Forsthoff gave it a derogatory label: "den forensischen Historismus."[15]

However, just as the Arendtian evocation of the incompatibility theory did not pass unchallenged, neither did Forsthoff's attempt to apply it on historical experts. Adolf Laufs, legal scholar and historian of law of the youngest generation, promptly stated: "Ernst Forsthoff has recently in this place debated the issue (. . .) of the processes against National Socialist war criminals in which historians appeared as experts. If contemporary historical research takes the form of the expert report, it becomes apodictic, claims Forsthoff (. . .) leading to 'the abolishment of contemporary historical research' in the Frankfurt example. (. . .) However, the statements of these experts in the court as contributions to the search for truth are not fundamentally different from other forms of scientific statements. (. . .) The testimonies of the historians in a criminal process are as little apodictic as those of scientists in any other discipline."[16]

Laufs was even taking the other extreme position, arguing for complete compatibility between the disciplines, emphasizing their mutual dependence:

> Both disciplines are connected (. . .) through the bridge of legal history. (. . .) Particularly tight is the connection between lawyers and a specific aspect of history: contemporary history. Contemporary history attempts to scientifically treat the epoch of its contemporaries. It shares with the administration of justice dangerous but also advantageous degree of closeness to the events and persons, which it evaluates and recognizes, as well as the other means of finding the truth, including living witnesses. Research in contemporary history is of help to the courts in very difficult and far-reaching processes against the criminals of the Nazi period: productive collections of sources and institutions

(what I have in mind is the Institute for Contemporary History), publications and well-known representatives of this discipline coming forth as experts—all of these are indispensable sources of knowledge. These considerations show that consulting contemporary historians as experts gives no cause for the uncertainty and worry about scientifically degenerated forensic historicism, as described by Forsthoff. There is absolutely no reason for this.[17]

The brisk nature of this exchange needs to be seen in context of the controversies about processing Nazi crimes that were shaking Germany at the time. In comparison to the over five thousand sentences in the first five postwar years, investigations in the FRG between 1950 and 1962 resulted in indictments against 12,846 persons, of which 5,426 were brought to court. However, 4,027 were acquitted, and among the, 1,399 sentenced, only 155 went to jail for murder.[18] It was clear that powerful forces, not the least within the judiciary, thought that even that was too much. An outside trigger was needed to shake such a scene, and indeed it came: "Due to the arrest of Adolf Eichmann, public interest in Nazi Crimes rose enormously."[19] Disenchanted insiders were encouraged to step up. One such was Barbara Just-Dahlmann, a prosecutor from Manheim, attached to Ludwigsburg Zentrale Stelle. She spoke with unusual bluntness at the Evangelic Academy in Loccum in November 1961 about the complexities surrounding the Nazi trials, enumerating their practical obstacles, including the lack of willingness of the police and judiciary to help the prosecutions. However, the only visible outcome was a disciplinary proceeding opened against her, despite support she rallied from organizations as different as the Council of the Evangelical Church in Germany, the Central Jewish Council in Germany, and the Socialist Democratic Party.[20]

Her own boss, Erwin Schüle, head of Zentrale Stelle, also came under pressure. Fully aware of the strength of inertia in the German judiciary, police, and security system, as well as of the tainted past of its dignitaries, he was searching for a less confrontational way to overcome the same problems. He was also building on the attention caused by the Eichmann case. Schüle used this opportunity to write in the journal of the Institute for Contemporary History in Munich: "In connection with the proceedings against the former SS-Obersturmbannführer Eichmann in Israel the question is often asked why was Eichmann not brought to justice by the German law enforcement authorities, and what was done and what is being done in the Federal Republic of Germany to prosecute such persons." To answer this question, Schüle recited the statistics on the postwar trials, claiming that "these few figures probably show very clearly that the German judiciary, when it again was capable of action has made intensive efforts in the pursuit of the Nazi criminals." He emphasized that the creation of the Ludwigsburg office attests to this readiness: "Since its inception, the office initiated systematic work on the main perpetrators amounting to a total of about 900 cases. Over half of this process has already been transferred to the responsibility of corresponding prosecutors and courts (. . .). Only in one of these procedures—the crimes committed in the concentration camps Auschwitz—the investigation was launched over 950 former members the Auschwitz camp administration investigations be performed. (. . .) Similarly, just to name a few examples, we examine crimes committed in Warsaw, Belzec, Treblinka, Sobibor, Hungary and elsewhere (. . .). The activity of the Central Office serves not only in the atonement of this injustice, but also provides information to the German People. Only now, through these systematic investigations will the German people learn about the monstrous crimes with which the Nazi thugs burdened their name."[21]

Such dramatic wording aimed to provide additional impetus for the prosecution of Nazi war crimes, which had been losing support even where one would expect it. On the pages of the same historical journal, one could read the much more pessimistic assessment of Karl Bader, a former prosecutor in Freiburg. Frustrated with the difficulties and failures in the prosecution of Nazi criminals, Bader resigned in 1951 from his position as Attorney General of Freiburg, where he had served since 1946. Taking the position of professor at Zurich University, he reflected in the journal of Munich's Institute for Contemporary History: "The legal system does not conduct criminal proceedings for the sake of history, but for the sake of punishing the wrong. Perhaps these proceedings taken by the German justice system can contribute to overcoming our unresolved past (which regretfully is a term that has been degraded to a mere buzzword). But they were not, and must not be undertaken for the sake of knowledge of the past."[22] Much like Arendt, Bader was developing his argumentation on the incompatibility of history and law, formulating convincing warnings:

> The legal order is overwhelmed when expected to deal with political history. Trials that are performed in order to provide evidence for historians are bad trials, bordering on show trials. (. . .) Criminal cases are dubious historical sources (. . .) in Anglo-American law perhaps more than in continental criminal procedure, because these forms of the judicial duel that take place there between prosecution and defense, and in a not unduly ritualized process struggle, make the exploration of the whole truth still less possible than in our type of proceedings. I specifically want to address the Nuremberg trials of war criminals, as they were not attempts at national, but rather of intergovernmental criminal justice, and (. . .) test cases for the beginning of a genuine international criminal law. But every criminologist or contemporary historian, who tried to create a comprehensive picture of the factual and legal events from the impressive series of volumes of the Nuremberg court reports, should know better. Single documents literally torn from countless official documents still do not amount to a picture of contemporary history."[23]

For the same reason, Bader was doubting the effects of the Eichmann trial "modelled on the basis of the Anglo-Saxon pattern (. . .). The forthcoming judgment in Jerusalem, therefore, notwithstanding all the commendable efforts to reach historical truth, cannot result in a complete picture. What puzzles me in the Eichmann trial, are not so much the individual procedural defects, at least in part healed, by subsequent aids, but the fact that there was no more serious effort to set up an international panel for the Eichmann trial. The line of international criminal law, which was set up by the Nuremberg trials, has therefore been interrupted."[24] However, this was hardly a satisfying position for a new generation of dissenters, such as criminologist Herbert Jäger, who was working on Nazi criminality. He was also concerned with their assertions that the legal system cannot catch up with crimes of such magnitude. Jäger however posed a rhetorical question regarding Arendt's standpoint: "Are we here taking about criminality at all, or has the extent of historical catastrophe, which escapes individual, moral and legally prosecutable responsibility, already been reached?" He had a ready answer: "A signal could have been and must have been sent through the Eichmann trial, that even such actions, the scale of which exceeds everyday criminality, are real crimes."[25] He advocated the necessary reforms in the German penal system directed toward more successful prosecution of the crimes of the Nazi period. Other voices joined, concerned about the approaching expiration of their statute of limitations in 1965.

In light of the forthcoming deadline, Ludwigsburg, staffed with eleven lawyers, started working at full speed, launching investigations and referring them to prosecutions at a staggering pace. Ludwigsburg opened 645 investigations encompassing over 10,000 potential suspects, of which 418 cases were taken over by different prosecutors' offices. However, only 64 such cases materialized as criminal trials, indicting 152 persons, leading to 33 acquittals, 19 life imprisonments, and 100 prison sentences of different lengths.[26] The future of the huge backlog of cases in the investigative stage remained uncertain, as the pending statute of limitations for murder was threatening to render them obsolete. In the face of such prospects, the German Democratic Republic adopted a law in August 1964 that abolished the statute of limitations for persons who committed crimes against peace, crimes against humanity, or war crimes between January 30, 1933 and May 8, 1945. The Western Allies were equally suspicious—anticipating the advent of procedural limitations, the French government abolished the statute of limitations for crimes against humanity on December 26, 1964.[27] The German government tried to respond to these initiatives by fivefold enlargement of the Ludwigsburg staff, which grew from 25 to 120 persons, with half of the staff as judges or prosecutors.[28] Additionally, the German government launched an international appeal for the submission of evidence of Nazi crimes before the expiry date in Germany, which was May 8, 1965.[29]

Many could not wait for this date to arrive, among them one of the ablest defense attorneys in Nuremberg, Otto Kranzbuhler, who reflected two decades after: "Thus they were political trials, or one might use the term 'historical trials' in which one political system, namely the democratic one, held court over another system, that is, the dictatorial one."[30] Expressing a number of legal and political objections, Kranzbuhler conceded that one of the aims of Nuremberg was

> the re-education and democratization of the German people. No one familiar with present day Germany will doubt that this process was largely successful. Whether the Nuremberg trials contributed to that result, or whether in view of their many faults they have rather impeded this development, is a difficult question, which I am unable to answer. Doubtless, the reaction of the general public in Germany to the Allied war crimes trials initially was that one had had enough of it; and the German legal administration for all practical purposes did not bother for years with the prosecution of real crimes committed in wartime, even after it became legally possible to do so. Only gradually, after the creation of a central prosecution authority for all offenses of this nature, did investigations and new indictments again begin. What had been left undone for years was now done with "German thoroughness." As a consequence, hundreds, if not thousands, of trials are still to be expected, mainly against people of lesser account who acted within the scope of their mission or orders. In considering these unfortunate prospects, I share the opinion of Sir Hartley Shawcross, the British Attorney General during the International Military Tribunal, who recently stated in a German periodical that he felt the time had come to put an end to these proceedings.[31]

There was no shortage of powerful counterarguments. "Let us pose the seemingly absurd question: what would have happened, if on one day Adolf Hitler had just popped up among us?" one could read in a powerfully titled article, "Do the Murderers Stay among us?" by Dietrich Strothmann. "Could he be put on trial? No. On 8 May 1965, such is the decision of the federal government, the statute of limitations expires."[32] Vigorous debate was sparked, with Fritz Bauer, Karl Jaspers, and many other public figures arguing for abolishment of the statute of limitations for murder.[33] Even Konrad Adenauer from his retirement also advocated the prolongation of the statute of limitations to his successor, West German Chancellor Ludwig Erhard.[34] Germany was not just pressed from within; its policies in this realm were scrutinized by its Eastern (Poland) and Western (France) neighbors. Under such pressure, on the proposal of the minister of justice, in March 1965 the Bundestag opted for a compromise measure. With 344 votes in favor, 96 against, and 4 abstentions, the Bundestag agreed to change the starting date of limitations to the year of the founding of the state, enabling the

Figure 6.1 Cover of *Der Spiegel* questioning the expiration of the statute of limitation
© 1965 *Der Spiegel*. http://www.spiegel.de/spiegel

prosecutions for murder until December 31, 1969.[35] The constitutionality of this decision was challenged, but in the meanwhile, the road for further legal reckoning with Germany's criminal past was once again reopened.

It remained to be seen whether this road would be taken. The interim was used for careful building of bridges between interested professionals and governmental officials. Just-Dahlman and her husband, Judge Helmut Just, were relentlessly trying to involve the professional community of legal scholars, in particular appealing to Professor Ernst Friesenhahn, the president of Deutschen Juristentag, the greatest and most reputed legal association, to put the topic of the Nazi trials on the agenda of its biannual gatherings.[36] The preliminary preparatory meeting, held in early April 1966 in Königstein near Frankfurt am Main, assembled more than a dozen jurists to debate the legal issues related to the crimes of Nazism. The central topic was the trials of the Nazi perpetrators—their scope and length, and in particular the judgments, which caused an uproar due to their lenience and the qualification of the accused as aiders and abettors, rather than perpetrators. Among the participants were a number of professors of law: Ernst-Walter Hanack, Jürgen Bauman, Claus Roxin, and the recently habilitated Herbert Jäger. Among the practitioners, prosecutors from the Nazi trials included Erich Schmidt-Leichner and Anton Roesen, but also defense attorneys engaged in the NS trials, like Gerhard Hammerstein and Konrad Redeker, as well as Adalbert Rückerl of Zentrale Stelle Ludwigsburg and Karl Lackner of the Ministry of Justice. The long shadow of the recently completed Frankfurt Auschwitz trial was looming over this meeting, as its *spiritus movens* Fritz Bauer was presented, as well as the presiding judge Hans Hofmeyer, attorney for the victims of this trial Henry Ormond, and Hans Buchheim, expert of the Institute for Contemporary History, the only invited non-lawyer. The meeting was held behind closed doors, as the participants felt the need for a candid exchange of opinions on the topic, which was causing such a public outcry.[37]

Judge Hofmeyer warned his colleagues about the mounting pressure on the judicial system. He expressed concerns about the number of potentially forthcoming processes and their length and warned in particular about the danger of bringing history to the courtroom: "One has to be clear about it, whether the object of the procedure or theme of the trial should be the guilt of the accused, or whether the entirety of the events in the background should be tackled in these processes. The Code of Criminal Procedure answers these questions clearly. The court cannot be summoned to provide historical documentation, and in such a way forestall the writing of history. If one would strip the process from all of these, no matter how interesting these historical matters may be, it would be possible to lessen the difficulties of these processes."[38] Expectedly, the prosecutors were opposed to this version of incompatibility between history and law, arguing for the necessity of a wider historical context in the courtroom. More surprisingly, some of the defense lawyers shared that view. Attorney Gerhard Hammerstein expressed "the unconditional need to bring historians into the trials. As a lawyer, you could not just say 'We will try to remember how it might have been,' but we had to have it explained by experts what were the circumstances of the time, in order to mete out justice to every perpetrator. Therefore I chose the topic: Which historians should be sought? How are they to be questioned? What does one ask them? And what is to be done with the acquired knowledge? Historical expertise was completely new."[39] Hans Buchheim was in the position to offer practical insights into the creation and deployment of historical expertise, leading Herbert Jäger, professor of criminal law from Frankfurt am Mein University, to a conclusion: "The epistemological value of these processes, as much as any criminological consideration of historical events, seems to me simply to consist of an individualization of history, that is a marking of the points in which world history hits upon personal history and leads to the fusion of historical and individual causality, therefore of contemporary history and criminology."[40]

Theoretical approval for the merging of history and law in these cases was followed by practical implementation through the work of Ludwigsburg, after a huge shake-up. The reason that Adalbert Rückerl represented Ludwigsburg at this meeting was that its head, Erwin Schüle, was facing revelations of his SA and NSDAP (Nazi Party) membership. The Ulm Einstzgruppen prosecutor and leader of Ludwigsburg Zentrale Stelle was under increased pressure in early 1966, with Soviet authorities alleging his participation in Nazi crimes. Investigations begun over this in Stuttgart produced no results, but he was increasingly becoming a target of Cold War propaganda and was forced to step down from Ludwigsburg in August 1966.[41] Nonetheless, his office, whose investigations encompassed inquiries into wartime activities of no fewer than 14,733 persons, used this interim period to pass on information to local prosecutions on a level that could hardly be ignored, as the subject concerned extermination programs in concentration camps under the infamous Operation Reinhardt.[42]

Rückerl inherited not only the cases, but also the inclination of his predecessor for cooperation with historians, entering together in this uncharted territory: "Particularly controversial, and often poorly understood, is the role of historians in the trials of the National Socialist perpetrators of genocide," notes Erich Haberer.[43] These trials involved crimes that were perpetrated on an unprecedented scale, but committed outside of Germany, leading to a number of obstacles: eyewitnesses were scarce, insiders silent, and documentation shattered. The testimonies of historians were expected to tie up many loose ends. The need for contextual evidence was greater than ever; so was the engagement of historians, who submitted their expert reports and appeared in courtrooms without the complications encountered in Frankfurt. The courts initially favored historians with previous testifying experience—Krausnick, Seraphim, and Buchheim testified in the Treblinka trial in April 1965.[44] However, the Sobibor trial in Hagen featured a historian of the new generation, Wolfgang Scheffler (1929–2008), who was habilitated on the persecution of the Jews and was an observer for the Federal Republic in the Eichmann case.[45]

After a shaky start, the historical expertise was firmly established in the German courts. Anchored into judicial practice, the practice outlived its creator, Fritz Bauer, who was found dead in his apartment on July 1, 1968. Helmut Krausnick's 1969 assessment attested to the lasting success of his endeavour to "open desire of German statesmen after 1945 to educate the general public on the subject of the origins and record of nazism, in order to further the development of democracy among the German people: that is to say, they wanted to use historical science primarily and directly as a means of political instruction. These politicians' expectations were, however, irreconcilable with the nature of scholarly institutions which they desired to set up (. . .). Only when it was possible, by reliably produced scientific research, to free the picture of our past both from the fog of national socialist propaganda and mythology and from the dubious additional twilight into which it had fallen in the cross-examinations and distorted visions of the Nuremberg trials, could genuine insights be discovered and convincing education be provided."[46] He summarized the impact of these developments on the remoralization of German historiography: "The relentless analysis of German contemporary history of the exclusion of all humanity from policy, as practiced by national socialism, must in the end also call into question the merits of a neutral 'historicism,' which threatened to turn 'tout comprendre' into 'tout pardonner.' "[47] With apologetic tendencies gradually abandoned, the road was open toward taking an unequivocal stand about the most atrocious aspects of the German past.

Washington to Selma: Crossing the Bridge

If Germany was struggling to address the issue of Nazi criminality, the U.S. was facing a watershed as well,. "The only mass experience that Western people have had within recorded history comparable in any way with Negro slavery was undergone in the nether world of Nazism".[48] Such 1959 comparison of Stanley Elkins would prove controversial, but was also indicative of the desire to addsress the legacy of racial inequality, hardly solved with the *Brown v. Board* decision. A decade after its rendering, 75% of school districts in the South were still segregated, and the situation was even more alarming where desegregation was underway: "The day after a federal court in New Orleans had ordered the desegregation of the public school system, newly elected Governor Jimmie Davis announced to the state legislature that his administration was sponsoring a series of bills."[49] Those bills were intended to revive the other cornerstone of segregation—obstruction of voting rights. The number of Black voters in the South was on the rise, from 750,000 in 1948 to 1.3 million in 1952.[50] So the intention was to put a stop to this. The promulgation of the Civil Rights Acts of 1957, promoted by the Eisenhower administration and adopted by the Congress after the longest one-person filibuster in the Senate's history, aimed to reaffirm the voting rights of Black Americans and to push them into the political process. However, the results were disappointing. In 1957 only 20% of Black Americans were registered to vote, and by 1960 the number of Black voters in the South was still dropping. The new Civil Rights Act of 1960 contained some improvements, including the extension of the jurisdiction of the federal courts toward the protection of voting rights, but the advancement was modest in Alabama, where the number of registered voting-age Black people rose only from 14.2% (1958) to 19.45% (1964), in Louisiana, from 31.7% (1956) to 31.8% (1965), and in Mississippi, from 4.4% (1954) to 6.4% (1964).[51] In these states poll taxes, literacy tests, and even special redistricting of voting areas prevented Black Americans from voting, but the courts were reluctant to challenge this practice, as apportionment was seen as a political matter, not a judicial one.

Coincidentally, the Warren Court was addressing a related problem in the case *Baker v. Carr*, concerned with the apparent lack of willingness of the Tennessee general assembly to reallocate the votes across the ninety-five counties of the state, unchanged since 1910 despite huge demographic changes in urban areas, due to an influx of migrants, who remained under-represented. The case was brought before the Supreme Court in 1962 and argued under the Equal Protection Clause of the Fourteenth Amendment. Archibald Cox, U.S. Solicitor General, supporting the appellants, insisted that there had to be a rational ground for representation, and that in Tennessee this rationality was lacking. This plea for rationality caused Justice Frankfurter to comment: "History very often isn't rational." The justices were curious to know what the historical reasons for inadequate allocation of votes were, leading Solicitor General Cox to comment: "I cannot speak with any great degree of knowledge about the political history of Tennessee." The representative for the state, Jack Wilson, attempted to relativize this approach, claiming that the motivation behind the lack of electoral reform was unclear: "What does history show? Is it true that the only thing that history teaches is that history teaches nothing?"[52] This probably did not sit well with Justice Frankfurter, who had written ten years earlier in another case about "modern cynicism that the only thing that history teaches is that it teaches nothing."[53]

However, the question of how to learn from history in the courtroom remained. From the outset of this case, the plaintiffs were looking into the legislative history of Tennessee: "We have set forth (. . .) the record of every proposal for reapportionment in the Tennessee legislature that shows that over and over again every bill for reapportionment since 1901 has been voted down."[54] They "set out to establish the total unwillingness of the Tennessee legislature to meet its constitutional duty and the corresponding inability of the people of the state to obtain relief through any alternative means, such as the initiative or referendum. To this end, they relied on Dr. Robert H. White, the state historian, who dug into old editions of the legislative journal, dating back to the 1870s, and methodically documented the recalcitrance of the legislature since the turn of the century."[55] Robert Hiram White (1883–1970), a graduate of the University of Chicago and the first historian appointed to the state of Tennessee, took his task very seriously: "The final two months before the three-judge hearing were occupied in assembling the proof. Dr. White was tired of the tedious task of checking page after page of journals grown yellow and dusty. He felt his labors were to be lost, anyway, and wanted to quit when, halfway through, he felt he had enough to prove the point. (. . .) And finally, on November 12, Dr. White delivered the final page of his research which he had been carrying on 'like the cat gnawing away the grindstone. (. . .) It is done. Am I glad!' "[56] He worked without payment or compensation. "For Dr. White, then in his seventies, the survey had been a labor of love. (. . .) He deeply believed in the cause. (. . .) On Thanksgiving Day, 1959, depressed by the news accounts which indicated that Judge Martin and Judge Boyd, at least, were going to rule against Baker, he wrote: "If I were not a sort of fool optimist, I would be ready to exclaim that justice and equity have lain down to weep! (. . .) I have always thought of equity as being the synonym of natural justice of inherent right. Now I wonder."[57]

However, three years later, in front of the nation's highest court in Washington, "Dr. White's meticulous research became vital when Baker v. Carr reached the high court, for it helped document the argument that Tennessee citizens of the United States could not find remedy at home. (. . .) Dr. White's research, with the luxury of time, expanded to an impressive, elaborately footnoted, *Documented Study of Legislative Apportionments in Tennessee, 1870–1957* by the time the case reached the Supreme Court." His historical expert report "was one of the most important documents prepared in the matter. He went back and checked the archives, even the journals of the various Senate and House committees of Tennessee every year that the legislature had met since 1870. (. . .) He documented the results in great detail. He further investigated the votes—who was voting which way—and documented which counties the legislators came from. The purpose and thrust of all this was to show the utter impossibility of obtaining any relief from the Tennessee legislature. That avenue was closed. Justice Brennan referred to this survey twice in his opinion."[58] Indeed, in the ruling that remanded the case to the lower courts, it was established that the reshaping of electoral boundaries with discriminatory purpose in mind is an issue under the jurisdiction of the federal, and an expert opinion of a Tennessee State Historian, Dr. Robert H. White, was duly footnoted. Consequently, participation of historians in similar cases continued, such as *Gray v. Sanders* (1963), in which James C. Bonner (1904–1984) supplied the plaintiff with an affidavit entitled *Legislative Apportionment and County Unit Voting In Georgia Since 1777*.[59] This tendency was brought to a logical conclusion in a "one man–one vote" principle expressed in the case *Reynold v. Sims* (1964). The majority opinion written by Chief Justice Warren concluded: "History has seen a continuing expansion of the scope of the right of suffrage in this country (. . .) The democratic ideals of equality and majority rule, which have served this Nation so well in the past, are hardly of any less significance for the present and the future."[60]

There was less unanimity over the new set of antidiscrimination cases, peaking with *Bell v. Maryland* (1964), concerning people arrested for sit-ins in segregated restaurants. As the Supreme Court requested the government's position, the Department of Justice produced a brief that was deeply grounded in history: "History and an appreciation of current institutions show that racial segregation in places of public accommodation cannot be viewed as merely a series of isolated private decisions (. . .) It is an inescapable inference that Congress, in recommending the Fourteenth Amendment, expected to remove the disabilities barring Negroes from the public conveyances and places of public accommodations."[61] However, the court split over this case, exactly along the lines of historical interpretation, resulting in no fewer than four opinions of nine justices over the meaning of the Fourteenth Amendment. The concurring opinion of Justice Goldberg quoted abundantly from Van Woodward's *Strange Career of Jim Crow* in an attempt to document "the American commitment to equality and the history of that commitment."[62] However, in the absence of a decisive ruling, the majority opinion was made public on June 22, 1964. Over a week later, the Congress practically resolved this question by adopting the Civil Rights Act.

During that tumultuous decade, the activity of the Warren Court was lionized and criticized at the same time.[63] Its use of history received particular attention. A historian noted at the time that "although it can only be speculation, an interesting question is raised as to whether the subsequent public castigation of the Court for relying upon the 'modern authority' of six sociological and psychological texts in rendering the famed 1954 integration ruling, Brown v. Board of Education, may not have had the effect of pushing it back toward the use of history and precedent in subsequent rulings, especially those calculated to arouse strong public emotions."[64] However, J.R. Wiggins warned that using historical argumentation proved no less controversial:

> The unfortunate muse, harried by subpoena, harassed by cross examination, subjected to *ex parte* proceedings, and lectured by the courts, has not spoken with a clear voice in every attendant proceeding. (. . .) Unfortunately, the general public is not so well aware of the accepted and acknowledged deficiencies of history written by lawyers. Because they are not forewarned against it, they sometimes take seriously its sweeping conclusions. Unless historians bestir themselves in the future, more energetically than they have in the past (. . .) history thereafter may become what the lawyers mistakenly said it was theretofore. The lawyers then will have become not only judges of the law and the judges of history, but also the makers of history.[65]

A wave of reexamination of the role of history in the Supreme Court reasoning was prompted. In the *American Historical Review* Paul Murphy drew "attention to the history profession's neglect of a vital area for which it is responsible, and about which it has done shamefully little in the last quarter century." His appeal to his colleagues to reclaim this territory was coupled with a number of warnings: "The Court has always used history; the founding fathers expected it to do so. What should bother the historian is the type of history (. . .) used in evolving a basis for an important constitutional ruling."[66] He concluded that

> in virtually all of these rulings, the Court, when it cited history, either relied upon archaic historical works of the earlier devotees of "revealed" history, turned to history written by non-historians, or trusted its own ability to reconstruct historical evidence from the sources themselves. The fact should disturb sensitive historians. Yet it should also force them to reassess the way the Court uses history and should challenge them to examine carefully what steps they can take to improve the situation. (. . .) Granted, then, there is little that the history profession can do to change the methodology of legal decision making. And with the Court using history, even if in nonacademic fashion, to attack many of the legal myths of a static society and thereby reach new and significant plateaus of social and economic justice, there is even less incentive to try. Yet, the historian can take positive steps that can be of relevance. If the Court is intent upon building new and dramatic legal structures to meet the requirements of a dynamic society, the historian can at least furnish it with complementary modern architectural materials, so that it does not have to rely upon crap lumber, salvage bricks, and raw stones for its buildings. (. . .) This certainly does not guarantee that the present Court will cease to be criticized when its decisions rely upon historical evidence for points of law, but should at least exempt us from the charge that we are not providing the Court with modern research findings, a charge that we cannot afford to ignore.[67]

He solicited a response from none other than Alfred Kelly, a constitutional historian who performed exactly this purpose in Brown v. Board of Education: "Murphy ignores the question whether the function of history as the historian writes it and that of history as written by the courts are reconcilable." He was of the opinion that "when a court ascertains the nature of the law to be applied to a case through an examination of a stream of judicial precedent, after the time-honored Anglo-American technique, it plays the role of historian. A historian might well say that in this process the court goes to the 'primary sources.' Further, when a court finds it necessary, as it frequently does, to inquire into the circumstances surrounding earlier judicial expositions of the law, it gets still deeper into the writing of history."[68] In Kelly's assessment, the Warren Court was neck-deep in exactly such activity: "In search of some adequate guiding principle upon which to support their libertarian interventionism in the social order, the reformist activists on the Court initiated a new era of historically oriented adjudication."[69] Kelly was unusually blunt:

> performing its self-assumed role as a constitutional historian, [it] has been, if not a naked king, no better than a very ragged one. From a professional point of view, most, if not all, of its recent historical essays are very poor indeed. (. . .) Too often they reach conclusions that are plainly erroneous. More often they state as categorical absolutes propositions that the historian would find to be tentative, speculative, interesting, and worthy of further investigation and inquiry, but not at all pedigreed historical truth. What are the reasons for this failure? In part, it would appear to derive from the radical difference in theory and process between the traditional Anglo-American system of advocacy and equally time-honored techniques of the scholar-historian. The Court, I submit, has attempted to sit on two stools at once and has fallen between them. It has confused the writing of briefs with the writing of history.

However, Kelly conceded that the nexus between history and law is here to stay, "as the essential nature of the judicial process is too close to that of history-writing for the Court to ever abandon entirely either the use of history or the writing of history. But a historian might observe that the historical evidence seems to indicate the Court's history to be the most dubious in those instances in which an appeal to the past has been recruited for the activist purposes of interventionist political implications. It is on those occasions that the worst kind of law-office history makes its appearance in the Court's opinions."[70] Profoundly influenced by his own experience in Brown v. Board of Education, Kelly was setting forth his own version of the theory of incompatibility, questioning the court's usage of history as well as the ability of historians to contribute. Similar thoughts were expressed by another rising constitutional historian, Charles Miller, who worried that "general history (. . .) takes the judges into fields where their training and knowledge may be limited. (. . .) By writing history into its opinions the Court contributes to the public's view of the American past as much as, and sometimes even more than, the professional historians and other historical writers do. (. . .) With the increased scope and power granted the Court by the use of history goes the increased responsibility in the handling of historical materials." He concluded that "the world of the judge is relatively unrestrained with respect to the use of history, compared to the worlds of the lawyer and the historian. Lawyers may lose poorly presented cases. But judges win them all. Historians rise and fall in their open society on the basis of the quality of their work."[71]

Doyens of historical scholarship, such as Henry Steele Commager, were troubled by similar issues: "To judge or not to judge, that is the historical question. Should the historian sit in judgment over the great drama of the past and the men and women who performed on that vast and crowded stage, exposing evil and celebrating virtue and demining and praising famous men? Or should he observe the historical processes with scientific detachment, and record them as automatically as a tape recorder, rigorously excluding personal, national, or religious considerations? Is he competent to perform either of these functions—the function of the judge, or the function of the impartial reporter? The problem is difficult and perhaps insoluble."[72]

However, while Commager was writing these lines, his younger colleagues were solving the problem with their feet. In early March 1965, civil rights protests turned violent in Alabama, where the state police were forcibly stopping the protestors from reaching the capital, Montgomery, from the city of Selma, seriously injuring dozens on a bridge, which became a spotlight of this struggle. Many public figures responded, and academics as well. Inevitably John Hope Franklin, alongside University of Chicago historian Walter Johnson, called upon their colleagues: "As historians of slavery, the Civil War and reconstruction," they asserted, "we believe it is high time for the issues over which Civil War was fought to be finally resolved. We join the march to Montgomery because we believe that the achievement of Negro voting rights will open the floodgates of freedom that will bring an end to the economic, social and political backwardness of the American South."[73] Among the historians who responded, around sixty actually made their way to Selma, among them Shaw Livermore from the University of Michigan, Donald Campbell of Dartmouth, and Roger Shugg of the University of Chicago; Harold Hayman from Rice University; William Leuchtenburg, Robert Cross, James Shenton, and Richard Hofstadter from Columbia University; C. Vann Woodward of Yale; and others. This was a rather heterogeneous group of professionals from some of the most prestigious institutions.[74] For some, like John Higham of the University of Michigan, such activism was self-evident: "We have today a major opportunity for revitalizing the moral relevance of historical scholarship," he had already written in 1962, arguing in the same year for no less than *The Reconstruction of American History*.[75] Others, like Richard Hofstadter, who abandoned their tumultuous interwar political commitments to become architects of postwar liberal consensus, were skeptical: "The activist historian who thinks he is deriving his policy from his history may in fact be deriving his history from his policy."[76] However, the plight of Selma was cutting through that detachment: "There are times when the intellectual feels obliged to make himself heard, and the present is such a time," said Hofstadter to the press.[77] Therefore, "the day before the march concluded, Hofstadter flew to Atlanta (. . .). The tension provoked in Hofstadter a kind of mordant humor. It was a typical gesture—self-deprecation as a tool to put others at ease. Leaving Montgomery on a bus loaded with historians, he cracked to William Leuchtenburg that if segregationists firebombed their vehicle, calculating junior faculty in search of jobs and professional advancement would rejoice."[78] Humor was, however, mixed with a keen sense of responsibility. According to John Hope Franklin, "it was en route to Tuskegee that the bus made a lurch around the corner and almost left the road. At that point, Richard Hofstadter stood and pleaded with the bus driver to be more careful: 'If your driving leads to an accident that kills us all, you will set back the liberal interpretation of American history for a century.' "[79]

Arriving safely, historians joined a crowd that swelled to twenty thousand marchers, reaching Montgomery on March 25. "We marched as historians," remembered Kenneth Stampp, Berkeley historian and author of the famed *Peculiar Institution: Slavery in the Ante-Bellum South* (1956), "but we were also coming as individuals."[80] Certainly their expectations varied: "It may be that we're reaching the end of an era," Vann Woodward optimistically informed the press. A cautious Hofstadter countered, "I think it's more of a beginning because actually we haven't got very far yet."[81] Yet they stood united. In order to highlight this aspect, they improvised on the spot. Without any common banner, they nailed a piece of cardboard on a top of John Higham's umbrella, resulting in a shabby but memorable inscription, "U.S. Historians," caught by Dennis Hopper's photo. "When by virtue of that impromptu sign someone recognized us as being historians, the order came own that since this was a historic event, we should be given a prominent place so that we could bear witness to the events about which historians would someday write.", remembers John Hope Franklin: Thereupon we were ushered to a place in the line of march not too far from the leaders."[82] They were there to hear Martin Luther King speaking from the steps of the Alabama State Capitol. His famous speech reminded everyone that "racial segregation as a way of life did not come about as a natural result of hatred between the races immediately after the Civil War. There were no laws segregating the races then. And as the noted historian, C. Vann Woodward, in his book, *The Strange Career of Jim Crow*, clearly points out, the segregation of the races was really a political stratagem (. . .) to keep the southern masses divided and southern labor the cheapest in the land."[83] Vann Woodward was in the audience. He reported listening to King in front of the Alabama State Capitol with mixed feelings: "I heard him read and endorse passages from the book as support for his crusade."[84] In turn, these historians endorsed the civil rights agenda.

A direct accomplishment that came out of Selma was the adoption of the Voting Rights Act, which prohibited literacy tests and included federal oversight on the process of voting registration. "When Congress passed the sweeping federal Voting Rights Act later that year, the participants in the movement felt that they had accomplished something very important.", concludes John Hope Franklin.[85] And indeed, its effects could be felt quickly—in 1965 Black registered voters in the South were 35.5% (29.3% in the deep South) as opposed to 73.4% whites. By 1967, the number of

Figure 6.2 U.S. historians in Selma

© Dennis Hopper, Courtesy of the Hopper Art Trust

registered Black voters rose sharply to 52.1%.[86] It was the time of quick transformations. "In the long view, which the historian of our trouble will one day take, the mid-1960's will appear as the time when desegregation was finally accepted and began to work in earnest in the South," wrote Alexander Bickel.[87] Thurgood Marshall's ascent mirrored this trajectory. Federal judge at the Court of Appeals from 1961, and Solicitor General from 1965, he was appointed in October 1967 to the Supreme Court as the first Black American to become a Justice, and also the last to be appointed to the bench presided by Earl Warren.

Historians who worked for him in the Brown case shared this trajectory, as in a fairly short time activism moved from the periphery to the core of their profession. In a leap so unprecedented as to deserve the front page of the *New York Times*, Franklin moved from Howard University in 1956 to become chair of the History Department of Brooklyn College, New York.[88] A professorship at the University of Chicago was to follow in 1964, at the department he chaired from 1967 until 1970. Along this path, he continued his engagement in the field of civil rights; however, he warned about the complexity of this nexus, which "involves a recognition of the difference between scholarship and advocacy. (. . .) There is also a place for advocacy, so long as the Negro scholar understands the difference. Recognizing the importance of the use of objective data in the passionate advocacy of the rectification of injustice, the Negro can assume this additional role for his own sake and for the sake of the community. When I wrote the first working paper to be used in the briefs of the NAACP in their school desegregation cases, I was flattered when the chief council, Thurgood Marshall, told me that the paper sounded very much like a lawyer's brief. I had deliberately transformed the objective data provided by historical research into an urgent plea for justice; and I hoped that my scholarship did not suffer."[89] He was actively searching and finding this delicate balance throughout his life—emerited at the Duke University, he was decorated with the Presidential Medal of Freedom in 1995.

This balance did not come so naturally to C. Vann Woodward, who continued his academic advancement at Johns Hopkins after publishing his set of lectures on the *Strange Career of Jim Crow* (1955), inspired in part by his participation in Brown vs. Board. However, his approach differed greatly, as is apparent from the review of Franklin's contribution to a volume called *The Southerner as American:* "Is it the proper function of the historian to 'overcome' the past? Does this not give him a moralistic role? Rather like the pacifist historians who 'turned away' from war? Can the historian ever properly reject the past? Reject myths and illusions about the past surely. But not the past, not even war, feudalism, slavery, or imperialism."[90] On the other hand, not many historians contributed more to undoing what he called the burden of Southern history, both in the classrooms of Yale where he moved in 1961 and on the streets of Selma in 1965. Yet he continuously worried about the radicalization of protests.[91]

Concerned about the future of the civil rights movement and critical toward the new generations of its activists, he expressed his concerns in an article entitled *What Happened to a Civil Rights Movement?*: "We have witnessed in our own time a rising tide of indignation against an ancient wrong, the slow crumbling of stubborn resistance, the sudden rush and elation of victory, and then the onset of reaction and the fading of high hopes." His concerns were an expression of a lasting commitment: "Because this time we were spectators as well as students of events, because one could sometimes say, 'I was there.' For we were all involved in some measure and could stake some claim to it as our movement, at least in the sense that it was the greatest social movement of our time."[92] Uncertain what the future would bring, Woodward had no doubt about the depths of a transformation: "For however future historians may explain it and whatever consequences they may attribute to it, we know that 1966—call it watershed or turning point—was a critical year in our history."[93]

A similar duality is discernable in his speech to the Organization of American Historians, whose president he became in 1968. Entitled *Clio with Soul*, his address reflected his doubts about the extent of the rereading of American history: "Will historians be able to absorb and control the outraged moral passions released and bend to the social purposes dictated without losing balance and betraying principle? Or will the historian's moral engagement compromise the integrity of his craft?" Concerned as he was, he was also not willing to abandon the ethical engagement of historiography. Reflecting well the consensus that American postwar historians were painfully building, he contradicted one of the interwar proponents of the incompatibility of history and law: "In spite of the warning admonitions of Herbert Butterfield and others about the moral interpretation of history, Negro history seems destined to remain the moral storm center of American historiography." Therefore, he confidently concluded that "the moral neutrality approach is no longer acceptable. Moral engagement ranging upward to total commitment now predominates."[94] The bridge was crossed, in Selma and beyond.

Going Contemporary, Going Comparative, Going Global

During the 1960s, as historiography was gradually abandoning its creed of distance and disengagement, a similar development was shaking the field of jurisprudence, questioned both about the relations between law and history in general, and particularly about the role of criminal trials in fostering a social change through the reexamination of the past. Whereas early in the decade Carl Friedrich was still adhering to a strict separation of historical work and jurisprudence, and Hannah Arendt was separating criminal procedure from examination of the past with same vehemence, it was clear that the intellectual space for judicial activism directed toward social change through righting the past wrongs was gradually reclaimed. Even Otto Kirchheimer, ever suspicious toward politicization of trials, treated Nuremberg as a noble exemption to that rule: "In spite of the Nuremberg trials' infirmities, the feeble beginning of transnational control of the crime against the human condition raises the Nuremberg judgment a notch above the level of political justice by fiat of a successor regime."[95] Further breakthroughs came with Judith Shklar's influential book *Legalism: Law, Morals and Political Trials* (1964). In a true theoretical watershed, she acknowledged that there are "occasions when political trials may actually serve liberal ends, where they promote legalistic values in such a way as to contribute to constitutional politics and to a decent legal system."[96] This was particularly the case in "a very rare situation in which there is no law, no government, no political order, and people have committed acts so profoundly shocking that something must be done about them. That was the setting of the Nuremberg Trial of the Major War Criminals." She concluded that "their main value lies in the historical facts about Nazi government they brought to light."[97] In her view, the idea was "eliminating the Nazi leaders in such a way that their contemporaries, on whom the immediate future of Germany depended, might learn exactly what had occurred in recent history."[98]

However, Shklar was not convinced that this mission had been accomplished. She felt that "history had to be tortured throughout in order to reduce the events to proportion similar to those of a model criminal trial within a municipal system."[99] In her view, that restricted the responsibility to a small circle of top perpetrators, amounting to a "conspiratorial view of history."[100] It was an outcome of "confrontation of two entirely different and incompatible notions of causality, the historical and the legal."[101] Shklar doubted that the presence of experts would rectify this deficiency. Noting that "the passion for this sort of 'scientific' expertise rests on quite the same ideological presuppositions as most American natural law theory," she criticized the belief that "expertise in the fact, in short, was the best means to legal justice as well. (. . .) The expert was expected to apply facts to settle conflicts." This belief, she argued, "explains such exercises as the Brandeis brief and Chief Justice Warren's citations of psychological tests in support of his decision in the segregation case."[102]

Shklar was no less skeptical toward historical expertise, using an example from postwar Germany: "In the wake of the celebrated Remer trial a number of eminent German theologians, historians and jurists joined to consider the entire theory of the right of resistance. All of them admired the conspirators of the July 20th movement. Yet in the end even the natural lawyers among them agreed that ultimately no general formulas applicable to all circumstances were available."[103] She added that "no amount of facts, however accurate, yields a decision or an agreement."[104] Additionally, she was fully aware that "the criteria of the historian and those of the lawyers are entirely different and not interchangeable."[105] Yet, she was not calling for separation of disciplines. On the contrary, she concluded that "the isolation of law from history, the notion of an integral legal history apart from that of society in general, is in itself one of the great oddities of legal theory."[106] In fact, her book was an urgent call to bridge "a considerable intellectual gulf separating jurisprudence from most other kinds of social theory. Many historians and political scientists, who have a real interest in law, in the legal profession, and in legal theory, find the lawyer's approach to these subjects irrelevant to and remote from their concerns."[107]

Such a call did not fall on deaf ears. Actually, "in the years after 1965, there was significant blurring in the dividing line between history and law and between law professor and historian (. . .) legal history developed into a legitimate academic field in law schools and history departments."[108] Her own school, Harvard University, was leading the way. Its political science graduate Charles Miller chose his topic for his seminal work, *The Supreme Court and the Uses of History*, because he felt that "it has not been given much attention by either historians or political scientists."[109] Historians were also rediscovering deep roots of connection between their discipline and legal studies through the work of Myron Piper Gilmore and Donald Kelley, who concluded that "the marriage of legal and historical studies in the sixteenth century provided one of the most enduring elements in the continuity of historicism from that age down to the present."[110] American historiography, fairly unburdened with the epistemological concerns that had beset the generation before and the generation after, was more likely to subscribe to Bruce Kuklick's description of its role:

> If the craft of the historian can be in part comprehended in relation to the theory, however, the historian will adopt the role of judge. He will behave as if he were attempting to put himself into the position of ideal observer and to use the feelings he has when making this attempt as evidence for how an ideal observer would react. On the basis of this evidence it could be said that the historian draws conclusions; his activity will be judgmental. Making much use of the language of law, historical discussion of human conduct will be replete with words like "verdict" and "judgment." This language, I shall say, is legalistic. In this judgmental role the historian will attempt to "make the case" for both sides of a controversy and will elaborate arguments that defend as well as denounce the person or action in question.[111]

This engaging trend found its particular expression in contemporary history. In a remarkably short span of time, questions besetting Stuart Hughes and Henry Commager about whether contemporary history exists and whether historians should write it were responded to by Louis J. Halle and Arthur Schlesinger, both agreeing with Richard Hofstadter: "The urgency of our national problems seems to demand, more than ever, that historians have something to say that will help us."[112] This tendency was by no means limited to the United States. "The 1960s acquired an historiographical mood," writes Michael Bentley

"It was a self-conscious decade."[113] At its beginning stood an edited volume *On the Track of Tyranny* dedicated to the anniversary of Wiener Library, whose director Eva Reichmann, the director of Wiener Library was hailing a growing trend of "the study of contemporary history as a political and moral duty."[114]. The editor Max Beloff remarked: "Some people will argue that to dwell on the grimmer aspects of the recent past can serve no useful purpose and helps only to engender or maintain hatreds that would be better buried."[115] Paul Klucke, former director of Munchen Institute for Contemporary History agreed that Paul Klucke, this special obligation stems from personal experience: "We are witnesses of great catastrophes of two world wars."[116] Alan Bullock summed up: "But why should the historian with so wide a field open before him, be under any special obligation to interest himself in the history of his own time? Because, if he does not, he leaves the field open to those who offer false and disputed versions of what has happened."[117] Gerhard Ritter, as a representative of an ourdated generation could only complain: "A strongly pragmatic tendency makes itself felt nearly everywhere. (. . .) What was once the pride of the historian (as of all genuine scholarship)—to pursue his science purely as an end in itself, exclusively for the sake of determining the truth—encounters the suspicion of being remote from life and thus fruitless."[118]

Contemporary historiography was increasingly exercised in an internationalized and growingly comparative context. The postwar resumption of International Historical Congresses, supported by UNESCO, was another telling transmitter of these tendencies. Already in the Rome Congress in 1955, while presenting a survey of central themes of American historiography, Oscar Handlin from Harvard University was warning against the researching of "institutions of politics, of economics or of religion as if their development were entirely self-contained and self-generating."[119] He found a particularly ready audience among the German and French historians presenting general surveys on the early modern and contemporary period, Gerhard Ritter and Pierre Renouvin, who agreed that an interdisciplinary and comparative approach secures stable ground for the objective assessment of the recent past.[120] This did not mean that the explosive potential of historical debates was any less, as discovered by A. J. P. Taylor and Fritz Fischer, whose iconoclastic writing on the origins of world wars brought their academic careers into jeopardy in the early 1960s. However, these conflicts were tellingly occurring within national historiographies, not between then. On the contrary, the bilateral and multilateral cooperation vested in pacifying those conflicts was another indicator of a mature, viable, and self-conscious field.[121]

Indicative of this change was a meeting in Wiener Library (also hosting the London Institute of Contemporary History from 1964), held in October 1966 in anticipation of reducing the ban on access to archival sources in Great Britain. It assembled over sixty scholars, invited to discuss the international state of the art of contemporary historiography. Hosted by Walter Laqueur, the event was attended by such names in contemporary history as Gordon Craig (Stanford University, California), J. B. Duroselle (Sorbonne), Alan Bullock (St. Catherine's College, Oxford), Paul Kluke (Universität Frankfurt), and Helmut Krausnick (Institut für Zeitgeschichte, München). The results of the meeting were published in an impressive volume, a true handbook widened to include contributions of authors from Eastern Europe and USSR, therefore giving an insightful overview of achievements in contemporary history and creating a roadmap for research in this field.[122]

Cooperation was an important element of that roadmap, both between historiographies and within disciplines. In that spirit, some attention was also given to the relation between history and law regarding the access to documents. Disciplinary differences were seen not as signs of incompatibility, but as a potential benefit. "Admittedly, the legal rules of evidence are necessarily different from the principle of historical inquiry, and 'the legally established facts' might therefore well differ from 'historical truth,' but as long as this is borne in mind there is no doubt that the documents, read together with the transcription of the proceedings in which they were discussed, are an incomparably better source than the documents alone," wrote Leo Cohn.[123] The usage of legal material was normalized, seen as by Alan Bullock simply as one of the segments "which combined, after the war, to give a sufficiently powerful impetus to the study of contemporary history to overcome the traditional objections and establish it as a difficult but accepted part of historical studies."[124]

Wiener Library's Institute for Contemporary History also attempted to institutionalize this momentum through the founding of a *Journal of Contemporary History*, whose first editorial note was very optimistic: "The idea that contemporary history could not and should not be written, prevalent between, roughly, the last third of the nineteenth century and the end of the Second World War no longer has many vigorous proponents. A more liberal view has prevailed (. . .). The historical journals of the nineteenth century excluded the 'discussion of unresolved problems of current politics' *(Historische Zeitschrift)*, announced that they would 'avoid contemporary controversies' *(Revue Historique)*, or even that they would refuse 'contributions arguing still burning questions with reference to present controversy' *(Historical Review)*. The *Journal of Contemporary History*, unlike its more distinguished predecessors, while not actively looking for controversy will certainly not eschew it; it will not shy away from the still unresolved questions of the recent past."[125]

To that end, in one of its first issues, the *Journal of Contemporary History* republished much of the state-of-the-art proceedings from the Wiener Library conference, even enlarging its grasp to encompass the authors from America. Optimistic tones also prevailed. "In the United States," wrote R.J. Wilson, "the professional situation of the historian is better in the 1960s than ever before."[126] His American colleague J.H. Hecter noted: "Another highly desirable transformation has been the emancipation of historiography from the limits imposed by nineteenth-century nationalism (. . .). For such historians a comparative approach, destructive of nationalist myopeia, has been a common response to their task."[127] Rene Remond was of the opinion that similar tendencies prevailed in France: "The history of the most immediate past enjoys such prestige among young historians looking for subjects for their doctoral theses (. . .). Thus contemporary history has ceased to be *terra incognita*."[128] Echoing their contributions, Hans Herzfeld summarized the troubled transformation of German scholarship: "The kind of research in contemporary history undertaken in Germany since the end of the Second World War has been determined by the completeness of the country's collapse, which put in question the entire concept of German history as previously held by the majority of historians, and confronted them with the task of 'mastering' the past in a fresh light, in order to give to a nation which seemed for a moment to be deprived of any history a new and clear understanding of the continuity and discontinuity of past and present." He concluded that the change amounts to "the reappraisal the 'nation-state' concept, which for too long played an exaggerated part in German thinking.[129]

Overcoming the parochial constraints of European historiographies became one of the recognizable facets of the *Journal for Contemporary History*, the other being engagement with controversial topics. Therefore it hardly comes as a surprise that in one of the first contributions from the U.S., authored by Robert Starobin, the point was made to emphasize "the centrality of institutions like slavery to long periods of American history, and regard the Negro as a key to the meaning of the American experience." Starobin critically examined the causes of this shift: "Their image was upgraded at home, in order, first, to defeat fascism, then to counter Soviet propaganda, and finally to woo the black nations emerging from European colonialism."[130]

The importance of the global dimension of his last argument was well recognized by Rupert Emerson: "Is there any other occasion on which so global and commanding a scheme of things was swept away in so brief a time?" he asked in a special issue of this journal, dedicated solely to colonialism and decolonization.[131] With a customary delay, historians also experienced what Harold McMillan called a "wind of change" in his 1960 speech, which materialized by the end of that year with the UN General Assembly Declaration on the Granting of Independence to Colonial Countries and Peoples, followed with the 1963 General Assembly *Declaration on the Elimination of All Forms of Racial Discrimination*. Notwithstanding frequent abstentions of Western countries, a rapid succession of documents that delegitimized both colonialism and racism as its ideological core continued in 1965 with the drafting of *International Covenant on Civil and Political Rights* and *International Convention on the Elimination of All Forms of Racial Discrimination*, which called for "effective measures to review governmental, national and local policies, and to amend, rescind or nullify any laws and regulations which have the effect of creating or perpetuating racial discrimination wherever it exists."[132] As these documents entered into force by the end of the decade, John Hope Franklin observed that in the nick of time the "affirmative position of the United States had the effect of removing it from the dwindling list of nations, such as South Africa and Rhodesia, that continue to adhere to a national policy of segregation and discrimination."[133] The struggle against racism was transgressing U.S. borders and was becoming a global yardstick.

Addressing the consequences of extreme violence brought about by the Second World War became an equally globalized effort. In 1968 the General Assembly of United Nations passed the Convention on the Non-Application of the Statutory Limitation to War Crimes and Crimes against Humanity. This Convention, "convinced that the effective punishment of war crimes and crimes against humanity is an important element in the prevention of such crimes, the protection of human rights and fundamental freedoms," abolished the statute of limitations for war crimes and crimes against humanity as defined in the Charter of the International Military Tribunal in Nuremberg, as well as the crime of genocide defined in the Genocide convention, "even if such acts do not constitute a violation of the domestic law of the country in which they were committed."[134] The signatories were mostly communist and non-aligned countries, with most Western powers abstaining or even voting against its wording, but affirming the principle, as the Council of Europe proposed and opened for signatures the similarly phrased

European Convention on the Non-Applicability of Statutory Limitation to Crimes against Humanity and War Crimes.[135] In the process, which was anything but linear, the national judiciaries of continental Europe picked up this task, establishing specific statutory clauses and different procedural elements, but also introducing new forensic elements in an attempt to struggle with the scope of the state-sponsored atrocities that occurred during the Second World War.[136] Global reckoning with the past was also obtaining a transnational dimension, in scholarship and the legal field as well.[137]

With an increasingly globalized recognition of the imprescriptibility of war crimes and crimes against humanity, as well as with equally globalized action against racial discrimination, the gulf between the proclaimed values of universal human rights and the realities of their postwar implementation was somewhat lessened. The ability to reckon with the wrongs of the past was increasingly seen as a token of transformation, and this yardstick was becoming increasingly globalized, and so was in fact the very practice of expert witnessing. Therefore, substantial change in relations between history and law achieved a tangible dimension. Two major barriers—historical distance and statute of limitations for offenses—gave way and created a new situation in which the past became a legitimate, indeed indispensable, field of legal interest. A turning point became a point of no return.

Notes

1 Carl Ioachim Friedrich, "Law and History," *Vanderbilt Law Review* 63 (1961): 1029.
2 See note 66 in Chapter II.
3 Hannah Arendt, "Reflections on Little Rock," *Dissent* 6.1 (1959): 50.
4 Hannah Arendt, "A Reporter at Large: Eichmann in Jerusalem I," *The New Yorker*, February 16, 1963: 40.
5 Ibid., 55–56.
6 Baron was a chairperson of Jewish Cultural Reconstruction, where Arendt worked as an executive secretary during the war. Despite their differing interpretations of Jewish history, they remained close friends. Liberles, *Salo Wittmayer Baron: Architect of Jewish History*, 8–9.
7 Hannah Arendt, *Eichmann in Jerusalem: A Report on the Banality of Evil* (London: Faber and Faber, 1963), 233.
8 Jacob Robinson, *And the Crooked Shall Be Made Straight: The Eichmann Trial, the Jewish Catastrophe, and Hannah Arendt's Narrative* (New York: Macmillan, 1965), viii. An early draft of this book is kept at the library of the NIOD Institute for War, Holocaust and Genocide Studies, Amsterdam, under the title *The Virtuous Criminal and the Victim's Crimes: Eichmann, Arendt and Jewish History* (New York, s.n., 1963), NIOD Library, DUI 6.221.
9 Robinson, *And the Crooked Shall be Made Straight*, 101.
10 Ibid., 36.
11 "The Formidable Dr. Robinson: A Reply", January 20, 1966. *The New York Review of Books*.
12 See Michael Ezra, "The Eichmann Polemics: Hannah Arendt and Her Critics," *Democratiya* 9 (2007): 141–165. Reactions on Arendt's book were rapidly assembled and published in German in F. A. Krummacher (ed.), *Die Kontroverse:*

Hannah Arendt, Eichmann und die Juden (München: Nymphenburger Verlagshandlung, 1964).

13 Hannah Arendt, *Auschwitz on Trial. Responsibility and Judgment* (New York: Shocken, 2005), 231–246.

14 Eugen Kogon, "Umwelt und Recht, " *Neue Juristische Wochenschrift* 41 (1965): 1901.

15 Ernst Forsthoff, "Der Zeithistoriker als gerichtlicher Sachverständiger," *Neue Juristische Wochenschrift* 13 (1965): 574–575. On Forsthoff's position and motivation see Dirk Van Laak, "Widerstand gegen die Geschichtsgewalt. Zur Kritik an der 'Vergangenheitsbewältigung.' " In Frei et al., eds. *Geschichte vor Gericht*, 16–25.

16 Adolf Laufs, "Zeitgeschichte und Rechtspflege: Eine Erwiderung," *Neue Juristische Wochenschrift* 33 (1965): 1521.

17 Ibid. 1522.

18 Rebecca Wittmann, *Beyond Justice: The Auschwitz Trial* (Cambridge, MA: Harvard University Press, 2005), 15.

19 Pohl, *Prosecutors and Historians*, 3. On the influence of the Eichmann trial in Germany, see the reactions of German public figures, highlights of press coverage, and public opinion polls assembled in Hans Lamm, *Der Eichmann-Prozess in der deutschen öffentlichen Meinung* (Frankfurt am Mein: Ner-Tamid Verlag, 1961).

20 "Der Vortrag in Loccum," in *Die Gehilften. NS Verbrechen und die Justiz nach 1945*, eds. Barbara Just-Dahlman and Helmut Just (Frankfurt am Mein: Athenäum, 1988), 40–46. The press naturally picked up on extreme, illustrative examples, including lenient bail (for example, one judge granted bail in the sum of 12,000 DM in a case involving 12,000 murders–one deutschmark per victim), and lenient sentencing (10 minutes for each killing), and showed open mistrust toward the way the German police handled these cases. Cf. John P. Teschke. *Hitler's Legacy: West Germany Confronts the Aftermath of the Third Reich* (New York: Peter Lang Publishing, 1999), 72–81.

21 Erwin Schüle, "Die Justiz der Bundesrepunlik und die Sühne nationalsozialistischen Unrechts," *Viertalsjahrhefte für Zeitgeshcichte* 4 (1961): 440–443.

22 Karl Bader, "Politische und historische Shuld und die Staatliche Rechtsprechung," *Viertaljahrshefte für Zeitgeschichte* 2 (April, 1962): 113.

23 Ibid., 123.

24 Ibid., 124.

25 Herbert Jäger, "Betrachtungen zum Eichmann-Prozess," *Kriminologie und Strafrechtsreform*, 3.4 (1962): 1, 11.

26 Similar concerns were also expressed in the best-selling work of Hannah Vogt, *Schuld oder Verhängnis? 12 Fragen an Deutschlands jüngste Vergangenheit* (Frankfurt am Main-Berlin-Bonn: Diesterweg, 1961). See also the debates edited by Karl Forster (ed.), *Möglichkeiten und Grenzen für die Bewältigung historischer und politischer Schuld in Strafprozessen* (Würzburg: Studien und Berichte der katolischen Akademie in Bayern, 1962) and Reinhard Henkys, *Die nationalsozialistischen Gewaltverbrechen: Geschichte und Gericht* (Stuttgart and Berlin: Kreuz Verlag, 1964).

27 Law Number 64–1326 of 26 December 1964, http://www.legifrance.gouv.fr/affichTexte.do?cidTexte=JORFTEXT000000684761.

28 Adalber Rückerl (ed.), *NS-Prozesse: Nach 25 Jahren Strafverfolgung: Möglichkeiten, Grenzen, Ergenisse* (Karlsruhe: C.F. Mueller, 1971), 21–23.

29 Robert A. Monson, "The West German Statute of Limitations on Murder: A Political, Legal, and Historical Exposition," *The American Journal of Comparative Law* 30.4 (1982): 610.

30 Otto Kranzbuhler, "Nuremberg Eighteen Years after, in Gunar Mettrouh," *Perspectives on Nuremberg*, 434.

31 Ibid., 443–444.

32 Dietrich Strothmann, “Bleiben die Mörder unter uns? Das Ende der Verjährungsfrist—ein Streit ohne Ende,” *Die Zeit*, 27 November, 1964.

33 Statements of over 200 public figures were carefully assembled and published by Simon Wiesenthal (ed.), *Verjährung? 200 Persönlichkeiten des öffentlichen Lebens sagen nein; eine Dokumentation* (Frankfurt am Main: Europäische Verlagsanstalt, 1965).

34 Teschke, *Hitler's Legacy*, 338.

35 Monson, *The West German Statute of Limitations on Murder*, 610. The 1965 law, parliamentary debates and the decision of the Constitutional court in Rolf Vogel (ed.), *Ein Weg aus der Vergangenheit: Eine Dokumentation zur Verjährung und zu den NS-Prozessen* (Frankfurt: Ullstein Verlag, 1969), 21–58.

36 Just-Dahlman, *Die Gehilften: NS Verbrechen und die Justiz nach 1945*, 176–236.

37 There are stenographic records of the meeting, but personal recollections of participants are gathered in Thomas Horstmann and Heike Litzinger (eds.), *An den Grenzen des Rechts, Gespräche mit Juristen über die Verfolgung von NS-Verbrechen* (Frankfurt am Mein: Campus Verlag, 2006). Some participatns published their contributions.

38 Hans Hofmeyer, “Prozeßrechtliche Probleme und praktische Schwierigkeiten bei der Durchführung der Prozesse,” in *Verhandlungen des sechsundvierzigsten Deutschen Juristentages, Essen 1966*, ed. Ständigen Deputation des Deutschen Juristentages (München und Berlin: C.H. Beck Verlag, 1967), vol. IIC, 38–44.

39 Horstmann and Litzinger, *An den Grenzen des Rechts*, 191–192.

40 Herbert Jäger, “Strafrecht und nationalsozialistische Gewaltverbrechen,” *Kritische Justiz* 2 (1968), 144.

41 “Die Errmittlung,” *Der Spiegel* 18 April 1966; “Der zweite Fall Schüle,” *Die Zeit* 16/1966.

42 Inge van Hulle, *When Judges become Historians: Rewriting Aktion Reinhardt in the Nuremberg Trials*, KU Leuven (2012), http://www.scriptiebank.be/sites/default/files/webform/scriptie/Thesis3.pdf, accessed on 21.2.2016.

43 Erich Haberer, “History and Justice: Paradigms of the Prosecution of Nazi Crimes,” *Holocaust and Genocide Studies* 19 (2005): 487–488.

44 A detailed description is in Michael S. Bryant, *Eyewitness to Genocide: The Operation Reinhard Death Camp Trials*, 1955–1966 (Knoxville: The University of Tennessee Press, 2014), 112–115, 170. This trend would continue, enabling Hans-Günther Seraphim to appear as an expert or to have his work referred to in judgments in no fewer than sixty-five proceedings after 1958. Helmut Krausnick, who testified in four more trials between the Ulm trial and the Frankfurt Auschwitz trial, went on to serve as an expert in twenty-eight further cases (1965–1983). Jacobsen and Martin Broszat testified visibly less, five more trials after the Frankfurt Auschwitz trial each, whereas Hans Buchheim submitted his reports, testified, or was quoted in forty-four more cases. The data is based on an overview compiled by Dick de Mildt, *List of Historians (Expert Witnesses) Mentioned in the German Trial Judgments Series Justiz und NS-Verbrechen: Sammlung deutscher Starfurteile wegen nationalsozialistischer Tötungsverbrechen, 1945–2012* (Amsterdam: Ex Post Facto, 2013). The numbers are not definitive, as they do not encompass the reports of experts made for the prosecutor but not used in court.

45 Wolfgang Scheffler, *Judenverfolgung im Dritten Reich* (Berlin: Colloquium Verlag, 1960). Wolfgang Schefller—Historiker, *Die Welt*, http://www.welt.de/welt_print/article2752840/Wolfgang-Scheffler-1929–2008-Historiker.html.

46 Helmut Krausnick, “Research and Research Institutes in Germany,” in *Contemporary History in Europe*, ed. Donald Cameron Watt (London: George Allen and Unwin Ltd., 1969), 166–167.

47 Ibid., 167. About the erosion of historicist legacy in Germany see Cf. Georg G. Iggers, "The Decline of the Classical National Tradition of German Historiography," *History and Theory* 6.3 (1967): 382–412.
48 Stanley M.Elkins, *Slavery: A problem in American institutional and intellectual life* (New York: Universal library, 1963), 104.
49 Payton McCrary, "Bringing Equality to Power: How the Federal Courts Transformed the Electoral Structure of Southern Politics," *University of Pennsylvania Journal of Constitutional Law* 5 (2003): 666.
50 The history of Black disfranchisement is in Bernard Grofman, Lisa Handley, Richard G. Niemi, *Minority Representation and the Quest for Voting Equality* (Cambridge: Cambridge University Press, 1992), 4–23. For a comprehensively overview see Morgan Kousser, *Colorblind Injustice: Minority Voting Rights and the Undoing of the Second Reconstruction* (Chapel Hill: The University of North Carolina Press, 1999), 12–68.
51 Grofman et al., *Minority Representation and the Quest for Voting Equality*, 15.
52 Audio recording and full text of oral argumentation can be found in the OYEZ Project, U.S. Supreme Court Media, Chicago-Kent School of Law, Baker vs. Carr, Oral Argument, part I, http://www.oyez.org/cases/1960–1969/1960/1960_6#argument-1, accessed on 21.2.2016.
53 Walter F. Murphy and Joseph Tannenhaus, *Comparative Constitutional Law: Cases and Commentaries* (New York: Springer, 1977), 147.
54 Gene Graham, *One Man One Vote, Baker v Carr and the American Levellers* (Boston: An Atlantic Monthly Press Book, 1972), 229.
55 J. Douglas Smith, *On Democracy's Doorstep: The Inside Story of How the Supreme Court Brought "One Person, one Vote" to the United States* (New York: Hill and Wang, 2014), 59–60.
56 Ibid., 162.
57 Ibid., 173–175. See Robert Hiram White, The Tennessee Encyclopedia of History and Culture, https://tennesseeencyclopedia.net/entry.php?rec=1500.
58 Graham, *One Man One Vote*, 158, 174.
59 Bonner was at the time chairman of the Department of History and Political Science at Georgia State College for Women in Milledgeville, Georgia. A manuscript of the report is in the James C. Bonner Collection, Special Collections, Ina Dillard Russell Library, Georgia College & State University, box 5–7. Fol.1–4. *County Unit System and Legislative Apportionments.* He published an James C. Bonner, "Legislative Apportionment and County Unit Voting In Georgia Since 1777," *The Georgia Historical Quarterly* 47.4 (December, 1963), 351–374.
60 Reynold v. Sims, 377 US 566 (1964). Historical reasoning in apportionment cases is studied at length by Miller, *The Supreme Court and the Uses of History*, 119–148.
61 Bell v. Maryland, 378 US 226 (1964), Supplemental Brief of the United States as Amicus Curiae, 11, 18, 136.
62 Disagreements in opinions are analyzed in Charles Miller, *The Supreme Court and the Uses of History*, 100–118.
63 Charles Wyzanski, "History and Law," *The University of Chicago Law Review* 26.2 (Winter, 1959), 237, 244; John G. Wofford, "The Blinding Light: The Uses of History in Constitutional Interpretation," *The University of Chicago Law Review* 31.3 (Spring, 1964): 502–533; Alexander Bickel, *Politics and the Warren Court* (New York: Harper and Row, 1965), 3.
64 Paul L. Murphy, "Time to Reclaim: The Current Challenge of American Constitutional History," *American Historical Review* 69.1 (October, 1963), 61.
65 J. R. Wiggins, "Lawyers as Judges of History," *Proceedings of the Massachusetts Historical Society* 75 (1963): 84, 104.

66 Paul L. Murphy. "Time to Reclaim: The Current Challenge of American Constitutional History," *American Historical Review* 69.1 (October, 1963): 64–65.
67 Ibid., 77–78, 79.
68 Alfred H. Kelly, "Clio and the Court: An Illicit Love Affair," *The Supreme Court Review* 1965 (1965), 121.
69 Ibid., 131.
70 Ibid., 154–157.
71 Charles A. Miller, *The Supreme Court and the Uses of History* (Cambridge, MA: Harvard University Press, 1969). 25, 195.
72 Henry Steele Commager, *The Study of History* (Columbus: Charles E. Merill, 1966), 60–61.
73 David S. Brown, *Richard Hofstadter: An Intellectual Biography* (Chicago: University of Chicago Press, 2006), 168.
74 John Hope Franklin gives insight into the creation of the appeal: "It was at this point that my colleague and the former chairman of our department at Chicago, Walter Johnson, suggested that historians should participate. Within a few days he and others had issued calls for historians to join the march, which some three thousand activists would start on March 21, to be joined by tens of thousands of supporters four days later outside Montgomery's city limits. Historians of the United States were the focus of his invitations, but others were welcome. Several of us from Chicago went, including Walter Johnson, Roger Shugg, Mark Haller, and myself. Other historians who came were C.Vann Woodward from Yale; Arthur Mann, of Smith College, who would join our department the following year; Bernard Weisberger, who had left Chicago for Rochester; John Caughey, John Higham, and Roger Daniels, who all travelled from UCLA; Samuel P.Hays, Pittsburgh; Rembert Patrick, Richard Hofstadter, and William Leuchtenburg, Columbia; Roger Hollingsworth, Wisconsin; Bradford Perkins, Michigan; Benett Wall, Tulane; and forty or more other historians." John Hope Franklin, Mirror to America, 237.
75 John Higham, "Beyond Consensus: The Historian as Moral Critic," *The American Historical Review* 67.3 (April, 1962): 617.
76 Richard Hofstadter. *The Progressive Historians: Turner, Beard, Parrington* (New York: Knopf, 1968), 464–465.
77 Jeffrey Newman, "Four CU Profs. Plan to Join Selma March. Historians Will Protest Voting Rights Denial," *Columbia Daily Spectator* CIX.88, March 23, 1965. Perhaps he was influenced by the fact that John Lewis, chairman of the Student Nonviolent Coordinating Committee, who was seriously injured during the infamous Bloody Sunday on March 7, had his book *The American Political Tradition* in his knapsack.
78 Brown, *Richard Hofstadter: An Intellectual Biography* 168–169.
79 Marotta Gary, *Afro-Americans in New York Life and History* 32.2 (2008): 85.
80 Brown, *Richard Hofstadter: An Intellectual Biography*, 169.
81 *The New York Times* and *The Atlanta Constitution* 23.3, 1965.
82 John Hope Franklin, *Mirror to America*, 239.
83 Martin Luther King, *Our God is Marching On!* https://kinginstitute.stanford.edu/our-god-marching.
84 C. Vann Woodward, *Thinking Back: The Perils of Writing History* (Baton Rouge: Louisiana State University Press, 1986), 92.
85 John Hope Franklin, *Mirror to America*, 240.
86 Grofman et al., *Minority Representation and the Quest for Voting Equality*, 23.
87 Alexander Bickel, *Politics and the Warren Court* (New York: Harper and Row, 1965), 3.

88 "Negro Educator Chosen to Head Department at Brooklyn College. Howard University Professor Will be First of Race to Hold That Rank Here," *New York Times*, February 15, 1956.
89 John Hope Franklin, "The Dilemma of the American Negro Scholar," in *Soon, One Morning: New Writing by American Negroes*, ed. Herbert Hill (New York: Knopf, 1969), 73–74.
90 Michael O'Brien, *The Letters of C. Vann Woodward* (New Haven: Yale University Press, 2013), 164.
91 Ibid., 241.
92 The article was first published in Harpers in January 1967, here reproduced from C. Vann Woodward, *The Burden of Southern History* (Baton Rouge: Louisiana State University Press, 1993), 167–168.
93 Ibid., 174.
94 C. Vann Woodward, "Clio with Soul," *Journal of American History* 65 (1969): 5–7. About gradual formation of postwar consensus on the subject of racial equality see Novick, *That Noble Dream*, 348–360. Its effect on historiography was scrutinized by Robert L. Harris, "Coming of Age: The Transformation of Afro-American Historiography," *The Journal of Negro History* 67.2 (1982):107–121.
95 Kircheimer, *Political Justice*, 341.
96 Judith Shklar, *Legalism: Law, Morals and Political Trials* (Cambridge, MA: Harvard University Press, 1964), 145.
97 Ibid., 153–154.
98 Ibid., 156.
99 Ibid., 147.
100 Ibid., 172.
101 Ibid., 194.
102 Ibid., 97, 101.
103 Ibid., 72–73.
104 Ibid., 91.
105 Ibid., 197–198.
106 Ibid., 80–81.
107 Ibid., vi, vii. This trend is remarkably persistent, as evidenced by similar concerns recently expressed by Richard Posner. *Divergent Paths: The Academy and the Judiciary* (Cambridge: Harvard University Press, 2016).
108 Neil M. Richards, "Clio and the Court: A Reassesment of the Supreme Court's Uses of History," *Journal of Law and Politics* (1997): 809–810.
109 Miller, *The Supreme Court and the Uses of History*, 2.
110 Donald R. Kelley, *Foundations of Modern Historical Scholarship: Language, Law, and History* (New York: Columbia University Press, 1970), 10. Cf. Myron Piper Gilmore, *Humanists and Jurists* (Cambridge: Harvard University Press, 1963).
111 Bruce Kuklick, "The Mind of the Historian," *History and Theory* 8.3 (1969): 319; Novick, *That Noble Dream*, 361–399.
112 Hofstadter, *The Progressive Historians*, 465–466. H. Stuart Hughes, "Is Contemporary History Real History?" *The American Scholar* 32.4 (1963): 516–525; Henry Steele Commager, "Should Historians Write Contemporary History?" *Saturday Review* 12 (February, 1966): 18–47; Arthur Schlesinger, "On the Writing of Contemporary History," *The Atlantic*, March, 1967: 69–74; Louis J. Halle, "What is Contemporary History?" *The Virginia Quarterly Review* 43: (1967): 566–579.
113 Michael Bentley, *Modern Historiography* (New York: Routledge, 1999), 137.

114 Eva Gabriele Reichmann, "The Study of Contemporary History as a Political and Moral Duty," in *On the Track of Tyranny*, ed. M. Beloff (London: Vallentine & Mitchell, 1960), 189–201.
115 Ibid., vii.
116 Ibid., 157.
117 Ibid., 73.
118 Gerhard Ritter, "Scientific History, Contemporary History, and Political Science," *History and Theory* 1.3 (1961): 262.
119 Karl Dietrich Erdmann, *Toward a Global Community of Historians* (New York: Berghahn Books, 2005), 227.
120 Ibid., 225–226.
121 Philipp Stelzel, "Working Toward a Common Goal? American Views on German Historiography and German-American Scholarly Relations during the 1960s," *Central European History* 41.4 (2008): 639–671; Jacques de Launay, *Major Controversies of Contemporary History* (Oxford, New York: Pergamon Press, 1965).
122 Donald Cameron Watt (ed.), *Contemporary History in Europe* (London: George Allen and Unwin Ltd., 1969).
123 Leo Kahn, "Some Problems of Research in European Archives," in *Contemporary History in Europe*, ed. Donald Cameron Watt (London: George Allen and Unwin Ltd., 1969), 341.
124 Alan Bullock, "Introduction," in *Contemporary History in Europe*, ed. Donald Cameron Watt (London: George Allen and Unwin Ltd., 1969), 13.
125 Geroge Mosse and Walter Laquer, "Editorial Note," *Journal of Contemporary History* 1.1 (1966): iii–iv.
126 R.J. Wilson, "United States: The Reassessment of Liberalism," *Journal of Contemporary History* 2.1, Historians on the Twentieth Century (January, 1967): 93.
127 J.H. Hexter, "Some American Observations," *Journal of Contemporary History* 2.1 (1967): 16.
128 Rene Remond, "France: Work in Progress," *Journal of Contemporary History* 2.1 (1967): 35, 37.
129 Hans Herzfeld, "Germany: After the Catastrophe," *Journal of Contemporary History* 2.1 (1967): 80–89.
130 Robert Starobin, "The Negro: A Central Theme in American History," *Journal of Contemporary History* 3.2 (1968): 37, 39.
131 Rupert Emerson, "Colonialisms," *Journal of Contemporary History, Colonialism and Decolonization* 4.1 (1969): 3.
132 Assembly *Declaration on the Elimination of All Forms of Racial Discrimination 1965*, www.un-documents.net/a18r1904.htm. *International Convention on the Elimination of All Forms of Racial Discrimination;* http://www.ohchr.org/EN/ProfessionalInterest/Pages/CERD.aspx, http://www.un-documents.net/a18r1904.htm., accessed on 22.2.2016.
133 John Hope Franklin, "The Negro since Freedom," in *The Comparative Approach to American History*, ed. C. Vann Woodward (New York: Basic Books, 1968), 173.
134 The text, the procedural history, and the signatories of the convention are available at the United Nations. Audiovisual Library of International Law, Convention on the Non-Applicability of Statutory Limitations to War Crimes and Crimes against Humanity, http://legal.un.org/avl/ha/cnslwcch/cnslwcch.html, accessed on 22.2.2016.
135 Council of Europe, *European Convention on the Non-Applicability of Statutory Limitation to Crimes against Humanity and War Crimes*, http://www.coe.int/en/web/conventions/full-list/-/conventions/treaty/082.

136 Debates in the United Nations over the Convention, as well as expressed reservations, are summarized in Jean-Marie Henckaerts and Louise Doswald-Beck, *Customary International Humanitarian Law* (ICRC: Cambridge University Press, 2005), vol. II, 4052–4073. The development of the principal of historical imprescriptibility is scrutinized by Antoon De Baets, "Historical Imprescriptibility," *Storia della Storiografia* 59–60 (2011): 128–149.

137 The transnational aspect of reckoning with the crimes of the Second World War on a European level is the subject of Norbert Frei (ed.), *Transnationale Vergangenheitspolitik: Der Umgang mit deutschen Kriegsverbrechern in Europa nach dem Zweiten Weltkrieg* (Göttingen: Wallstein, 2006). The importance of the transatlantic connection, and in particular U.S.-German historiographical cooperation, is signaled in Philipp Stelzel, "Transnationalism and the History of Historiography: A Transatlantic Perspective," *History Compass* 13.2 (2015): 78–87. The general striving toward formulation and practicing of global history in that period is described by Dietrich Erdmann, *Toward Global Community of Historians*, 267–275. The relevance of these developments for the globalization of historical expert witnessing is underlined by Ramses Delafontaine, *Historians as Expert Judicial Witnesses in Tobacco Litigation: A Controversial Legal Practice* (New York: Springer, 2015), 45–64.

Bibliography

Arendt, Hannah. "Reflections on Little Rock." *Dissent* 6.1 (1959): 45–56.

Arendt, Hannah. "A Reporter at Large: Eichmann in Jerusalem," *The New Yorker*, 16 February, 1963.

Arendt, Hannah. *Eichmann in Jerusalem: A Report on the Banality of Evil*. London: Faber and Faber, 1963.

Arendt, Hannah. "The Formidable Dr. Robinson: A Reply," *The New York Review of Books, 20* January, 1966.

Arendt, Hannah. *Responsibility and Judgment*. New York: Shocken, 2005.

Bader, Karl. "Politische und historische Shuld und die Staatliche Rechtsprechung." *Viertaljahrshefte für Zeitgeschichte* 2 (April, 1962): 113–125.

De Baets, Antoon. "Historical Imprescriptibility." Storia della Storiografia 59–60 (2011): 128–149.

Bell v. Maryland, 378 US 226 (1964), Supplemental Brief of the United States as Amicus Curiae.

Beloff, M., ed. *On the Track of Tyranny*. London: Vallentine & Mitchell, 1960.

Bentley, Michael. *Modern Historiography*. New York: Routledge, 1999.

Bickel, Alexander. *Politics and the Warren Court*. New York: Harper and Row, 1965.

Bonner, James C. "Legislative Apportionment and County Unit Voting in Georgia Since 1777." *The Georgia Historical Quarterly* 47.4 (December, 1963): 351–374.

Brown, David S. *Richard Hofstadter: An Intellectual Biography*. Chicago: University of Chicago Press, 2006.

Bryant, Michael S. *Eyewitness to Genocide: The Operation Reinhard Death Camp Trials, 1955–1966*. Knoxville: The University of Tennessee Press, 2014.

Commager, Henry Steele. *The Study of History*. Columbus: Charles E. Merill, 1966.

Commager, Henry Steele. "Should Historians Write Contemporary History?" *Saturday Review* 12 (February, 1966): 18–47.

Delafontaine, Ramses. *Historians as Expert Judicial Witnesses in Tobacco Litigation: A Controversial Legal Practice*. New York: Springer, 2015.

Douglas, Lawrence. *The Memory of Judgment: Making Law and History in the Trials of the Holocaust*. New Haven: Yale University Press, 2005.

"Der zweite Fall Schüle," *Die Zeit*, 15 April, 1966.

"Die Errmittlung," *Der Spiegel*, 18 April, 1966.

Elkins, Stanley M. *Slavery: A problem in American institutional and intellectual life*. New York: Universal library, 1963.

Emerson, Rupert. "Colonialisms." *Journal of Contemporary History*, Colonialism and Decolonization 4.1 (1969): 3–16.

Erdmann, Karl Dietrich. *Toward Global Community of Historians: The International Congresses and the International Committee of Historical Sciences 1898–2000*. New York: Berghahn Books, 2005.

Ezra, Michael. "The Eichmann Polemics: Hannah Arendt and Her Critics." *Democratiya* 9 (2007): 141–165.

Forster, Karl, ed. *Möglichkeiten und Grenzen für die Bewältigung historischer und politischer Schuld in Strafprozessen*. Würzburg: Katolischen Akademie in Bayern, 1962.

Forsthoff, Ernst. "Der Zeithistoriker als gerichtlicher Sachverständiger." *Neue Juristische Wochenschrift* 13 (1965): 574–575.

Frei, Norbert, ed. *Transnationale Vergangenheitspolitik: Der Umgang mit deutschen Kriegsverbrechern in Europa nach dem Zweiten Weltkrieg*. Göttingen: Wallstein, 2006.

Frei, Norbert, Dirk van Laak, and Michael Stolleis, ed. *Geschichte vor Gericht. Historiker, Richter und suche nach Gerechtigkeit*. München: Verlag C. H. Beck, 2000.

Friedrich, Carl Ioachim. "Law and History." *Vanderbilt Law Review* 63 (1961): 1027–1048.

Gary, Marotta. *Afro-Americans in New York Life and History* 32.2 (2008): 82–86.

Gilmore, Myron Piper. *Humanists and Jurists*. Cambridge: Harvard University Press, 1963.

Graham, Gene. *One Man One Vote, Baker v Carr and the American Levelers*. Boston: An Atlantic Monthly Press Book, 1972.

Grofman, Bernard, Lisa Handley and Richard G. Niemi. *Minority Representation and the Quest for Voting Equality*. Cambridge: Cambridge University Press, 1992.

Haberer, Erich. "History and Justice: Paradigms of the Prosecution of Nazi Crimes." *Holocaust and Genocide Studies* 19 (2005): 487–519.

Halle, Louis J. "What is Contemporary History?" *The Virginia Quarterly Review* 43 (1967): 566–579.

Harris, Robert L. "Coming of Age: The Transformation of Afro-American Historiography." *The Journal of Negro History* 67.2 (1982):107–121.

Henckaerts, Jean-Marie and Louise Doswald-Beck, eds. *Customary International Humanitarian Law*, vol. II: Practice. ICRC: Cambridge University Press, 2005.

Henkys, Reinhard. *Die nationalsozialistischen Gewaltverbrechen: Geschichte und Gericht*. Stuttgart and Berlin: Kreuz Verlag, 1964.

Herzfeld, Hans. "Germany: After the Catastrophe." *Journal of Contemporary History* 2.1, Historians on the Twentieth Century (1967): 79–91.

Hexter, J. H. "Some American Observations." *Journal of Contemporary* History 2.1, Historians on the Twentieth Century (January, 1967): 5–23.

Higham, John. "Beyond Consensus: The Historian as Moral Critic." *The American Historical Review* 67.3 (April, 1962): 609–625.

Hill, Herbert. ed. *Soon, One Morning: New Writing by American Negroes*. New York: Knopf, 1969.

Hofmeyer, Hans. "Prozeßrechtliche Probleme und praktische Schwierigkeiten bei der Durchführung der Prozesse," in *Verhandlungen des sechsundvierzigsten Deutschen Juristentages, Essen 1966*, vol. IIC, 38–44, ed. Ständigen Deputation des Deutschen Juristentages. München und Berlin: C.H. Beck Verlag, 1967.

Hofstadter, Richard. *The Progressive Historians: Turner, Beard, Parrington*. New York: Alfred A. Knopf, 1968.

Horstmann, Thomas and Heike Litzinger, eds. *An den Grenzen des Rechts, Gespräche mit Juristen über die Verfolgung von NS-Verbrechen*. Frankfurt: Campus Verlag, 2006.

Hughes, H. Stuart. "Is Contemporary History Real History?" *The American Scholar* 32.4 (1963): 516–525.

Hulle, Inge van. *When Judges Become Historians: Rewriting Aktion Reinhardt in the Nuremberg Trials*. KU Leuven (2012). http://www.scriptiebank.be/sites/default/files/webform/scriptie/Thesis3.pdf (accessed on 21.2.2016).

Iggers, Georg G. "The Decline of the Classical National Tradition of German Historiography." *History and Theory* 6.3 (1967): 382–412.

Institut für Zeitgeschichte, Archivdatenbank. http://archiv.ifz-muenchen.de./

International Convention on the Elimination of All Forms of Racial Discrimination, http://www.ohchr.org/EN/ProfessionalInterest/Pages/CERD.aspx; http://www.un-documents.net/a18r1904.htm.

Jäger, Herbert. "Betrachtungen zum Eichmann-Prozess." *Kriminologie und Strafrechtsreform* 3.4, Heft (1962): 73–83.

Jäger, Herbert. *Verbrechen unter totalitärer Herrschaft, Studien über nationalsozialistchen Gewaltskrimianlität*. Olten: Freiburg in Breigsgau, 1967.

Jäger, Herbert. "Strafrecht und nationalsozialistische Gewaltverbrechen." *Kritische Justiz* 2 (1968): 143–157.

James C. Bonner Collection. Dillard Russell Library, Georgia College & State University, Special Collection Finding Aids, Spring 2–4 (2015), Box 5–7, Fol. 1–4. http://www.gcsu.edu/library/sc/collections/jcbonner/index.htm.

Just-Dahlman, Barbara and Helmut Just. *Die Gehilften: NS Verbrechen und die Justiz nach 1945*. Frankfurt am Mein: Athenäum, 1988.

Kelley, Donald R. *Foundations of Modern Historical Scholarship: Language, Law, and History*. New York: Columbia University Press, 1970.

Kelly, Alfred H. "Clio and the Court: An Illicit Love Affair." *The Supreme Court Review* 1965 (1965): 119–158.

King, Martin Luther. Our God is Marching On! https://kinginstitute.stanford.edu/our-god-marching.

Kircheimer, Otto. *Political Justice: The Use of Legal Procedure for Political Ends*. Princeton: Princeton University Press, 1961.

Kogon, Eugen. "Umwelt und Recht." *Neue Juristische Wochenschrift* 41 (1965): 1901–1902.

Kousser, Morgan. *Colorblind Injustice: Minority Voting Rights and the Undoing of the Second Reconstruction*. Chapel Hill: The University of North Carolina Press, 1999.

Kuklick, Bruce. "The Mind of the Historian." *History and Theory* 8.3 (1969): 313–336.

Krummacher, F. A., ed. *Die Kontroverse: Hannah Arendt, Eichmann und die Juden.* München: Nymphenburger Verlagshandlung, 1964.

Lamm, Hans. *Der Eichmann-Prozess in der deutschen öffentli Meinung.* Frankfurt am Mein: Ner-Tamid Verlag, 1961.

Laufs, Adolf. "Zeitgeschichte und Rechtspflege: Eine Erwiderung." *Neue Juristische Wochenschrift* 33 (1965): 1519–1521.

Launay, Jacques de. *Major Controversies of Contemporary History.* Oxford, New York: Pergamon Press, 1965.

Law Number 64–1326 of 26 December, 1964. http://www.legifrance.gouv.fr/affichTexte.do?cidTexte=JORFTEXT000000684761.

Liberles, Robert. *Salo Wittmayer Baron: Architect of Jewish History.* New York: New York University Press, 1995.

McCrary, Payton. "Bringing Equality to Power: How the Federal Courts Transformed the Electoral Structure of Southern Politics." *University of Pennsylvania Journal of Constitutional Law* 5 (2003): 665–708.

Mettraux, Guénaël. *Perspectives on the Nuremberg Trial.* Oxford: Oxford University Press, 2008.

Mildt, Dirck de. *List of Historians (Expert Witnesses) Mentioned in the German Trial Judgments Series Justiz und NS-Verbrechen: Sammlung deutscher Starfurteile wegen nationalsozialistischer Tötungsverbrechen, 1945–2012.* Amsterdam: Ex Post Facto, 2013.

Miller, Charles A. *The Supreme Court and the Uses of History.* Cambridge, MA: Harvard University Press, 1969.

Mirror to America. *The Autobiography of John Hope Franklin.* New York: Farrar, Straus and Giroux, 2005

Monson, Robert A. "The West German Statute of Limitations on Murder: A Political, Legal, and Historical Exposition." *The American Journal of Comparative Law* 30.4 (Autumn, 1982): 605–625.

Mosse, George and Walter Laquer. "Editorial Note." *Journal of Contemporary History* 1.1 (1966): iii–iv.

Murphy, Paul L. "Time to Reclaim: The Current Challenge of American Constitutional History." *American Historical Review* 69.1 (October, 1963): 64–79.

Murphy, Walter F. and Joseph Tannenhaus. *Comparative Constitutional Law: Cases and Commentaries.* New York: Springer, 1977.

Newman, Jeffrey. "Four CU Profs. Plan to Join Selma March. Historians Will Protest Voting Rights Denial." *Columbia Daily Spectator* CIX.88 (23 March, 1965).

NIOD Institute for War, Holocaust and Genocide Studies. *The Virtuous Criminal and the Victim's Crimes: Eichmann, Arendt and Jewish History.* New York: s.n., 1963, DUI 6.221.

Novick, Peter. *That Noble Dream: The "Objectivity Question" and the American Historical Profession.* Cambridge: Cambridge University Press, 1993.

O'Brien, Michael. *The Letters of C. Vann Woodward.* New Haven: Yale University Press, 2013.

OYEZ Project, U.S. Supreme Court Media, Chicago-Kent School of Law, Baker vs Carr, Oral Argument, Part I. http://www.oyez.org/cases/1960–1969/1960/1960_6#argument-1.

Pohl, Diether. *Prosecutors and Historians: Holocaust Investigations and Historiography in the Federal Republic 1955-1975*, conference paper "Justice and the Holocaust," Yad Vashem, Jerusalem in December 2006.

Posner, Richard. *Divergent Paths: The Academy and the Judiciary.* Cambridge: Harvard University Press, 2016.

Rene, Remond. "France: Work in Progress." *Journal of Contemporary History* 2.1, Historians on the Twentieth Century (January, 1967):35–48.

Reynold v. Sims, 377 US 566 (1964).

Richards, Neil M. "Clio and the Court: A Reassessment of the Supreme Court's Uses of History." *Journal of Law and Politics* 13 (1997): 809–890.

Ritter, Gerhard. "Scientific History, Contemporary History, and Political Science." *History and Theory* 1.3 (1961): 261–279.

Robinson, Jacob. *And the Crooked Shall be Made Straight: The Eichmann Trial, the Jewish Catastrophe, and Hannah Arendt's Narrative.* New York: Macmillan, 1965.

Rückerl, Adalbert, ed. *NS-Prozesse. Nach 25 Jahren Strafverfolgung: Möglichkeiten, Grenzen, Ergenisse.* Karlsruhe: C. F. Mueller, 1971.

Scheffler, Wolfgang. *Judenverfolgung im Dritten Reich.* Berlin: Colloquium Verlag, 1960.

Scheffler, Wolfgang-Historiker. *Die Welt.* http://www.welt.de/welt_print/article 2752840/Wolfgang-Scheffler-1929–2008-Historiker.html.

Schlesinger, Arthur. "On the Writing of Contemporary History," *The Atlantic*, March, 1967: 69–74.

Schüle, Erwin. "Die Justiz der Bundesrepublik und die Sühne nationalsozialistischen Unrechts." *Viertalsjahrhefte für Zeitgeshcichte* 4 (1961): 440–443.

Shklar, Judit. *Legalism. Law, Morals and Political Trials.* Cambridge, MA: Harvard University Press, 1964.

Smith, J. Douglas. *On Democracy's Doorstep: The Inside Story of how the Supreme Court Brought "One Person, One Vote" to the United States.* New York: Hill and Wang, 2014.

Starobin, Robert. "The Negro: A Central Theme in American History." *Journal of Contemporary History* 3.2 (1968): 37–53.

Stelzel, Philipp. "Working toward a Common Goal? American Views on German Historiography and German-American Scholarly Relations during the 1960s." *Central European History* 41.4 (2008): 639–671.

Stelzel, Philipp. "Transnationalism and the History of Historiography: A Transatlantic Perspective." *History Compass* 13.2 (2015): 78–87.

Strothmann, Dietrich. "Bleiben die Mörder unter uns? Das Ende der Verjährungsfrist—ein Streit ohne Ende," *Die Zeit*, 27 November, 1964.

Teschke, John P. *Hitler's Legacy: West Germany Confronts the Aftermath of the Third Reich.* New York: Peter Lang Publishing, 1999.

United Nations. Audiovisual Library of International Law, Convention on the Non-Applicability of Statutory Limitations to War Crimes and Crimes against Humanity. http://legal.un.org/avl/ha/cnslwcch/cnslwcch.html.

Vogel, Rolf, ed. *Ein Weg aus der Vergangenheit: Eine Dokumentation zur Verjährung und zu den NS-Prozessen.* Frankfurt: Ullstein Verlag, 1969.

Vogt, Hannah. *Schuld oder Verhängnis? 12 Fragen an Deutschlands jüngste Vergangenheit.* Frankfurt am Main-Berlin-Bonn: Diesterweg, 1961.

Watt, Donald Cameron, ed. *Contemporary History in Europe*. London: George Allen and Unwin Ltd., 1969.
Wiesenthal, Simon, ed. *Verjährung? 200 Persönlichkeiten des öffentlichen Lebens sagen nein; eine Dokumentation*. Frankfurt am Main: Europäische Verlagsanstalt, 1965.
Wiggins, J.R. "Lawyers as Judges of History." *Proceedings of the Massachusetts Historical Society*, 75 (1963): 84–104.
Williams, Juan. *Thurgood Marshall: American Revolutionary*. New York: Random House, 1998.
Wilson, R.J. "United States: The Reassessment of Liberalism." *Journal of Contemporary History* 2.1, Historians on the Twentieth Century (1967): 93–105.
Wittmann, Rebecca. *Beyond Justice: The Auschwitz Trial*. Cambridge, Mass: Harvard University Press 2005.
Wofford, John G. "The Blinding Light: The Uses of History in Constitutional Interpretation." *The University of Chicago Law Review* 31.3 (1964): 502–533.
Woodward, C. Vann, ed. *The Comparative Approach to American History*. New York: Basic Books, 1968.
Woodward, C. Vann. "Clio with Soul." *Journal of American History* 65 (1969): 5–20.
Woodward, C. Vann. *Thinking Back: The Perils of Writing History*. Louisiana State University Press, Baron Rouge, 1986.
Woodward, C. Vann. *The Burden of Southern History*. Baton Rouge: Louisiana State University Press, 1993.
Wynn, Neil A. *The Afro-American and the Second World War*. London: Paul Eleck, 1976.
Wyzanski, Charles. "History and Law." *The University of Chicago Law Review* 26.2 (1959): 237–244.

Implications

From the Classroom to the Courtroom and Back

We live in an age of transitional justice, marked by the unprecedented demand to address historical wrongs. Whether through academic debates and truth commissions or lustration procedures and criminal trials, our encounters with the past invariably appear in a complex, high-profile context in which law, politics, history, and memory intertwine. This tectonic shift has affected a number of disciplines that traditionally deal with the past, challenging their practitioners to rethink the purpose of their work. The history profession, which in the meantime has experienced thorough transformations toward the contemporary and comparative study of the past, was prompted to consider the implications of that change. It called on historians to take an ethical stand regarding the atrocious past, and compelled some to take the stand and testify in proceedings aimed at undoing the consequences of historical injustices.

There is no shortage of scholarly reflections over this process, yet they are scattered around different historiographies and jurisdictions. Due to this lack of communication, there is only a very limited benefit from previous experiences in the creation, deployment, and reception of historical forensic contributions. To use a recent example, "when historians in Australia were approached by legal teams in native title and other cases from the mid-1990s (. . .) few were aware of these debates." Consequently, "some of them found the experience extremely confronting, and at times dispiriting (. . .), their sense of professional esteem challenged either by their dealings with legal teams or by their experience of hostile cross-examination."[1] Some of these surprises could have been avoided in the light of the experiences of U.S. historians involved in more than half a century of Native Indian litigation. The importance of this learning curve is apparent—one thinks of visible improvements through a string of cases in front of the International Criminal Tribunal for the former Yugoslavia or the relevance of the fiasco of the Zundel case in Canada for the success of the *Irving v. Lipstadt* trial in London.[2] As a rule, isolated cases produce repetitive debates, whereas keen attention to the previous uses of historical forensics holds constructive potential.

What lessons then can we draw from the troubled history of historical forensics? It would be just too convenient to conclude this book with a number of proscriptive statements about the present and future of historical expert witnessing. Such a conclusion, however, would not do justice to the complexity of the phenomenon, as on this topic, the last word does not belong to this author, but to prospective experts making that call. Whether historians decide to testify is, and will remain, their own choice according to their understanding of professional responsibility. One can only agree with Peter Mandler that "in a liberal profession in a liberal society, there can be no single definition of that responsibility, and no-one is entitled *ex officio* to decide upon it." This is, as he observes, "not to say that historians have no place in the courtroom; only that they ought to go in without illusions about their place and authority there."[3] However, illusions too frequently prevail among historians, jurists, and the wider public. These illusions range from a vision of a historian as an ideally impartial expert to his evil twin: the biased witness who compromises professional standards for the sake of unscholarly gratification or publicity. An oscillation between extremes was bound to shape the dynamic, interesting, and occasionally enraged, but generally ineffective and disconnected discussions described in this book. Bringing them together, a comparative overview of historical expert witnessing allows for the extrapolation of a number of points of relevance, aimed to foster informed decisions of the participants of this venture and enhance better understandings of their role.

Firstly, there is nothing inherently wrong with historical expert witnessing. There is hardly a branch of scholarship that assumed its forensic application unchallenged. Disputed courtroom expertise is as old as expert witnessing, and neither "hard" nor "soft" sciences have been spared such feuds. Glancing at the rapid professionalization of human knowledge at the turn of the century, coupled with the standardization of the legal process, one observes a general tension between the law and science, which reaches its height in the institution of expert witnessing. The institutionalization of this tension amounts by no means to an ideal solution, but rather presents an ongoing attempt to functionally rectify relations between law and science. These shifting modes of human experience are powerful forces that shape contemporary societies. Therefore, the constant flux of their refinements reveals many inconsistencies in the legal process, as well as many methodological uncertainties in scientific knowledge, particularly in the realm of the social sciences and humanities. Hence the debates over forensic applications of the sciences tend to turn into a battle for legitimacy of any given branch of human knowledge. Much of the *Sturm und Drang* surrounding historical expert witnessing comes from general disregard for the troubled history of forensic expertise and its manifestations in different legal and historical contexts. Only against such a background can one assess whether historical expertise brings any specificity to the generally strained relationship between science and law. History was among the last of the branches of human knowledge to take the stand, and the debates on the merits and the purpose of the practice do stand out even within the quarrelsome world of expert witnessing. Repetitive and disconnected, these discussions echo throughout the age of extremes, during which historical expert witnessing never managed to completely normalize itself. It is therefore fair to conclude that history took the stand belatedly and faced more obstacles, bringing a particular edge.

Where do the obstacles come from? A rather self-evident but too frequently overlooked point is that, for better or for worse, law and history are intrinsically intertwined. Hence the multilayered relationship: laws shape and at the same time reflect reality. They are simultaneously the agents and outcomes of history. Legal systems bear witness to past developments and break open paths for future developments. Scaled down to a courtroom, this duality is thus manifested in a similar duality: "While the Supreme Court frequently makes history through its landmark decisions, it also often uses history to reach them," writes Neil Richards.[4] This is not solely a prerogative of the highest legal fora. Analyzing a wide number of both famous and obscure criminal cases, Gerry Simpson concluded that "the performance of a war crimes trial is both situated in history and yet seeks to transcend it."[5] Trials use and produce historical documents, and consequently both revisit and create history at the same time. Such activity is, however, also a subject of historical scrutiny. These multiple, sensitive junctions frequently tempt jurists to act as historians, or historians to assume the role of judges, advocates, and prosecutors.

It would be hasty to conclude that the confusion would be resolved if jurists and historians would simply stick to their own area of expertise, because these overlaps are not simply occasional disciplinary trespassing. Concealed by the compartmentalization of knowledge production characteristic of the nineteenth century, this strong link was rediscovered at the turn of the century in several landmark trials, with historians such as Gabriel Monod and others jumping from their classrooms to the courtroom to testify on behalf of the Captain Dreyfus cause. Equally dramatic were debates such as the *Kriegsschuldfrage*, in which people like Justus Hashagen and Hermann Kantorowicz invested their reputations, careers, and lives. Hence the activities of history writing and justice rendering were brought together, and were more frequently than not on a collision course characterized by deep misunderstanding. In the strange battle for primacy, interwar historians started commenting on legal affairs; this, in turn, spread to fields traditionally explored by history. The response to this utilization came in the shape of attempts to keep history and law apart, shared by both idealists and relativists, presentists and historicists, as well as political, social, and cultural historians alike. The implicit treating of history and law as "odd bedfellows," which was common for thinkers as diverse as Benedetto Croce, Michael Oakeshott, and Robin Collingwood, grew into an influential theory of incompatibility, though never fully explicated. Equally diverse practitioners, like Herbert Butterfield, Marc Bloch, Johan Huizinga, and Charles Beard, would readily subscribe to it, hence significantly delaying the forensification of historiography.

The first cracks in this theory of incompatibility seem to be in its very foundations, as even its strongest proponents felt uneasy about the possibility of a complete divorce between history and law, particularly with the outbreak of the Second World War, the terrible crimes of which called for a response. How to account for these atrocities? Documenting violence on such a vast scale was a huge challenge for postwar historiography, expressed in the collapse of the customary disciplinary notion of historical distance. Legal imagination was equally challenged with rendering appropriate punishment. Expressed through the advent of international criminal law in Nuremberg, such legal activism guided historically minded prosecutors like Robert Jackson, Telford Taylor, and Robert Kempner in an attempt to put a criminal past to trial. Over time, it transformed into a demand for a massive rereading of history in accordance with the concept of universal human rights, prompting a strong remoralization of history and blurring the line between a courtroom and classroom.

As history entered the courtroom, historians were to follow, sooner or later. The Eichmann case and the Frankfurt Auschwitz trial of the early 1960s presented a globaly visible stage on which they performed. However, such trials are powerful beams that overshadow important groundwork. According to Devin Pendas, "the turning point in most cases seems to have come rather earlier, in the late 1950s, and it might therefore be more accurate to argue that the shift to a more critical juridical politics of the past was a cause of the political and cultural upheaval of the 1960s than a consequence."[6] Indeed, somewhat below the radar, the German courts have experimented with historical expertise at least since 1949, mostly for apologetic purposes, but sometimes with surprising turns. The careful brinkmanship of the zealous prosecutor Fritz Bauer in the 1952 Remer case and the strategizing of his more cautious colleagues like Erwin Schüle in the Ulm trial led to the first expert testimonies of historians like Hans Günther Seraphim and Helmut Krausnick. These breakthroughs coincided with the creation of new historical institutions, such as the Institute for Contemporary History in Munich, with a mandate to assemble documentation related to the Nazi past, and Zentrale Stelle Ludwigsburg, the prosecutorial unit tasked with steering the war crimes investigation. With this gray zone between law and history significantly enlarged, a model of cooperation between contemporary historians and the judiciary was gradually forming, enabling historians to take a more direct role in the courtrooms.

In what at first glance seems only a coincidence, historians have become expert witnesses in legal proceedings on the other side of the Atlantic, in the U.S., where no less dramatic changes were on the agenda during the 1950s. Prompted as well by the postwar sensibilities, many social scientists took part in antidiscrimination litigation spearheaded by the NAACP's strategist

Thurgood Marshall, in an effort to curb educational segregation based on racial prejudice. In conjunction with the judicial activism of the Supreme Court under the Justice Earl Warren, this tendency resulted in the growing engagement of historians in the courtrooms. In the famous *Brown v. Board of Education*, the court directed the parties to produce historical evidence, leading the NAACP to assemble an impressive team of historians (Alfred Kelly, C. Vann Woodward, John Hope Franklin, Howard Jay Graham . . .) whose interaction with the legal team led to the creation of a joint brief. Received with mixed reactions, historical forensic contribution became fully institutionalized, if not recognized as such, by the mid-1960s, and historians became growingly engaged in a number of proceedings, from to the cases in front of the Indian Claims Commission (Basil Chapman, Thomas LeDuc) to voting rights cases. Interestingly, historical forensics was taking root in both those quintessentially defeated and the quintessentially victorious countries of the Second World War. Notwithstanding the differences between the legal systems, this rooting was accompanied by remarkably similar doubts expressed by Hans Rothfels in German and and Henry Steele Commager in American context. Still, figures like Hans Günther Seraphim and John Hope Franklin jumped at the opportunity, prompted by the activism of historically minded attorneys. In both contexts, they confronted substantial criticism, but did ultimately fight to carve out some space for the historical profession, in both adversarial and inquisitorial procedures, to produce forensic contributions in the trials aimed at addressing the wrongs of the past.

Certainly, there were differences as well, stemming both from the structure of legal systems and the subject of the proceedings. The nature of the crimes of the Nazi regime in conjecture with its demise by force and the inquisitorial nature of continental criminal law produced the trials in which experts were summoned by the judges. As historians, they testified about the general background in which crimes were committed. The other paradigm, born in the competitive environment of the adversarial courtroom, was different, yet no less engaged. In the U.S., reckoning with the past was predominantly occurring through civil cases in which historians partook on different levels, analyzing nineteenth-century treaties with the Indian tribes or documenting patterns of abuse of voting rights. This shift in the nature of historical forensics occurred gradually, progressing from the mere authentification of documents as performed by Gabriel Monod and his colleagues in the Dreyfus trial toward the contextualization of the most dramatic events in their respective society. In both systems, the factual findings of historians from the recent or more distant past were bound to attract considerable attention, as well as criticism, as they were tapping into the cleavage between the proclaimed standards and their neglect in reality. For academics typically shielded with a professional distance, this was a whole new experience. Some historians, like Salo Baron or Alfred Kelly, were scorched by this process, whereas others, like Hans Buchheim or John Hope Franklin, successfully integrated their new commitments into their professional developement. For some, like Percy Schramm or C. Vann Woodward, testifying was a one-time excursion, whereas a new cohort of historians, like Helen Hornbeck Tanner or Wolfgang Scheffler, grounded their careers in the process. Yet, despite the uniqueness of their personal experiences, and the differences in legal and political contexts, they all had to fight an uphill battle to legitimize their position against the prevailing skepticism about this mode of interdisciplinary cooperation.

These early improvisations with historical forensic contribution were transformed into recognizable courtroom expertise through a decisive chain of events, unleashed with the trial of Adolf Eichmann in Israel and in a coincidentally mounting case against the Auschwitz personnel in Germany. Despite significant differences in the legal systems of Germany and Israel, resemblances between the engagement of historians in the Eichmann trial and the Frankfurt Auschwitz trial are striking. The two courts were in fact telling the same horrible tale from two different perspectives—striving to reach the top in Jerusalem and struggling to reveal the bottom in Frankfurt. In both cases, such a task called for a wide assessment of the political context in which the crimes had occurred. Therefore in both cases the prosecution envisaged historians as experts tasked to overcome the limitations of adjudicating collective crimes in a single criminal trial. Upon the invitation of Israel's Attorney General Gideon Hausner, a sole historical expert, Salo Baron, testified in Jerusalem and was briskly cross-examined. Prosecutor Fritz Bauer, equally interested in using the Frankfurt trial to write a first draft of history, opted for a collective effort. He contacted the Institute for Contemporary History and commissioned multiple expert reports by Helmut Krausnick, Martin Broszat, Hans Buchheim, and Hans-Adolf Jacobsen with the aim of painting a broad and layered canvas on the systemic criminality of the Nazi state, in order to properly contextualize the individual responsibility of the defendants on trial. During these trials, historians left behind the auxiliary production of forensic contribution and moved into the spotlight of the courtroom. In both cases, their reports were tendered as evidence and incorporated into the judgments, albeit quite restrictively. Interestingly, in both Jerusalem and Frankfurt the judges felt uneasy about historical expertise, attempting to delineate law from history in their judgment, but ultimately grasping the advantage of shared responsibility for shouldering these massive historical trials in the face of mounting criticism.

Harsh criticism came indeed, from liberal and conservative critics alike. Whereas Hannah Arendt criticized the prosecution's attempt to turn the Eichmann trial into a venture in historical pedagogy, Ernst Forsthoff specifically challenged the involvement of historians in Frankfurt. These debates were particularly embittered as they were led under the shadow of statute of limitations for murder and other offenses, which was to render crimes of the Nazi period unprosecutable in the Federal Republic of Germany from 1965 onward. Exactly due to this urgency, a number of public figures, like Simon Wiesenthal, Fritz Bauer, and Karl Jaspers, argued for the abolishment of that statute of limitations, leading to its postponement. In this interregnum a number of new trials regarding Treblinka, Sobibor, and other camps were launched, with visible involvement of German historians. These efforts were vindicated on a global level with the UN General Assembly resolution, which in 1968 called for abolishing the statute of limitations for war crimes and crimes against humanity.

An equally dramatic development was under way in United States. The Warren Court (1953-1969) was revolutionizing the political process in its vital points, from desegregation to voting rights. Its constitutional interpretation frequently relied upon historical argumentation and expert evidence provided by historians, causing a new debate about the relation between history and law. However, against the background of civil rights protests, which obtained significant support from public intellectuals—and notably a number of historians who marched alongside Martin Luther King in Selma in 1965, including John Hope Franklin, C. Vann Woodward and Richard Hofstadter—the space for disciplinary cooperation widened. It was additionally legitimized by the growing awareness of the trails' tranformative potential that was emerging in the works of Otto Kircheimer and Judith Shklar, easing the burden of those professionals who not only took a moral stand, but also took the stand in the courtroom.

The conjunction of all these factors, alongside liberalizing archival laws and the methodological maturing of contemporary historiography, created stable preconditions for a thorough reshaping of the role of expert historians and the normalization of their forensic contributions. However, it did not lead to automatic recognition, as every new zone of common interest for courts and historians was likely to trigger the old arguments about disciplinary (in)compatibilities. This the more so as "it is pretty well recognized now that the canons of evidence and argument that prevail in the courtroom are different from those that prevail in the classroom, and that, as a result, historians often come off badly when they are dragged into judicial proceedings. In courtrooms, facts are ascertained and then measured up against the law. In classrooms, facts are ascertained and then interpreted. While superficially similar, these processes are in reality very different."[7]

As this journey from the classroom to the courtroom and back becomes more frequent, the need for careful positioning in this arena grows. A trial is a highly structured environment, governed by its own rules. They significantly differ in criminal versus civil cases, inquisitorial or adversarial procedures, common or continental law, international or national jurisdiction. Grasping these nuances is a necessary, but by no means sufficient, requirement for successful expertise. Much unlike in the classroom, the contribution of historical forensics constitutes only a part of the complex mosaic of judgment, framed by the institutional requirements of a legal process. What one sees in the courtroom is just the tip of the iceberg. The imperfections of this process are clearly at odds with the social expectations, all the more so as the topics that reach the court are typically of wider public concern.

This results in a "gap between the experts and the popular expectations of what they can deliver. When important questions arise in public debate that involve recent historical controversy, it is only natural to turn to contemporary historians—in the same way that people would consult a doctor when ill, or a mechanic when the car breaks down. (. . .) This is a view of history which is highly simplistic and misleading (. . .). Misunderstandings about the role of history and the historian have serious implications for the practice of history, especially at the time when the 'historical expert' has come to play an increasingly active role in public and political debate."[8]

This trend is likely to persist, as high emotion stakes of such cases unavoidably lead to their politicization, making them potentially defining moments in the political and intellectual history of a community, like the Dreyfus affair, Holocaust cases, or the Selma march. Therefore, however large the temptation to partake, the risks are equally high. At the end of the day, "there can be no one historical account that renders perfect justice, just as there is no judicial outcome that can capture the complexity of history," notes Charles Mayer, who also reminds that despite existing tension, shouldering this responsibility is a necessity, as "the historian would like to do justice; the judge must establish some version of history (. . .). If good judges and historians shun these tasks, they will be taken on by prejudiced or triumphalist ones."[9]

Historians therefore continue to perform on this precarious institutional crossroad between history and law. Bridging the two fields, the reflective expert can indeed ease the disciplinary tensions, contributing both to advancing the legal process and to furthering scholarly understanding. The forensic historian can sometimes act as a powerful superconductor between past realities and present concerns. In less fortunate cases, the expert plays a far less helpful role, exacerbating the tension into an unbridgeable gulf. The past of historical forensic expertise points in both directions. Its present ever more so. The very day this manuscript was finished, a historian testifying at the Khmer Rouge Tribunal in Cambodia described his experience as "a cold torture."[10] At the same time on another side of the globe, a German court in Munich resolved an overdue case of Cold War political murder, after more than three decades with the help of two expert historians.[11] There are reasons to believe therefore that accelerated academic exchange can contribute avoiding some of the pitfalls and fostering greater understanding of this sensitive disciplinary junction, which has emerged as a continuous litmus test of the social role, epistemological privilege, and professional ethics of writing history.

Notes

1 Ann Curthoys, Ann Genovese and Alex Reilly, *Rights and Redemption: History, Law and Indigenous People* (Coogee, N.S.W.: University of New South Wales Press, 2008), 15, 10.

2 See the evolution from monumental to microhistorical expert witnessing in the ICTY in Richard Ashby Wilson, *Writing History in International Criminal Trials* (Cambridge: Cambridge University Press, 2011), 112–139.

3 Peter Mandler, "The responsibility of the historian" in *Contemporary History on Trial. Europe since 1989 and the Role of the Expert Historian*, ed. Harriet Jones, et al. (Manchester: Manchester University Press, 2007), 12, 16.
4 Neil M. Richards, "Clio and the Court: A Reassessment of the Supreme Court's Uses of History," *Journal of Law and Politics* 13 (1997): 809.
5 Gerry Simpson, "Didactic and Dissident Histories in War Crimes Trials," *Albany Law Review* 60.3 (1997): 801.
6 Devin O. Pendas, "Seeking Justice, Finding Law: Nazi Trials in Postwar Europe," *The Journal of Modern History* 81 (2009): 362–363.
7 Mandler, "The Responsibility of The Historian", 15.
8 Harriet Jones, Kjell Östberg, and Nico Randeraad, "Conclusion" in *Contemporary History on Trial: Europe since 1989 and the Role of the Expert Historian* (Manchester: Manchester University Press, 2007), 193–194.
9 A. Sarat and T. Kearns (eds.), *History, Memory and the Law* (Ann Arbor: University of Michigan Press, 2002), 1.
10 George Wright, "Historian Accuses Tribunal Lawyers of 'Cold Torture'", The Cambodian Daily, 3 August, 2016. https://www.cambodiadaily.com/archives/french-historian-accuses-tribunal-lawyers-of-cold-torture-116200. Historian in question is Henri Locard.
11 Sven Milekić, "Yugoslav Spy Chiefs Jailed for Life", Balkan Insight, 3 August, 2016. http://www.balkaninsight.com/en/article/yugoslav-spy-chiefs-murder-verdict-perkovic-mustac-08-03-2016. Historians in question are Bernd Robionek and Christian Axboe Nielsen.

Bibliography

Curthoys, Ann, Ann Genovese and Alex Reilly. *Rights and Redemption History, Law and Indigenous People*. Coogee, N.S.W.: University of New South Wales Press, 2008.

Jones, Harriet, et al., eds. *Contemporary History on Trial: Europe since 1989 and the Role of the Expert Historian*. Manchester: Manchester University Press, 2007.

Milekić, Sven. "Yugoslav Spy Chiefs Jailed for Life," Balkan Insight, 3 August, 2016. http://www.balkaninsight.com/en/article/yugoslav-spy-chiefs-murder-verdict-perkovic-mustac-08-03-2016.

Pendas, Devins O. "Seeking Justice, Finding Law: Nazi Trials in Postwar Europe." *The Journal of Modern History* 81 (June, 2009): 347–368.

Richards, Neil M. "Clio and the Court: A Reassessment of the Supreme Court's Uses of History." *Journal of Law and Politics* XIII (1997): 809.

Sarat, T. Kearns, ed. *History, Memory and the Law*. Ann Arbor: University of Michigan Press, 2002.

Simpson, Gerry J. "Didactic and Dissident Histories in War Crimes Trials." *Albany Law Review* 60.3 (1997): 801–839.

Wilson, Richard Ashby. *Writing History in International Criminal Trials*. Cambridge: Cambridge University Press, 2011.

Wright, George. "Historian Accuses Tribunal Lawyers of 'Cold Torture'", *The Cambodian Daily*, 3 August, 2016. https://www.cambodiadaily.com/archives/french-historian-accuses-tribunal-lawyers-of-cold-torture-116200

Index

www.ingramcontent.com/pod-product-compliance
Ingram Content Group UK Ltd.
Pitfield, Milton Keynes, MK11 3LW, UK
UKHW022001180926
475701UK00003B/142
* 9 7 8 0 3 6 7 2 6 4 0 5 5 *